FROMMER'S

BELGIUM

ARTHUR FROMMER

GW00502371

The views expressed in this book, and the judgments made, are solely those of the author, and do not necessarily reflect those of Sabena Belgian World Airlines or the Belgian Tourist Office.

Published by Prentice Hall Trade Division
A Division of Simon & Schuster, Inc.
Gulf + Western Building
One Gulf + Western Plaza
New York, NY 10023

ISBN 0-13-559352-2
ISSN 1040-9378
Manufactured in the United States of America.

*Although every effort was made to ensure the accuracy
of price information appearing in this book,
it should be kept in mind that prices
can and do fluctuate in the course of time.*

CONTENTS

MAPS

A Request for Comments

The best of books is a collaboration between author and reader. In subsequent editions of this guide, we hope to supplement our comments and recommendations with yours. If you have suggestions or reactions of any sort, won't you let us know of them? Send your letters to: Arthur Frommer, c/o Prentice Hall Press, One Gulf + Western Plaza, New York, NY 10023.

A Note About Prices

Quite obviously, inflation occurs in Belgium as it does everywhere else. In researching this book, I've tried hard to obtain up-to-date prices, but even the most conscientious researcher cannot keep up with subsequent revisions of those rates. Anticipate the possibility of 5% to 10% increases, especially if you will be using this book in 1990.

A Note About Currency

I've converted Belgian francs into U.S. dollars at the rate of 36 Belgian francs to one U.S. dollar. Since the dollar currently buys a bit more than 36 francs, and is predicted to strengthen even further, you may find—to your pleasant surprise—that dollar costs during the time of your visit are lower than the levels set forth in this book. Let's hope so, in any event.

THE GLITTERING NATION OF BELGIUM

■ ■ ■

. . . And why it is often bewildering

It never fails to amaze. To stun you, as if with a physical impact. You round the corner of a perfectly ordinary street—in Ghent, in Brussels, in Tournai and Bruges, in Antwerp, in Mons, in even a tiny village like Damme—and suddenly there rushes towards you a mammoth, medieval square. Soaring belfry towers of the 1200s, flying red-and-yellow heraldic flags. Giant Gothic Cathedrals surging with vertical line into the sky above. Turreted town halls adorned with streaming pennants. Intricately sculpted cloth halls and guild houses of the 1300s, the 1400s. Again and again and again, on every visit, in an experience that never grows stale, you react with physical thrill to the most radiantly beautiful City Squares in all the world—in Belgium.

In a country where sunshine is seen less often than the greyish light of the North Sea, the predominant impression is nevertheless one of color. It is color that best recalls a Belgian vacation:

the bright, vibrant reds and greens of Flemish masterworks of the late Middle Ages, the Memlings and Van Eycks, the Breugels and Rubenses, found in no fewer than 16 major museums; the warm, orange-yellow glow glimpsed through the casement windows of more restaurants per capita than anywhere else on earth, their interiors brightened by dancing firelight from open hearths, their entrances stacked with displays of red lobsters and black mussels, of exotic fruits and burgundy-colored wines; the festive rose-and-lavender stripes of canvas bath huts in serried rows along the 70-kilometer beach of the Belgian coast; the muted cream-colored lights of elegant casinos; the yellow arcs of light cast over the nation's entire highway system at night.

And although the country of which we speak is not among the wealthiest of Europe, far from it, yet the word "riches" springs to the mind of most discerning visitors: riches of culture and art, culinary riches, riches of music and theatre, of verdant forests and mountains, riches of turbulent history, riches found here in such profusion that hundreds of thousands of tourists from neighboring European countries flock to Belgium each year, and regard it as one of the great treasures among travel destinations.

THE PUZZLING OVERSIGHT: Why, then, don't more Americans, from both north and south, more Japanese and Australians, more adventure-seeking tourists from other distant continents, travel through Belgium on their holidays in Europe? The answer, I suggest, lies in the character of tourism, and not in the nation called Belgium.

In travel, as in life, the good comes hard, the best requires an effort. Such sights as the Eiffel Tower are easy. Piccadilly Circus is easy. The Golden Gate Bridge is easy. The greater number of tourists travel to easy destinations already familiar from a thousand novels, films and picture books, to spectacles requiring no advance preparation for their enjoyment. They come, they see, they exclaim with pleasure, and then move on to still other easy sights—but to what end, and with what lasting rewards?

For the non-European, Belgium is not always an easy nation to admire and understand. Although it, too, possesses attractions that overwhelm even the untrained eye—the Grand' Place of Brussels is the supreme example—its sights are often cerebral, its culture profound and complex, its history unfamiliar, its pleasures designed for the avidly curious, for persons seeking growth and understanding, and not for the casual throngs that create travel statistics. Belgium requires an effort—but what rewards that effort brings!

THE FIRST BROADLY EUROPEAN NATION: Belgium requires an effort, and brings a reward, first, because it is probably the least nationalistic, and most broadly *European,* of all the nations of the Old World—and therefore the herald of a new and unfamiliar sort of European state, the source of an emerging and still difficult-to-comprehend new European outlook that can profoundly affect the lives of all of us (as we'll be exploring later in this book). Its people display none of the often distinctive national attitudes by which we recognize the Spanish, the Italians, the French, the Germans, the English; they are a quirky mixture, at once cautious and cynical, intensely practical, averse to flights of patriotic fervor or stubborn stands, courteous to the stranger, and most important, endowed with a sense of proportion about themselves, their nation, their place in history and in the contemporary world. Put simply, they have a sense of humility; in even the wealthy, upper strata of their nation, they affect none of the *haute grandeur* that afflicts one or two other European peoples. If you'd like a personal experience of this, simply walk as a tourist into any of the greatest of Belgian restaurants—say, the Villa Lorraine of Brussels, whose very name causes celebrated food critics to quiver: to your astonishment, you are treated like a human being, led courteously to a table, aided with the menu and your selections, dealt with in a fashion virtually unique to the Belgians, and found today in few other nations.

How it happened

Given the history of Belgium, this sense of proportion and humanity could not have developed otherwise, for Belgium has gained these attributes through dramatic events. For ten centuries, and as recently as 1944, its strategic position between Britain, Germany and France made it the continuous battleground for other peoples' wars, the punching bag of great nations, never conquering but always conquered, periodically subjugated, invaded, occupied, bombarded and pillaged, passed like a pawn from one Noble House to another, owned in turn by the French, the Spanish, the Austrians, the Dutch, denied statehood until 1830, and then again invaded and violated in two great World Wars. Is it any wonder that few Belgians are raving nationalists, or given to patriotic bombast? Or that many Belgians profess not even to know their National Anthem?

Belgium is also the most European of all European nations because every great movement of European history, every major personality, most of the multiple cultures and nations of Europe, have marched across Belgium and left their imprint. Why was this small country such a focus of attention? Again: location. Belgium lies directly on the classic east-west axis, the equally traditional north-south axis, of European trade and military movements. So everyone passed through: German merchants and French kings, Julius Caesar and Napoleon Bonaparte, the shippers of English wool and Italian spices, Spanish inquisitors and Dutch Calvinists, Desiderius Erasmus and Karl Marx, Counter-Reformation and colonizing capitalists, Austrian Hapsburgs and King Henry VIII of England (the latter corpulent gentleman physically seized the Belgian city of Tournai and himself presided over giant banquets there)—all of these were experienced, in the most direct manner, by generations of Belgians, whose society became, in many respects, as European as it was Belgian.

It was undoubtedly the European character of Belgium that caused it to be chosen, in our own times, as the original capital of the European Common Market, of the European Steel and Coal Community, of EURAtom, of NATO and SHAPE, and of today's powerful European Community, headquartered in Brussels. In turn, the very presence of these bodies in Belgium, attracting an immense emigré population, has further heightened its international character. Today, an astonishing 25% of the population of Belgium's capital, Brussels, are foreign—a large part of them made up of highly-educated, high-income, multi-national lobbyists, diplomats, advocates and journalists (with their families) who pay court to the European Community, and the executives (with their secretaries and families) of the literally thousands of multi-national corporations that have established their headquarters in the receptive heart of Belgium. Elsewhere are found the military elite (with their families) of a dozen nations staffing NATO in Brussels and SHAPE near Mons/Bergen, again with their attendant journalists, supplicants, support population and spies. So great is the ratio of this foreign colony to total population that the newcomer is often smothered in a blanket of emigré clubs, finds it difficult to break out (into indigenous Belgian life) from a bewildering array of Yale and Oxford alumni groups, foreign-language children's schools, Gilbert and Sullivan societies, English community theatres, Young Conservatives, and Physicians for Social Responsibility. How large is the foreign community of Belgium? Well, on the newsstands of Belgium, an English-language weekly, *The Bulletin,* published for the emigrés, sells 30,000 copies each week; on the very same newsstands, the best-selling of the French-language Belgian weeklies, *Pourquoi Pas?,* sells only 60,000 copies a week!

So there you have it: a new kind of international state, an almost stateless and broadly European state, requiring an effort to understand, but utterly fascinating as a mirror of modern and future society.

THE TOURISTIC NATION OF THE HIGH MIDDLE AGES:
Belgium requires an effort, and brings a reward, secondly, because its chief touristic sights are associated with the most widely confused and under-appreciated era of human history: the late Middle Ages of Western Europe. Don't misunderstand: modern life is also abundant in Belgium, and there are enough casinos and beaches, theatres and boutiques, sociable restaurants, discos and hippodromes to satisfy the most jaded playboy. But the supreme tourist attractions of Belgium are those, nevertheless, of the High Middle Ages. Just as one travels to Egypt to view an ancient civilization thriving millenia before Christ; just as one visits Greece primarily for the sights of a later, classic civilization; just as one then follows the chronological human story to Rome for evidence of an Empire that flourished shortly before and after the beginning of the Christian Era; and just as one voyages to Amsterdam for the seventeenth century, or to Paris for the nineteenth century; in the same manner, one travels to Belgium primarily to view the achievements of a society whose peak of importance, whose dominance on the world stage, occurred during one particular period, roughly between the years 1100 and the early 1500s. And therein lies a problem. The bulk of mankind—those from outside of Europe—regard that period as one of unrelieved darkness—and therefore dull. This involves a monumental misjudgment, and one that needs to be examined.

Why we went wrong

In the history courses pursued by most of us, the Fall of the Roman Empire was followed by an uninterrupted period of social decline (the "Dark Ages"), until—in a grand awakening—the Western World thrilled to the notions of the Italian Renaissance, and resumed its progress. This theory, advanced in far more sophisticated and less blatant fashion by the Swiss historian, Jacob Burckhart, has caused millions of partially-educated persons to regard the thousand years in Europe from the 6th to the 16th century as the unrelieved "Dark Ages".

"Dark Ages" there most assuredly were, but the Middle Ages—from the fall of the Roman Empire to the impact of the Italian Renaissance upon northern Europe—fall into two distinct halves, of which only the first (from around 500 to 950 A.D.) can be said to have been "Dark". Commencing around the year 1,000, Europe experienced an extraordinary resurgence of commercial, artistic and intellectual activity that made of the ensuing five centuries—the so-called "High Middle Ages" or the "Late Middle Ages"—a period of remarkable progress and, in certain areas of life, remarkable beauty. When you have made your first visit to the Belgian city of Bruges, and walked, tingling and open-mouthed, through a ravishing medieval metropolis extending over several square miles of Gothic splendors and irridescent, tapestried brilliance, you will suddenly realize that all your prior notions of human history were possibly mistaken, and that mankind may have *declined,* in some aspects, in the years since the great Belgian cities reached the apogee of their existence in the High Middle Ages (this, indeed, is the fiercely-held view of a Belgian museum curator in the domain of Bokrijk, whom we'll be meeting in later pages of this book). You will also discover, in the course of your stay, that these High Middle Ages were the source for, and have a sensitive association with, much of the art of our times, our day-to-day commercial practices and codes, our theology and legal systems, our hospitals and universities, much of our architecture, arts and crafts. The travellers who ingest this lesson, and use the opportunity of a Belgian trip to delve more deeply into a great human era, soon find that never again do they look at the world in quite the same way, soon discover that they have grown in aesthetic and intellectual powers. And then they glow, inwardly, as again and again they enjoy the rich delights of Belgium.

All this takes an effort—but what rewards that effort brings!

WHAT SORT OF EFFORT? Not so long ago, people who delved into medieval studies made me exceedingly nervous. When a bright, young couple announced, in my presence, that they were flying the Atlantic to spend three weeks among the Romanesque churches of northwest Spain, I flushed with envy and chagrin. How had they acquired such refined tastes? What years of study had they devoted? What arcane learning, what Latin motets?

Belgium taught me differently. For the splendors of the Belgian Middle Ages are so strong and evident that only the merest refresher of information once taught to all of us, is needed to appreciate them. In the motto of a medieval Flemish nobleman, Louis de Gruuthuse, "plus est en vous"—you already know more than you think, you are capable of more than you dream. In the short two chapters ahead, we set the historical background for your visit to Belgium. Naturally, they can be skipped by those who have delved deeper into the history and institutions of Europe than did the quick survey courses taught to most of us.

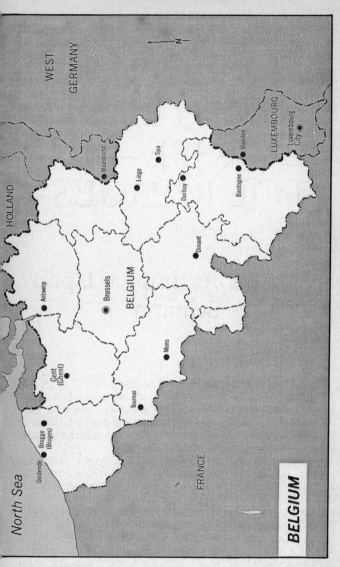

CHAPTER I

A HISTORY OF WESTERN EUROPE—IN FOUR PAGES

□ □ □

. . . And Its Impact Upon Belgium

The year is 476 A.D. In the West, the Roman Empire has fallen, and barbarian Germanic tribes sweep unchecked over a largely undefended continent. Visigoths and Ostrogoths, Vandals and Huns, roam to and fro, sacking and burning, pillaging city and countryside alike, causing devastation to both the material and intellectual resources of Europe.

Life becomes atomized. Cities decline. People cluster for protection about the fortified castles or manors of local lords. An absurdly decentralized form of government—the system of feudalism (from "feodalité"—faithfulness)—emerges. In exchange for protection, men pledge their services, a portion of their income, to a local lord, of whom there are thousands. He, in turn, pledges similar services to a higher lord, while those below spin off a part of their domains or their promise of protection to persons on yet a lower level ("subinfeudation") in exchange for services and "faithfulness". At the top of the chain: a few scattered kings, but they reign in name only. At the bottom: serfs, virtual slaves, bound to the land. Three days out of six, they labor for their lord, tilling *his* fields, tending *his* flocks, some giving up their brides, as legend would have it, to the lord's "right of the first night".

For brief periods of time, a particular warlord or two achieves something more. In the area of Europe that is now France and Belgium, a sixth-century, Frankish leader named Clovis (he will be succeeded by Pepin, and by Charles Martel) establishes the ambitious "Merovingian Dynasty" (we'll see traces of it in Belgium), but later Merovingians lapse into brotherly conflict, and they have little impact upon the life of people. In the year 800, an abler king, the great Charlemagne, conquers large parts of Europe, is named "Holy Roman Emperor", establishes the brief "Carolingian Renaissance"—we'll see traces of it, too, in Belgium—on a continent where, by that time, scarcely anyone knows how to read or write. But Charlemagne relies for the administration of his realm upon semi-autonomous lords whom he calls "Counts" (we'll be meeting the "Counts of Flanders" in later pages of this book), and upon his death, and in ensuing years, these local officials exercise absolute powers, soon ending the days of the Carolingian kings. Upon their demise, in the mid-800s, a new series of barbarian invasions erupts—by Vikings, Saracens and Magyars—and Western Europe sinks to a nadir of despair in the 900s. The continent lies devastated. As the year 1000 approaches, wandering evangelists predict the "end of the world".

THE REVIVAL OF CITIES: And then: a spark. From some deep inner wellspring of energy and determination, mankind revives. And the instrument of their revival is the City—the fortified city. From manors and farms, they flock to cities seeking protection behind high walls, but also freedom from feudal bonds. There they associate themselves in "communes"—self-governing groups that negotiate with local counts and princes. Quite literally, the communes purchase their collective freedom from these lords, and record the transaction in a written "charter", a parchment. They build, in their cities, high belfry towers to symbolize the newly-won liberties, and into the belfries they place iron boxes containing the charters. Around the belfry towers they have built walls, successfully designed, at long last, to repel barbarian invasions. The walled cities are called "bourgs", their inhabitants "burghers" or "bourgeois". If a serf should succeed in remaining within these city walls for a year and a day, he automatically wins his freedom, becomes a "bourgeois".

And where do these new cities develop most fully, and in the greatest profusion? In two places: in the key sea and river locations of northern Italy—Venice, Pisa, Genoa—and in a section of northwest Europe now known as Belgium. In Belgium, in the "High Middle Ages" of the 12th and 13th centuries, the cities of Bruges, Ghent, Brussels, Antwerp, Tournai, Liège, Courtrai, Ypres, become the dominant urban centers of northern Europe.

Thirteenth century Bruges was then larger and more important than London. Ghent was itself the largest city of northern Europe except for Paris. The University of Louvain, south of Brussels, vied at a later time with Oxford, Cambridge, Paris, as a great center of medieval learning. The city-states of "Flanders", as the west of Belgium was then generally known, dominated the life and commerce of northern Europe. Manufacturing cloth out of wool imported primarily from England; developing, in the process, the world's first urban proletariat (in turbulent Ghent); shipping its immensely-famous Flemish cloth (primarily from Bruges) to cities throughout the known world; housing foreign merchants (again primarily in Bruges) in an embryonic "European Economic Community" (even then), these same Belgian cities set the tone and shaped the forms of Western urban life as it has been experienced ever since. The Western city was largely born in Belgium in the 1100s and 1200s of the current era.

And it was from Belgium that the people of northern Europe set out to develop trade and commerce with nations of the East. When, in 1095, an ambitious Pope, Urban II, issued his electrifying call for a Crusade to wrest the city of Jerusalem from infidel Moslem hands, his appeal stirred the blood of a courtly young knight named Godfrey living in a castle atop heights of the little Belgian city of Bouillon, in the Ardennes (we'll be visiting that enchanting castle in later pages). Godfrey of Bouillon proceeded to pawn his lands and castles with the potentate of another Belgian city, Liège, and with the funds from that mortgage, from the town of Bouillon, he recruited and supplied the international army that led the great First Crusade—the most successful of all the several Crusades—and one that opened, for a time, trade routes with countries of the Levant.

From the optimism and tangible results of that international effort, and from Cities, grew a revived Europe of flourishing commerce, improved agriculture, surging religious belief, and unparalleled artistic achievement, all the hallmarks of the High Middle Ages of the 12th and 13th Centuries. And as Europe passed through the less promising 14th century, slowed by a Black Plague (1348–1350) that reduced its population by a third, and entered the dynamic 15th century, Europeans consolidated their gains by developing, in some areas, large and powerful national states. In France, in England, in Spain, strong monarchs claiming absolute authority began to centralize the exercise of power; in Germany, a confusing collection of local dukes and barons granted increasing powers to the so-called Holy Roman Emperor of the German states. And in Belgium? Well, that was a different story. Let us now leave our four-page History of Western Europe, and follow the rest of the European story solely through the eyes of Belgium, first back-tracking a bit.

CHAPTER II

A HISTORY OF BELGIUM—IN NINE PAGES

□ □ □

. . . What You'll Need to Know to Appreciate Its Current-Day Sights

Both before, during and after the time when France, England and Spain became strong national states, Belgium remained an area ruled by widely-scattered local lords, none of them wielding as much power as did the great Medieval cities in their midst. The area was not even called Belgium, but was known instead by the names of its major "counties" (ruled by a count) and "duchies" (ruled by a duke): Flanders, Brabant, Liège, Hainaut. Except for a fleeting reference in Caesar's Commentaries to the fierce "Belgii" tribes of northwest Gaul (58 B.C.), whom Caesar saluted as the bravest of all his enemies, the word "Belgium" scarcely existed, and was not again to be heard until the year 1830.

879 TO 1384 A.D.: THE FRAGMENTED LAND

Imagine a Belgium cut very roughly into four quarters.

FLANDERS: By the year 1100, the northwest quarter of what is now Belgium (the area of Ghent and Bruges, of Ypres, Kortrijk and the Coast), was firmly established as "Flanders", ruled by the Counts of Flanders. Big, strong men who wielded forty-pound swords and lived in giant, drafty castles (we'll visit one in Ghent), these Counts of Flanders received their "Fiefs" (their powers, their lands) under the feudal system from the Kings of France, of whom they were theoretically "vassals" (servants, sub-tenants)—but such vassals you would not want to have! Constantly at odds with the French monarchs, constantly turning back efforts of France to annex poor Flanders, they remained in power only by staying constantly in motion, now darting to Paris to mollify the French court, now dashing to secret meetings with the French-hating English, now spurring their steeds to put down an urban uprising here, to assist a political murder there. As if France were not enough of a cross, they faced the obstinacy of their own Flemish "city-states", on whom they had earlier bestowed the municipal privileges so proudly enshrined in the great belfry towers.

Ghent and Bruges, so rich and eminent in the 1200s and 1300s that they scarcely recognized the Counts' authority, were continually rebellious, continually independent. When a French King, in 1127, sought to name the successor of a childless Count of Flanders, the cities of Flanders rejected the choice and themselves forced selection of Thierry of Alsace as the new Count. When, in 1302, an exasperated later French King, Philip the Fair, finally decided to do away with Flanders, to invade its territory, to arrest the Count and incorporate his rich possession into France, the cities of Flanders again revealed where power lay. From looms and butcher shops, from dye-ing vats and blacksmith sheds, the laborers of Bruges, Ghent, Ypres and Kortrijk, inspired by weaver Jan Breydel and butcher Pieter de Coninck (whose statues now stand in the Market Square of Bruges), sallied forth to meet the French, having first murdered various wealthy patricians in their towns, supporters of France. For the awesome battle ahead, they armed themselves (in part) with ugly, little "goedendags" (how-do-you-do's), small spiked balls of iron on four-foot chains which they swung violently in circles about their heads. And thus equipped, on a muddy field outside the town of Kortrijk, this motley group of artisans and craftsmen met and defeated the badly-generaled flower of French chivalry—two thousand knights in mirror-like armor on brightly-caparisoned horses, all slashed to pieces by the "goedendags". That night, from the field of battle, several hundred golden spurs were retrieved from the heels of the fallen French knights, and the immortal "Battle of the Golden Spurs" gave notice to all the world of the might and determination of the Flemish cities. Though they continued to try, violently and repeatedly, French kings failed ever again to annex Flanders into France, the feat being finally performed (and then for only a short time) by the republican armies of the French Revolution in 1789.

BRABANT: The northeastern quadrant—the upper right-hand side—of what is now Belgium, was then Brabant, ruled by the Dukes of Brabant, who enjoyed a far easier situation than did the Counts of Flanders. Vassals of the easy-going and rather powerless "Holy Roman Emperor" of Germany ("neither Holy, nor Roman, nor an Emperor", quipped Voltaire), these Dukes were spared the gentle attentions of French kings, the constant fear of annexation. And the cities of Brabant—Brussels, Louvain, Mechelen (Malines), Antwerp—were at that time far less developed than Ghent or Bruges, less populous, less contentious and unruly. The result: a rather warm feeling of regard between the Dukes and the people of Brabant, the emergence even of a form of constitutional monarchy limiting the Dukes' power (the "Charter of Kortenberg", the "Joyeuse Entree"), and the relative absence of those periodic bloody revolts and massacres, violent demonstrations and wars, intrigues and conspiracies, that made a Marxistlike battleground out of Bruges and Ghent, in Flanders.

LIÈGE: The southeastern quadrant (very roughly speaking)—the lower right-hand corner—of what is now Belgium, was a strange entity ruled by an ecclesiastic, the "Prince-Bishop of Liège", in turn nominated by, and a vassal of, various kings of neighboring Germany. A priest, yet at the same time a secular prince, he ruled his "Prince-Bishopric of Liège" (which included the great Forest of the Ardennes) from the French-speaking city of Liège, then (as now) populated by surely the most fiercely independent people of Europe (we'll be meeting those feisty, contemporary Liègeois in later pages of this book). Among the more-or-less typical events of their stormy history: a particularly galling defeat in battles with Brabant, following which the entire city of Liège was razed to the ground in 1468 (but it rose again).

HAINAUT: And finally, the approximate southwestern quadrant of what is now Belgium was, from the 12th through the 14th century, the French-speaking County of Hainaut, fief of the Counts of Hainaut, who were (very loosely) vassals of the Counts of Flanders. Dotted here and there, and elsewhere, in this fragmented land: the County of Namur, the Duchy of Limburg, and even a portion of the Duchy of Luxembourg that overlapped a southern section of present-day Belgium.

Taken altogether, this was less a country than a simple mess! A monumental stew! But a fascinating cross section of colorful Europe.

1384–1477: BEGINNINGS OF COHESION

Enter now, into this vast, buzzing, blooming confusion, the flamboyant Dukes of Burgundy, descendants of the brother of a French king. From their rich capital of Dijon, they rule the French province of Burgundy—but they are anxious to become kings in their own right, of a real country—and their eyes fall on Belgium. In 1369, in a dynastic wedding of awesome implications, Philip the Bold (Duke of Burgundy) marries Margaret of Male, only child of Louis of Male, the Count of Flanders! On Louis' death in 1384, Margaret inherits Flanders, and her husband combines it with Burgundy. Later, Margaret inherits Brabant from a doting aunt, and so that, too, falls into the realm of the Burgundian dukes. They, in later years, inherit Holland on their own, purchase Namur on favorable terms, marry a daughter of the Wittelsbach clan, who just happens to own the County of Hainaut. Suddenly, most of what is today Belgium and most of what is today Holland becomes combined into one entity—the Burgundian "Netherlands" ("low countries")—which in turn is attached to French Burgundy.

The Age of the Burgundian Dukes (nearly the entire 1400s)! It is one of the grand eras of Belgian history, prosperous, relatively calm (by the standards of those days), and prolific in artistic and political achievement. Except when they are savagely repressing uprisings by—you guessed it—the men of Ghent, or repelling periodic invasions by the French (against whom the Burgundians had turned) and others, the Dukes devote themselves to creating modern administrative structures for the areas they rule, supervised by several celebrated "chancellors" (whom we'll be seeing in the great paintings of that time, in later chapters of this book). They support the arts with lavish endowments from a seemingly-bottomless treasury. They preside over a remarkable flowering of Flemish painting—by Memling, Van der Weyden and Van Eyck, among others—and enliven the social scene with giant festivals, tournaments, jousts, and absurdly monumental wedding ceremonies. French "joie de vivre" pervades the Netherlands! In the field of commerce, they exhibit their distaste for the increasingly narrow policies of the established merchants in Bruges and Ghent, by favoring the newer cities of Brabant. The Flemish "capitals" of Ghent and Bruges almost imperceptibly begin a slow decline; the cities of the east—Brussels, Antwerp, Mechelen (Malines) and Louvain—surge forward and enjoy their greatest age.

And then: tragedy. As the 15th century draws to a close, the last of the Burgundian Dukes—Charles the Bold—overreaches, is militarily defeated in Alsace and Lorraine, loses the Duchy of Burgundy to the French king. Only the Burgundian Netherlands (Belgium and Holland) are left, and now the French move towards a goal hungrily desired for centuries. To Mary of Burgundy, surviving child of the Duke, the French king delivers an ultimatum: marry the Dauphin (eldest son) of France—and thus bring the Netherlands into France! She responds by writing to Maximilian of Austria, son of the Hapsburg emperor of Austria: marry me (and keep the Netherlands free)! In 1477, Mary of Burgundy marries Maximilian of Austria, and Belgium (after the usual, routine battles on her territory, this time between Austria and France) becomes a province in the empire of the Austrian Hapsburgs, ruled (ultimately) from Vienna.

1500–1555: THE AGE OF CHARLES V

Today they are quaint nomadic nobles exiled to the casinos of various resort cities, barred from even entering onto Austrian soil; at that time, the Hapsburgs were rulers of the world. Through a succession of deaths and marriages too dreary to relate, the Hapsburg prince who ruled the Netherlands (Philip the Fair, son of Margaret of Burgundy and Maximilian of Austria) subsequently inherited Spain from his wife (as well as Sardinia, the southern part of Italy, and Spain's possessions in the New World). Thereupon, Philip's seven-year-old-son—Charles—who had been born in Ghent in 1500 (as you'll hear from everyone in Ghent) inherited the Hapsburg empire of Austria and Hungary from his grandfather, and was later elected Holy Roman Emperor of Germany. The result: a personage who ruled over greater domains than any human being before or since—the great Charles V (Charles Quint), who spent his childhood in the Belgian city of Mechelen (Malines).

He ruled this vast territory for 40 years (1515 to 1555), in almost continual movement at the head of his armies, dashing repeatedly from Spain to Austria, from Flanders to northern Italy, fending off Turks in the East, the French in the West, occasionally paying attention to Belgium, but increasingly pre-occupied with a more important domestic concern: the Protestant Reformation. In Germany during the reign of Charles V, Martin Luther had nailed his 95 theses to the church door at Wittenberg, attacking corruption in the Catholic church, the indolent and sybaritic lives of Pope and monks, the cynical sale of indulgences. In Geneva, John Calvin had established a militant Protestant church intent on replacing the Roman Catholic creed with an austere brand of fundamentalist belief. The latter movement spread in particular from Switzerland to Belgium, as fiery Calvinist orators preached in the forests outside Bruges and Tournai, Mons and Ghent, Antwerp and Liège, to increasing thousands of Protestant converts. Though Charles attempted to suppress the outbreak—by summoning Luther to the Diet of Worms, by prosecuting individual "heretics"—his Flemish upbringing, his Flemish tolerance, if you will, made it impossible for him to act decisively. By 1555, exhausted, depressed and uncertain, he resolved to abdicate his throne in favor of his son, Philip II of Spain. Thereby was set the scene for one of the most dramatic struggles in human history: The Revolt of the Low Countries (today's Belgium and Holland) against the Catholic armies of Spain.

1556–1648: THE REVOLT OF THE NETHERLANDS

The ceremony of abdication: it was an event of high drama, staged like the preview of a coming attraction. It gathered into one resplendent throne room of Brussels' Palace of the Coudenberg (see paintings of the event) all great participants in the tragedy about to unfold. A weary Charles V entered the hall leaning on the arm of William of Orange, a Flemish/German nobleman whose quiet, assured presence was to earn him the nickname of "William the Silent". Behind him walked Philip II of Spain, about to be given half the world. Upon the conclusion of his father's emotional farewell, he replied in Spanish that he could speak neither French nor Dutch, and would therefore have his own address read by another. It was an inauspicious start for the new ruler of the Low Countries. At his side stood the burning-eyed, black-bearded Duke of Alva, Philip's most famous general. In the audience were two particularly prominent Flemish noblemen of considerable authority in the Netherlands: the Count of Egmont and the Count of Hornes.

Within months of Philip's accession, the smouldering religious controversy of the times erupted into daily incidents. In Tournai, a Protestant zealot burst into the city's cathedral, snatched the Host from an astonished priest, crushed it beneath his foot, and screamed to the congregation: "Misguided men! Do ye take this mere thing to be your Lord and Saviour?" (He was immediately tied to a spit, and roasted slowly to death over a low flame). To this and similar provocations, Philip responded from Madrid with the only tool he knew to use: the Inquisition, now reinstated throughout the Netherlands. A remote Spanish king, single-minded, without pity, ruling a faraway people he neither understood nor respected, escalated a religious dispute into a flaming conflict. Yet Protestantism continued to spread. When Philip seemed to hesitate, in 1566, in his campaign against heresy, the emboldened Protestants chose the moment to strike back. In one single, amazing month, in an act known as the "Iconoclastic Fury", they broke into hundreds of churches throughout the Low Countries, smashed statues and religious imagery, destroyed whole religious structures, burned works of art, opened tombs, and danced around the bonfires of church furniture.

(As you travel through Belgium more than 400 years later, you will still see evidences of the "Calvinist fury" of 1566: empty niches on the facades of cathedrals from which statues have been removed; smashed and disfigured ornamentation on the capitals of columns. Invariably, your Belgian tour guide will make cryptic references to the "iconoclasts" who caused this destruction, and when you inquire as to who these "iconoclasts" might be, your guide will uneasily shift her feet, stare down at the ground, then refer to an odd group of people who once harboured unusual beliefs. As a typically polite Belgian anxious to avoid offending even a single member of the tour group, she will do everything to avoid admitting that those strange "iconoclasts" were Protestants pure and simple—in this case, Calvinists. The word "iconoclasts" scarcely appears in a single, non-Belgian history of the Revolt of the Netherlands.)

The very next year, Philip struck back, and hard, sending the cruel Duke of Alva with an army of 10,000 Spanish troops into the "Spanish Netherlands". Alva made no concessions, avoided no extremes, imprisoned thousands of Flemings, executed hundreds of others; and then, in his most dramatic turn, arrested the popular Counts of Egmont and Hornes (both Catholics), and brought them to the Grand' Place of Brussels six months later to be decapitated in front of the Maison du Roi. Their crime? To have urged conciliatory policies on Philip, to have temporized with the Protestant outbreak and sought accommodation with it.

War broke out. Armies raised by William the Silent clashed with Alva's men. Other noblemen, most of them by now Protestants, raised private armies of their own. Earlier, they had been called "beggars" by a Spanish courtier speaking to a regent of Spain: "What, madam? Are you afraid of these beggars?" Now they proudly adopted the term. There were "sea beggars" raiding the coast, seizing Spanish ships; there were "wild beggars" cutting off the noses of monks and priests.

The war lasted for 80 years (1568–1648). It was perhaps the cruelest conflict in all of human history. Prisoners on both sides were slaughtered without mercy. Whole cities were starved into submission, then erased (with their inhabitants) from the ravaged earth. Soldiers cut the heart from the still living body of a captured enemy, bit into the still pulsating organ, used extraordinary tortures. In 1576, two Spanish regiments went berserk in Antwerp —the "Spanish Fury"—slaughtering thousands of Flemings. Tens of thousands more immediately emigrated to Britain, France and Germany. In the course of the war, William the Silent was assassinated by a Catholic fanatic, and succeeded by his son, Maurice of Nassau, an abler general. Alva was succeeded by Alessandro Farnese and others. By 1648, exhaustion—and smaller towns lying in ruins, populations depleted—compelled a final truce. The seven provinces in the north of the Low Countries won their independence from Spain, and became the largely-Protestant nation of Holland. The provinces to the south remained the "Spanish Netherlands" or the "Catholic Netherlands", under the continued rule of Spain—and returned to the Church. The River Scheldt leading from Antwerp to the sea was closed to Flemish shipping, and a weakened Flanders slid for a time into economic decline.

1648–1830: CONTINUED FOREIGN DOMINATION

We can telescope the next near-200 years. Defeated in their bid for independence, a helpless plaything of larger nations, the provinces that are today Belgium moved successively from one occupying power to another. The Spanish were succeeded by the Austrians, the Austrians by the French, the French by the Dutch. But foreign "protection" failed to spare Flanders and Wallonia from continual war. Time and again, foreign armies (especially the royal armies of France) marched against Belgium, pummeled Belgian cities (see our Brussels chapter for one such episode), plundered its warehouses, used Belgium as the battleground for conflicts with *other* nations. The French Revolution annexed Belgium to France, moved Belgium's proudest works of art to the Louvre, again destroyed and pillaged churches and monasteries. When the French, led by Napoleon, were finally defeated in 1815 at Waterloo (in Belgium), Belgium was again denied its independence by the Great Powers, and forced into a merger with Holland, but as the distinctively junior partner in it. It was not until 1830 that the Belgians were finally able to cast off the Dutch, expel all foreign troops from their land, declare their independence as "Belgium" (a name used for the first time since the days of Julius Caesar), and choose an uncle of Britain's Queen Victoria as the nation's first "King of the Belgians" ("Le Roi des Belges"): Leopold I.

1830–1989: THE "DYNASTY"

Under the as-yet short dynasty of five kings to date— Leopold I, Leopold II, Albert I, Leopold III, Baudouin I— Belgium has fared a bit better in the field of war-and-peace, but only by a tiny degree. After 84 years of unprecedented development in the 19th and early 20th centuries, Belgium was again ravaged, its neutrality cruelly violated by Germany in 1914 at the start of World War I. Sweeping through Belgium on that classic invasion route, in its attempted conquest of France, a German army at first overwhelmed the Belgian forces, but was then bravely resisted by a surviving Belgian army personally led by Albert I, the "soldier king", who tenaciously held on to a thin strip of Belgian territory near Ypres for all four years of the war. Throughout that time, Belgium suffered extraordinary privations, and the plight of "starving Belgium" was decried throughout the world.

In 1940, it happened again. A German "blitzkrieg" against France quickly swept over Belgium, and once more the Belgians endured foreign occupation for four long years, as well as considerable destruction and loss of life, not only at the outset of the war, but in the liberation of Belgium that ended it. (See our chapters on the Ardennes for the briefest indication of the suffering of Belgian civilians in World War II.)

With peace, Belgium quickly snapped back. In the 1960s, despite its withdrawal from the former Belgian Congo (now Zaire), Belgium experienced an "economic miracle," leaping forward in every industrial field. In the late 1970s and 1980s, it declined into a business "crisis" (the word used by the Belgians for the current period) that is perhaps beginning to level off. In all post-war years, it has been a leading advocate of European unity, a United States of Europe. Given its history, could it want anything else?

And there you have it: *The History of Belgium in nine Pages.* Though it's an absurdly minimal basis for understanding Belgium, it's supplemented by the history of particular Belgian cities in the chapters to come, and by further analysis in the pages ahead.

CHAPTER III

SIX KEYS TO BELGIUM

□ □ □

Religion, Art, Language, Food, Politics, Commerce

We began with history, for history opens the door to Belgium. It starts to dispel the confusion that every first-time visitor feels on encountering a country that is almost totally unfamiliar, one that rarely appears in novels or films. With history, we begin to understand the pattern of Belgian cities, their proud belfries, their alternating national styles, the marvelously "frozen" character of "art cities" that ceased developing, and remained gloriously medieval, when other stronger nation-states put a halt to the growth of divided Belgium. Through history, we appreciate the diffidence of the Belgians, their urge—after so many centuries of invasion and subjugation—to "lie low", to remain unobserved.

To history must now be added a dollop of sociology—Belgian traditions, concepts, attitudes, institutions. Most are extremely simple to grasp, yet often overlooked or inadequately understood on the occasion of one's first visit.

THE ROLE OF RELIGION

Belgium, first, is a Catholic country, influenced by the religion into which more than 90% of its population are born. Its royal family is the last remaining Catholic monarchy in all of Northern Europe. Though complete religious freedom prevails, evidences of religion are more than usually apparent, particularly in northern Flanders, where small street shrines to the Virgin Mary are repeatedly found in areas where people live. Public religious ceremonies, outdoor religious processionals, celebrations of saints' days, all intensely colorful and exotic, take place in every Belgian community, just as they did in the great "Age of Faith", the high Gothic period, when the cities of Belgium reached the apogee of their existence. And religion continues to assume greater significance here than in most other northern European countries.

But now to confound matters. Though everyone is a Catholic, not everyone is a believer, and controversy over the role of the Church runs like a basic theme through much of recent Belgian life. Two of the three major political groupings of Belgium were originally organized (in the 1800s) along religious lines, the Liberal Party taking an anti-clerical stance, the Catholic Party allied to the Church, both in constant conflict over the role of the Church in public education, state aid to religion, the work of charitable institutions. Today, though the Liberal Party can be conservative at times on economic issues, it strongly supports the right to abortion, and takes similar anti-Church stands on other social issues. Though the Catholic Party has long since changed its name to "Social Christians" or "Christian Democrats", many of the older Belgians you meet in the course of your trip will continue to refer confusingly to the "Catholic Party" and to refer to a politician as a "Catholic"—as if the others weren't! The third major cluster of Belgian political parties is Socialist—also anti-clerical and free-thinking in their initial orientation.

We have referred to the "Age of Faith". From the 11th century through much of the 17th century, the people of Flanders and Wallonia, like those throughout most of Europe, held fierce and unquestioning beliefs, adhered to a literal reading of the Bible and the lives of Saints, regarded the outbreak of Plague in the 14th century as a direct visitation of God on earth. So heartfelt and intimate were the concepts of heaven and hell, the events of the Bible, that Flemish artists chose to portray them as occurring in Flemish towns. Biblical figures, in settings of the Middle East, wore the medieval doubloons, jerkins and caps of Bruges and Ghent! Your own appreciation of the art and architecture of historic Belgium will be aided if you refresh your memory, before arriving, with the historical development of Christianity in Europe, the episodes of the New Testament, the lives of the major Saints, particularly as laid down in the "Golden Legend" (Legenda Aurea). For it is only then that the paintings in galleries, the relics in museums, the sculpture on buildings, will become comprehensible to you, in this once-intensely religious land. And it is only by understanding the fervor of that "Age of Faith" that you will fully appreciate that most magnificent architectural achievement of Belgium: the Gothic cathedral.

THE GOTHIC CATHEDRAL: In every Belgian community of any size, there is a Gothic cathedral or a Gothic church (when the church is the seat of a Bishop, it becomes a Cathedral). You will be seeing many of them, and to enjoy the experience requires an effort at understanding.

The Gothic cathedral was the skyscraper of ancient times, but unlike the skyscraper, its construction was an act of the purest idealism. It represents a breathtaking leap in the evolution of architecture, an attempt quite literally to re-create the grandeur of God on earth. Imagine how awesome was the size and height of the Gothic cathedral in relation to the two-story and three-story homes that comprised the remainder of most medieval towns. The efforts required to construct each one are almost unimaginable today, enlisting the work and resources of whole communities, and several hundred years of building.

Prior to the Gothic age, in the five centuries from the fall of the Roman Empire to the year 1000, the style of church construction was "Romanesque", modeled after the Roman structures of Italy, relatively squat, with thick, load-bearing walls and small windows, and with rounded forms throughout: rounded arches, rounded ceilings, rounded apertures.

Around the year 1150, first in northern France, then in what is now Belgium, the builders of churches adopted a radically different approach designed to endow those structures with gigantic windows flooding their interiors with color-filtered light. They shifted the loadbearing function to soaring pillars or "piers", going higher than ever before. Between the pillars they hung massive windows of illustrated stained glass, surrounded by "tissue-thin" walls. To reinforce the pillars—enabling them to support roofs towering far above—they build much lower, parallel piers or pillars outside—so-called "buttresses"—at key points, connected to the interior pillars by stone arches known as "flying buttresses". Like the intricate network of a "tinkertoy", the whole was endowed with enormous strength and steadiness, despite the unprecedented height of the structure and its thin walls and vast windows.

Their designs made use of the vertical line, stretched upward towards heaven, soaring high in a near-state of ecstasy. The rounded form was replaced by the point—pointed roofs and spires, pointed arches and windows, pointed Gothic vaults in place of rounded ceilings, always the point aimed at the skies. Exterior were then covered by an embroidery of stone, a frenzy of statuary, a pattern of granite tracery resembling the most intricate lace. All throughout Belgium in the 12th through the 15th centuries, people labored with zeal to build the new Gothic-style cathedrals. Often they did so on the foundations of former Romanesque churches. Always they regarded the work as the single most pressing obligation of their lives.

The parts of the Gothic cathedral

As you tour the cathedrals and churches of Belgium, you will be assaulted by unfamiliar terms and descriptions of their various parts; cathedral tour guides love to impress with their architectural precision, but the matter is far more simple than they would imply.

The Gothic church is designed, when seen from above, to have the shape of a cross—a cross whose long beam usually runs from west to east. The long, western section of that beam is known as the "nave", and is where the congregation stands or sits to worship. The crossbeam is called the "transept". There is a north transept and a south transept. The shorter, eastern segment of the long beam, beyond the transept, is known as the "choir", probably because the choir is usually placed there to sing during services. The extreme, eastern end of the choir is almost always rounded, and is known as the "apse". Around the apse is usually a series of chapels, and the intervening aisle where one walks up one side of the choir, around the apse, and down the other side of the choir, is known as the "ambulatory". In later chapters of this book, we'll be using these terms to locate key paintings, statues and sculptures in the major cathedrals of Belgium. We won't become any more technical than that, and in particular, we won't make any use of those confusing terms that relate to vertical segments of a cathedral—"clerestory", "triforium", "tympanum", "arcade".

The Gothic cathedral! When medieval people embarked on their construction, they knew they would not live to see their completion, because the average cathedral required from one hundred to two hundred years to build. Yet they labored mightily—some craftsmen for decades on end—cutting endless blocks of stone from quarries, dragging them for tens of miles to the site, shaping each piece by hand, hoisting them to windy heights on crude platforms using the rope of heavy windlass machines, trudging hundreds of steps upwards each day, all without benefit of electric or steam power, structural steel or, in some instances, even nails. In Belgium, they did this as early as the 1100s (in Tournai), and what they built has survived for as many as 800 years to enchant and edify the visitor of today. In nearly every instance, the major cathedrals serving the modern religious needs of Belgium, and which you now will be visiting, were built in the 13th, 14th, and 15th centuries, the products of a religious zeal about which we can only wonder.

THE "BEGUINAGE": A last, and rather odd, religious institution is found in those same Belgian cities possessing great cathedrals: the Beguinage. In Bruges and Ghent, in Louvain and Tournai, women of the Middle Ages wishing to retreat from the hurly-burly of ordinary life, but unwilling to take the vows of nuns, went to live in female communities maintained apart from normal neighborhoods, usually in a complex of townhouses surrounding a peaceful, grassy square. They became "beguines", and although they occasionally left the area to venture into the market square, they generally led a peaceful and contemplative life within the "Beguinage", some of which would lock their gates at night. Though the movement has disappeared, and actual nuns now inhabit most of the "Beguinages", they remain among the most attractive sights of Belgium, a thought-provoking institution, and an important example of the historic role of religion in Belgian life.

THE ROLE OF ART

Art, in the form of paintings, art attracting countless generations of travellers from around the world, art in a flood of masterworks far greater than the country's size would ever warrant, art of Rubens and Van Eyck, of Bruegel and Magritte, is among the greatest lures of Belgium. It is the reason why professors of art and museum curators all flock to Belgium and spend weeks drifting in a trance from one museum to another. It is the reason why college sophomores drop their knapsacks at Brussels' Gare Centrale, and go rushing to the "Musée de l'Art Ancien"—before choosing a hostel! An eruption of creative genius—in the form of paintings —has taken place in every Belgian century starting with the 15th, with the possible exception of a fallow 18th century, when activity subsided a bit.

History again provides part of the explanation. It is history which reminds us that the first large cluster of cities to emerge in a revived medieval Europe were those of Flanders (now Belgium) and of Italy. Here, then, was the wealthy underpinning for art, the patronage of artists. To the prospering cities of Flanders, made wealthier still by the later largesse of the Dukes of Burgundy, artists flocked to seek their fortunes from royal commissions. Bruges and Ghent, Antwerp and Tournai, Brussels and Ypres, were the places to be. Later still, in the 17th century, the merchants of Antwerp, the increasingly wealthy tradesmen of Brussels, besieged the studios of Rubens and de Vos, Van Dyck and Jordaens, begging for portraits of themselves and their families. From a giant market for art, genius emerged, and every major Belgian city became associated with a masterful native son: Brussels with Bruegel, Ghent with the brothers Van Eyck, Bruges with Hans Memling, Tournai with Robert Campin and Rogier van der Weyden, Antwerp with Rubens, Louvain with Dirck Bouts, Ostend (in much later times) with James Ensor. And tourists today concentrate on the work of those figures in the cities they blessed with their presence.

THE FLEMISH "PRIMITIVES": The most important impact was made by those Flemish artists who painted in the 1400s—the "primitives". They sought to become a mirror to reality, to portray both people and nature exactly as they appeared to the human eye, without classical distortions or embellishments, showing light in the precise way it fell upon objects, creating luminosity and shadows. To do so, they became the first group of painters to make a major use of oils—clarified oils, almost transparent—as the solvent for their pigments of color (in place of the egg whites or egg yolks that others had used to mix with pigments in the "tempura" method of creating paint). In the early 1400s, Jan van Eyck learned to make these transparent glazes, through which light could penetrate, causing colors to glow.

The "Primitives", as well as most later Flemish artists, painted on wooden panels, which they first covered with a ground chalk polished to create a gleamingly smooth surface. They then created colors by laboriously applying successive layers of paint to the same spot. To create purple, for instance, they would first apply a light blue, let it dry, apply then a darker blue, then add touches of red to the areas desired as purple. Through all three of the painstakingly applied, transparent layers, light would penetrate to the panel underneath and rebound to the viewer's eye, resulting in the brightest of tones, the most glowing effects. The works of the "primitives" are marked by the brightness of their colors, a radiant effect which attracts you to them from many yards away. They depict people and objects as if in a photograph, reproducing the tiniest detail. Impelled by religious belief, an almost inhuman drive, such towering Flemish figures as the brothers Van Eyck, Hugo van der Goes, Hans Memling, Dirck Bouts, Robert Campin, Rogier van der Weyden, Petrus Christus, Quentin Metsys, Hieronymus Bosch, would devote long months, even years, to a single work, occasionally employing brushes with but a single hair to make the infinitesimally small lines that captured reality. Yet though they "photographed" man and nature, the results were other-worldly, silent and still, mystical, the enhanced products of genius.

Why were they called "primitives"? As you travel through Belgium, various explanations will be fobbed off on you by Belgians embarrassed by the term. You will be told that "primitive" also means "first", and that these were the first to use oils, or to portray certain themes. In actual fact, the term "primitive" was used in its natural, critical sense by Italian painters of that time—led by Michelangelo—to stigmatize the Flemings as crude in their failure to reproduce classic shapes and harmonies, to endow their works with the graceful, flowing lines and composition of the dream-like Italian approach. But though the initial reaction was harsh, many Italian painters stayed on to master the new Flemish methods, and to express a sneaking admiration for the colors the Flemings achieved.

The art of the altarpiece

The theme of the "primitives" of the 1400s was almost always religious, commissioned for churches and chapels, and only occasionally does one discover a "stand-alone" portrait of a wife or a patron. Often a painting would be requested to serve as the backdrop for an altar, "curving" about it, and therefore painted on three-or-more separate panels hinged to open and close. If made of three panels, it was a "triptych". If made of five or more, it became a "polyptych". The central panel or panels portrayed the main theme; the side panels or back panels depicted either secondary themes, or, more often, were used to repay the donors or financial patrons of the painting by depicting them. On the left panel you will see the male-donor kneeling with his male children, their patron saint standing protectively alongside, or else you will see a kneeling churchman. On the right panel, you will see the female donor kneeling with her daughters, a patron saint alongside, or else you will see the nuns who financed the painting. Sometimes, as in the case of the van Eyck's remarkable "Adoration of the Mystic Lamb", the donors appear on back panels, which become front panels when the painting is shut—presumably, in ancient times, on weekdays, preliminary to the grand opening of the "triptych" or "polyptych" on the occasion of a high mass. The "Mystic Lamb" is a polyptych, so celebrated that art experts refer to it as "The Ghent Altarpiece"—as if there were only one!

THE "SEVEN WONDERS" OF BELGIUM: When tourist officials sought in 1978 to use art as a theme for attracting visitors to Belgium, they dramatized the subject by asking a panel of experts to select the seven outstanding, native, artistic works of the country. The exercise was, of course, a bit absurd, in a country possessing hundreds of acknowledged masterworks. And it was made further suspicious by the fact that the winning Seven consisted of a carefully balanced three from Flanders, three from Wallonia, and one from Brussels. Nevertheless, as a means of reminding us about the artistic treasures of Belgium, it was a pleasant competition, and it is fun to keep the Seven Wonders in mind as you travel from place to place (we'll actually be visiting all seven in later chapters of this book). They are (in no particular order): (1) Bruegel's "Landscape with the Fall of Icarus" in Brussels; (2) Rubens' "Descent from the Cross" in Antwerp; (3) The Van Eycks' "Adoration of the Mystic Lamb" in Ghent; (4) Nicholas of Verdun's "The Shrine of Our Lady" in Tournai; (5) Renier of Huy's "Baptismal Fonts" in Liège; (6) Hugo of Oignies' "Goldsmith's Treasure" in Namur; and (7) Hans Memling's "Shrine of St. Ursula" in Bruges. Watch for "the Magnificent Seven"!

THE ROLE OF LANGUAGE

Belgium is the meeting place in northern Europe of the Latin and Germanic cultures; it is the important buffer state between France and Germany. It was populated in the south by Celtic tribes speaking a later-Latinized language that became French. It was populated in the north by Frankish invaders speaking a form of low German called Dutch.

Today, an invisible "linguistic line" runs across the whole of Belgium, from east to west, splitting the nation almost precisely in half. South of the line ("Wallonia"), people speak French and are called "Walloons". North of the line people speak Flemish (which is nothing other than Dutch, with a distinctive accent; in its written form, it is indistinguishable from Dutch), and they are called "Flemings". In places where the linguistic "line" cuts through a populated area, you can cross a street—from one sidewalk to another—and suddenly encounter signs, billboards, the speech of people, that have changed from French to Dutch. You can drive along a highway that swings back and forth from one area to the other, and as you do so, the city to which you are driving changes names on the highway signs: from "Liège" to "Luik" (the same city) or from "Antwerpen" to "Anvers" (which is the same Antwerp).

Within the Flemish northern half of the nation is carved out, quite confusingly, the city of Brussels, officially bi-lingual but predominantly French. At the city limits in the area of the Atomium in Brussels, you need only walk across the street and suddenly everyone is speaking Dutch (Flemish) instead of French! And then, to confuse matters more, there is a small border enclave in the east of the country where everyone speaks German.

The linguistic question is an ever-constant theme of Belgium, troubling and vexatious to the Belgians, odd and of no great importance to tourists, a travel curiosity that lends flavor to the country. But the problem of bi-lingualism has now arisen in other nations (Canada, the United States, among them), and the long Belgian experience with it is of increasing interest to political scientists from around the world. In its origins, the language question involved an element of positive discrimination against the Flemish half of Belgium. The language of the commercial and political elite was French, the steel mills and coal mines of French-speaking Wallonia gave economic pre-eminence to the so-called "francophones"; university education, government proceedings, were conducted in French, and Flemish defendants could be made to participate in trials conducted in a language they could not understand. Thereupon, the Flemings fought back, beginning late in the last century, increasingly in modern times, and today the situation has sharply reversed itself. Flanders has more than half the population of Belgium, is currently enjoying a shift of industry to it, conducts courses at its great University of Leuven (Louvain) entirely in Dutch, insists on absolute, mathematical parity in the governmental use of the two languages. When switchboard operators answer the phone in the Belgian Senate, they say "Le Senat/De Senaat" on Mondays, Wednesdays and Fridays, "De Senaat/Le Senat" on Tuesdays, Thursdays and Saturdays!

Because nearly everyone in the Belgian tourist industry speaks English (hoteliers, restauranteurs, sightseeing guides), you won't personally be affected by the language issue, but you'll be fascinated by it as you travel through Belgium, pondering the ever-present effort, in every field, to accommodate the cultures of two different linguistic groups in the same country.

THE ROLE OF FOOD

Food as a Solace and Joy, a sensual delight, never to be taken for granted, but to be sung and extolled—that, too, is a strong theme of life in Belgium. No matter what their station, high or low, Belgians take enthusiastic, demonstrative relish in food. They talk about it, boast about it, devote long hours and a considerable portion of their budgets to consuming it, take extraordinary pains in preparing it, make celebrities out of chefs who excel at it.

And when Belgians speak about their restaurants, they cease being courteous Belgians. They drop all pretence to modesty. They state loudly and firmly that the level of cuisine in Belgium is the highest in the world—higher, in particular, than the norms maintained by their competitive neighbors from across the border, the French. Belgium's leading food critic, Henri LeMaire, made it official in a recent edition of his prestigious guide. I can now state "without hesitation", he wrote, "without foolish nationalism", that "we in Belgium eat better than the French." Those renowned French chefs like Pierre Troisgros? "We have four of his equal. Alain Chapel? Good . . . but I know at least three Belgian chefs as skilled as he . . . Paul Bocuse? We can export at least a dozen like him! . . . Per square kilometer, Belgium has the most top class restaurants . . . We do things better."

Is the food of Belgium in fact the best in the world? While all of us can remember memorable meals in numerous countries, it is hard to recall having eaten as consistently well elsewhere as in Belgium, in both cheap restaurants and costly ones, at both sidewalk carts and silver tureens. While I for one am not yet ready to choose between Belgium and France, I am stumped to recall any recent extensive trip in which meal after meal, day after day, has been as scintillating—yes, that's the word for them—as on similarly extensive trips through Belgium.

Part of the credit for consistent good eating goes to the three, cheap staples of popular Belgian dining: mussels, french fries and beer. Steamed mussels are a classic of Belgium, flavored with seaweed and leeks, juicy and tender, eaten almost weekly by a vast number of the Belgian population. The french fries of Belgium? They're doubly ethereal! And served not simply in restaurants, but from sidewalk stands, to be eaten like popcorn as one strolls along, from a paper cone covered with a dollop of mayonnaise.

(Why can't the rest of the world make french fries as they do in Belgium? The technology seems simple enough. The potatoes are undoubtedly the same. Some Belgians suggest the secret lies in preparing the potatoes twice: once at low heat to thoroughly cook the insides, after which the potatoes are drained and dried, then reimmersed into oil at high heat to complete their golden brown "outsides".)

And then there is Belgian beer, or rather "beers", three hundred varieties of them, some aged and dated, some with yeast settled to their bottoms, some "lambic" in category and sweet, others "trappist" (abbey-brewed) and grainy, all available in a remarkable range of brands in the cheery beer cafes of Belgium (in which only beer, and never hard drinks, may be served). "The Bordeaux and Burgundies of Belgium are Beer". Belgians drink beer in greater volume than any people other than the Germans.

And Belgian chocolate! You buy it in sacks of 100 grams apiece, the best course being to request an assortment, from irresistible "chocolatiers" located, seemingly, on every street corner and lane. "Next to Belgian chocolate," said a Belgian chocolate maker, "American candy bars taste like sand". (On all other topics, the same gentleman is modest and given to understatement.)

In the better restaurants, you may be surprised to find appetizers occasionally priced at the same levels as main courses. Appetizers here are no "throwaway" to pass the time, but fanciful creations, as carefully presented as a Japanese flower arrangement, a proud and often unique dish of the establishment serving it. If the total cost of both appetizer and main course, or three courses, is beyond your budget, then share the appetizer course with your dining companion. Belgian portions are invariably mammoth—"French in style, German in quantity", said a wit—and it is not unusual for Belgians to request either a half portion (at half price) or a single portion shared by two. As for the prices on Belgian menus, they already *include* both service charge and tax, and there is no obligation to leave other than a modest tip. Because of that inclusion, which saves the 15% or 20% that one adds to the check in certain other countries, the cost of dining in Belgium is refreshingly reasonable by the standards of those other nations.

As you'd expect, much of this book deals with restaurants and food—the ever-present theme of Belgium, the sensual backdrop to almost every other image or experience.

THE ROLE OF POLITICS

The contemporary life of Belgium—its government and politics, its approach to modern problems—is also a valid subject of tourist interest, but one made a bit difficult by the division of the country into two cultural/linguistic communities: the Dutch-speaking Flemish and the French-speaking Walloon. In 1980, the national government of Belgium was partially "regionalized". Most cabinet positions, most major departments—not including foreign affairs, defense, finance, of course—were reconstituted into two identical cabinet positions and departments, one for Flanders in the north, one for Wallonia in the south. The legislature of Belgium, in addition to meeting as a national body, now meets periodically split into two components: a "Flemish council" and a "Walloon council". Earlier, the major political parties of Belgium had each split into a separate Flemish or Walloon party; and there are additional political parties operating solely in the Brussels region, and still other parties formed entirely on the basis of linguistic issues. The result is an "alphabet soup" of political parties almost incapable of being grasped by the casual visitor to Belgium, but important to know, if only to decipher the newspaper headlines in the course of your stay. Despite its inner divisions —which find their counterparts in most other nations—Belgium continues, from the standpoint of the outside world, to function effectively as one nation, an interesting commentary on the many permissible forms of political organization.

In all other respects, Belgium's political structure is quite similar to that of its nearest neighbors: France, Germany, the Netherlands. It is a welfare-state, with heavy involvement of government in economic matters. Price and wage controls have been in effect for many years. Medical costs are reimbursed almost in full to every Belgian resident. A number of basic industries (steel, ship-building) are government-owned. Persons discharged by their employers are guaranteed up to nine months' severance pay, depending on length of service. Both government and private pension plans are widespread. Unemployment compensation is generous, in the current-day traditions of northern Europe. Though Belgium may *seem* an ancient land of belfry towers and market squares, its policies are as modern and advanced (or as retrograde, depending on your point of view) as those of nearly every other industrial, developed nation of Western Europe.

THE ROLE OF INDUSTRY AND COMMERCE

As recently as 1970, little Belgium was rated as the 9th largest industrial power of the world. That point needs emphasis as another corrective to the image that tourists otherwise receive. In a country that, to the visitor, seems exclusively composed of chefs and waiters, resplendent art galleries and peaceful farms, an awful lot of people are laboring at the very tasks that made economic powerhouses of the Flemish cities in the 12th and 13th centuries! The nation lives from international trade. Its exports on a per capita basis are the highest in the world. Its commercial successes are legion. It was Belgians who built the Paris subway, and Belgians who founded the Club Méditerranée. And all over the world, railway cars and modern lathes, navigation equipment and printing machines, bear a "Made in Belgium" mark.

You won't, of course, see any of this on your own trip (unless you sign up for various factory visits); the industry of Belgium is quite effectively concealed in areas to which tourists rarely go. And although the pages ahead contain brief descriptions of such commercial phenomena as the port and diamond industry of Antwerp, the coal mine "museums" outside Liège, the engineering marvel of the Ronquières canal, we've obviously concentrated on the pleasures and culture of Belgium, and not on its workaday life. Still, it's important to have a rounded picture. Though Belgium may no longer be 9th in the world among industrial nations, it remains a country of surprising commercial significance, a nation of hard-working—as well as hard-playing—people. Festivals and processions, restaurant feasts and taverns filled with revelers, are simply the leisure-time outlets of an energetic lot that work diligently in the *non*-mealtime hours!

THE "GUILDS": For historical, touring purposes, you'll want to remember that virtually all economic activity in the Middle Ages of Belgium was channeled through a maximum of 52, carefully-delineated "Guilds", which each possessed a monopoly over activities in a particular craft: shoe-making, tallow-boiling, carpentry, even the painting of pictures ("the Guild of St. Luke's", in which Rubens was entered). Each exercised stringent controls over admission to the craft, required long years of apprenticeship and training, examinations for passing from the status of "journeyman" to "master", inspections of even mature work to insure adherence to standards. Each provided benefits and security for its members, sometimes even arranged marriages to fellow guild members, engaged in so many comprehensive activities that they were as frequently known as "corporations" as by the name of "guilds". And it is these organizations, of course, whose handsome, gilded headquarters will be found around many a market square of the key Belgian cities.

TWO KEYS TO THIS BOOK: On those market squares (or nearby) of nearly every Belgian city of any size, are tourist offices stocking free city maps, all of a size many times as large as a page of this pocket-sized book. Because small maps in this book's dimensions would have been of little use to you, we've omitted all but an occasional map from this book, and suggest that you pick them up from the tourist office upon arrival in each city.

Prices in the pages ahead are set forth in Belgian francs. When we have also provided U.S. dollar equivalents, we have converted Belgian francs into dollars at a conservative exchange rate of 36 to the dollar. Since the Belgian franc is currently selling at nearer 39 to the dollar, that 36-to-one ratio should leave an adequate "cushion" and might even result in some pleasant price surprises.

After preparation enough, Brussels awaits.

CHAPTER IV

BRUSSELS: THE HUB AND THE HEART

□ □ □

BRUSSELS

WATERLOO

LEUVEN

It is all of Europe in one city. Not simply one style or era, but all styles and eras. The medieval and the Renaissance. The Austrian neo-classic and the Spanish flamboyant. The French 19th century and the modern skyscraper. The accents and tones, in the very sounds that you hear, of both the Latin-influenced languages of Europe (here, the French) and the Germanic strains (here, the Flemish, or Dutch)—a rare, bi-lingual city. And not only do you see all of Europe here, and hear much of Europe here, but the very people that you meet—in a metropolis where a full one-quarter of the population is foreign—are from every corner of Europe, mixing and mingling in a setting that was always a crossroads for both invasions and trade. Brussels is not simply the nominal capital of Europe, it is fast becoming the true capital of Europe, and shows that status in a hundred, intriguing ways.

THE CAPITAL, TOO, OF BELGIUM: From the travel features of a lifetime of Sunday newspapers, you have probably learned of its richest sights long before now. They include the grandest of all the great City Squares. And restaurants so numerous as to make you dizzy. And subways decorated with modern art. And great museums of ancient art. And open-air markets of antiques and foods, of secondhand fashions and leather-bound books . . . and "chocolatiers" . . . and bakers of pastries sublime . . . and beery cafes.

Brussels is all of these . . . but it is more.

It is Bruges. And it is Ghent. And it is Antwerp and Liège. And Mons. And Tournai. Because Brussels is also a hub, a base for short day excursions, a geographical phenomenon unequalled on earth, a metropolis so centrally located that the lures and attractions of a dozen other great cities are also the attractions of remarkable Brussels.

THE HUB AND THE WHEEL: Look first at a map. In a country whose major art cities are arranged like the points on an oval circle, Brussels is located in the very center of the circle—and almost ridiculously close (30 miles or so) to most of those towns.

In the time that some of us spend commuting from home to work, we can travel from Brussels to Ghent (40 minutes away). In the hour that one drives from central London to Windsor Castle (which we all associate with London), one can go by train from Brussels to Bruges, or to Liège, or Tournai. In the 35 minutes needed to reach the Palace of Versailles from most Parisian hotels, a tourist from Brussels can be in Antwerp or Mons. In a sense, therefore, the attractions of those cities are also the key sights of Brussels: the Home of Rubens in Antwerp, the "Adoration of the Mystic Lamb" in Ghent, the Cathedral of Tournai, are all part of the inventory of Brussels. Though the avid sightseer will want to stay overnight or longer in those other cities of Belgium, the visitor limited to Brussels alone can also quite easily see them. When that fact is understood (and some tourists never grasp it), the nature of a stay in Brussels becomes not simply satisfying, but staggering—offering more choice and variety, more visits of genuine importance, more museums, galleries, historical sites, theatres and shops than in cities eight times its size. And requiring a far longer stay than is normally planned. As we now turn to the rich treasures and activities of Brussels itself, keep always in mind that Brussels virtually *includes* Bruges, Ghent, Antwerp, Mechelen, Leuven, Liège, Tournai, Mons, Binche, Namur and more—each reached in an hour-and-less from each of three railroad stations in the center of Brussels: Nord, Centrale and Midi. No other city on earth possesses such proximity to so many places of renown.

THE CAPITAL WITH A HUMAN FACE: But it is Brussels itself that most intrigues us. And yet puzzles the visitor to it. For it is utterly unlike—in fact, the diametric opposite—of what it should be.

By all reasonable expectations, Brussels should be a rather forbidding city, an historic seat of government somewhat haughty and imperious. It possesses all the ingredients for such a condition. It is 1000 years old, and a million persons in size. The language of most of them is elegant French. It was the 15th-century court of the flamboyant Dukes of Burgundy, and later of the regal Charles V. It is the capital of historic Brabant, and of the Belgian State. It is the emerging capital of the European community, and a capital of food for the world's gourmets.

In touristic terms, it enjoys all the superlatives. The world's greatest city square (in its gilded **Grand' Place**). One of the greatest of all art collections (in its **Musée de l' Art Ancien**). The world's most remarkable restaurant street (**Petite Rue des Bouchers**), and one of the greatest of all parks (**Forêt de Soignes**) and battlegrounds (**Waterloo**). It has palaces and royal guards, formal squares surrounded by neo-Classic colonnades, horse paths and esplanades leading to a giant triumphal arch. It *should* be filled with insolent doormen and arrogant maitre d's, with Balenciaga-clad matrons leading poodles on a leash, and by intimidating police at the imposing entrances to government buildings.

And yet Brussels is none of this. It is the most democratic of cities, the antithesis of "snob", always human in countenance, down to earth. Its sights impress but never (except for the Grand' Place) overwhelm. Its people and institutions are modest in their bearing, avoiding overstatement and illusions of grandeur, respectful and welcoming to the outsider. The greater part of its structures show little ostentation: the city's finest restaurant is on a modest square, the chic-est shops behind understated facades, the scale of entertainment sized to human proportions, in part consisting of small, beer-serving cafes to which the outsider is admitted without hesitation. Here are no surging crowds pouring into subway entrances, or massive traffic jams, or fleets of cars roaring about plazas and traffic circles. There is time for strolling, an absence of unremitting urban pressures, and even the faces of shoppers are without anxiety or strain.

It is a browsers' city. One wanders without plan from place to place, enjoying unexpected sights, intriguing small structures, a modest but ancient church or specialists' museum, a small open-air market with stands for raw mussels or hot snails, a gallery of paintings or books. One walks into a tiny shop staffed by a single proprietor who sells collections of stamps, or old coins or postcards, or ancient engravings and prints, in settings almost consciously cluttered, pleasantly shabby. One peruses the merchandise without pressure and at length, or with the assistance, if requested, of the elderly shop-keeper, an expert in numismatics or antiquarian books who makes no attempt to impress or overwhelm. One wanders into government buildings and is courteously shown around. One steps into cheery cafes and takes a beer without feeling unwanted. On the first day there, amid occasional splendor, one is relaxed, and at home.

Why is this? It is history—the peculiar history of Belgium—that has softened the appearance, moderated the grandeur, affected the attitudes of resplendent Brussels. Recall that for the last 500 years, the Belgians have been among the few people—are perhaps the only people—never to have entertained ambitions of world domination, or to feel themselves omniscient, powerful, or especially favored in resources or good fortune. Brussels in particular has been subjugated or occupied, bombarded or otherwise dominated, through much of that time, by every major European power other than the Scandinavians, the Swiss and the Italians. The vicissitudes of time, the knowledge of misfortune, has given a sense of proportion—a human face—to Brussels, eliminating the regal arrogance that undoubtedly prevailed in the 15th and 16th centuries. What results from all this is the best of both worlds: spectacle without snobbery, the grand vista of the European civilization without patronizing condescension. And make no mistake about it: though Brussels is calm and down-to-earth, it is nonetheless filled with splendor and exotic sights, a city of almost "theatrical" delight for the tourist prepared to accept it on its own terms.

THE RICH THEATRE: When the French poet, playwright and stage designer Jean Cocteau first saw the Grand' Place of Brussels, he called it "un riche théâtre", in fact "le théâtre le plus riche au monde" (the richest theatre on earth). In a sense, all of Brussels is a theatre, a stage set displaying the entire story of Europe.

It has no consistent appearance. A 19th-century train station overlooks an architectural "island" of the 15th and 16th centuries. 20th-century skyscrapers stand at the head of 19th-century boulevards. A square of 18th-century elegance is flanked by a 15th-century Gothic church. Turn-of-the-century "art nouveau" stands short steps away from a 17th-century step-gabled townhouse. Architectural development never stopped in Brussels, nor was architectural uniformity ever enforced. Within a tourist area measuring no more than a mile and a half in each direction, you walk from "play" to "play", changing eras with dizzying rapidity, changing dramatic treatments as you discover the most elegant districts situated just to the side of shabby ones, high-priced couture short steps from "friture" (french fries) stands.

You see these sights as in the short compass of an enclosed theatre, not in the vasty expanse of a film. Though there are broad boulevards, especially in the higher-income "upper part" of the central city ("haut de la ville"), the greater part of Brussels is a place of short, narrow streets, often winding or slightly curved, sometimes opening into a small square, only soon to close again, rarely affording broad vistas of light, or the panoramas of lengthy avenues. Because of this, and apart from the Grand' Place, few sights of Brussels "hit you over the head"; they sneak up upon you; they gradually emerge; they are like theatrical vignettes, small and colorful scenes featuring every major "player" on the European stage, from Peter Breugel to Napoleon Bonaparte, from Lord Byron to Victor Horta, from Charles V and Philip II to Jacques Brel; they display such varied physical highlights as to require an effort for their appreciation. But once understood, they are—like the best of dramas—enthralling. And the best means for acquiring that understanding is through a short review of history.

HISTORY AND ORIENTATION: It all began with a river called the *"Senne"* (but not to be confused with the "Seine" of Paris). Prior to the time when 19th-century city-planners covered it up, the Senne ran in a slightly-angled north-south direction through a marshy valley in the center of Brabant, in the heart of what is now Belgium.

For our limited purposes, the top of that river originated at what is now the **Place Rogier** of Brussels near the city's **Gare du Nord** (North Station), while the bottom end emerged at the South Station (**Gare du Midi**). The course it traversed is, very roughly, along that one lengthy boulevard bearing different, successive names—**Boulevard Adolphe Max, Boulevard Anspach, Boulevard Lemonnier**—that runs today from north to south through the center of Brussels. Though no one else in Brussels uses a single, generic name for them, we'll invent one and call these streets-built-over-the-river "Les Grands Boulevards". (Don't ever speak those words to a taxi driver!)

Several hundred yards to the east of the river (now: "Les Grands Boulevards") were hills, ascending sharply to a massive plateau. And on the side of these hills were once swiftly-flowing, mountain-like streams plunging downhill to the river. One of these—the *Rollebeek*—began in a hillside area of "sables" (sands), hence known as the **"Sablon"**, and plunged downhill into the Senne. Today, "le Sablon" is an important square of ravishing beauty, and the "Rollebeek" a picturesque, cobblestoned street lined along its downhill plunge with exquisite antique shops and medieval-style restaurants.

Along this river and on the sides of its flanking hills, a small trading settlement existed as far back as the times of the Frankish invasions of the late 300s. Christianized in the 7th century, the inhabitants of that settlement built a small hillside chapel dedicated to the archangel Michael, who had cast out the Devil from Heaven. The successor of that chapel, the imposing, two-towered **Cathedral of St. Michael,** stands on precisely the same hillside site today. Already the town was becoming known as *"Bruocsella"*—"a place in the marshes"—the marshes extending far up the side of the hills along the river.

Brussels in the late Middle Ages

It became a city in the year 977, when Charles of Lotharingie, the disaffected youngest son of a French king, placed a fortress there. Breaking with the family, he had pledged allegiance ("vassalité"—vassalage) to the Holy Roman Emperor of Germany, receiving in return a part of the "legacy of Charlemagne"—the land of "Lower Lotharingia"—which included what later was to be the Duchy of Brabant. As the Duke of Lower Lotharingia, his successors automatically became Counts of Brussels and Louvain, and later Dukes of Brabant. Fifteen of them—from Lambert I in 1015 through Jean III in 1355—presided over the development of Brussels as a rich commercial city specializing in the most luxurious forms of cloths and tapestries ("la draperie Bruxelloise"), other high quality crafts. From their castle on the **Coudenberg Hill** (where now you find the "Place Royale" and a part of the Park of Brussels), they also cast their lot, for the main part, with a handful of rich patrician families ("les lignages") in the struggle for control of the city waged for more than three hundred years against the workingmen of the crafts guilds of Brussels. That conflict periodically erupted in battles and insurrections, horrible punishments (in which strike leaders were buried alive) and privations, and generally resulted in victory by the patricians, who maintained the upper hand until well into the 15th century. In this regard, the history of Brussels differed radically from that of Bruges and Ghent, where the Guilds were victorious at an early stage of the same struggle. Cloth-trading Bruges and cloth-making Ghent were also far more important cities than Brussels in that time of the 13th and 14th centuries, reaching the height of their influence, size and fame in those years. It is perhaps because of this that the present-day aspect of Bruges and Ghent is a far older one than in Brussels, and one finds 12th-century, 13th-century and 14th-century structures in Bruges and Ghent of the sort and size that are virtually nowhere to be seen in Brussels.

At last, Brussels soars

In the 15th century, it became Brussels' turn. For now the immensely wealthy, pleasure-loving, art-appreciating Dukes of Burgundy enter onto the scene, consolidating their rule over almost all of what is now Belgium, and gradually shifting their capital from Dijon in France to a city they vastly preferred: the newly-prosperous, fast-growing Brussels.

As Bruges and Ghent declined (for reasons discussed in the chapters to come), Brussels soared. Artists and artisans poured into a city that was becoming rich and resplendent under the royal patronage of those lavish-living, gesture-loving Dukes. The Market Square of Brussels, partway between the river and the start of the hills, became a true **"Grand' Place"**. The increasingly-wealthy Guilds placed their headquarters buildings around the Square. An extraordinary **Town Hall** ("Hôtel de Ville") arose along one side, its construction requiring a full fifty years of the 1400s. Periodically, the Square erupted with silken, heraldic banners and flags, bleachers and pavilions for viewing the medieval tournaments and jousts of which the Dukes were so fond. On one memorable day, the young Charles the Bold (later the Duke of Burgundy) broke 18 lances in a single afternoon!

The 1500s were the second of the two centuries in which the power and eminence of Brussels reached their peak. In northern Europe, the mighty Charles V made Brussels the site of his most important councils and gatherings, the unofficial capital of a far-flung, world empire. The city swelled in size, prospered and shone, became especially renowned for its great tapestries which recorded all occasions of note. By this time, the Grand' Place was host to a yearly *"Ommegang"* ("walk-around", described later in this chapter), a procession of its colorfully-garbed city officials, nobles and guild members, its militia and its theatre troupes, which paraded for Charles V and his son, Philip II of Spain, in a particularly brilliant example of civic pride in 1549. From the Grand' Place, that procession snaked its way uphill to the majestic Church of the Sablon, on what was now the **Place du Grand Sablon** standing on that once-sandy expanse along the side of Brussels' eastern hills.

Though the second half of the 16th century was to be a far less happy time for Brussels—a period of continual religious conflict between Protestant and Catholic, witnessing vandalism and destruction of religious edifices by Protestant iconoclasts, the arrival of the occupying army of Spain's infamous Duke of Alva, the decapitation of Brussels' leading noblemen, the Counts of Egmont and Horne—the city continued to flourish. And throughout the more placid years (for Brussels) of the 1600s, its streets erupted with Baroque buildings, its outskirts with outposts of the Counter-Reformation—convents and abbeys, churches without number—as Brussels became the capital of the "Catholic Netherlands", that portion of the "Spanish Netherlands" (Belgium and Holland) that had remained loyal to Church and Spain.

. . . Until leveled by the French

And then: disaster. As the 17th century neared its end, so did the power of Spain in northern Europe. Weakened by military adventures and imperialistic expansion, Spain soon found that its "colonies" in Flanders and Wallonia were targets for the ambitions of the "Sun King" (Le Roi Soleil), Louis XIV of France. As his armies moved into the west of what is now Belgium, other European powers—the English, Swedes, Austrians, certain princes of Germany, even Holland—allied themselves to check the French advance, and Belgium again became a battlefield for more than forty years (roughly from 1667–1715). In 1695, in one of those casual acts of genocide so continually directed against Belgian cities over the centuries, King Louis XIV directed his chief of staff, the Marshal de Villeroy, to create a "distraction" by destroying Brussels. The object: to divert the Allies' attention from their seige of Namur! Villeroy and his armies dragged 18 giant cannons and 25 mortars to the heights of Anderlecht overlooking Brussels, and for nearly 48 hours, proceeded quite casually to rain down more than 4,000 shells upon a completely defenseless city, destroying several thousands of houses, 16 churches and other major buildings, and the entire Grand' Place except for the Town Hall. It was a fate similar to that suffered by Liège two centuries earlier, and to be suffered by Ypres in World War I and by Tournai in World War II, and explains why the appearance of the greater part of Brussels, Liège, Ypres and Tournai is today so very different (and more modern) than that of a largely-untouched Bruges or Ghent.

The re-building of the Grand' Place

The resilience of Brussels! Infuriated by the destruction of their market square, the city government ("la Magistrat") and the

Guilds of Brussels resolved to re-build the Grand' Place even grander than before. And they agreed to build according to a plan that would regulate the height of buildings and coordinate the designs of façades into a relatively-uniform display of fancifully-Baroque fronts of the "Italo-Brabant" style. In less than four years, from 1695 to 1699, in a flowering of architectural genius rarely seen either before or since, the draftsmen and builders of Brabant created one of the great sights of Europe: the **Grand' Place** of Brussels, to which we'll be returning for a closer look at a later point in this chapter. Victims so greatly imposed upon by military might, found their revenge—in Art. And emerged victorious over the greater power of their neighbors.

Brussels in more recent times

For most of the next 130 years, the people of Brussels turned inwards, weary of the disputes of kings, the tiresome marauders into their homes, the great power rivalries that so disturbed their peace. In the early-to-late 1700s, under the rather gentle rule of the Austrians (who had, by decision of the major powers, replaced the Spanish as Belgium's masters), the people of Brussels subsided into rather conservative habits and attitudes that distressed a visitor among them in 1740, the great Voltaire of France. "I am in a sad city", he wrote. "Un vieux pays d'obedience, Privé d'esprit, rempli de foi" (an ancient country of obedience, lacking in spirit, full of faith). The people of Brussels, with perhaps a greater wisdom of suffering, turned to beautifying their city. They surrounded the **Place Royale,** during this time, with those perfectly-symmetrical, neo-classic buildings that so refresh the eye when you walk uphill towards them from the Grand' Place (those graceful buildings, unaltered over the centuries, now contain such varied institutions as Lloyd's Bank and the Museum of Modern Art). They laid out the adjacent and enchanting **Park of Brussels** on the Coudenberg Hill. Within the lower city, 15,000 ladies patiently worked on the quiet production of lace renowned throughout the world. The entire population patiently endured a re-occupation of the city by the French, under Marshal de Saxe, from 1746 to 1748. They flocked then to welcome back their genial Austrian ruler, the playboy-sportsman Charles of Lorraine, who kept a benevolent watch over matters until 1780.

In 1789, the calm ended. The excitement of the French Revolution reached Brussels, resulted in the declaration of an independent Belgium by one faction, riotous disputes throughout the city with conservatives loyal to Austria, the brief occupation of Brussels by Austrian troops, and then the annexation of Belgium (and

Brussels) by the Revolutionary French Government, whose supporters proceeded to pillage the Cathedral of St. Michael and Ste. Gudule, to abolish the Guilds, scatter the bones of Dukes from up-ended tombs, destroy statues and other vestiges of "l'ancien regime". Brussels became the capital of a minor French "département"; various churches underwent transformation into "Temples of Reason"; and the Maison du Roi, on the Grand' Place, was renamed the "Maison du Peuple" (House of the People). Later, the emergence of Napoleon as Emperor of the French led to a moderating of the Revolution; but the defeat of Napoleon, and his escape from Elba, brought foreign troops back to Brussels in June of 1814.

It was like the re-run of a hundred imaginary movies. A great confrontation was about to take place. Napoleon had regrouped and re-animated the French armies. The British, Prussians and Dutch marched to destroy the re-born French. And to where did everyone proceed, almost without hesitation? To France, or to Germany? Of course not. They came to *Belgium,* Belgium the eternal Battlefield! And specifically: to Brussels, where a vast expanse of fields outside the neighboring village of *Waterloo* provided the site for one of the greatest battles of all time. With Napoleon defeated, the Congress of Vienna in 1815 re-drew the map of Europe, awarding Belgium to Holland; and for the next 15 years, the Belgians again endured rule by a foreign nation.

1830: An independent Belgium

When the Belgian Revolution finally occurred, it broke out in Brussels—and under the most colorful of circumstances. On the 25th of August, 1830, in the classic and imposing **Théâtre de la Monnaie** near the Grand' Place, where major operas and ballets are performed to this day, an opera called "La Muette de Portici" was playing to a packed house. In its second act, a tenor walked to the footlights to deliver the stirring aria, "Amour Sacré de la Patrie" (Sacred Love of Country). The audience exploded into tumultuous applause. Their shouts and cries carried to a crowd strolling in the square outside, and soon all of Brussels erupted into revolutionary fervor. Roaming bands of aroused residents broke into the homes of Dutch sympathizers and pillaged their contents, formed a volunteer militia, raised the newly-designed Belgian flag, sang a newly-composed anthem, "La Brabançonne". On the 23rd of September, the Dutch king responded by dispatching an army of 14,000 men to put down the rebellion. They were met by a hastily-supplied army of Brusselians, aided by a number of firebrands rushing up from Liège, and in a four-day battle that centered on the Park of Brussels, the Dutch were defeated. After a thousand years of fragmentation, division and foreign rule, an independent, unified Belgium had been created, in Brussels, in 1830.

19th-century Brussels

The capital at last of a nation, and under its own royal dynasty, Brussels took major leaps forward in population and development, proceeding to astonish the rest of Europe. In 1835, it was the first city on the continent of Europe to enjoy a railway line, connecting it to the city of Mechelen. In 1847, it became the first European metropolis to construct a spacious, glass-enclosed shopping arcade, the still-existing, still-elegant "**Galeries Saint Hubert**", a block from the Grand' Place, the very model for later indoor urban arcades ranging from London to Milan; they all copied "le passage Bruxellois". In the 1870s, Brussels constructed the largest building erected in the 19th century in Europe. This was the 16,000-square-meter **Palais de Justice**, designed by architect Joseph Poelaert in combined Greek/Roman style for the top of "Gallows Hill" overlooking the low-income Marolles district of Brussels (and deliberately placed there, some claim, to over-awe and subdue the unruly residents of that section); it still looms over the city from that site. Starting near that giant edifice, great curving boulevards were placed atop the heights of the hills overlooking the lower city. And then, to cap off a century of remarkable achievements, and after first opening the great, secular **Free University of Brussels** ("Université Libre de Bruxelles") and the neo-classic "**Musée de l'Art Ancien**", the city proceeded to hold not one, but three, World's Fairs or Expositions—in 1880, 1888 and 1897—at the newly-created Park of the "**Cinquantenaire**" (pronounced "san-con-tuh-nayr"), a monumental triumphal arch raised in 1880 to celebrate the 50th anniversary of the independence of Belgium, and flanked by two equally monumental exhibition halls that today serve as major museums of Brussels.

To such a growing, vital, vigorous city, there flocked the political exiles or emigrés of a dozen other countries. Victor Hugo fled here from France in 1851, took an apartment on the Grand' Place, and pronounced himself "tout ébloui de Bruxelles" (completely dazzled by Brussels)—with such a view, how could he fail to be! Karl Marx, expelled from Paris in 1845, moved to Brussels for a three-year stay, and therefore undoubtedly composed the "Communist Manifesto" in the Belgium capital (while thinking, presumably, about Ghent). Both he and other socialist leaders, among them the eminent Proudhon, attended meetings in the

"House of the Swan" (Maison du Cygne) on the Grand' Place, which currently and ironically houses one of the city's most expensive restaurants, upstairs. Already, Brussels was becoming the most international of all cities, open to every influence, receptive to every tendency in art, in architecture and politics. No wonder it presents such a varied appearance today!

20th-century Brussels

Our own century began brilliantly in Brussels with the flowering there of an architectural style almost unique to it—"art nouveau", whose most perfect practitioner was Victor Horta; we'll visit his masterworks in later pages of this chapter. In the ensuing fifty years, Brussels twice experienced cruel occupation for long years by German troops, in both World Wars I (1914–18) and II (1940–44), the latest in that historically endless series of humiliations visited upon the Belgian people; courageous acts of resistance by the city's mayors ("bourgmestres") and its residents are recorded in proclamations and exhibits hanging in the Town Hall on the Grand' Place.

Between the wars, the city continued to erect magnificent new structures: among them, the **Basilica of Sacré-Coeur** on the Koekelberg Hill, which is the fourth largest Christian edifice in the world (after St. Peter's in Rome, St. Paul's in London, Notre Dame des Fleurs in Florence); the **Palais des Beaux Arts** by Victor Horta on the hill ("mont des Arts") arising at the eastern side of the Grand' Place. But it was in the post-war year of 1958 that Brussels began to erupt in every district with those modern constructions that today create such a varied city, such a controversial and arresting, but vital, contrast between the traditional and the new, the low-lying and the high-rise.

1958 was the time of the monumental, post-war World's Fair of Brussels in the district of Heysel. It was surely among the greatest of the World's Fairs to be held in this century, with the most memorable of all theme symbols: the towering **Atomium** (a molecule of iron expanded by a factor of billions), still standing and in perfect operating and visiting condition today (with all escalators running, all exhibits still as they then were). That vastly optimistic 1958 exhibit of science and technology set off a burst of creative building that made a virtual construction site of much of Brussels throughout the 1960s. Simultaneously, the decision to make Brussels the headquarters city of the European Community, of N.A.T.O., and of scores of attendant international organizations and business firms, caused still more excavation, scaffolding, and disruption . . . all followed by more than fourteen years of subway construction starting in the early 1970s, and continuing almost to the present time, ripping up streets, disfiguring graceful boulevards, forcing tourists to tread their way warily upon plank-covered sidewalks and through the din of riveters' jackhammers, the choking dust of concrete mixers.

By 1988—with only pockets of continuing construction in the central city—the job was completed. And the tourist in 1989 and 1990 now sees a far different Brussels than was the case before.

If you were a visitor to Brussels in those construction-disturbed years of 1973–87, you'll need to give the city another look. Because you never really saw it! Brussels is Brussels again! Its downtown streets are clear of giant girders and deep trenches. Its boulevards are open and enthralling. Beneath them runs Europe's most modern subway system speeding between stations adorned with modern art. The streetcars are also largely underground. The key shopping thoroughfare of the center city—the **Rue Neuve**—has become a bustling but pleasant strolling-street for pedestrians only. At its head stands a furturistic, multi-level shopping center —"City 2"—of great verve. Except for touches of road renovation near the Place Rogier and at the Place Louise (probably complete by the time of your visit), Brussels is, at long last, Brussels again. And patches of modern architecture throughout the city now set off the varying examples of development—the succession of the centuries—the evolution of Europe itself—which mark the physical appearance of a city that experienced much, and never ceased to change.

THE PEOPLE AND THE TOWN OF BRUSSELS: In the technical terms of Belgian government, Brussels is an "agglomeration" (an aggregation, a "consolidated city") of 1,000,000 persons living in 19 separate and self-governing "communes", of which only one—a heart-shaped district in the very center, no more that 1½ miles in diameter—is the actual, traditional city of Brussels ("Bruxelles" to the French, "Brussel" to the Flemish). Twenty-five percent of the population are non-Belgian foreigners of widely-differing status: the sophisticated civil-service elite of the European Economic Community, the low-income North African "guest workers" performing industrial and manual tasks. Though there is considerable industry in Brussels, it is all in the Western portion of the "agglomeration" through which tourists rarely pass.

It is rather in the museums, shops, restaurants, hotels and theatres of that single, "heart-shaped" district in the very center of the "agglomeration" that tourists spend nearly all their time—and everyone calls it a "heart-shaped" district, even though the straight, horizontal line at the top of the "heart" gives it the better-described shape of jockey shorts on a human body. However described, the central district or commune has the concave *form* of a three-sided bowl. In the center ("centre de la ville") and to the west it is flat; along its northeastern, eastern and southeastern sides, it rises up along the side of hills into the area known as "haut de la ville" (upper Brussels). The flat part, where the River Senne once flowed, is the site of the "Grands Boulevards" and the "Grand' Place". Halfway or so up the hills are the Cathedral, the Sabena Air Terminal, Central Railroad Station, Palais des Beaux Arts, and Museum of Ancient Art. Further up, on the very tops of the hills, are the start of elegant residential quarters, boulevards, office buildings, the Royal Palace. Returning to the flat portion: the *North Station* ("Gare du Nord") is at the top of the "heart" (or jockey shorts); the *South Station* ("Gare du Midi") at the bottom.

Within the city, dual languages reign. All street signs and place names are in both French and Dutch. So are menus, museum descriptions, posters and advertisements. On television, channels alternate between the two languages, and all foreign movies carry dual sub-titles, in French and Dutch. But in the hotels, in the restaurants and the larger shops, English and several other languages are all well spoken, and it's in English that we now embark upon the search for rooms and meals.

HOTELS OF BRUSSELS

In the top categories, they are almost all of post-World War II construction, modern and with every comfort, yet far less expensive than their counterparts in other major European capitals. For a room that would be priced at $140 in Paris, you pay only $95 in Brussels; for what would cost $95 in London, you pay $65 in Brussels. In all the city, there are currently only three hotels whose room rates exceed 7000 francs ($194) per room, and the costlier of the three goes up to a top of 8,800 francs ($244), far less than at deluxe hotels in London, Paris or Rome. Like Brussels itself, the hotel scene is calm and unpressured, lacking the grand pretentions and haughtiness of so many other large cities.

The hotels also mirror the increasingly international flavor of Brussels. Prior to World War II, the very top rank consisted of four Belgian-owned hotels: the **Palace, Metropole, Atlanta** and **Astoria.** Today, the six leading hotels bear such distinctly non-Belgian titles as **Hilton, Sheraton, Hyatt, Ramada, Amigo** and **Royal Windsor.** Of the six, four are American-operated, one belongs to Chinese investors, and only the Amigo is managed by a thoroughly-Belgian group! And the French—those Belgium-coveting French—are here as well, this time with the best of Brussels' moderately-priced hotels, a gleaming, new, construction known as the **Arcade Sainte-Catherine**. But regardless of the owner's nationality, the hotel staffs you'll encounter are almost entirely Belgian, multi-lingual beyond even normal European abilities, kind and direct in their dealings with guests, always aware that you, not they, are the person to be served. As in the restaurants—a phenomenon you'll soon be experiencing—Belgian courtesy is always observed.

Most hotel rates in Brussels (except occasionally in the very highest categories) include continental breakfast, service charge and Value Added Tax. Because you almost certainly will be staying overnight in Brussels—and should stay much longer—you'll need a fairly thorough review of the available choices. My own highly-personal ratings—from de luxe to budget (and below)—follow now in generally descending order of category and price.

THE VERY BEST: Two hotels—one modern (the Brussels Hilton), one traditional (the Amigo)—lead all the others. But though the 183-room **Amigo**, 1 Rue de l'Amigo (phone 511-5910), has the centuries-old appearance of the Spanish Renaissance, blending perfectly with the setting of the ancient Grand' Place only one short block away, it was built in 1958, and admits to no lack of modern comfort. Far from it, this is a thoroughly de luxe operation, with emphasis on close personal attentions by a large staff, the 24-hour availability of services. It is, however, a quiet, understated hotel maintained for people of highly-developed, good taste, with only a single, subdued bar, a small restaurant, no nightclub or other like features. Public areas display oriental rugs on flagstone floors, Brussels tapestries and landscape paintings on elegant, moulded, white walls; rooms are done in traditional, country-style furnishings, with fairly narrow twin beds, but with giant bathrooms having bidets and all else. The key attraction is location—just behind the Town Hall, a block from the Grand' Place—and most windows look quite thrillingly at the turreted roof of that 15th-century structure. A subsidiary attraction are the quite moderate prices for a hotel of such standing: from 3600 to 5850 francs ($100 to $163) for a twin-bedded room with breakfast for two, service charge and Value Added Tax, from 2800 to 5300 francs ($78 to $147) for a single with breakfast, service and tax.

The city's other contender for top honors is the **Brussels Hilton,** 38 Boulevard de Waterloo (phone 513-8877), gracefully-elegant, a 30-story, slab-sided skyscraper of nearly 400 rooms, along that high-altitude boulevard to the east of the central city that is definitely "haut de la ville" (the "height of the city", "upper Brussels") in more than a purely physical sense: starting from here, along that broad, "elevated" boulevard, are the most expensive shops and great shopping names of Brussels, operating in the main from behind heavy grills or narrow glass windows in stocky granite buildings that once were mansions. Across the boulevard are film theatres and still more shops, restaurants, and the start of an upper-income district of office structures and apartment houses. Throughout the Hilton chain, this is known as a "Flagship", a training ground, the pursuer of impossibly high standards by a staff that is starched and correct. Rooms are modern, spacious, air-conditioned and of the best Hilton standards, with wide, hard beds; and prices are high (by Brussels levels) but reasonably so: 6800 to 7500 francs ($189 to $208) for single rooms with breakfast, 8000 francs ($222) for most double rooms with breakfast, service and tax—although they technically range as high as 8700 francs ($241), the latter, however, for two floors of specially-designed "Givenchy rooms", all in brown suede and leather, as if lifted from a Playboy-style dream. There is a sauna, but no swimming pool. The choice you make between this and the Amigo, in seeking the very best of Brussels' hotels, is influenced solely by your own preferences as between the modern and the traditional, the showy and the subdued.

THE TOP RANK—JUST BELOW THE TWO BEST:

Down a step, but very good indeed, are the Sheraton, Hyatt and Royal Windsor, which some would rank in that ascending order.

The 600-room **Brussels Sheraton,** at 3 Place Rogier (phone 219-3400), many stories high, is almost of the physical standard of the Brussels Hilton. Its large and modern guest rooms are tastefully designed and have small "living areas" (couch or easy chairs with cocktail table), as well as every modern convenience (in-house video movies, individually-adjusted air conditioning), and there are multiple restaurants, bars and cafes, in addition to that treasure which the Hilton lacks—a top floor, indoor swimming pool, solarium and health club attended by numerous chic types from both within the hotel and without. If the Sheraton were located in "upper Brussels", it would attract the very same spiffy sorts that lend such a special atmosphere (not a better one, simply a distinctively different one) to the Brussels Hilton. Instead, the Sheraton was built at the Place Rogier, at the start of the broad, middle-class shopping and entertainment boulevards ("Les

Grands Boulevards") of Brussels, at a time when the district north of the Place was being demolished for creation of a multi-skyscraper "World Trade Center". When work on that partially-abandoned project ceased in the mid-1970s, it left a vast blight, a part of which resumed its earlier life as the red-light district of Brussels (a valid sight-seeing attraction, incidentally). Though the Sheraton itself is on a perfectly proper square, well-located in walking distance to shops, theatres and the Grand' Place, it lacks the favored "milieu" of the Hilton, and attracts normal people like you and me: tourists, business visitors. Still, it is a high-quality, slickly-maintained hotel, third best in Brussels, and charges precisely 7290 to 7500 francs ($203 to $209) for twin-bedded rooms (wide, firm mattresses), including breakfast, service and tax.

The **Hyatt-Regency Brussels** at 250 Rue Royale (phone 217-1234), at the side of the Botanical Gardens (but on an otherwise unprepossessing street), is up that steep hill from the Place Rogier, on the way to "haut de la ville", and is actually quite well located for reaching and enjoying both the lower center city and the elegant uplands. More than 300 rooms in size, and totally new, it is covered or endowed throughout with marble and mirrors, fancifully-exotic crystal chandeliers, soft and modern brown-leather chairs, numerous restaurants and cafes, and best of all, well-designed rooms of modern comfort (in-room movies, etc.), the standard of Brussels' Hilton and Sheraton, but generally smaller in size. Rates are uniformly 6000 to 6300 francs ($167 to $175) for either single or double rooms, including service and tax, but with breakfast additional.

Hotel Royal Windsor, 5 Rue Duquesnoy (phone 511-4215), is another of the new and modern, or recently built, hotels that today account for the greater part of Brussels' hotel industry, and this one enjoys a location as exciting as the Amigo's, a short 2½ blocks from the Grand' Place, in "L'Ilot Sacré" (the Sacred Isle) of Brussels' origins. It literally gleams, a recently constructed block of burnished-wood interiors and polished copper fittings, ingeniously designed to complement the older structures of the Grand' Place area. It also operates high quality public facilities—a richly-Victorian restaurant, an Edwardian club and bar, a typically English pub—and equally well-furnished rooms (275 of them) with sparkling fixtures of considerable elegance. Though rooms are compact, they are quite comfortable, and their access to superb public facilities perhaps warrants the highest room charges in Brussels: a standard 7500 francs ($208) single, 8800 francs ($244) double, but *including* a mammoth buffet breakfast of costly ingredients taken in a downstairs restaurant (or a continental variety served to your room), service charge and Value Added Tax.

THE REMAINDER OF THE MAJOR FIRST CLASS HOTELS:

As you've noted, all the hotels we've cited are of modern, post-war construction (although two—the Amigo and the Royal Windsor—are in traditional, or near-traditional, style). Yet as we now descend to a slightly less costly category of first class hotels, they continue to consist of recently-constructed hotels in five of the eight instances. Brussels may be an ancient city, but the overwhelming number of its hotels are modern and up-to-date. My own highly personal rating of the next eight, in descending order of desirability, is the following:

Arcade Stephanie, 91 Avenue Louise (phone 538-8060), on the upper-class portion of that high-income shopping boulevard in "upper Brussels" (haut de la ville), near parks and tree-lined walks, leads the list. It is so futuristic in style and furnishings that its lobby is lined in stainless steel! Looking like a glass office building, its 140 units consist of kitchenette suites with space age furnishings, moulded plastic chairs with contour-shaped cushions, even dishware of the most advanced, hand-crafted styles. And the hotel itself boasts an indoor swimming pool (one of two in Brussels to do so). Rates are 5490 francs ($153) for the two-room-suites, including breakfast, service and tax.

Hotel Bedford, 135 Rue du Midi (phone 512-7840), consisting of 250 first class rooms, all with TV, radio and direct dial phones, comes as a distinct surprise as you walk from the area of the Grand' Place down the somewhat shabby and quaint Rue du Midi lined with the shops of stamp collectors and dealers in ancient coins. Squeezed between far older structures, no more than five blocks from the famous square, is suddenly this marble-lined structure of quality totally unlike its outdoor setting. Rooms are fairly compact, but not unusually so; furnishings and standards are of modern motel levels; rates (including continental breakfast, service and tax) are a reasonable 3760 to 4200 francs ($104 to $117) double, 3020 to 3350 ($84 to $93) single. And though your immediate surroundings aren't especially attractive, you are but the shortest stroll, never requiring transportation, from the color and glitter of the Grand' Place and its surrounding restaurant streets ("l'Ilot Sacré").

The 245-room **Brussels Europa,** 107 Rue de la Loi (phone 513-7820), member of Britain's Grand Metropolitan chain, is a glass-and-stone high-rise off a motorway that courses through an office district near the headquarters building ("the Berlaymont") of the European Economic Community off the Rond-Point Schuman. It was obviously placed here to house visitors and conferences associated with the E.E.C., and although its public facilities —including its particularly acclaimed "Beefeater Restaurant"— are as adequate as any other, it is not close to sites of touristic interest (other than the E.E.C. building) and should be considered only as a high-quality alternative if other hotel choices are full. High quality it most certainly is, with rooms in "British modern" —solid and proper, with green-accented tones—renting at 5900 francs ($164) for a double with breakfast, 4900 francs ($136) for a single with breakfast, including service charge and tax as well.

The **Brussels Ramada,** 38 Chaussée de Charleroi (phone 539-3000), in a long but low, six-story, modern building on a streetcar-street a five-minute walk from the fashionable Avenue Louise, in "upper Brussels", is of standard Ramada quality, possessing all the comforts (including modern, wide beds with firm mattresses) but presenting them in somewhat dull fashion, like a hundred other hotels you've seen. America plunked down in Brussels! Still, you may be homesick for such familiar sights. And comforts are there, though somewhat pricey at the rate of 4950 francs ($138) per double room, including breakfast, service and tax.

Jolly Hotel Atlanta, 7 Boulevard Adolph Max (phone 217-0120), is the revised, refurbished and now newly-modern version of the long-established and rather grand Atlanta Hotel, on that 19th-century, major shopping boulevard in "centre ville" (central Brussels) that runs from the Place Rogier to the "Bourse" (Stock Market) in front of the Grand' Place. Its 250 rooms are now "Italian modern" under management of the famed Jolly hotel chain of southern Italy, and possess such surface touches as mini bars in each room and bedside TV controls; once-traditional public facilities and lobby are now "functional modern", rather slick. Rates are 4900 francs ($136) single, 6000 francs ($167) double or twin, including breakfast, service and tax—which is overly high by Brussels standards, but a real value by comparison with other European cities for a location such as this.

Hotel Metropole, 31 Place de Brouckère (phone 217-2300), brings us at last to a thoroughly old-fashioned hostelry (an increasing rarity in constantly-changing Brussels). Near the Jolly Atlanta, and in the very center of "Les Grands Boulevards" to which we've referred, it is Brussels' classic hotel from the very late 1800s, 500 rooms in size, and site of the famed Brussels Conference on Physics in 1911, commemorated by a lobby photograph of the assembled Max Planck, Albert Einstein, Marie Curie, Ernest Rutherford, Hendrick Lorentz and others, as they pondered here the theories that led to nuclear fission. What a superb vestige of the past is this hotel—to be seen by every visitor to Brussels—all gilt and marble, with Greek columns and green palms, decorated ceilings, lofty spaces; a bit musty in parts, with rather standard furnishings in the large guest rooms, wide corridors; a thoroughly European experience for travellers who don't demand the ultimate in modern comfort but like atmosphere and fairly reasonable rates: 4400 to 5000 francs ($122 to $139) for a twin room with private bath and breakfast, 3600 to 4200 francs ($100 to $117) for a single with bath and breakfast, always with service and tax included.

Hotel Pullman Astoria, 103 Rue Royale (phone 217-6290), was once *the* hotel of Brussels. Built in 1909 in the style of the "Belle Epoque" (with a dash of the Art Nouveau thrown in), and almost consciously modeled after the celebrated Hotel Adlon of Berlin, it was to Brussels as the Ritz was to London, the Negresco to Nice, the Charidge to Paris. And it is still a spectacular sight in its public places, with its Louis XV furnishings, Corinthian columns, textured marble. Guestrooms upstairs are all recently redone, and while not quite of de luxe standard, they're attractively and comfortably furnished. Single rooms rent for 3920 francs ($109), doubles for 5840 francs ($162), but not including breakfast, which is 420 francs ($12) more. In the days of its glory, the Emperor Hirohito stayed here, and another perennial guest, the Aga Khan, took milk baths in his tub each morning.

The 100-room **Hotel New Siru,** at the Place Rogier (phone 217-7580), is yet another of the major first class hotels, and among the best values in this category. At its central location alongside the Brussels Sheraton, it's a thoroughly refurbished version of the once-popular Siru, but "refurbished" is too mild a word—it's been gutted and re-done in thoroughly modern form as of early 1988, and although most guestrooms are compact in size, they're so ingeniously and light-heartedly designed, in such futuristic fashion (halogen lamps, art deco headboards, humorous wall murals) as to lift your spirits. So will the rates: only 2180 francs ($61) for a single with private shower and breakfast, 2660 francs ($74) for a single with private bath and breakfast, 3090 francs ($86) for a twin with private shower and two breakfasts, 3490 francs ($97) for a twin with private bath and breakfasts.

And there you have, in three groupings, 13 of the top hotels of Brussels, ranked according to my own purely personal tastes, in descending order of preference. The selection is by no means all inclusive, and omits several Avenue Louise hotels (the **Tagawa, Mayfair,** others), as well as those near the Airport of Brussels (the quite sumptuous, 300-room **Holiday Inn Airport,** with king-sized beds and free sauna and pool; the 126-room **Hotel Sofitel;** the **Sheraton Airport,** others). It omits as well the giant President Hotel near the World Trade Center (occupied primarily by business visitors to Brussels), as well as several other relatively-recent hotels (such as the **Fimotel, Alfa Sablon,** and others) that are currently battling the longer-established properties for inclusion in the top ranks. In a book as small as this, it obviously isn't possible to list or describe everyone.

Now let's look at the smaller hotels of Brussels, which are frequently less expensive but often of similar standard and comfort to the better-known names. Many—in keeping with Brussels' recent emergence as the capital of Europe—are brashly modern creations with rooms decorated in "far out" contemporary styles, and with kitchenette facilities included for those many visitors on week-long or several-week stays in the Belgian capital.

THE SMALLER HOTELS: Hotel Archimede, at 22 Rue Archimede (phone 231-0909), leads the list in this next category, and misses inclusion in the earlier grouping only because of its relatively small size, 56 rooms. But what rooms! Designed with panache—a wildly-eclectic assortment of far-out lamps, beds, chairs, desks and other furnishings—it's a thorough *gestalt* of contemporary visions, and enhances the sophisticated humor of its appearance with such touches as a life-sized mannequin of a maitre d' stationed near the lobby entrance, a series of nautical portholes pasted on walls of the basement dining room. The stylish Galila Barzilai-Hollander, who also operates the New Hotel Siru at the Place Rogier (see above), is the creative force here; she oversees a trendy clientele who receive exquisite service, all in a different sort of Brussels location just down the street from the star-shaped headquarters building of the European Community. Double rooms rent for 4400 francs ($122), including a buffet breakfast for two; singles for 3750 francs ($104), again with that buffet.

Much cheaper is the brand-new, 60-room **Hotel Arlequin,** 17 Rue de la Fourche (phone 514-1615), in the heart of Brussels' "L' Ilot Sacre" (the Sacred Isle) of medieval streets lined with restaurants, just to the side of the Grand' Place. But with a location like that, and spectacularly-modern rooms of beige or light grey decor, the low-price structure is probably intended only for a first year of operation (1989) and will undoubtedly take an upward leap in 1990. Still, for early-bird guests, rates are only 1300 francs ($36) single, 1800 francs ($50) for a large double bed, 1900 francs ($52.77) per twin, 2400 francs ($53) for a triple, always with breakfast included, and often for rooms with an awesome view of the Town Hall towering over a jumble of ancient roofs. Though the main address is as given above, I prefer the entrance just off the "restaurant street" of Brussels—the Petite Rue des Bouchers—down a passageway next to No. 14 on the street.

The 40-room, newly-constructed **Hotel l'Agenda,** at 6 Rue de Florence (phone 539-0031), down the street from the important Avenue Louise, in upper Brussels ("haut de la ville"), is just such a gem, its rooms furnished in the most brightly-modern style, each with mini-bar, color TV and completely equipped kitchen (not kitchenette, but *kitchen*), of which half look out onto a quiet, inner courtyard with giant tree; numerous Japanese and Italian business visitors stay here, enjoying 24-hour room service, and yet they pay only 3300 francs ($92) for a double so equipped (with fairly narrow twin beds, true), without breakfast, but with service and tax included. And Rue de Florence, off the large avenue, is a pleasant, semi-residential street.

The 55-room **Hotel Alfa-Louise,** at 4 Rue Blanche (phone 537-9210), again only short steps from the Avenue Louise, is more of the same: a gloriously modern, clean-lined, glass-sided building of colorfully-decorated rooms with private bath and color TV, this time providing kitchenettes only to guests staying more than one week; for those who don't, there's a delightful, seventh-floor breakfast room. Rates are 3250 francs ($90) twin, 2850 francs ($79) single, *including* breakfast, and of course including service and tax.

And then there's the quite remarkable **Hotel-Residence Manos,** at 100 Chaussée de Charleroi (phone 537-9682), in this very same district of "upper Brussels" near the Avenue Louise. This one is for readers appreciative of imaginative design and of what a designer can do with an opportunity: two fairly old, adjoining structures on a rather plain street, where one gasps with admiration after entering through a courtyard-like entrance into a lavishly-decorated, living room bar and garden that serves as "frontispiece" for 24 sophisticated, large rooms or duplex-style "apartments" (the latter quads, and equipped with kitchens). All are again intriguingly decorated, some like a New Orleans bordello (and that comment is meant in a highly complimentary sense). Doubles are 2675 francs ($74), without breakfast, but with service and tax; apartments used as triples are 3175 francs ($88) on the same basis; apartment quads 4380 francs ($122)—a top value; and a single drawback is the lack of an elevator in these buildings lovingly converted into hotel use. The Manos is just up the street from the Brussels Ramada.

If all three of these moderately-priced selections are full, then try the 42-room **Hotel La Cascade,** at 14 Rue de la Source (phone 538-8830), 2½ blocks from the Manos, 2915 francs ($81), for a double with breakfast, service and tax included). And if La Cascade is full, you'll find a nearly identical value (because it provides full American or English-style breakfast in its room rates, guaranteed to fill you till evening), at the extremely modern, much larger (260 rooms) **Hotel Delta,** at 17 Chaussée de Charleroi (phone 539-0160), back near where you found the more exciting Manos: 3200 francs ($89) twin, 2700 francs ($75) single, including that large breakfast, service charge and tax.

Something cheaper? We now move downwards a notch, to the budget variety of Brussels hotel.

THE BUDGET-PRICED HOTELS OF HIGH QUALITY:
Easily the most exciting hotel to come along in years is the 234-room **Arcade Sainte-Catherine,** Place Ste. Catherine (phone 513-7620), near the so-called "Fish Market" area of Brussels (which is actually a section of seafood restaurants), and just a very short walk from the Grand' Place. The Arcade chain, once confined to locations in France, is a joint venture by major French companies seeking to create modestly-priced, in-city, "two star" hotels by using every recent advance in construction, engineering and design. The Arcade Sainte Catherine is their Brussels achievement. Its 234 rooms are triangularly shaped, with bathrooms at the outer wall, not next to the door as in most hotels (thus gaining an additional two square meters in space). Moulded, plastic furniture in bright orange or green supplies the decor; doubles are converted into triples and quads by pulling down upper bunk beds fitted into the walls; stall showers are in bathrooms; grocery shopping carts used for taking your luggage upstairs; ingenious exterior design of the large, seven-story building conforms with the more traditional appearance of surrounding buildings; a children's play area is maintained downstairs; payment is made on arrival rather than departure. In utterly modern surroundings of quite reasonable comfort and pleasant appearance, you pay (including breakfast, service and tax) 2035 francs ($57) per twin room with private facilities, 1750 francs ($49) per single, 275 francs ($7.64) extra, including breakfast, for children. From the "Bourse" (Stock Market building) in front of the Grand' Place, simply walk across the Boulevard Anspach (one of the "Grands Boulevards"), and three short blocks further in, to find the Place Ste. Catherine.

Almost as large (151 rooms), just as well-located, but as old as the Arcade Sainte-Catherine is new, is Brussels' **Hotel Central,** at

3 Rue Auguste Orts (phone 511-8060)—and central it is: directly across the Boulevard Anspach from the Bourse, and therefore only 200 yards or so from the Grand' Place. A stately, but somewhat weary, 19th-century building houses these 151 rooms stuffed with heavy, old-fashioned furnishings. Those with bath rent for 1900 to 2300 francs ($53 to $64) double or twin, breakfast for two included, for 1600 to 1750 francs ($44 to $49) single, again with breakfast (and always with service and tax as well).

The secret of a good hotel, said a wise hotelier, is "location, location and location". Around the corner from the Grand' Place, at the start of the "Mont des Arts" (Hill of the Arts), the 28-room **Hotel La Madeleine,** 22 Rue de la Montagne (phone 513-2971), occupies one of the most exciting locations in Brussels. (Don't be disturbed by the kitchen behind the reception desk.) In this remarkable situation of period buildings with Baroque gables, all near art galleries and collectors' shops (old manuscripts, old postcards), the elevator-equipped hotel provides perfectly respectable and quite charming accommodations, with private bath, for 1795 francs ($50) per twin-bedded room, 1295 francs ($36) single, breakfast, service and tax included.

Finally, on that same Place Rouppe that houses Brussels' finest restaurant (Comme Chez Soi; see our restaurant discussion below), a 10-minute walk down the Rue du Midi from the area of the Grand' Place, the 24-room **Hotel Windsor,** 13 Place Rouppe (phone 511-2014), occupies a relatively modern building in which it offers rooms of a solid, tourist-class standard for 1530 francs ($46) double, with breakfast, service charge and tax included. From your windows, you look right out, yearningly, at Comme Chez Soi!

Let's next go to the *cheap,* but suitable, hotels of Brussels.

BRUSSELS' THOROUGHLY RECOMMENDABLE CHEAP HOTELS: Pension Osborne, 67 Rue de Bosquet (phone 537-9251), off the restaurant-lined Rue Jourdan, itself off the lovely Avenue Louise, charges only 1000 to 1350 francs ($28 to $38) for a double with bath and breakfast, 900 to 1200 francs ($25 to $33) for a single with bath and breakfast. **Les Bluets,** nearby at 24 Rue de Suisse (phone 538-4428), is still another "tourist residence" with comparable rates.

Back in lower Brussels ("centre ville") on the Place Rouppe, **A La Grande Cloche,** 10 Place Rouppe (phone 512-6140), opposite the famed "Comme Chez Soi" restaurant, is one of those oft-encountered older hotels of Belgium found perched over a tavern, with weather-beaten, much worn rooms resembling Van Gogh's at Arles, but utterly respectable and appealing to the more adventurous brand of tourist to Europe. Twin-bedded rooms with private shower are only 1450 francs ($40), including breakfast for two, service and tax, and the same without that makeshift shower (a cubicle placed in the room) are only 1150 francs ($32), again with service, tax and continental breakfast for two. Place Rouppe is not only the departure point for buses to Waterloo and Anderlecht (home of Erasmus), but it is no more than 10 minutes on foot from the area of the Grand' Place.

YOUTH HOSTELS OF BRUSSELS: Though preference is given to travellers of student age in summer, people of any age may stay at the five, welcoming youth hostels of Brussels—the word "youth" having been given the broadly-Belgian definition of "young in spirit", not young in chronological years. In fall and winter, a great many savvy oldsters (the kind who ferret out all sorts of "underground" travel values) head with smug expressions for the best of Brussels' student establishments, which also happen to be among the best of the world's youth hostels. One is operated by the French community of Belgium, the other by the Flemish—but both are open to all visitors of any background at all.

The French version is the brand-new **"Jacques Brel" International Accommodations Center,** at 30 Rue de la Sablonniere (Place des Barricades, near the Place Madou), phone 218-0187, in an elegant square of period buildings in the "upper Brussels" section of the city; it's near everything. Totally modern, but designed to resemble the 19th-century mansions it adjoins, the Jacques Brel offers 131 beds in doubles, triples, quads and 6-bedded or 12-bedded dorms. These rent, including breakfast, for 550 francs ($15.27) in a room used as a single, for 450 francs ($12.50) per person in twins, for 375 francs ($10.40) per person in triples or quads, and for only 330 francs ($9.17) per person in the dorms. There's a one-time charge of 90 francs ($2.50) for sheets. Facilities include an excellent restaurant and snackbar, meeting rooms and lounge, a highly-qualified staff, a well-stocked bulletin board, the best of beds and lockers. Run, do not walk; but better yet, take the metro to "Madou" or "Botanique".

The alternate, modern hostel is a Flemish-run wonder known as the **J. H. Bruegel,** at 2 Rue St. Espirit off the Boulevard de l'Empereur (phone 511-0436), alongside the Notre Dame de la Chapelle church, ten minutes on foot from the Gare Centrale (Central Station). Less than five years old, an architectural marvel that uses odd protrusions, ingenious angles, abstract shapes and geometric forms to resemble a building of the Middle Ages (and thus harmonizes with the fascinating, old district in which it is found—a proof that modern construction need not disturb the appearance of older districts), the 125-bed, four-story Bruegel is otherwise modern inside, with self-service evening cafeteria (open to all from 6 p.m. to 7:30 p.m.), elevators, comfortable lounge covered with college-style bulletin boards and posters, and both single, twin, quad, and dormitory-style (12 to a unit) rooms, costing 550 francs ($15.27) single, only 450 francs ($12.50) per person twin, 375 francs ($10.40) per person quad, only 330 francs ($9.17) in the double-decker dorm—always including breakfast. However: you pay 60 francs ($1.67), one-time only, for sheets (if you haven't a sleeping bag), 80 francs ($2.22) for a temporary youth hostel card (if you aren't already a member). From your base at the Breugel, you are only a few minutes from the daily flea market of "les Marolles" at the Place du Jeu de Balle, an equal distance from the elegant precincts of the Place du Grand Sablon; and to these and all other noted sights of Brussels, you'll be directed by a dedicated English-speaking staff of young Flemings headed by a long-experienced, youth affairs specialist, Mark Wyttenhove.

The larger (180 beds), far more basic **"CHAB" Hostel,** at 6 Rue Traversière (phone 217-0158), around the corner from the Botanical Gardens and the Botanique metro stop (and very well located, as you'll soon come to understand), occupies a big, rambling structure of 1930s construction, on an old, old street, but it is no less exciting for all that! Directly across the street, CHAB also operates the summer-only (June 10 to September 10) **"Sleep Theatre"** (the floor space remaining, after seats have been removed, of a small playhouse) where backpackers place their sleeping bags for the cheapest price in all of Brussels: 170 francs ($4.72) per night, not including breakfast. Inside CHAB, accommodations are standard youth hostel level (rooms consisting of beds and nothing else), but 36 out of 43 rooms are private doubles, triples and quads renting for 420 francs ($11.67) per person double, 370 francs ($10.27) per person triple or quad, including a quite adequate breakfast. Beds in the remaining 10-person dorms are 280 francs ($7.77), again breakfast included. Since CHAB has no official hostel affiliations, it requires no membership card, and also —like the Brel and Bruegel—takes persons of all ages. High recommendation.

The fourth of the hostels is another old structure (covered, inside and out, with murals of 1920s aviators, peace symbols and other exotica) known as the **Sleep Well,** 27 rue de la Blanchisserie (phone 218-5050), marvelously well located near the Place Rogier, the Gare du Nord (North Station), the pedestrians-only shopping street of Brussels (Rue Neuve), and the Jacques Brel Foundation (of which more later). Another rabbit warren of rooms and dorms (with also a pleasant lounge in back, adjoining a sprightly breakfast room), its units are mainly doubles renting for 380 francs ($10.55) per person, breakfast included, and there are six dormitories housing either five persons at 330 francs ($9.17) apiece, ten persons at 270 francs ($7.50) apiece, or twelve and more at 180 francs ($5) apiece, breakfast included. To this, add 50 francs for the one-time rental of fresh sheets.

And finally, in Upper Brussels, ("haut de la ville"), using the Porte de Namur or Luxembourg metro stations, you'll find the building (and adjoining summertime camp site) of **La Maison Internationale,** 205 Chausée de Wavre (phone 648-8529), where most rooms are singles, of all things, renting for 340 francs ($9.44) breakfast included (another 24 rooms are doubles for 290 francs ($8) per person, including breakfast), and tents outside house summertime (June to September) backpackers for only 200 francs ($5.55) a night. Sleeping indoors, add 50 francs ($1.39) for the one-time rental of sheets.

ROOMS IN PRIVATE HOMES OF BRUSSELS—"LA ROSE DES VENTS":

We end our discussion of lodgings with a different, but very typical, form of Belgian hospitality: bed and breakfast, in a family setting, with residents who make their homes available as much to meet and converse with travellers from around the world as to earn the rather meager sums they charge for such facilities. Belgium possesses the "bed-and-breakfast" organization to end all others, in the form of Simone Blancke-Hinnekens' **"La Rose des Vents"** (the "Windrose" or Compass), at 9 Avenue des Quatre-Vents, 1810 Wemmel (Brussels) (phone 02/460-34-59).

In later portions of this Brussels chapter, and in other city chapters still ahead, you'll be reading about a broad array of Belgian organizations that offer free hospitality services to visiting foreigners: free nature walks, free tours of Brussels ("Meet the Brusselians"), free visits to Belgian homes. Though La Rose des Vents must charge for its members' room accommodations ($34 to $42 for most double rooms, per night, breakfast included), its major aim is to tap a Belgian resource: the enjoyment that so many Belgians derive from meeting travellers, from revealing the glories of Belgium to them, from thus promoting world understanding. Though Denmark is the European nation most famed for such attitudes, Denmark's "Meet the Danes" programs can't compare in scope and variety with those of Belgium.

La Rose des Vents will place you in private homes not only in Brussels, but in other Belgian cities. Its delightful descriptive literature lists such opportunities as a house outside Bruges, for instance, "alongside a quiet canal lined with leaning poplar trees. . . . Trudo, our host, is retired. He is a mathematics and drawing teacher, tall and straight like a poplar tree. His wife, Ghislaine, is younger, and still a teacher at kindergarten". Or else a Brussels residence at the edge of the sylvan beauties of the Forest of Soignes, "large and comfortable and surrounded by an extensive garden; you can relax and read in a cosy chair on the lawn. Ann and Yvan have four children. Yvan is a commercial manager and has an extensive education . . .". Or else a house 10 minutes from downtown Brussels, whose "Madame . . . is a most pleasant woman of style and polish, in her fifties. Her former profession of social worker has developed her natural pleasure in human contact and in being helpful. Monsieur . . . is a chemical engineer who speaks English . . .". Or else a home located on the heights of Waterloo outside Brussels, overlooking the battle site: "Mr. . . . is 35, and his young wife, Muriel, is 30. Their two little twin sons, Gregory and Xavier, are 3. They live in a brand new house and look forward to years of embellishing their happy nest and making new friends".

At these, and many other similar homes and apartments, all carefully screened to eliminate quarrelsome types and other psychological problems, Mrs. Blancke-Hinnekens will book you for long or short stays, arrange group visits, student exchanges, all other forms of hospitality services. Her one-time booking fee is $29, and a letter ahead is best advised for the most attractive homes out of her inventory of delights!

With lodgings secured, the sensual glories of Brussels—led by food!—await.

THE EXTRAORDINARY RESTAURANT SCENE

We could be relatively restrained in discussing the hotels of Brussels; though excellent and varied, they are no better, no worse, than in a dozen comparable towns. But the food of Brussels—that's another matter! Experts generally agree that Brussels is matched only by Paris and Hong Kong as the Greatest Restaurant City on Earth. And Belgians will claim that among the three, Brussels leads!

It is a defensible case. The restaurants of Brussels—an astonishing 1500 of them—have been acclaimed for a century by every noted critic both in Belgium and abroad, and by all the publications of gastronomy. In the greatest of Brussels' restaurants, you soar with the angels; in the least of them, in even the plainest cafe, you find dishes always tasty and attractively presented. After that single first meal, your taste buds come alive with the anticipation of each new restaurant visit—you look forward to mealtimes, as you do on a great cruise ship or in a top resort hotel. You find that food vies for your attention with ancient architecture, theatre and art!

The *grande cuisine* of Brussels! Among the residents, it is the constant topic of conversation. It is discussed as heatedly as sports or politics. At a cocktail party, a cluster of worried people will argue whether the once-famed Restaurant Ravenstein is staging a successful comeback, or whether Restaurant X has declined. At a civic meeting, an official will whisper excitedly about an expanding restaurant chain, or advise a colleague that the Beaujolais Nouveau has just arrived at the dining spots off the Avenue Louise. In this arena, all the customary modesty of Belgium disappears. Normally mild and courteous people will flare up at a foreigner's suggestion that any city of France could compare in cuisine. For them, Brussels is the unchallenged pinnacle of patés, the apotheosis of endives, the summit of sauces, the *wunderkind* of wine!

As you'd expect, the choices in restaurants are staggering. But rarely fraught with peril—you nearly always eat well, and at prices considerably less than in the challenging cities. There is no such thing in Brussels, realistically, as a $150 per person level at the top establishments, as there is at Paris' Tour d'Argent or Lasserre's, for instance. In even the several "greats"—**Comme Chez Soi, Villa Lorraine, Bruneau, Romeyer's**—you eat quite well for 3000 francs ($83). And you enjoy high culinary quality (by which I mean meals prepared in the classic style of the "haute cuisine") in large numbers of establishments charging 1500 francs ($42) and 1000 francs ($28) per average meal; as well as exceptionally tasty meals (though not at all classic ones) in those charging 750 francs ($21) and less.

Generally speaking, the restaurants of Brussels are *clustered* in five distinct areas (though also widely scattered everywhere else): (1) Along the *Petite Rue des Bouchers* and intersecting *Rue des Bouchers* off the Grand' Place (and you are required to eat at least one meal in this area at the peril of being judged not to have visited Brussels—it is the most awesome restaurant street of the world!); (2) On the now-landlocked "Quays" jutting off from the *Place Ste. Catherine* and known as the "Marché aux Poissons"—the fish market; (3) On and off the elegant *Place du Grand Sablon;* (4) On and just off the *Rue Haute* above the "Marolles" (and especially on that segment of it near the Porte de Hal); and (5) on the streets just off the *Avenue Louise* near the Place Louise, in "Upper Brussels" ("haut de la ville"). We'll first discuss a number of outstanding individual restaurants of Brussels (many of which are nowhere near the above areas), and then we'll describe the characteristics and typical establishments of the Five Areas. And we'll proceed, with some exceptions, in generally *descending* order of cost, starting with the most expensive; if those cause dismay, take heart and show patience—we end with delightful bistros charging 250 francs ($7), 300 francs ($8.33), and less.

THE "OLYMPIANS", AT 2500 FRANCS ($69) TO 3000 FRANCS ($83) FOR A THREE-COURSE "EVENT":
The equivalent of any culinary star of Paris, and (say the Belgians) perhaps superior to many of the great names in the City of Light, are at least the following, five, widely-scattered "institutions":

First, and virtually in a class by itself, **Comme Chez Soi,** at 23 Place Rouppe (phone 512-1921 or 512-3674), a short, six-block walk down the Rue du Midi from the area of the Grand' Place. Its proprietor, Pierre Wynants, is not simply regarded as Belgium's top chef, he is venerated, referred to in lowered voice and with awe, for his lifetime of constant innovation and experimentation alike to a Picasso. You enter into a single, narrow room on the slightly-elevated ground floor of an elegant townhouse, finding banquettes and turn-of-the-century, oval mirrors set into mahogany wall panels; 14 tables only; and then, incongruous in its modernity but welcome and thrilling to every serious gourmet, a giant clear-glass wall at the end of the room, affording an unobstructed view of the gleaming, superbly-equipped kitchen, of Mr. Wynants, and of his considerable staff (almost outnumbering the diners) of acolytes/chefs. If you are three or more persons dining together, you can order one of the three set, four-course menus for either 1600 francs ($44), 2350 francs ($65), or 3500 francs ($97); all three start with the renowned, whipped-meat "Mousses Wynants" (imagine roast goose or smoked ham pulverized to the consistency of whipped cream) and include such odd but perfectly complementary combinations as "Le poussin des marchés de Provence et sa béarnaise d'ecrivisses" (chicken of Provence cooked in a sauce of crayfish). Otherwise, you order à la carte, beginning with the "mousses Wynants" (450 francs), then choosing a classic fish combination of, say, sole and lobster "en cardinal" (1150 francs) or "supreme de bar à la vapeur" (steamed bass, a specialty, in a basil-flavored sauce that invades your senses like a great symphony, 1100 francs), proceeding finally to a climactic main dish of, say, "La cassolette de ris de rognon de veau à la moutarde gantoise" (casserole of sweetbreads and veal kidneys in mustard of Ghent, another renowned item, only 925 francs). Eminent food critics apply one word to such plates: "Perfection". A tip: although you can rarely obtain an evening reservation at the small Comme Chez Soi without phoning several days in advance, you will almost always find a lunchtime table by phoning a day in advance. Closed Sundays, Mondays and the entire month of July.

Villa Lorraine, at 75 Avenue du Vivier-d'Oie (phone 374-3163 or 374-2587), is as large as Comme Chez Soi is small, an expansive and gloriously beflowered three rooms of brown-and-rust tones, wicker chairs, under a vast ceiling skylight, and all in a park-like setting surrounded by the forestry of the Bois de la Cambre; take a cab there. Dishes are classically French, presented with the ceremony of a Cathedral from reheated chafing dishes at your table, and a four-course menu, served to as few as two persons, is 2500 francs ($69) per person, plus wine, and includes quail as the main course. Though the atmosphere is one of gracious elegance, and a visit here is an important, dressy occasion, you will be received with great cordiality and given considerable assistance with the extensive menu of classic, time-honored dishes, a bit less innovative than at Comme Chez Soi. And you may share courses if you're determined to taste a stratospherically-priced item, like "Le Foie Gras aux Truffes et Vin de Malvoisie à la Façon de Barrier"; Villa Lorraine will, on request, bring one course and two plates! My own recent 2500 francs ($69) meal there (including wine) remains shimmering in the memory; creamy goose liver paté (shared), hot oysters in a heavenly white sauce, cold crayfish, partridge with apples, strawberries chantilly, demitasse. But now let's assume that you don't wish to spend 2500 francs ($69) for any meal, although you're anxious to experience the celebrated, three-star Villa Lorraine. Solution: you go there weekdays at lunch! Rarely mentioned, but always the case, is that Villa Lorraine serves a set, three-course, lunchtime "menu" (you must specifically request it) for only 1500 francs ($42) per person, with two choices per course, enabling a party of two to sample several of the restaurant's most acclaimed dishes. And for wine? At lunch only, you may ask the wine steward—he will do it—to bring you a carafe of open wine—not a bottle—for only 250 francs more. The celebrated Villa Lorraine—whose specialties include "Homard au Four Beurre rose" (oven-baked lobster with butter rosé) and "Caneton de Bresse aux Figues confites à la Façon de Virgile" (chicken from the province of Bresse, where they are raised in darkened coops and fed mashed corn in sour milk, with preserved figs, all truly in the style of Vergil)—is closed Sundays, and through most of July.

The three other supreme dining experiences of Brussels? They are at **Restaurant Bruneau,** 73 Avenue Broustin (awarded three Michelin stars in 1988; expect to pay about 3000 francs—$83—for a "tasting menu" with wine); at **Pierre Romeyer,** 109 Chaussée de Groenendaal (phone 657-0581 or 657-1777), Brussels-Hoeilaart, a beamed-ceiling, lodge-like setting in the midst of the Forest of Soignes, where you'll pay around 2850 francs ($79), including wine, for the average meal, this time perhaps of "Huitres au Champagne" (oysters in champagne), "Truite au Bleu à ma Façon" (barely-grilled trout in Romeyer's own personal style), "Ris de Veau Brillat-Savarin" (sweetbreads as they were done by the master, Brillat-Savarin), a dessert wagon ("Charrette") of 26 different selections, closed Sunday evenings, Mondays, and February; and at **Eddie van Maele,** 964 Chaussée Romaine, Brussels-Wemmel (phone 460-6145), the dean of the "Nouvelle Cuisine" of Brussels, inventive, lightly-sauced, lightly-steamed and fresh, a melange of exotic flavors, presented on the plate like an abstract painting or a Japanese flower arrangement. Closed Sunday evenings, Mondays and July.

THE "SILVER MEDALISTS" JUST BELOW THE TOP, AT 2000 FRANCS ($56) PER AVERAGE MEAL: At

least two dozen restaurants enjoy this next honored rank in Brussels, of which the following are only representative examples:

L'Ecailler du Palais Royal, 18 Rue Bodenbroek (phone 511-9950 or 512-8751), near the top, left-hand side (looking uphill) of the Place du Grand Sablon, is Brussels' finest seafood restaurant (it serves nothing else) and one of the greatest fish-preparers of the world; even the most prosaic, often-tasted dish, emerges as a Belgian masterpiece revealing flavors rarely known. The daily special in particular—averaging 700 francs ($19.40) and listed in a box on the long, green fish at the center of the menu—is an especially fanciful concoction of fish, sauce and exquisite vegetable that blend perfectly. It should always be ordered by at least one in your party. Best preceded by a half-dozen Colchester oysters for 525 francs; accompanied by a bottle (for two people) of a white Bordeaux (choose the Chateaux Reynon 1985, at 775 francs the cheapest on the list, yet perfectly marvelous); and followed by a 350-franc dessert, and tea, your meal and your check will total around 2000 francs ($56) per person, service included. Reservations are needed but if tables are filled, you'll be placed in a comfortable seat at the room-long bar, where Brusselians of great chic are often found savoring the paper-thin Scotch salmon, the popular fish known as "lotte" with the chewy consistency of a lobster (always a satisfying choice). Closed Sundays and the month of August.

En Plein Ciel, on the 27th floor of the Brussels Hilton, 38 Boulevard Waterloo (phone 513-8877), a modern, high altitude room larger than a basketball court and enjoying a stunning view over all of Brussels, is another of the Belgian "greats", the legacy of an outstanding Hilton hotel manager who has since been transferred to work similar miracles in Asia for the American chain. Here you have the classic "haute cuisine" prepared by several specialist chefs (including one of Belgium's few female sauce chefs, a young American who puts in 12-hour days here), served in a highly formal, even haughty atmosphere, unusual for Belgium and designed perhaps to overcome the American connotation. You can spend 2000 francs ($56) very quickly, on appetizers averaging 700 francs (cold lobster and white asparagus, duck livers, smoked trout in a rainbow-jelly of vegetables), main courses for 840 francs (filet of rare beef covered with creamy goose paté and truffles, a side "bouquet" of colorfully-sauced vegetables), desserts for 350 francs (flaming crepes); but you might be better advised to order the three-course, table d'hote menu for 2400 francs ($67), including half a bottle of champagne (it starts with smoked salmon crisscrossed with young, Belgian asparagus, goes on to a juicy fish filet covered with a white wine sauce prepared by that young expatriate in the kitchen, and includes a beef main dish), or, if you are with a party of people all willing to have the same meal, the seven-course, 2675 francs ($74) per person "Menu Gourmand" served only to an entire table: smoked trout in vegetable jelly, then sole in a vichyssoise, crayfish with caviar, hot duck liver paté in sweet vinegar, sweetbreads of lamb in estragon sauce, with potatoes au gratin and baby vegetables, a choice of classic cheeses of Belgium, then your pick from a groaning dessert trolley, all of the highest *niveau* (level). A passing insight into blind, nationalistic prejudice: this major restaurant, respected by every Belgian food critic, is not even listed, let alone starred, in the *Guide Michelin!* It is closed Sunday evenings, and Saturdays for lunch.

La Maison du Cygne, at 2 Rue Charles Buls (phone 511-8244), on the second floor of the magnificently-gilded "House of the Swan" overlooking the Grand' Place, is world famous, not simply for its enthralling view of the great square, but for a burning dedication to the classic recipes and dishes of the "haute cuisine" unaltered by modern touches or dietary fads. Because it is filled at lunch with corporate presidents, diplomats, and others of that ilk, you will, in an unusual switch, find reservations easier at dinner time, when you should dress to the teeth, and prepare by fasting the entire day, for your dinner in this intensely elegant setting of velvet and flowers, thick carpets and hushed-voiced staff. Prices are broad in range, permitting meals of widely varying levels, but generally settle into a level of 350 to 400 francs for exquisite soups, 700 and 800 francs for most appetizers (smoked fish in jelly, eels in green sauce, Belgian shrimps, melon with Parma ham), 850 to 950 francs for most main courses (lamb Estragon, juicily-rare Tournedos with green peppercorns, veal sweetbreads), with several fine fish and chicken dishes at a lower 600 francs (duckling with tiny onions and brown sauce, scallops of lotte). Supplemented by a good wine, dessert and coffee, you will spend just under 2000 francs ($56) per person, although by careful ordering you can spend considerably less—but shouldn't. How often will you be dining at a Maison du Cygne? It is closed Saturdays for lunch, all day Sundays, and from mid-to-late August.

THE STILL-SERIOUS RESTAURANTS, CHARGING 1500 FRANCS ($42) PER AVERAGE MEAL: Restaurant Ravenstein, at 1 Rue Ravenstein (phone 512-7768 or 513-3269), just up the hill from the front of the Grand' Place, on your way to the Place Royale, occupies the only surviving small palace of those many noblemen who flocked to the court of the Dukes of Burgundy; it is a ravishing, reddish/brown-brick, 15th-century step-gabled complex, and its elegant, subdued Flemish interior of copper-hooded fireplaces, maple panelling, cut-glass chandeliers, promises the most European of dining experiences. Why, in such a distinguished setting, are the prices so relatively inexpensive? Because the restaurant suffered a devastating decline several years ago, and is now, under new management, fighting its way back to eminence, inviting former clients to forgive-and-forget with meals priced most attractively. There is actually a 1500-franc ($42) dinner that includes champagne; a three-course lunch for only 725 francs ($20); but an à la carte, four-course meal of the restaurant's classic French specialties, tempered a bit by the modern styles of the nouvelle cuisine, will mount just barely to 2000 francs ($56) when wine and coffee are included. Take care of the days of operation (the Ravenstein is open weekdays only, and is closed in August), enter with cautious expectations and prayer, and you may be witness to a new Phoenix arising to fame!

La Sirene d'Or, 1A Place Ste. Catherine (phone 513-5198), is on the little, church-lined square just off the huge, elongated square known as the "Marché aux Poissons"; its specialties, fittingly, are fish, its most celebrated dish is "La Bouillabaisse Grand Marius", a garlic-laced stew of fresh fish and lobster for 1250 francs ($35). With dessert and wine, that Bouillabaisse makes the perfect centerpiece of a 1600 franc ($44) meal. Although there's also a five-course "menu du chef" here for 1300 francs ($36)— soup, asparagus with sweetbreads, lotte with bouquet of vegetables, cheese, then a fruit tarte—you'll want, on your one visit, to try the unique à la carte dishes, expensive-but-worth-it at 690 francs for fish Waterzooi (also a stew), 790 francs for a classic Sole Normande, 745 francs for numerous other varieties of fish, preceded by all the standard appetizers, and priced to total (with dessert, wine and coffee) around 1500 francs for three courses. Because proprietor Robert van Duuren was once chef to Albert, Prince of Liège, brother of King Baudouin—you'll eat almost like a king! And although the clientele of this sumptuous room often consists of the most svelte Brussels models and their custom-suited escorts, other affluent types, the matre d' will actually open the door and invite you in, if he spots you hanging about undecided. Imagine that happening in establishments of similar category in other capitals! Closed Sundays, Mondays and the month of August.

Le Palais Royale of the Hotel Astoria, 103 Rue Royale (phone 217-6290), on the street running between the Place Royale and the Palais de Justice, is Europe As It Once Was, a stunningly extravagant room in brocaded satin wall panels, crystal chandeliers, candlelit tables, vaguely 19th-century, and in the turn-of-the-century landmark hotel of Brussels. Its meals (of standard French cuisine) are also distinguished, and the combination of gracious setting and carefully prepared cuisine makes for a grand evening, priced at around 1500 francs ($42) for three courses, wine and coffee. While the restaurant also displays a 1280-franc ($36) menu, including pre-dinner aperitif and unlimited house wine, it is from "la carte" that you'll order its several most memorable dishes, including a featured "quenelles de brochet" (pike) served with curry and ginger. Monday through Friday are the only days of operation.

A STAND-OUT AT 1250 FRANCS ($35) PER MEAL:
Restaurant Scheltema, 7 Rue des Dominicains (phone 512-2084), is a less costly seafoods alternative to the prestigious L'Ecailler du Palais Royal or Sirene d'Or. An always-crowded, bustling establishment in the restaurant-packed section of the "greatest restaurant street in the world" (see below), off the Grand' Place, its specialties are seafoods and fish (though its menu goes

beyond them), its premises so packed that you come here only for a serious, voracious attack on those denizens of the deep, and not for calm conversation. Appetizers average 300 to 360 francs (fishermen's soup, fresh marinated herrings, grey shrimp of the North Sea); main dishes range from 680 to 800 francs (sole and lobster surrounded by creamy mashed potatoes, Bouillabaisse, grilled turbot with béarnaise sauce, many other more complex fish dishes); and with wine included (and careful ordering), you'll spend about 1250 francs ($35) for an excellent savory meal of the freshest possible ingredients, given the volume of traffic that the restaurant enjoys. Scheltema is youthful and lively, but serious and skillful in its approach to the sauces and other accompaniments for worthy seafood. Open till 12:30 a.m.; closed Sundays.

A SAMPLING OF THE 1000 FRANC ($28) ESTAB-LISHMENTS: Aux Armes de Bruxelles, 13 Rue des Bouchers (phone 511-2118 or 511-5598), on the horizontal bar of the T-shaped "greatest restaurant street in the world" (see below), off the Grand' Place, is that area's classic restaurant of general appeal, serving every conceivable Belgian/French food item from steamed mussels (it pioneered in bringing them to Brussels) to entrecote steak, from beef stewed in beer to luscious chicken pot pie ("Vol au Vent de Poularde"). It offers these scores of possibilities from a large, glossy menu—a veritable "cram course" in French-language menu items—on which most appetizers are priced at 185 to 325 francs, most main courses of chicken, fish or beef at from 385 to 585 francs, often for less, thus easily permitting a 1000 francs ($28) meal of three courses, including wine. Consider, in particular, the home-made fish soup for 220 francs, with croutons, shredded cheese, and a garlicky mayonnaise ("soupe de poissons", with "rouille"); the Baltic herring for 155 francs; the quarter-grilled chicken with béarnaise sauce for 310 francs; the steak with pepper and cream sauce ("Steak au Poivre Vert Crème") for 495 francs; the marvelous side orders of fine string beans ("haricots verts fins") for 155 francs; the house red wine ("vin rouge de dejeuner") at 450 francs per full bottle). Many visitors choose "Aux Armes de Bruxelles" for their first experience with the famed mussels dishes and mussels casseroles of Brussels—prepared here in eight different ways, of which the "Moules spéciales (marinières)" with french fries, at 395 francs, are the standard dish—but I wouldn't; "Aux Armes de Bruxelles" is too elegant, too gracious for that. But though its several large rooms are attended quite formally by waiters in white jackets and epaulets, a quarter of its Belgian guests are in sweaters, with open

collars (while others are fairly formally dressed). All things to all people, in food and setting—that's "Aux Armes de Bruxelles"! Closed Mondays and the month of June.

The restaurants off the Avenue Louise

Patronized by a trendy crowd of rising young professionals anxious to eat well, but within reasonable price limits, these are a number of 1000-franc-averaging bistros clustered on the small sidestreets off the impressive Avenue Louise (a high income shopping boulevard) near the Place Louise. The latter is a point on that hilltop boulevard encircling the eastern side of inner Brussels, in the area known as "haut de la ville" (the upper city); it looks down upon (in more ways than one) the "centre de la ville" (central city). One of the five major concentrations of restaurants in Brussels, its members are typified by the **Restaurant "Al Piccolo Mondo,"** at 19 Rue Jourdan (phone 538-8794), with its stylishly-dressed patrons in their 20s and 30s crowded into a tasteful setting of brick arches, wood-burning fireplaces, old paintings on the walls, and reasonably-priced Italian specialties: hors d'oeuvres from 235 to 295 francs, spaghetti alle vongole (with clam sauce) for 355 francs, saltimbocca alla Romana for 430 francs, veal cutlets Milanaise 410 francs. With wine and dessert, you'll almost always spend just about 1000 francs ($28) per person. Across the street, **Meo Patacca**, at 20 Rue Jourdan (phone 538-1546), offers more of the same from a lengthy menu of Italian items, to a similarly chic clientele, for similar prices (try its 690-franc "menu" of three courses, not including wine). Both it and Al Piccolo Mondo stay open until 1 a.m., every day of the week. Down the street, **Au Boeuf Gros Sel**, at 8 Rue Jourdan (phone 538-1195), is again in the 1000 franc ($28) range for full meals, and offers normal French meals of beef and veal, as well as an outstanding "cassoulet toulousain" for 485 francs, a long-simmered, dry-ish brown bean stew with sausages much favored hereabouts; while **Restaurant La Vigne**, at 6 Rue Jourdan (phone 538-1207), is the Avenue Louise's seafood specialist in the 1000 franc per-three-course range, serving seven major varieties of mussels ("les moules"): simply steamed for 295 francs, "au vin blanc" (in white wine) for 320 francs, "provençale" (with tomatoes and garlic) for 320 francs, "au fenouil" (with fennel and cream) for 365 francs, "poulette" (with cream) for 385 francs, "parquée" (raw) for 365 francs, "au gratin" (with cream and cheese, a more limited number of mussels) for 245 francs. And you can, in the Brussels-style tavern decor of La Vigne, eat for considerably less than 1000 francs through careful ordering.

The restaurants of the "Fish Market"

We have earlier referred to the elongated square around the corner from the Place Ste. Catherine, whose "quays" were once the docks for boats entering the waterway that ran through that long and broad space. Because fresh fish stores are interspersed among restaurants along both sides, the area is still known as the "Marché aux Poissons" (Fish Market). And although we've already singled out several higher-priced establishments there, and will later be discussing several low-cost wonders there, the majority of "Fish Market" restaurants fall squarely into the 1000-franc ($28) per meal category, of which may own personal choice is the small **Cochon d'Or** at 15 Quai au Bois à Bruler (phone 218-0771), whose every dish is a delight to the taste. It actually offers a set, four-course menu for 795 francs, which wine will increase to almost exactly 1000 francs, and that includes fish soup to begin, then a choice of smoked eel, tiny shrimp, oysters or snails (all with interesting, carefully prepared sauces), then your selection of eight different main courses, of which the "Coquelet Clamart"—an entire small chicken soaked in wine, then roasted—is outstanding, as are the half lobster "Belle-Vue", or thickly-cut lamb chops with creamed vegetables, the platter of cold sea foods, the "Royal Arcachon aux Pousses Pierres" (tender fish filets in a heavenly white/yellow sauce, with mashed potatoes). A ripe and oozing brie cheese is offered for dessert. Closed Sunday evenings, Mondays, and the month of September. Reserve. Diagonally across the square, 38 Quai-aux-Briques (phone 511-3044 or 511-3116), with its glassed-in kitchen in full view of diners, serves *six* courses and a half-bottle per person of house wine (red or white) for a total of 950 francs ($28.50), and though the dishes here are far less complex than at Cochon d'Or, more dependent on natural flavors than on the saucier's art, they are nevertheless mouth-watering: fish paté or scallops to begin, then fishermen's soup, then half a fried sole, then either an entrecôte steak in champagne sauce or half a lobster flambé in whisky, followed by a plate of cheeses, then mandarin-orange ices, with the wine thrown in. Closed Sunday evenings and all day Mondays.

Other Fish Market restaurants similarly-priced: the large **Restaurant Cheval Marin**, 25 Rue Marché aux Porcs (phone 513-0287) at the very end of the Quai, closed Sunday evenings (three courses for 925 francs); **La Minque**, 58 Quai au Briques (phone 511-8589), closed Sunday evenings; and **La Baramoule**, 27 Quai au Bois à Bruler (phone 218-4997), closed Sundays and the first half of June (busy and attractive, it offers a four-course "choix du gourmet" for 850 francs, plus wine). But try Cochon d'Or, first, for flavor, Le Castel de Rhodes for value; and bear in mind that most Fish Market restaurants are quite naturally oriented to fish specialties.

Upon the Grand' Place

Finally, **Casa Manuel**, at 34 Grand' Place (phone 511-4747), directly on the great square at the corner of the Rue Chair et Pain, is a leading Spanish/Portuguese restaurant of Brussels, priced at these levels. With appetizers at 250 francs (on the average), paella Valenciana and other Spanish/Portuguese main courses at 480 francs, and desserts for 130, your average three-course meal with wine will amount to slightly under 1000 francs. Order a bottle of the white, slightly-bubbling, Portuguese "Casal Garcia," exhilarating, for 540 francs.

THE SPECTACULAR BRAND OF BRUSSELS RESTAURANT CHARGING ONLY 750 FRANCS ($21) PER MULTI-COURSE MEAL WITH WINE: Restaurant Jacques, at 44 Quai aux Briques (phone 513-2762), is the seafood bargain of the Fish Market area described above, a large and old-fashioned cafe serving à la carte only but at remarkable item-by-item prices: soup of the day for 75 francs, mixed salad 70 francs, filet of herring 120 francs, fish soup 170 francs, snails 150 francs, steamed mussels marinères only 300 francs (among the cheapest in Brussels), sole meunière 480 francs, turbot or lotte 560 francs, desserts 110 francs. Here you can eat the "fruit of the sea" till you burst, and still spend well under 750 francs.

Hippopotamus, 2 Rue Capitaine Crespel (phone 512-9362), corner of Avenue Toison d'Or, is the widely popular, superbly modernistic, steak "king" of Brussels, located quite appropriately almost directly across the broad Boulevard Waterloo/Avenue de la Toison d'Or from the Brussels Hilton in "haute de la ville" (upper Brussels). It offers every known form and variety of steak (and pictures each on the menu to aid your choice): entrecote, rumpsteak, "faux filet", everything but T-bone steak, is priced never higher than 460 francs (and other thinner cuts—again graphically illustrated—are 375), leaving 370 francs (from your 750-franc budget) for appetizer, dessert and wine. The latter, ordered in a pitcher ("Pichet Hippo"), is only 165 francs; while creme caramel at 90 francs and brie or camembert at 120 francs are excellent desserts. A 750-franc meal is the precise target of this colorfully decorated, large and trendy restaurant, suitable for a top occasion and not at all institutional. Incidentally, you order your steak (which comes with Belgian french fries) either "bleu" (very rare), "saignant" (rare) or "à points" (medium rare); because of their considerable thickness, certain varieties cannot be made "bien cuites" (well done). Open daily except Mondays (and Sunday evenings) until 11:30 p.m., Friday and Saturday evenings until 1 a.m.

L'Atomium, in one of the balls of the 300-foot-high symbol of the Atom on the former World's Fair grounds of Brussels, in Heysel, houses the Grand Lunchtime Buffet of Brussels—three large tables of superbly tasty hors d'oeuvres, cheeses and desserts —of which you partake in unlimited quantities for a total of 550 francs ($15.27), including coffee, while gazing out through portholes over the vast, park-like grounds, seeing the soccer stadium, the Chinese Pavilion of the Royal Park (where lives the king), the Church of Laeken and the planetarium, much more besides. Knowing by this time the food prowess of Belgium, you can imagine the quality of their smorgasbord-style buffets! You dine on herrings, smoked fish and eels, all varieties of cold meats including tangy ham of the Ardennes, on deviled eggs, pickled beets, bean sprouts, lightly peppered potato salads, juicy ripe tomatoes, celery and peppers; for dessert you take watermelon and pineapple chunks, fresh strawberries with chantilly cream, luscious eclairs and chocolate cakes. For 100 francs more, you can then have a supplementary hot plate chosen from a selection of ten (which include a grilled lobster—"homard grillé aux herbes"—for a further supplement), and by a final expenditure of 280 francs for a half-bottle of wine, you end with a bill of 930 francs (if you've taken the superfluous, hard-to-finish hot course) or of only 830 francs ($23) if you've dispensed with the warm plate, but stayed with the wine. You take an elevator directly to the restaurant, and to reach the Atomium you either board trolley ("pre-metro") 81 from the Place Rogier, or the metro to Bockstael. The buffet is available noon to 2:30 p.m. only, closed Sundays.

Restaurant Adrienne, at 1A Rue Capitaine Crespel (phone 511-9339), across the street from the Restaurant Hippopotamus (see above), and therefore across the broad boulevard from the Brussels Hilton in elegant "upper Brussels", is operated by the same people who manage "L'Atomium" and offers the very same, moderately-priced food extravaganza: an unlimited buffet of fancy and colorful ingredients for 550 francs, a hot plate for an additional 100 francs, wine (a good, young Beaujolais) for 100 francs per glass, this time both at lunch and in the evening, in a quiet, splendid structure surrounded by garden terraces and verandahs. Hors d'oeuvres heaven! Closed Sundays, and public holidays.

Restaurant L'Athenian, 15 Grand' Place (phone 512-4198), at the "uphill" end of the great, central square, up a short, outdoor flight of steps, is my own favorite among the many Greek restaurants of Brussels; for one thing, it enjoys much the same view as the glittering Maison du Cygne a few doors away! The Greek cuisine is an unusually flavorsome, underrated one, that must be eaten in a prescribed order. Though a complimentary plate of fresh olives and sharp green peppers is immediately put before you as you begin to order, you must nevertheless start with fresh, cold "meze"—Greek hors d'oeuvres—which are 345 francs for one person, but only 445 for three persons, 660 for three persons, 760 francs for four: olives and feta cheese, a giant whole shrimp, breaded and fried calamares (squid), stuffed vine leaves (with cold rice), lettuce and sliced onions, a sharp yogurt-type sauce called "tzatziki", the heavenly "tarama salata" of sour cream flavored with fish roe, sliced tomato, sharp green peppers—a virtual meal in itself and a true "appetizer" that leaves your mouth tingling, your appetite sharpened, for the main course. Those (the main course) are pictured in color photographs insert into the menu, and include "brochette" (shish-ke-bab) of lamb with cream-covered salad for 320 francs, shrimp swimming in a smooth cream sauce ("scampis maison") for 385 francs, lamb chops (cotes d'agneau) with a copious salad for 385 francs, "Moussaka" (ground meat and eggplant, layered with mashed potatoes, slathered with sauce béchamel topped with bread crumbs, all oven baked to become "au gratin") for all of 320 francs, a giant "brochette" accompanied by tzatziki, feta cheese and olives for 450 francs—the latter the costliest item on the menu. With a giant "Dame Blanche" (vanilla ice cream flooded with hot chocolate sauce) for dessert, half-a-carafe of wine, the "meze" to begin, and a normally-sized brochette main course, your check will amount to about 750 francs ($21). Open daily until midnight, weekends until the dawn, this is a colorful "taverna" of red candlelit tables and stucco walls with friezes of classic Greek scenes, Zorba music constantly on the loud-speakers, imparting the spirit of Dionysus and Bacchus to the colorful Grand' Place. Somehow it all fits.

BRUSSELS' "LITTLE WONDER" RESTAURANTS CHARGING ONLY 500 FRANCS ($13.88) PER MEAL:

To eat well at this level, you rush to that dazzling district of Brussels off the Grand' Place: "the greatest restaurant street in the world!" It is as much a sightseeing attraction as Waterloo or the Mannekin Pis, and includes several subsidiary and equally narrow streets whose criss-crossing pattern covers a tiny area known as the "Ilôt Sacré"—the Sacred Isle. Preserved and safeguarded as a great treasure of the world, it is a place of medieval city life enjoyed intact, a labyrinth of cobblestoned streets so narrow you can almost touch both sides at once, surging with life and color, the kind of area that 15th-century burghers knew, and down which they led their merchandise-laden donkeys, or caroused, or dueled. The "Ilôt Sacré!" Few such sections have survived to our day, and fewer still have remained so commercially active—with Brussels standing alongside Lisbon's Alfama, the narrow alleys of Venice and Florence, Athens' Plaka, as among the few such examples.

Walk downhill on the Grand' Place until, halfway along the square, you turn right through the narrow Rue Chair et Pain for one block, cross the Rue Marché aux Herbes, and enter the **Petite Rue des Bouchers**. This is the tiny giant of a street, continuously lined on both sides with restaurants until it meets the intersecting **Rue des Bouchers,** and that, too, is lined with restaurants on both sides, and on the extensions of it: the **Rue Grétry** and the **Rue des Dominicains**. There are more than sixty restaurants altogether in this short expanse. And what restaurants! Colorful beyond imagining, each with distinctive color themes created by table lights and dancing fireplace flames, casting a glow that suffuses the pavements with red-and-yellow hues which bounce off the outdoor displays of red lobsters and black mussels, tomatoes and yellow eggplants, green seaweed and gray fishermen's nets. It is a scene from Bruegel, strangely medieval or at least from another age, sensual, happy—and unforgettable. It must be experienced at least once in your stay, visiting restaurants that serve every conceivable item of the Belgian/French cuisine, some emphasizing seafoods, other grilled meats. Though some are in the 750- and 1000-franc ($21 and $28) range for meals (including the Restaurant Scheltema and Aux Armes de Bruxelles earlier discussed), others charge as little as 500 francs ($13.88) for three courses and wine. Still others, normally in a higher range, are forced by competitive pressures to supplement their costlier à la carte prices with specially-reduced "Menus"—a "menu" being a set, three-course meal offered at one comprehensive price. As you walk down this "greatest restaurant street of the world" in 1989, you'll pass at leastadozenrestaurantsofferingthree-course"menus"for400francs or less. Supplemented by wine or beverage for 100 francs, that rate results in 500 francs ($13.88) for a complete meal.

The restaurants hereabouts that *always* offer such prices, start with the **Restaurant Chez Richard**, at 37 Petite Rue des Bouchers (phone 511-6110), charging 450 francs ($12.50) for its *four*-course menu of soup, appetizer, main course and dessert, with the right to select mussels/casserole as the main course. Add a pitcher of white wine, and the total is 500 francs. Nearby, the "**Bigorneau**", at 2A Petite Rue des Bouchers (phone 511-9859), is the perennial source of a three-course meal for 420 francs ($11.67). On the intersecting Rue des Bouchers, both the **Restaurant Le Petit Belge** at no. 8 and the **Restaurant Savarin** at no. 7 serve four-course meals throughout the year at 450 and 475 francs, respectively, and both maintain à la carte prices (appetizers for 150 francs, numerous main courses for 250 francs) that permit a 500-franc meal, while the exciting **Restaurant Shanghai**, at 25 Rue des Bouchers (phone 511-2508), charges only 395 francs for a four-course Chinese menu, permitting you to add a rather good wine within the 500-franc limit.

The *special* offers by the better restaurants are even more exciting. On a recent *high season* day, the quite stunning **Restaurant La Petite Rue**, at 12 Petite Rue des Bouchers (phone 511-6300), charged 445 francs ($12.36) for soup, fondu parmesan, grilled steaks with french fries, and dessert. **Restaurant Le Trouvère**, at 11 Petite Rue des Bouchers (phone 511-3275), charged 525 francs ($14.58) for a four-course "menu du Pecheur" (fisherman's menu) that began with fish soup, and included Ostend eels on toast. With its yellowish glow throughout, its big garden in back with actual banana tree ("Des bananes dans L'Ilot Sacré?" asked a newspaper), Le Trouvère is an especially exciting place. And among a dozen other such offers, **La Bergerie**, at 22 Petite Rue des Bouchers (phone 511-5752), was displaying (on a blackboard outside), a 495 francs ($13.75) price for its own three, set courses. While no one can guarantee that the very same restaurants will be offering cut-rate "menus" at the time of your visit, at least a dozen establishments on the street will always be doing so; simply walk up and down, and look for the headline-sized signs that announce the special value.

Finally, at that point where the "restaurant street" (Petite Rue des Bouchers) meets its complementary "restaurant street" (Rue des Bouchers), you have the 50-year-old, mussels-featuring "institution" of the "Ilot Sacré", the quite remarkable **Chez Leon**, 18 Rue des Bouchers (phone 511-1415), serving hundreds of thousands of pounds of mussels each year, on two busy floors, usually in big, iron pots filled also with celery, onions and seaweed, and accompanied by heaping mounds of golden, Belgian, french fried potatoes, that are known collectively as "speciales" or as "Moules spéciales" and cost a surprisingly high 395 francs per pot and accompanying fries. Chez Leon also serves an especially tempting and well-priced ensemble of these ingredients in its two-course "menu" called "Le Complet de Chez Leon" (announced via a small box tucked into the front of its menu): a tomato stuffed with the small "grey shrimp" of the North Sea, "un speciale" of the mussels and fries, and a glass of draft beer, all for a total, including tax and service, of 525 francs ($14.58). But ordering à la carte from other menu items will generally slightly exceed our 500-franc limit, unless you share plates—which can easily be done; they are massive in portions. This is not a venue for restful dining or atmosphere; more a giant "fritture" than a restaurant, it supplies paper tablecloths only, straight-backed, lightwood banquettes, stone floors, a bustling atmosphere in which hundreds and hundreds of Belgians and tourists are served each day. But the quality of its food is high, and its mussels (as well as its fish soup) are classic. Open daily, continuously from noon to 10:45 p.m.

But keep in mind: mussels and french fries for considerably less than the 395 francs charged by Chez Leon are offered by nearly a dozen other restaurants in the same area. And although Chez Leon will claim that its higher price is justified by the quality of its mussels, not simply by its crowd-attracting reputation, the others will hotly dispute that point. In any case, you can obtain steamed mussels ("les moules", "moules casseroles") and french fries for a low 250 francs ($6.94) at the **Restaurant Le Petit Belge**, at 8 Rue des Bouchers; for only 295 francs ($8.19) at the **Restaurant Bigorneau**, 2A Petite Rue des Bouchers; for 340 francs ($9.44) at **Restaurant Savarin**, 9 Rue des Bouchers; and for 350 francs at **Restaurant Richard**, 37 Petite Rue des Bouchers.

THE BELGIAN "MIRACLES" OF BRUSSELS CHARGING 240 TO 300 FRANCS ($6.67 TO $8.33) PER FULL, MULTI-COURSE MEAL:
We descend here to undreamed-of-levels, but without the slightest regret: in Brussels, even the backpackers dine regally! For less than you'd pay for a meager plate in other countries, you receive colorful, wonderfully-tasty, multi-course meals in this city of one million gourmets.

The Spanish "wonders" of the Rue Haute
The meals are most exotic, and incredibly priced, at a string of six, adjoining Spanish restaurants (and one across the street)— perhaps the largest cluster of rockbottom-priced Spanish restaurants outside of Spain—on the **Rue Haute**, at the corner of the Boulevard de Waterloo, near the Porte de Hals. (This is all an easy walk from the Sablon, a manageable one from the Grand' Place.) In rooms decorated like a Spanish tavern, with swords, paintings, bullfight posters and a raised stage for the inevitable flamenco guitarists, a restaurant like the **Alicante** (my own personal favorite),

at 411 Rue Haute, open seven days a week, serves Soupe Julienne, a lamb brochette with rice provencale, and dessert, for a total of 240 francs ($6.67), service included! It offers four other three-coursers for from 200 to 250 francs ($5.56 to $7), eleven four-course "menus" for 290 to 340 francs ($8 to $9.44). Choose Gazpacho Andaluz (the cold soup classic of Spain), then anchovies with vinaigrette sauce, then sole meunière with golden, molten-liquid french fries, and a fruit tart dessert, and you'll pay a total of 295 francs ($8.20). **Restaurant Torremolinos**, next door at 405 Rue Haute, even provides a free aperitif to start, as well as flamen-co beginning at 8 p.m., and yet charges only 280 francs ($7.77) for chicken croquettes to begin, then steak provencale with fries and dessert; or 330 francs ($9.17) for mixed salad, dessert—and paella Valenciana! It also asks only 280 francs ($7.77) for mussels casserole and all the french fries you can eat ("à volonté"). Next door, **El Rincon**, at 403 Rue Haute, looking like a Madrid "tapas" bar with its Moorish arches and tiled floor, charges only 260 francs ($7.22) for fish soup, then grilled steak with fries and salad; while the dignified **Casa Campo** at 399 Rue Haute, and the Portuguese **Restaurant Mar Bravo**, at 397 Rue Haute, offer à la carte rates of a moderate level for Spanish and Portuguese specialties. Cheapest of all is **Restaurant Villa Rose ("Casa Lucas")**, last of the six, where gazpacho is only 80 francs ($2.22), Spanish omelette 120 francs ($3.33).

Imagine the competition between these six Spanish wonders as they cater to the most cost-conscious of the city's residents. It is as if Brussels were here enjoying a 400-year-late revenge for the misdeeds of Philip II!

A Belgian "miracle" on the Grand' Place

In the very center of town, nestled away in the vaulted, med-ieval basement of a gilded structure on the Grand' Place, no less (uphill side), Belgium provides its own classic dishes at near-unbelievable rates, in "**Au Caveau d'Egmont et d'Hornes**", 14 Grand' Place; you find the room with difficulty by peering down-stairs at that address, only 30 yards away from the super-costly "Maison du Cygne" (Restaurant of the Swan). Though plates are presented in fairly crowded comfort, on oilcloth-covered tables, one pays only 200 francs ($5.56) for soup, ground steak, Belgian french fries and a vegetable; only 230 francs ($6.39) for soup, pork cutlet, fries and vegetables; only 290 francs ($8) for soup, roast chicken, fries and salad; only 130 francs ($3.61) for a fine tomato omelette. The adjoining "**'t Kelderke**" cellar restaurant looks similar in category, but is actually more expensive, though still moderate; a heavy, cream soup with bread for 150 francs ($4.17), most main courses for 295 francs and 325 francs ($8.19 and $9), a two-kilogram pot of steamed mussels with fries (enough to share among two persons) for 400 francs ($12). To find a similarly-priced alternative to the more remarkable "**Au Caveau d'Egmont et d'Hornes**" simply walk half-a-block off the lefthand, "uphill" side of the 'Grand' Place to "**Au Gateau Royal**", at 15 Rue de la Colline, serving filling Italian dishes for only 160 francs ($4.44) (spaghetti "Bolognaise"—i.e., with meat sauce; or a tomato-cheese-oregano "Pizza Margherita" for that price), and open "non-stop" from 11:30 a.m. to 10 p.m., daily except Wednesdays. And finally, for a simple sandwich on the Grand' Place, you can try **Stella Grand' Place'** at 24, where "tartines" (long slices of rye bread covered with various toppings) of cheese (fromage), ham (jambon) or "Americain" (raw, spiced hamburger) are 75 francs ($2.08) apiece.

The Turkish "miracles" on the Chaussée de Haecht

Brought here by the "guest workers" who now account for so much of Belgium's labor force, the Turkish cuisine has captivated the refined palates of the city. And though the larger part of Brussels' Turkish community has occupied the rather shabby area near the Gare du Midi, where you probably won't want to go, a smaller number have opened restaurants in the much more refined precincts of the Chaussée de Haecht, which runs roughly parallel to the Rue Royale, an easy walk from the Hyatt Hotel, in the "upper Brussels" section of the city. This is in the commune of Schaerbeek, a decent, safe area of town that's increasingly marked by the gaudy, colorful signs of wonderfully-inexpensive Turkish restaurants serving the tasty dishes of Anatolia—somewhat like the Greek cuisine (with moussaka, roast lamb and stuffed vine leaves on every menu), but with added Turkish touches: yogurt used in place of cream, shish kebabs throughout, cucumbers). If you're like me, you'll love every taste of these sharp and slightly sour morsels, and find them a refreshing change of pace. And you'll pay the most modest amounts for them. With care, you can order two big courses for about $8; or a three-course dinner with wine, coffee, and a liqueur at the end for under $14.

That precise repast can be had at the colorfully-illuminated **Restaurant Izmir**, 89 Chaussée de Haecht, open seven days a week, with live music on Friday and Saturday evenings. For 495 francs ($13.75), you start with a "salade russe", then dig into an "Ankara kebab", end with "kazan dibi" (a fruit dish), and receive both wine, coffee and a brandy along the way. Most à la carte appetizers are only 90 francs ($2.50), most main courses are 180 and 210 francs ($5 and $5.84 for grills—"kebabs", oven-baked lamb or moussaka), a wide variety of desserts for 85 francs ($2.36).

The big and exotic **Pala Restaurant**, 85 Chaussée de Haecht, offers much of the same: entrees and soups for 85 and 95 francs ($2.36 or $2.64 for lentil soup, string beans in oil, tarama salata, cucumbers and yogurt, stuffed vine leaves), main courses like grilled chicken or doner kebab and rice for 165 francs ($4.58) or 195 francs ($5.42). Waiters here are particularly kind and attentive.

Or you can walk down the street to: the **Restaurant Bergama**, at 121 Chaussée de Haecht (soup 75 francs, appetizers 80 and 90 francs, grills 190 and 220 francs), where you can also splurge on a 645-franc banquet (choice of aperitifs, then assorted hors d'oeuvres, roast lamb or mixed grill, pastries for dessert, and a half-bottle of wine per person); the **Restaurant Sahbaz**, at 102 Chaussée de Haecht; or to the slightly-more-costly **Restaurant Sultan** at 94 Chaussée de Haecht.

And the quick meals on the Rue Neuve

The always-active, popularly-priced shopping street of Brussels is the **Rue Neuve** running parallel to the "Grands Boulevards" from a starting point near the Place Rogier. It is today barred to traffic along its entire length, and therefore thronged by lively, happy crowds who converge in particular upon the large **Inno Department Store**, located at a mid-point of the street, and open daily (except Sundays) until 6:30 p.m., until 7:30 p.m. on Fridays. Maintaining the same times of operation (which permit you to squeeze in an early evening's shopping after a hard day at the museums, or at Waterloo or Bruges), the Inno's 3d floor, self-service cafeteria charges only 35 francs (97¢) for soup and bread, only 40 francs ($1.11) for a portion of those heavenly, Belgian french fries (and 23 francs more for a giant glob of the chef's sauce béarnaise on top of the french fries), only 169 francs ($4.69) for "vol au vent" (chicken pot pie), 175 francs ($4.86) for a quarter of a roast chicken and fries. While Inno isn't nearly as cheap as others we've named, it's a speedy, modern and attractive facility, in which you see all offerings spread out vividly before you. And near the entrance to the cafeteria is Inno's poster shop selling all the most famous René Magrittes (Belgium's celebrated surrealist) for 200 and 250 francs ($5.56 and $6.94) apiece.

Even faster, cheaper food is available in a "village" of colorful food shops on the bottom level ("niveau 1") of the multi-floor, modern shopping center called "**City 2**", at the very head of the Rue Neuve near the Place Rogier. At a counter called "**Intermez-**

zo Domini", you have a giant blood sausage (un "boudin"),
mashed potatoes and sauerkraut for 130 francs ($3.61); while
"**City Steak**" serves up a juicy ground variety with heaping
mounds of french fries for 160 francs ($4.44), and "**King Sand-
wich**" supplies tasty spreads on crusty rolls for 40, 45, and 50
francs ($1.11, $1.25 and $1.39).

PICNIC MEALS, LATE-NIGHT MEALS: Occasionally in

travel, it's fun to vary the usual routine of taking meals at a restaurant, with a picnic meal of cold ingredients, purchased at a grocery
or from the food counters of a department store, and then consumed upon a park bench or along a river's bank. In Brussels,
where these cold ingredients reach sublime heights, it's part of the
experience to have such a meal! And nowhere can you find a broader and more exotic spread of ingredients than at the big, underground, supermarket of "**City 2**", described above: luscious
cheeses in indescribable varieties, carefully basted and flavored
roast chickens at 180 francs ($5) apiece, olives of a dozen species,
rolls in a score of forms, cheap wines from all over (as little as 25
francs for a full bottle), and creamy patés at 160 francs ($4.44) per
kilo (but you need only a quarter of a kilo—"deux cents
cinquante grammes, s'il vous plaît"). What non-European city of
a one-million population could come up with a similar array?
"City 2" is open from 10 to 7:30, Fridays until 8:30.

Late-night dining? Of the many Brussels restaurants open till
the wee hours, **L'Altro Mondo**, on the Rue Grétry, a block from
the Grand' Place, is an always-reliable, moderately-priced Italian
restaurant which keeps serving until the dawn. Or try your author's Greek favorite, the **Restaurant Athenien**, at 15 Grand'
Place, which stays active until at least 1 a.m. There are more.

THE BEER OF BRUSSELS: In addition to the bars that serve

several hundred varieties of beer—something every large Belgian
city possesses—Brussels provides in every bar its own, unique,
sweet-tasting, "lambic" beers brewed from wheat and barley, that
ferment without yeast and simply from the bacteria descending
from the city's air. These are known as "*gueuze*" (pronounced
"gyoo-zeh" or "ger-zeh", a rather warm beer of fruity flavor),
"*kriek*" (mixed with cherries and therefore sweeter), and "*faro*"
(mixed with an additive of sugar candies); all three are acquired
tastes not to everyone's liking, and sometimes requiring several attempts before the craving sets in. If you'd like to try one of these
strange-tasting beers, you can dart from the Grand' Place to the
plain and very traditional wood-panelled "brown bar" nearby
known as "**A La Mort Subite**" ("Sudden Death"), at 7 Rue

Montagne-aux-Herbes-Potagères, where the faro is 45 francs ($1.25), gueuze 65 francs ($1.81), kriek 75 francs ($2.08), a plain, non-Brussels beer only 35 francs (97¢), and a "trappiste"—one of the grain-tasting, monk-brewed elixirs, which everyone likes on the first try—65 francs ($1.81). At this large and well-known bar frequented by all classes and conditions (and which took its name from a double-or-nothing game played there, not from the effects of its beer!), you take the beer best with a "tartine beurré"—a foot-long slice of home-made, wholewheat bread covered with sweet butter. How does "gueuze" taste? Like a cross between beer and sweet Asti Spumante champagne, or like beer diluted by a bit of ginger ale; and you will like it best on the third try!

The largest variety of beers in all of Brussels—more than 300 selections, listed on a 20-panel, typed, blue-paper menu that everyone takes away as a collectors' item—is offered by the **Cafe-Taverne "Le Jugement Dernier"**, at 165 Chaussée de Haecht, not far from the Hyatt-Regency Hotel (but a plain and homey large bar, not at all forbidding). Tipped by a long-time patron to order the "Saint Idesbald Blonde" at 70 francs ($1.94), I had a long draught of the most intoxicating brew of my life! Some order only the "seasonal" beers available in certain months only, or only those from the province of Hainaut or West Flanders, or beers perfumed with honey, or aged to a proper maturity—and if you infer from all this that the people of Brussels are nuts about beer—you're right!

Properly housed, fed and lubricated in Brussels, we turn now to pleasures of the mind:

DAYTIME BRUSSELS—THE 21 GREAT SIGHTS

In this capital of the ultimate European nation, we now begin a book-long adventure—into European history and contemporary life, into religious and political ideas and conflict, into new forms of culture and commerce. We do that via the sights, an impressive but sometimes daunting array. In other Belgian cities—in the chapters ahead—it's easy to outline the six or seven highlights that immediately come to mind as the goals of every tourist. In Brussels, so numerous are the city's attractions that it's necessary first to reduce what's available into manageable form, to winnow out the merely-significant and focus on the important.

Every great city has statues and plazas, government buildings and parks, memorial columns, law courts and universities—and so does Brussels, but you'll hear nothing about them in this condensed book. Rather, we're interested in the *unique* sights of Brus-

sels, or in the distinctively Belgian, in visits that open our eyes
and enlarge our minds, that teach while entertaining, or provoke
and challenge settled ideas. Of the latter, there are 21 major daytime sights or categories of activities associated with Brussels, of
which six are indispensable, and should always be scheduled by the
first-time visitor; while the remaining fifteen are for "optional" selection according to one's tastes or special interests.

The "big six" are: (1) Brussels' astonishing **Grand' Place** and
L'Ilot Sacré (which in turn possesses eight subsidiary sights: the
Town Hall, Maison du Roi, the "Restaurant Street", Mannekin
Pis, Galleries of St. Hubert, Beer Museum, Lace Museum, and
"rubbing statue" of Everard t' Serclaes); (2) Brussels' remarkable
Museums of Ancient Art and Modern Art;" (3) the city's
Breugelian **"Open-Air Markets"**, (4) The unique **Atomium;** (5)
the still-trembling **battlefield of Waterloo**, and (6) **At least one,
full-day excursion to the "Art Cities"—Bruges, Ghent, Antwerp or Tournai** (not to take advantage of one's stay in Brussels
for a quick jaunt to these treasures is a tragic neglect).

The remaining fifteen? They are: (7) the **"Cinquantenaire
Museums"**; (8) the **architecture of "Art Nouveau"**; (9) the **Mu-
seum of Central Africa;** (10) **"Art in the Subways"**; (1) **"Royal
Brussels"**; (12) the **Jacques Brel Foundation;** (13) the **Castle of
Gaasbeek;** (14); the **Home of Erasmus;** (15) **"Autoworld";**
(16) the **"Browsing Streets"**; (17) the **Cathedrals;** (18) the **Specialists' Museums** (Musical Instruments, Posts and Telegraph,
Musée de Bellevue, etc.); (19) the **Forest of Soignes;** (20) the
headquarters of the **European Community;** (21) the program for
"Meeting the Brusselians"—people as the main (and accessible)
attraction of a major European capital.

The always notable 22nd attraction? Eating! Let it never be
forgotten that the culinary arts are a Brussels-achievement equal to
any, and that you come here also to enjoy memorable daytime
meals, in outstanding restaurants, at affordable cost. We'll quickly
begin with that initial sight where both types of art—visual and
culinary—are at hand, and in profusion.

THE "GRAND' PLACE" AND "L'ILOT SACRÉ": If you
were asked to name the top two or three sights in all of Europe,
you would include the **Grand' Place.**

You do not and cannot see it from afar. You must first walk
through a narrow, cobblestoned street that gives no hint of what
awaits, but suddenly opens onto this great enclosed plaza, flanked
on all four sides by the gilded, ornamented, flag-bedecked houses
of the ancient Guilds of the Middle Ages, and by the city's fairy-

tale Town Hall. And if you are like most visitors, you instantly stop, as if yanked by a string, mouth agape, silent, and you are consumed by the beauty and age of one of the most extraordinary of all attractions. The market square of Brussels as early as the 12th century, the Grand' Place is today revered as among the greatest summations of medieval architecture and society—though it is not strictly medieval (except for its 15th century Town Hall), but rather medieval with a Renaissance (or Baroque) updating.

The Rebuilding of a Market Square

You will recall from our earlier short history of Brussels that in 1695, under orders from Louis XIV, the French Marshal de Villeroy directed his gunners to pulverize the central city of Brussels—he told them, in particular, to use the spire of the city's famous Town Hall as their aiming point. Astonishingly, the Town Hall (built in the 1400s) survived the deliberate carnage (though it suffered interior damage), but the guild houses around the square, and the Masion du Roi, were all razed to the ground. It was an act of violence, as Napoleon was to say more than a hundred years later, "aussi barbare qu'inutile" (as barbaric as it was useless). But it galvanized the magistrates and guilds of Brussels into rebuilding the Grand' Place even grander than it was before. In three-and-a-half years, from 1695 to 1699, on the sites of what had been destroyed, they rebuilt the Guild Homes in approximately the same locations, shapes and sizes as before, but with all-stone facades (they had been partially wood before), of almost uniform height, and with fanciful, decorative touches of the new Baroque designs (the "Italo-Flamand") of the 17th century adorning the top-most gables of the structures. It was as if these proud craftsmen were thumbing their noses at the Great Powers of Europe. In a triangularly-shaped, large, gold inscription under the roof of the "House of the Tailors" (third up from the Maison du Roi, on the left-hand side as you face uphill; you can read it quite easily from ground level), these unassuming Belgians who normally sat with crossed legs atop a cloth-strewn table, patiently plying their needles on someone's silk jacket, proudly proclaimed "QUAS FUROR HOSTILIS SUBVERTERAT IGNIBUS AEDES, SARTOR RESTAURAT PRAESIDIBUSQUE DUCAT" (That Which the Enemies' Hostile Fire Destroyed, We the Tailors Have Restored and Offered in Tribute to the City's Magistrate)!

The Town Hall—"Tower" of the Grand' Place

Start with the Town Hall ("Hotel de Ville"). It survived the bombardment of 1695, and is essentially the same, sumptuous,

Gothic, medieval structure built in the early 1400s under the Dukes of Burgundy. Have you ever seen a modern structure to compare with it, in beauty of proportion, in lightness, in harmonious detail? Look especially at the tower, surmounted at the very peak of the spire with a 16½-foot-high gilded statue of St. Michael, patron saint of Brussels, sword drawn, atop a vanquished Devil. Square in shape for its first five stories, it then becomes an open construction—a framework of stone ribs—in its next three octagonal stories, before assuming a pyramidal form to culminate at St. Michael. It is as airy as the castle tower of a fairy tale, showing the sky between its stone ribs, and seems to float in the heavens towards which it soars.

The tower replaced an earlier Belfry tower, which pre-dated the Town Hall. When construction began in 1402, that Belfry Tower marked the furthest limit of the building. When it was then decided, in 1455, to extend the building, only a small space was available for the right-hand wing (as you face it), accounting for the difference in length of the two wings (and the off-center position of the tower). The heavy stone walls of the Belfry Tower also required the placing of an off-center entrance archway underneath the new tower. The assertion that this was an architectural mistake, which caused architect Jan van Ruysbroek to commit suicide when he allegedly discovered the "error," is simply a Brussels joke that has been told for centuries to dismayed tourists (it fooled me for years).

The original entrance to the building was at the staircase flanked by the two lions of Brabant, one holding the escutcheon of St. Michael; young couples walk down those steps on Saturday mornings following their civil weddings inside. On both sides of the lions are scalloped arcades connecting to pillars; but two arcades have no pillars beneath, ending instead in tightly-compressed bas-relief sculptures that simply "hang" in the air—they're called "pendentives". Look closely at them. One tells the story of the righteous Judge Herkenbald who executed his own nephew for the crime of rape. You see the rape, the Judge slitting the nephew's throat, the Judge on his own deathbed receiving Divine approbation for this impartial act of justice. The other tells of Brussels alderman Everard t'Serclaes, who opposed the territorial ambitions (threatening to Brussels) of the Lord of Gaasbeek, owner of the famous castle outside Brussels. He was set upon by henchmen of the infamous noble, who cut off his tongue and right foot, and left him to die on a deserted road outside the city. The pendentive depicts the bloody deed, and underneath shows the Devil carrying off the Lord of Gaasbeek's soul to Hell.

The main entrance to the Town Hall today is the large archway under the tower, directly above which are statues of the five major patron saints hereabouts. St. Michael is in the center, his sword above the devil; at his side to the left (looking at the statues), the nearly naked St. Sebastian (patron of the archers), St. Christopher (patron of the arquebusiers), and to his right, St. George (patron of the cross-bowmen, here killing the dragon), and a kneeling St. Gery, the eminent churchman of Brussels. Above these saints, in a semi-circle, the seven prophets and a scribe —the latter in a robe of the Capuchin monks, writes on a scroll; sculpted in the 15th century, these are the most remarkable of all the sculptures of the Town Hall, but they are copies of originals displayed in the museum of the Masion du Roi directly across the Grand' Place.

INSIDE THE TOWN HALL: The remaining, front facade of the Town Hall is profusely covered with dozens of sculpted figures of royal personages, like a vast picture gallery. These are all the rulers of Brabant up to nearly the end of the 15th century, always in chronological order: the Carolingian emperors starting with Charlemagne; the "Mayors of the Palace"—Pepin, Herstal, Charles Martel—who became Merovingian rulers; the Dukes of Brabant from Godfrey I to Jeanne and Wenceslas; the Dukes of Burgundy; often their wives, brothers, and sisters are shown alongside. Since some are portrayed rather abstractly, and not in an exact likeness, and because a lengthy, complex listing would be required to locate each one, we won't try. We do advise you to go inside the Town Hall, where you'll find dozens of oil portraits of the same and later rulers, in a succession of richly resplendent halls, chambers and antechambers used by the Burgomaster and Aldermen of the city of Brussels. Indeed, the chief impression you'll take away from an inside visit is of the rather gentle, warmhearted treatment of Brussels towards the former foreign rulers of Belgium! You'll see giant paintings of various emperors of Germany, the Empress Maria-Theresia of Austria, Charles of Lorraine and several archdukes of Saxony, Napoleon, William I of the Netherlands, a bewildering array of potentates, dukes, protectors and governors who came and went in the history of Belgium: how tolerant the treatment of them! But in giant, priceless Brussels tapestries (bearing the "BB" logotype of Brussels— "Bruxella in Brabantia")—and other panoramic paintings, you'll see scenes of the great moments of Brussels, and of its more recent mayors and Belgian royal figures.

Finally, immediately on entering the Town Hall, you will

read the two great poster proclamations of resistance (in French and Dutch) by its mayors on the eve of German occupation in both World Wars I and II. They show the heights to which those two languages can ascend, when animated by passion and courage. "Quoi qu'il arrive" (whatever happens), wrote Mayor Adolphe Max in 1914, "ecoutez la voix de votre bourgmestre. Il ne trahira pas" (listen to the voice of your mayor. He will not betray you). "Vive la Belgique libre et indépendante! Vive Bruxelles!" And similarly: pay no heed to the decrees of false collaborators, wrote Joseph van de Meulenbroeck in 1940. "Je suis, je reste et resterai le seul bourgmestre legitime de Bruxelles!" (I am, I remain, and I shall remain the only legitimate mayor of Brussels!).

Guided tours of the interior of the "Hotel de Ville" (Town Hall) of Brussels costing 50 francs ($1.39), are operated daily except Saturdays, from 9 to 1 on Mondays, from 9 to 4 p.m. Tuesdays through Fridays, and from 10 to 1 and 2 to 4 on Sundays. But the facade is free to viewing around the clock. Along with the town halls of Leuven and Bruges, this is the preeminent town hall of Belgium, and one of the greatest in the world.

The Guild Houses of the Grand' Place

From the Town Hall and its Brabantine-Gothic facade, let's now proceed *counter-clockwise* around the square. What we are viewing, in essence, is the genius of the "Italo-Flamand", or the Baroque, superimposed upon the forms of the Middle Ages. Note that on most of the houses, three stories of pillars decorate each front, and follow on a uniform succession of styles from bottom to top: Doric, Ionian, Corinthian.

Crossing the Rue Charles Buls from the Town Hall, we first encounter the smallest structure on the square, the exquisite **"House of the Star"** (with a star on top) built, quite incredibly, on stilts. It originally wasn't. Torn down in the mid-1800s by misguided civic officials to widen the street next to the Town Hall (thus gravely harming the architectural unity of the Grand' Place), it was later rebuilt by wiser minds, but on columns to permit carriages and the like to pass underneath. Beneath the arcade created by those columns is the reclining, metal sculpture of the dying **Everard t' Serclaes**, Brussels' greatest civic hero, whose arm and thigh are rubbed for good luck (and are thus shiny gold) by every well-informed passerby. In the 1300s it was t' Serclaes who led the militia that freed Brussels from occupation by the French-admiring Count of Flanders; t' Serclaes himself tore down the Count's flag from where it flew in front of this very house. Attacked while traveling on a country road, and cruelly multilated by hirelings of the Lord of Gaasbeek, the dying t' Serclaes was carried to this House of the Star, which fittingly commemorates his sacrifice today with the "rubbing statue" in bas relief against the wall. There, too, are plaques to the great Charles Buls, a mayor of Brussels in the late 1800s, who (among other things) restored the "House of the Star" and did much to preserve ancient Brussels.

Next door to it (still moving counter-clockwise): the **House of the Swan** (home of the Butchers' Guild), with a giant swan on front, designed in the classical French style of the man who destroyed the Square, Louis XIV, and not at all Flemish, Italian or Baroque. It is an odd exception (along with the House of the Fox — "Renard") to the generally curvaceous, Baroque designs of the Square. Statues representing Agriculture, the State of Plenty, and the Butchers, stand along the roof.

Next door to the "Swan" is the richly flamboyant "**House of the Brewers**" ("the Golden Tree"), with unmistakable beer hops climbing up the columns, the helpful inscription "Maison des Brasseurs" (House of the Brewers) along its front, and an equestrian statue of the popular Charles of Lorraine (Austrian governor of the Low Countries) atop its gable. Beer lovers! Here you will find the cheapest beer in Brussels, by simply paying 50 francs ($1.30) to visit the cellar-sited "**Brewery Museum**" in this building, open 10 to noon and 2 to 5, on Saturdays only from 10 to noon, and closed Sundays; press the bell for admission, tour the ancient instruments of brewing, view the interesting short technicolor film on brewing, and after all this, you'll be given a "free" glass of draft beer, which will have cost you the 50 francs admission.

Now turn to the long, continuous building at the top, uphill side of the square: the "**House of the Dukes of Brabant**", whose busts adorn the 19 pillars at the immediate top of the ground floor portion. Higher up are colored emblems of the Guilds that occupied these six, connected houses (see the six doors, up the outer staircase) built in the style of one large Italian palace: the Masons, the Cabinet Makers, the Millers, the Tanners, the Wine and Vegetable Merchants, the "Four Crowned Crafts" ("les Quatres Couronnés"; sculptors, stone cutters, roofers and masons) — you should be able to connect each emblem to the appropriate craft. On the roof of the building: four giant vases emitting flames of burning oil — an allegory of the yearning for peace (for which Brussels continued to yearn in vain since 1695).

Turn now (counter-clockwise) to the side of the Square on which stands the Maison du Roi. On the block above that structure, third from the left (i.e., the middle building) is the "**House**

of the Tailors" we referred to earlier, with its stirring, Latin inscription in the triangular portico under the fanciful, Baroque gable. Atop the gable stands St. Boniface with outstretched arms; in his other arm, he holds a shield adorned with Golden Scissors, symbol of the tailors' guild. Downstairs, over the door that presently leads to the firelight-lit tavern on the ground floor, is a bust of St. Barbara, patron saint of that Guild. The two buildings to the left are classic examples of the hodge-podge of styles—Italian/ Brabantine/Baroque, the detailed precision of the Flemish given excitement and movement by fanciful, Italian shapes—that came together so miraculously to create the ravishing beauty of the Grand' Place. On the facades of one are leering theatrical masques inspired by the Commedia dell' Arte of Italy.

Next comes the combined Gothic/Renaissance **Maison du Roi**, originally built by the Emperor Charles V in the 1500s for various communal purposes (tax collection, courts, prison), then rebuilt in the 19th century in neo-Gothic style to approximate the earlier structure. Because Charles was also king of Spain, it was soon called the House of the King, though he never lived there. So seriously have the building arts declined in our own times (from what they were in the Middle Ages) that the building scarcely compares, either in beauty or in the way it has aged, with the 500-years-older Town Hall across the Place (in my view). We'll return to the important **Communal Museum** inside the Maison du Roi (House of the King) in just a bit.

The best for last. On the downhill end of the Square, the lavish frenzy of the Italian/Flemish explodes into a gilded fairyland, strangely beautiful, in which the Guilds used allegorical symbols —an elegant touch—to advertise their own importance. From left to right, looking downhill, you first see the "**House of the Haberdashers**" on the extreme left, topped by the statue of St. Nicholas, patron saint of merchants, with staff. Underneath, on the top floor, four buxom caryatides (maidens performing as pillars) display the world's wealth: wool, wheat, the vine, flowers. Atop the ground floor are five striking figures: the middle one is Justice, blindfolded, a scale in one hand, a glorious Sun above him. The continents, two by two, stand on each side of him: Africa (ebony and ivory on a turtle shell) and Europe (the horn of plenty) on one side, Asia (an elephant's tusk) and America (gold, the European image of recently-discovered America) on the other. Next, the "**House of the Boatmen**", its facade covered with emblems of sailing, its gable consisting of the richly-decorated stern of a 17th century ship. At the very top, two lions guard the heraldic shield and image of Charles II of Spain. Lower down: sea horses, fish scales, and a horn, for the alternative name—"Maison du Cornet" (Horn)—of the building. Next door: the **"House of the She-Wolf"** ("Maison de la Louve"), serving the Guild of the Archers, who placed a golden Phoenix arising from the Ashes atop the roof, to symbolize the re-birth of the Grand' Place and Brussels. The profession of archery is symbolized in the triangular pediment, in which Apollo shoots the Serpent with his arrows. Statues of Peace, Strife, Falsehood and Truth adorn the third floor; the bas-relief of a she-wolf suckling Romulus and Remus, founders of Rome, is over the door. Next door: the incredibly gilded and ornate **"House of the Cabinet Makers"** ("le Sac"), designed quite appropriately to resemble an enormous and elaborate wooden chest. A compass stands atop the gable; while tools of the Guild decorate the railings over the bottom floors. Above the door: the emblem of a sack. Next door: the **"House of the Grease (or Tallow) Merchants"**, with its great variety of columnar styles, some twisted (the only such on the square), others plain and classic. Blue shields over the ground floor contain images of Wheelbarrows ("les brouettes")—the other identifying name for the building in the Middle Ages, when there were no street numbers—and in a niche of the Gable stands St. Gilles, patron saint of these candlestick-makers. Finally, at the extreme right, with a small cupola tower on top, the corporate **"House of the Bakers"**, with a bronze bust of St. Aubert (patron saint of the Bakers' Guild) in papal hat, above the door, King Charles II of Spain further up, allegorical statues of Wind, Water, Agriculture and Fire along the railing on the roof, and the golden nymph of "Fame" blowing her horn while balanced on one precarious foot, above everything else.

La Grand' Place! What gives it such impact? Perhaps it is the fact that it is totally enclosed. Once inside it, the modern world disappears. And one is immersed in the flow of history, the stages of the world; one senses what people can occasionally accomplish, working together, and impelled by the kind of idealism that resulted in this stupendous achievement.

Le Musee Communal (City Museum) in the Grand' Place

The rich history of Brussels, which reflected major trends in European life, is partially displayed within a city museum maintained in the Maison du Roi, and in plaques affixed to it. It was directly in front of the Maison du Roi that the Counts of Egmont and Hornes were beheaded in 1568 by troops of the Duke of Alva, pursuing policies dictated by Philip II of Spain to repress all stirrings of religious dissent and political independence within the Netherlands. Egmont—hero of Beethoven's soaring "Egmont Overture"—had served Philip II with utmost loyalty, attempting in the most agonized fashion to preserve the king's authority while tempering his policies. Though Brussels, and the provinces of what later became Belgium, remained firmly Catholic and even remained within the Spanish Empire for another hundred years, the people of Brussels never forgave this affront to their national dignity. A large inscription on a pillar at the entrance to the Maison du Roi calls Egmont and Hornes, without equivocation, "victimes de despotisme et de l'Intolerance de Philippe II."

The Communal Museum fills all three floors of the Maison du Roi. It is particularly rich in paintings, maps and engravings (found on the second floor) of the city's history in the 19th century. It is here, too, that one finds the amusing "Salle Mannekin Pis" containing nearly 400 costumes donated from around the world —from baseball uniforms to samurai robes—for the two-foot-high statue of the impudent Mannekin Pis caught relieving himself (see below). But the museum's most important collection are its paintings, sculptures, "retables" and tapestries on the second floor. These include the priceless "**Cortege de Noces**" (Wedding Procession) by Pieter Bruegel the Elder, depicting two lines of Brabantine peasants—one male, one female—walking in the countryside just outside Brussels to a marriage ceremony. The bride is obviously that same, plumpish, young lady with reddish-brown hair seated in Bruegel's equally-renowned "Wedding Feast" ("De Boerenbruiloft") now hanging in the Museum of Fine Arts in Ghent. But which is the groom? Is he the man between the two trees? Or is he beyond the left-hand margin of the painting? And to what conceivable figure does he relate in "De Boerenbruiloft" (see our Ghent chapter)? Across the room: the anonymous triptych of the early 1500s, "**Les Quatres Couronnés**" (the Four Crowned Trades), a tribute to the hewers and sculptors of stone who built both Cathedrals and homes; in the central panel, four of these sculptors, masons, stone cutters and the like reject the demand of an astonished pagan emperor to work on the statue of a pagan god, and are martyred, becoming the sainted "Quatres Couronnés". And there is also here "**The Martyrdom of Saints Crespin and Crepinier**" by a Brussels master of the year 1500, as well as the weatherworn originals of the statues of prophets and scribe, the capitals of columns, now adorning the facade of the Town Hall across the way. There are also great Brussels tapestries, including two fragments of the celebrated woven wall-hanging that tells of the legend of the Antwerp maiden,

Beatrix Soetkens, who (in response to a celestial command) stole a statue of the Virgin from an Antwerp church, transported it by boat down the River Sennes to Brussels, and deposited it within the Church of Notre Dame du Sablon on Brussels' Place du Grand Sablon (see our later discussion of this church and the legend).

THE RETABLE DE SALUCES: The most extraordinary work in the Communal Museum is surely the part-painted, part-sculpted **"Retable de Saluces"** created from 1505 to 1510 in a nameless atelier of Brussels. A "retable" is a one-foot-thick wooden wall sculpture of several large panels (of which the outer or upper ones are often paintings). This one, an amazingly vivid succession of seven sculpted New Testament scenes—from left to right, (1) The Presentation of the Virgin at the Temple, (2) The Marriage of the Virgin, (3) The Annunciation, (4) The Nativity, (5) The Circumcision of the Infant Jesus, (6) The Adoration of the Magi, (7) The Purification of the Virgin—was produced for the chapel of a rich Italian family living in the town of Saluces. Retables of Brussels were famed throughout Europe in the 14th and 15th centuries for many of the same reasons that brought acclaim to the Flemish "primitives" in the 15th century: exquisite precision of detail, little household features and instances of "genre" that brought humanity to the scenes of exalted personages. The Retable of Saluces (Brussels bought it back from Italy in 1894) portrays an entire biblical world bursting with life, in a pageant of adorable, little, doll-like creatures under a forest of filigree-like, Gothic columns. Playful touches abound: a tiny monkey crouching beneath the stairs, in scene number one; tiny angels holding protectively to the richly-brocaded robe of the Virgin—they seem to have flown here from a canvas by Memling or Van der Weyden (see the paintings in Bruges and Tournai), in scene number two. In scene number three, look at the wind-blown robe of the angel; the deep folds of the robe of the Virgin caught studying a text. The detail of each scene could absorb us for hours; the obvious love and fervor which animates each tableaux is a hallmark of the medieval "Age of Faith", when people had no doubts, and believed with zealous fervor. Imagine creating such a masterpiece for the closed chapel of a private family, never to be seen by another person! (The sculptor is thought to be the son of the Brussels sculptor Jan Borman, who did the equally large and grand "Retable of St. Georges" now displayed in the "Royal Museums of Art and History" portion of Brussels' Cinquantenaire Museums complex; see below.)

Alongside the sculpted retable are the painted portions of it —same size and shape, and probably intended to cover the sculpture—but this time devoted to the less-frequently-depicted life of Joseph; from left to right, it presents such scenes as the Birth of Joseph; the Apprenticeship and Acts of Charity of Joseph; the Marriage of Mary and Joseph; Joseph's Dream; the Census at Bethlehem; the Life at Nazareth; Joseph's Death.

It seems appropriate that the Retable of Saluces should appear near to the triptych of the "Quatres Couronnés" extolling the work of Brussels' ancient sculptors, stone fitters, masons and roofers. For it was men such as these—sculptors of wood—who created the Retables of Saluces. In medieval times, the craftsmen of Brussels had concluded that their best defense against competition was the stringently-high quality of their work—"la bonne qualité" (high quality), "travail bien fait" (work well done)—enforced by inspections, rules and strict procedures of apprenticeship and qualification as "master craftsmen." The painstaking detail and precision that went into this retable constructed for private ownership in a foreign land, is a first example of the qualities of the Middle Ages that we'll have occasion to encounter time and time again in the later chapters of this book.

The "Musée Communal" (City Museum) in the Maison du Roi on the Grand' Place charges admission of 50 francs ($1.39), except on Sundays when it is free, and is open weekdays from 10 to noon, and 1 to 5, weekends from 10 to noon only.

L'ILOT SACRÉ: The narrow, cobblestoned streets immediately around the Grand' Place, and their overhanging old houses, have been carefully preserved in recent years, reverentially treated, and referred to quite chillingly as "L'Ilot Sacré"—the "Sacred Ile" in the midst of Brussels. Each bears the medieval designation that characterized the merchants who tended to cluster in their specialties along that street: Rue du Marché aux Herbes (Street of the Herb Market), Rue des Chapeliers (Street of the Shoe Makers), Rue Marché aux Fromages (Street of the Cheese Merchants), Rue Chair et Pain (Meat and Bread Street), Rue des Harengs (Herring), Rue au Beurre (Butter), Rue des Brasseurs (Brewers). Each is now lined with colorful restaurants, shops and souvenir stores, the former catering as much to residents of Brussels as to tourists, and it is here that you find the "Greatest Restaurant Street in the World" referred to by me in our restaurant section above. From the Grand' Place, walk down the Rue Chair et Pain at the bottom (downhill) side of the Maison du Roi, cross the Rue Marché aux Herbes, and you are suddenly on the alley-like "Petite Rue des Bouchers" leading to the wider Rue des Bouchers (Street of the Butchers), both of them combining into the lusty, colorful and very Breugelian "Greatest Restaurant Street in the World", a must-see even for people lacking the time to dine in Brussels. Turning right on the Rue des Bouchers, you then walk into one of the three wings of that glass-enclosed **Royal Galleries of St. Hubert** of the 19th century, which touched off the construction of other, highly-decorative, enclosed shopping arcades in other European cities. It contains not simply a string of prestigious shops, but a large dancehall, an important legitimate theatre, a large cinema, several chocolate stores, various coffee/beer/pastry bars, and two trendy restaurants. It should be seen.

The Lace Museum

Now return to the Grand' Place, and walk down the Rue Charles Buls at the uphill end of the Town Hall. Two blocks along, on this street lined with lace shops, you'll turn left for 30 yards on the Rue de la Violette to the three-story **Lace Museum** (Musée de la Dentelle), at 6 Rue de la Violette, charging admission of 50 francs ($1.39). It is open weekdays from 10 to 12:30 and 1:30 to 5 (winters until 4 only), weekends from 2 to 4:30 only, and deals with that 17th century (and earlier) industry of Brussels which once employed more than 15,000 practitioners of the highly-demanding, incredibly-laborious art, and continues to be pursued, on a much reduced scale, in the Brussels of today. On its second and third floors, you'll not only see exhibits of the most elaborate and accomplished lace, the kind requiring hundreds of hours of patient hand weaving, but also paintings of various noble figures wearing lace of great intricacy that peeks from underneath collars and cuffs. And suddenly you'll remember all those portraits you've seen of European counts and dukes, duchesses and princes, adorned with yards and yards of lace, all produced painstakingly, over months of time, and for an absurd pittance, by whole armies of exploited female Belgian lacemakers. Just as most of us have never thought of the lives that went into those casual cuffs, it is even less likely that the regal wearers ever gave them a thought! If you'll be travelling on to the lace-making shops or other art museums of Belgium, you might first want to spend an hour in Brussels' Lace Museum.

The Mannekin Pis

If you'll return now to the Rue Charles Buls and continue along it, you'll find that the street becomes the Rue de l'Etuve and leads, in just a few steps more, to the corner fountain occupied by the immortal, but tiny, bronze statue of a little boy urinating into the air from a cocky stance atop a ledge of the fountain. Until the early 17th century, a stone statue dating back to the mid-1400s occupied the same niche and performed the same office; it was known then as "little Julian". In 1619, the Brussels sculptor Jerome Duquesnoy created a bronze replacement which all the world now knows as the "Mannekin Pis".

After whom is the little boy modeled? There are at least a dozen competing legends. One is of the little boy-hero of Brussels—Julian—who, using his natural resources, extinguished an incendiary bomb thrown into the street by enemy troops. Another tells of the peasant who came with his little son to a Brussels festival, lost the child in the crowd, found him five days later, and expressed his thanks by sculpting a statue of the boy as he looked when rediscovered: the Mannekin Pis. Still another claims he is the son of a nobleman who attempted to seduce the virtuous Ste. Gudule. Heaven's punishment was to condemn his son to remain always a child, and always relieving himself (a poor explanation of the sweet little statue). Stolen from his niche on numerous occasions, and the subject of other incidents too numerous to describe, Mannekin Pis is today treated as the symbol of Brussels' ironic, impudent outlook, a mirror of the impiety and cynicism of its average resident. Somehow he fits, and it is hard to imagine him standing on the stately squares of those other European cities that have occasionally sought to dominate the world. Instead, in a Brussels that has witnessed every misfortune, suffered every indignity, and lost all illusions, Mannekin Pis is an artistic summation.

THE MUSEUMS OF ANCIENT AND MODERN ART:

On the first full day of your stay in Brussels, either a full morning, or the full afternoon, should be set aside for the Grand' Place, L'Ilot Sacré, and their associated museums, shops and inside visits; the remainder of that day, and perhaps a bit of any unused half-day, can then be enjoyed in the heady setting—a feast for all the senses—of the single classical building at 3 Rue de la Regence that houses both "**Le Musée de l'Art Ancien**" (Museum of Ancient Art) and "**Musée de l'Art Moderne**" (Museum of Modern Art). From the Grand' Place, walk out the exiting street of the uphill, left-hand side of the Square, and then turn right towards the imposing hill that flanks the side of "L'Ilot Sacré." Walk directly up that hill ("le Mont des Arts"—Mount of the Arts) through the gardens of the modern library known as the "Albertina" (on your right), the Palace of Congresses (on your left) to the classical square overlooking the city, known as the "Place Royale"; surrounded by stately, white buildings of the city's 18th-century Austrian era, with an equestrian statue of crusader Godfrey of

Bouillon set incongruously inside (see our later chapter on Bouillon, in the Ardennes), this was the site of the city's former medieval palace of the Coudenberg. Today, the Royal Park of Brussels is to the left, the King's Royal Palace to the upper right; but sharply to the right, a short walk down the Rue de la Regence, is that major structure that ranks quite easily among the greatest art museums in all of Europe—the Prado in Madrid, the Louvre in Paris, the Kunsthistorisches in Vienna, the Uffizzi in Florence.

On its ground floor and upper floors, the building is the famed Museum of Ancient Art. Then, in an adjoining structure—but reached from the same main entrance—a downward-heading escalator brings you to the seven "subterranean" floors of the Museum of Modern Art. Though seemingly underground, they actually front onto floor-to-ceiling windows flanking the former slope of the hillside outside (a remarkable architectural feat). Thus, natural light illuminates works of the renowned Belgian surrealists, symbolists and neo-impressionists that constitute such a major Belgian contribution to all the world's modern art. And admission to the Museum of Modern Art (open 10 to 1 and 2 to 5) is also completely free.

The Museum of Ancient Art

We'll be returning in a few pages to those subterranean masterworks of modern art. Regardless of your own tastes, and because of its importance, you should begin with the older collection.

The Museum of Ancient Art is a large collection, the home of at least 40 towering masterworks and hundreds of major secondary pieces. You can return time and again—never too often—each time to delight in another series of rooms, a different period, a formerly-overlooked grouping of paintings. Unlike numerous other museums of art in other Belgian cities, it does not specialize, but offers a bit of everything, a broadly eclectic selection, sometimes a bit confusing, and larger than the more compact displays in other Belgian cities (although Antwerp's Royal Museum of Fine Arts is nearly as sizeable and important, especially for its far more numerous collection of Rubens). But though it shows works from the brush of nearly every major Flemish and later Belgian master from the 15th century on, Brussels' Museum of Ancient Art is pre-eminently the museum of one man—Pieter Bruegel the Elder, and the dynasty of Bruegels he spawned.

PIETER BRUEGEL (1525–1567): A revolutionary, a painter of the common man, an artist-philosopher who delivered sadly gentle commentaries on the ways of the world, Bruegel is today acclaimed as one of the greatest artists of all time, though for centuries he was disparaged and dismissed as a mere "peasant painter." His accomplishments were monumental. Prior to Bruegel, virtually all paintings were of religious scenes or allegories. If they portrayed ordinary life at all, they do so in tiny patches seen through the casement windows of cathedrals or other holy structures. Landscapes in particular were almost totally subordinated to sacred themes (except perhaps in the Van Eycks' "Adoration of the Mystic Lamb").

Bruegel made mankind and the natural world the major theme of his paintings. He virtually invented "genre" art—the painting of everyday life. He created monumental landscapes that alone provided the theme for an entire painting. In depicting the activities of ordinary people—their weddings and festivals, their work in the fields—he proclaimed the worth of the common man. He preached an egalitarian message, performed an almost revolutionary act. He may have gone further. In the troubled time of religious conflict through which he lived—the saddest years in all the history of the Low Lands, witnessing inquisition and executions at the stake, the arrival of occupying foreign armies and repression of free conscience—many of his paintings may be read as cries of protest against the forces of repression. In biblical scenes portrayed as if they took place in Flemish villages, the armies and authorities he included there can be seen as the Spanish troops of Philip II—although the latter point is hotly disputed by some art experts.

Although his surviving work amounts to only 40 paintings and a hundred or so etchings, they span a remarkable range of artistic themes and styles. There are, of course, the scenes of peasants swilling, and of villagers dancing, of wedding processions, and hunters returning homeward through bleak and frigid wintry snows. Yet there are also classical mythologies of almost abstract composition—witness his "Landscape and the Fall of Icarus". There are biblical events set as in a Flemish village. And fantastical visions of heaven and hell directly influenced by Hieronymus Bosch. In his lively portrayals of village life, there is so much significant detail and tiny vignettes that some art lovers bring magnifying glasses to the museums in which these Bruegels hang, and spend hours peering at small portions of each canvas.

What little we know of Bruegel's life is derived from a short essay written by a near-contemporary. He was born somewhere in Brabant, received his art training in Antwerp, where he then worked for the foremost etchings printer of that city, and later moved to Brussels, possibly to escape involvement in the sharp (and dangerous) religious conflicts of the 1500s, but also to marry the daughter of another prominent artist of that time. He is described as a friend of leading humanists, who frequently accompanied him on excursions into the countryside to witness the weddings and banquets of the village folk. Within five years of his death, he became the father of two sons later to become important artists: Pieter Bruegel the Younger (known as "Hell" Bruegel) and Jan Bruegel (known as "Velvet" Bruegel). Following his death, and except as perpetuated by his sons, the realistic artistic traditions he established moved on primarily to Holland and to such painters as Vermeer, while Belgium was captivated by the radically different, florid and curvaceous, Italianate styles of the Baroque, as produced with such drama by the great Peter Paul Rubens.

More than that we do not know. In succeeding centuries Pieter Bruegel was virtually forgotten by the art world, or denigrated. Today he is acknowledged as a Titan of art, the master of Brussels, the only painter to whom Brussels' Musée de l'Art Ancien pays the supreme tribute of hanging a lofty sign over the entrance to Room 31 housing his major works. In giant gold letters duplicating his signature, on a brown background, it proclaims: BRVEGEL.

ROOM 31: Five works only. One is a tiny portrait of a man yawning; only a genius could have compressed such expression into so minuscule a space. The second is a badly-preserved "Adoration of the Magi" done in fading, tempera paints (egg yolk with pigments), and kept behind glass in a chemically treated atmosphere. Here are no fairytale kings in royal vestments, but real people come from afar after a long, dusty journey to attend on the Child. The third is the turbulent "Fall of the Rebel Angels" influenced by Bosch but endowed with a never-before, and never-again-duplicated, sense of motion, as the angels and their opponents seem to cascade down and then to rebound fluidly upward, in constant, gentle movement, on a static canvas covered with irridescent colors—it is a "change of pace" work having nothing in common with the bulk of Bruegel's other paintings. The fourth is the renowned "Census at Bethlehem", making the biblical city into a Flemish village set in the snow, populated by common people working, playing, lining up to be counted; Mary and Joseph are tiny figures in the foreground, barely emphasized, unnoticed in the life of the town. There is a brooding tension about the scene—the prologue to momentous events about to transpire. There is a house in ruins, a shelter for persons suffering from the plague, a hollow, decaying tree, numerous other items of fascinating detail. And then there is the fifth work, which people travel from all over the world to see. It has been named one of the Seven Marvels of Belgium, and it is:

"LANDSCAPE AND THE FALL OF ICARUS": A solitary ploughman is carefully cultivating a strip of land along a sun-bathed Mediterranean Sea. Below him a day-dreaming shepherd is gazing at the sun, leaning on his staff, surrounded by sheep. At the extreme bottom right, a fisherman casts his line. Near him a Portuguese man 'o war is slowly passing, its sails bulging with the wind. A mythical city glitters in the distance near jagged mountains of stone. And suddenly we see legs—two tiny legs—flailing from out of the sea.

They are the legs of Icarus, who has attempted to soar too high. Imprisoned with his father Daedalus by Minos, the tyrant of Crete, the two had determined to escape by using wax to affix wings of feathers to their backs. As the Greek poet Ovid relates the mythical tale, the father had warned the son neither to fly too low, for then humidity would make the wings too heavy, not too high, for then the sun would melt the wax. But Icarus had been so enraptured by the flight that he went ever higher, and the prediction materialized—the sun melted the wax, the feathers dropped off, and Icarus plunged into the sea.

But why aren't the figures in the painting paying attention to the boy's plight? Didn't they hear his cries as he fell from above? Don't they realize he is drowning? The fisherman is only feet away. The ship is passing blithely by. The ploughman, unconcerned, and the shepherd, gazing into the heavens, are deep into their own concerns, oblivious to the tragedy of a fellow human being. Bruegel is telling us of the life that goes on in the face of the great historical moments. He depicts the disregard shown by ordinary people to even the greatest of human dreamers, the persons who seek to achieve, to reach, to aspire, and whose failures pass unmarked by humanity at large. Everyday life continues on its placid course while some people, seeking freedom, pay a price for it. Though endless speculation can be set off by this monumental inquiry squeezed into a small canvas, I like W. H. Auden's reaction to it in his poem, "The Museum of Fine Arts" based directly on Bruegel's masterpiece: "About suffering they were never wrong,/The Old Masters: How well they understood/Its human position; how it takes place/While someone else is eating or opening a window or just walking duly along . . ."

Solely as an achievement in design and painting, the work is extraordinary: look closely at its magnificent composition, at the crossed diagonals created by its landscape and figures. See his use of proverbs in an otherwise abstract work: the barely-perceived purse with a knife through it (the symbol of human folly) lying just below the ploughing horse, the head of a reclining figure lying under the trees to the left ("the plough stops for no dying man"). Along with the Van Eycks' "Mystic Lamb" in Ghent, Rubens' "Descent from the Cross" in Antwerp, Memling's "Shrine of St. Ursula" in Bruges, Nicholas of Verdun's "Reliquary of our Lady" in Tournai, others, this is truly one of Belgium's "Magnificent Seven", and a wondrous attraction of Brussels.

THE SONS OF PIETER BRUEGEL: Emerging from the door at the side of the "Icarus", you find yourself in Room 32, and immediately confront the copies and adaptations of his father's work done by Pieter Bruegel the Younger ("Hell Bruegel") (1564–1638); some of the elder's paintings, of which the originals are lost, have survived only because of the many copies to which the younger Bruegel devoted much of his life. Here is the magnificent "Kermesse Flamand" (Festival of Flanders) whose dozens of detailed vignettes are like a picture book of medieval life; look carefully at the religious play staged upon a platform in the middle of the crowd. Here, too, is the "Massacre of the Innocents" (like an old sepia photograph, the killing of all children in a Flemish village by a sinister army led by a man in black; though a re-telling of the New Testament gospel, some take it to depict the passage of the Duke of Alva and his Spanish army through the Low Lands). Note how the son's copies are more graphic and explicit, with more distinct lines—and yet ultimately how they fail to measure up to the sublime talents of the father (though these paintings remain masterpieces judged solely on their own attributes). To complete your viewing of the museum's Bruegels, walk then down the long, narrow space of rooms 32 to 34 into Rooms 45 and 44 near the very entrance to the floor. There you find "Winter Landscape with Skaters and a Bird Trap" by Bruegel the Elder; another "Massacre of the Innocents" by Bruegel the Younger; and then Bruegel the Younger's lusty "Outdoor Wedding Dance", superbly composed, with grim, teeth-set peasants engaging in what seems almost to be an obligatory dance; though some are drunk, none are smiling, and one wonders whether Bruegel is here commenting on the harshness of the peasants' life. You will of course wish to purchase a reproduction downstairs, as a memento of your communion with Peter Bruegel.

A GALAXY OF ARTISTS: Though Bruegels are the chief attraction, dozens of other renowned paintings grace the Museum of Ancient Art, from all major phases and eras of Flemish painting, a bit of everything. We can group them best by artist:

Peter Paul Rubens (see our Antwerp chapter for discussion of his life, style and work), 1577–1640, is represented in Brussels' "Ancien Art" Museum by several major works, but he is displayed not nearly as well as in the Antwerp Fine Arts Museum, and his paintings are confusingly hung, the monumental works upstairs, the smaller but equally outstanding paintings in downstairs locations. Upstairs, at the heads of stairs or corridors, badly reflecting light and difficult therefore to enjoy, are his giant "Adoration of the Magi", "Ascent to Calvary", "Martyrdom of St. Livinius", with all their surging life flung over vast expanses of canvas, their muscular men and buxom, curvaceous women. All three were meant to hang in mammoth Gothic churches, in Tournai, Affighem and Ghent, respectively. Downstairs are his more obvious works of genius: "Heads of a Black Man" (four facial studies on the same canvas of one whose race was rarely seen in the Belgium of that time, and quite obviously provoked Rubens to awe and wonder); "Christ and the Adulteress"; "Landscape and the Hunt of Atalante" (where the very forest seems to be dancing and alive); the superb "Portrait of Peter Pacquius" (a sage and sly lawyer who had become Chancellor of Brabant; his eyes follow you as you scan the face); "Portrait of Helene Fourment" (Rubens' saucy, blonde and very young second wife); the unfinished "Miracles of St. Benedict"; and in the same room, nearly a dozen small studies in yellow, red and brown, dashed off in preparation for larger canvases and ceilings destined for the royal court of Spain ("The Fall of Icarus", and several other tiny, mythological sketches preserved in a small case) and an English banqueting hall ("Wisdom Triumphing Over War and Discord"); see also his preparatory sketch, "The Martyrdom of St. Ursula", a scene literally carpeted with the bodies of fallen virgins glowing with silvery holiness (see our Bruges chapter for discussion of the legend of St. Ursula). (And think of how even this genius engaged in the most painstaking, tedious, preparatory sketches and laborious experiments before flinging paint upon his most monumental canvases.)

The disciples of Rubens (notably **Anthony Van Dyck** and **Jan Bruegel**), and others who painted in roughly the same period, are found in rooms adjoining the works of the master. The great portraitist and student of Rubens, Van Dyck (1599–1641), is represented by several canvases, of which his "Portrait of the Sculptor Frans Duquesnoy"—the Flemish sculptor holding a moulded satyr's head as the symbol of his profession, and looking proudly into the eyes of an artistic equal, one he knows understands him, the painter—is outstanding. And note Van Dyck's "Portrait of a Jesuit", "Portrait of a Genoese Lady and her Daughter", "Rinaldo and Armida" and "Crucifixion". . . . "Still Life" (jewelry, outshone by exquisite flowers painted with rapture), in the same room, is by Pieter Bruegel's younger son, Jan (known as "Velvet" Bruegel), 1568–1625, who made a specialty of such subjects, and was often asked by Rubens to paint the flowers and jewels appearing on the latter's canvases. And again in the very same fascinating room: several towering works by Antwerp-born, but Holland-residing, **Frans Hals** (1580–1666) ("Children's Group", "Portrait of Johannes Hoornbeek"), by **Cornelis de Vos of Antwerp** (1586–1651) ("The Artist and his Family"); by Dutchman **Nicholaas Maes** (1634–1693) ("Man in a Felt Hat"); and even by **Rembrandt** (1606–1669) ("Portrait of Nicolas van Bambeck", painted a year before he did "The Night Watch"; notice the lavish lace).

Dirck Bouts (1415–1475), and other Flemish "primitives" of the 15th century, are back upstairs, near the Bruegels. You must not fail to see Bouts' two-panel re-telling of the legend, "The Justice of Emperor Otto", in Room 13, with its strangely elongated figures, but all of the other hallmarks of the "primitives" style: the faces of real men and women, the cloths and stones and trees and furniture of actual life and nature depicted with an almost photographic realism, the luminous tones achieved by nearly transparent oil paints, the blindingly bright reds, blues and greens, the almost mystical stillness and static, other-worldly holiness of figures frozen into a "pose" of magnificent composition. Here, in the uncompleted "Execution of the Innocent Man" panel at the left, the Emperor Otto has been deceived by his wife into ordering the be-heading of a courtier. The far more beautiful "Fire Ordeal" panel at the right shows the wife of the be-headed man, cradling his head in one hand, and calmly and without pain holding a red-hot poker in the other (ordeal by fire) to prove to the Emperor and astonished onlookers that her husband was innocent; whereupon the Emperor orders his own wife to be burned at the stake, as shown at far rear. Yet the sad eyes of the widow record the irrevocable death of her innocent spouse. The consummate beauty and composition of the second panel, the subtle expressions of emotion on the faces of the participants, are a great achievement of the master of Louvain, whose magnificent "Last Supper" we'll soon be viewing in Louvain.

Hans Memling (1435–1494), one of the greatest of the primitives, is in Room 14, and although his grander and more flamboyant works are found in Bruges, you'll find his "Portrait of Barbara van Vlaendenbergh" (a strongly handsome, blonde matron of the times), his "Portrait of a Man", and especially his "Martyrdom of Saint Sabastian", to be enthralling. The last named is a violent scene of assassination by archery, yet neither the saint nor his assailants betray the slightest emotion as the arrows pierce the martyr's body, as if both were in a mystical communion, cooperating in his holy end.

Rogier van der Weyden (1399–1464), that earliest of "primitives" from Tournai, is in Rooms 11 and 12, with his "Pieta", his "Portrait of Laurent Froimont", "Virgin and Child", and especially his magnificent "Man with the Arrow" (a knight, in the year when he was elected to the Order of the Golden Fleece, its emblem around his neck).

Hugo van der Goes (1440–1482), that most other-wordly of the "primitives", is in several rooms, as is: **Quinten Matsys** (Room 22) (1465–1530); the **"Master of Flemalle"** (1400s, probably Robert Campin of Tournai, a contemporary of the Van Eycks, and the teacher of Roger Van der Weyden; his "Annunciation", a preliminary attempt at the central panel of his later and greater "Merode Altarpiece", is found here in Brussels' great museum); **Jan Gossart** (1478–1532) (don't miss his "Portraits of a Donor and Donatrice" in Room 25, two narrow, side panels of a triptych, depicting a handsome, young, very self-satisfied and unquestioning couple); **Gerard David** (1450–1523); **Jan Mostaert** (1473–1555); **Bernard van Orley** (1488–1541); and numberless other Flemish greats. And especially, there is—

Hieronymus Bosch (1450–1516), known also (in French-speaking parts of Belgium) as Jerome Bosch, first of the "Belgian surrealists", with his flying fishes dropping bombs on exploding villages, his cracked-eggshells concealing scenes of sexual frenzy, his half-human/half-animal creatures, is also here. Though Bosch's greatest works have gone to other galleries (see his "Garden of Delights" in Madrid's Prado), his outstanding "Temptation of St. Anthony" is in Room 17, a painting well worth close study. Remarkably, the very same room contains one of the few standard, non-grotesque works of Bosch, his "Christ on the Cross", almost modern in its abstraction and design.

At least two hundred other Flemish masterworks are hung in this important museum of Brussels, and scarcely a single painting of second rank. If you will walk through its rooms in calm and measured fashion, seeking to follow a chronological path by observing the signs, you will enjoy, as it were, a silent and immensely moving "conversation" with past masters, men of astonishing talent, who not only recorded the attitudes of their time, but transcended those themes with deeper insights and visions of their own—the mark of great art.

The Museum of Modern Art

Brussels' "Musée de l'Art Ancien" displays paintings from the 14th through the end of the 18th-century. Brussels' "Musée de l'Art Moderne" picks up the thread from the nineteenth century to date. It is a staggering collection, among the world's most important, and it is brilliantly displayed on that series of "subterranean" floors flooded by natural light that we described at the start of this section. Because they are all below ground level of the Museum of Ancient Art, each of the Modern's floors is marked by a "minus" and then its number: "-3", "-4", "-5", and so on. And although you'll want to view all seven, you should keep in mind that Magritte is on "-6", Delvaux on "-5", Alechinsky (pure 20th century) is on "-8", and Constant Permeke—the great proletarian painter—on "-5".

But start with the traditional and symbolist works of the important, 19th-century Belgian, James Ensor (his almost-miraculously-advanced and modern "Les Masques Singuliers" of clowns, his traditional and much acclaimed "La Musique Russe" of a lady at the piano while a seated man listens). Then, perhaps, go on to Constant Permeke, seeking out the famous, crude and blockheaded couple, "Les Fiancés" (the Fiancées), or Permeke's more explicit works of social protest: a dusk-time scene of Walloon workers marching off on strike preceded by a red flag.

But all this is prologue to the areas displaying the two leading Belgian surrealists of contemporary times: Rene Magritte (1898-1967), and Paul Delvaux (1897-). The latter is discussed in our section on the Belgian Coast dealing with his museum there. Here he is represented by perhaps his very best-known works: "La Voie Publique" (Public Thoroughfare, a reclining nude with her clothed attendants, all incongruously placed in an Art Nouveau room opening onto a night-bathed streetcar station) and "Pygmalion" (the nude who embraces a stone, male statue, while clothed and hatted figures walk by).

And then Magritte. Though you may never have viewed one of his full-scale works, Rene Magritte is already familiar to you, for his powerful images have been shamelessly copied by advertising agencies the world over. Here is the painter of conservative men in bowler hats, their faces entirely obscured by a large, shiny apple; of city streets that are pitch-dark in the blinding glare of a noontime sun; of clouds drifting from an open sky into the window of a closed room that badly needs airing; of a giant fish standing upright next to a sea-and-sky of infinity. His paintings tell of anxiety and isolation in the modern world, of stultifying homogeneity and the inability to communicate, especially in that famous canvas of the group of identical persons staring wordlessly through a window into an open room. These are visions that speak to our subconscious; they have not one but multiple, possible explanations; and it is our sub-conscious, rather than our logical mind, that instantly grasps their meaning. Magritte, whose work is associated with Brussels (but see his murals in the Knokke casino discussed in our Belgian Coast chapter), is represented here by his very greatest paintings: "L'Empire des Lumières" (that night-lit house on a dark canal, under a bright, daytime sky); "Le Mariage de Minuit"; "L'Homme du Large"; "La Saveur des Larmes" (a decaying and corrupted dove); "La Recherche de la Verité" (a ball, a fish, a scene of infinity).

Several hundred other, major, modern works are presently on display (don't miss Roger Raveel, he of the Brussels subway Station Merode), virtually all by Belgian artists; They perpetuate that almost mystical explosion of artistic talent which began more than six hundred years ago, in one small nation, and has continued almost undiminished down to the present day.

As noted before, both the Museum of Modern Art, and the Museum of Ancient Art, are open daily except Mondays from 10 to 5 (with differing closing hours for lunch). They are entirely free of admission charge.

THE MULTIPLE OPEN-AIR MARKETS OF BRUSSELS:

You are now on a cobblestoned square covered with blankets or strips of canvas, or—in the tonier locations—with portable stands topped by gaily-striped, green-and-red awnings. And what do you see? Old magazines, postcards and gramophone records of the 1930s. The helmet of a Belgian soldier of the 1890s. Exquisite antiques, ancient cameos, second-hand leather jackets, scarcely-used wedding dresses, fresh Belgian endives and raw mussels on the half shell, tiny canaries to be carted away in paper Dixie cups punched with air holes. What all these products have in common is their frequent appearance in the clamorous, lively, immensely entertaining **open-air markets** of Brussels, as much a sight-seeing attraction (for the tourist) as places to shop.

The tradition of open-air markets doesn't simply survive in Belgium, it *rages* in Belgium, it pervades the life of every city large and small on at least one day of the week. The largest of the markets is the one held on Sundays along the fabled River Meuse of Liège (see our Liège chapter), but the most frequent of the open-air markets, and the most numerous types of them, are found in Brussels. One (on the **Place du Jeu de Balle** in the central Marolles district) takes place *every* day of the week. Another (on the far more elegant **Place du Grand Sablon**) is held on Saturdays and Sundays. A third and a fourth take place on Sundays in the web of streets adjoining the **Gare du Midi** (South Station) and on the **Grand' Place**, respectively. Each affords an absorbing glimpse into the life and popular culture of Belgium and Europe (not to mention the quite remarkable shopping opportunities they also provide), and each is a relic of past times well worth viewing, intensely human and personal—a highlight of your stay.

Sundays in Brussels

Because all four of the markets take place on Sunday mornings (until 2 p.m.), Sunday is a day of particularly high excitement in Brussels—for you can easily go to at least three of the four if you awake early enough and wear your best walking shoes. Start at the Grand' Place, where a unique Sunday morning **"Bird Market"** —endless varieties of live robins, larks, parakeets and canaries, even chickens and roosters, in sharply defined species bred to duplicate themselves, and all for purchase by families and avid bird fanciers of Brussels for as little as 150 francs ($4.17)—is an odd sort of market, small by comparison with the others, but pleasant to combine with a coffee at a cafe of the Grand' Place. On occasional Sundays, the "bird market" is expanded to include crafts displays (weavers, ceramicists, silk-screen artisans), but dates can't be predicted in advance. Half an hour should suffice for the ordinary tourist, though obviously not for ornithologists and enthusiasts.

Now exit from the Grand' Place at its "uphill" end, and walk halfway up the further hill to the broad boulevard ("Boulevard de l'Imperatrice", "Boulevard de l'Empereur") that runs directly in front of the Sabena Air Terminal and the Gare Centrale (Central Station). Turn right along that boulevard and in less than a hundred yards you'll pass the Rue Lebeau on your left, which curves further uphill to the elegantly lovely **Place du Grand Sablon** surrounded by antique shops (and streets of antique shops), chichi coffee bars and restaurants, trendy boutiques. You are now among the "beautiful people", the well-heeled "Yuppies" (Young, Upwardly-Mobile Professionals) of Brussels, who congregate and converse in several attractive restaurants and bars, and look on indulgently at the somewhat older types who patronize the canvas stands of the elegant **"Antiques Market"** ("Marché des Antiquités") that takes place every Saturday (until 6 p.m.) and Sunday until 2 p.m. in the center of the Place du Grand Sablon.

These are small antiques and artifacts, not furniture (which you'll find in the larger stores along the square), perfect for purchase by tourists, and range from books, lithographs, old photo albums and postcards, canes, musical instruments and serving dishes, to silver cutlery, items from Zaire (the former Belgian Congo), paintings, helmets, pistols, spurs, suits of armor, and fists of mail. Simply looking at them is like perusing the history of Belgium! Prices are moderate, not rock-bottom, and attract a middle-class clientele, in contrast to both the younger and older bargain-hunters who flock to the third great market in the "Marolles" a short walk away.

Now, walking downhill on the Place du Grand Sablon, exit the square via the downhill, left-hand side, and keep walking downhill to the broad, popularly-priced shopping street known as the Rue Haute, as different from the Sablon area as a street could be. In Brussels, the Poor co-exist just alongside the Rich! Turn left down the Rue Haute (or down the roughly-parallel Rue Blaes), walk five tiny blocks down the Rue Haute to the Rue des Renards on your right, and walk down that latter ancient street to the lively, low-cost, massive **"Place du Jeu de Balles"**—the daily flea market of Brussels (operating on Sundays until only 2 p.m.). Here, from a thousand Belgian attics and basements, are the fascinating cast-offs and throwaways that create shopping (and viewing) excitement for Belgians from miles away (some come from as far as Tournai) and North African "guest workers"—the latter clothing themselves, and equipping their flats, with the indescribably numerous items arranged on the cobblestoned "floor" of the square: bed-pots and old gramophones, ancient TV sets and albums of the late Queen Astrid, variety so rich as to defy description. If Pieter Bruegel were living today, he would be painting the old men in striped and hooded cloaks, working people from Turkey and Morocco, who go picking their way for a choice piece of merchandise, among the tourists and Belgian students who throng the square.

Chances are that your visits on foot to these three grand markets won't leave sufficient time for a trip (by subway or taxi) to the fourth: the sprawling, Sunday-morning (until only 1 p.m.) **"practical market"** (of vegetables, fruits, meats, Mediteranean-type delicacies, new but inexpensive clothing) so heavily patronized by the North African residents of Brussels in the streets just alongside the Gare du Midi (South Station). Because so many items are sold to be consumed on the spot, it is a gustatory experience, in addition to an exotic sight, and an updated version of scenes that were once painted, in this city of Breugel, by the great 16th-century artist of the common man.

The four Sunday-morning markets of Brussels! They make the city into a giant open-air Fair, equalled only by the similar, Sunday-morning activity of Liège.

Saturdays in Brussels—and Other Days as Well

On Saturdays, one enjoys a condensed version of the Sunday scene, in the form of the *two* markets held on that day: the Place du Grand Sablon market (all day), and the completely contrasting market of the Place du Jeu de Balles (directly below the Palais de Justice) operating until 2 p.m. Every remaining day of the week, the "Place du Jeu de Balles" market is in operation (again until only 2 p.m. daily), but in slightly reduced fashion from its full scale on Saturdays and Sundays—still an exciting event. Thus, you can see at least one of Brussels' remarkable open-air markets from Mondays through Fridays, two on Saturdays, four on Sundays. On weekdays, tourists visiting the Place du Jeu de Balles take advantage of its many snack facilities for an open-air lunch. You can buy french fries at a "friture" for 40 francs (and as he serves them to you, the "friture man" pops one into his own mouth); pick up meat sandwiches for only 30 francs at the nearby **Charcuterie** (butcher shop) **Den Duim**, 242 Rue Blaes; drink one of 20 varieties of unusual Brussels beers (gueuze, kriek, faro) at **L'Ettekijs**, on the Rue des Renards running off the square (40 to 50 francs per unusual glass); order patés and rolls at **Le Palais de la Volaille** (Chicken Palace) directly on the square; or dine in enclosed splendor at the cheap **Chez Marcel** on the square, asking the mustached Marcel for a bowl of vegetable soup, a "pistolet beurré" (long, hard loaf of bread slathered with butter), and beer, for all of 70 francs ($1.94). While elegant museum curators from around the world gaze at the Bruegels in the Musée de l'Art Ancien, *this* is where old Peter Breugel would now be spending his time!

THE ATOMIUM: In the fourth "must-see" of Brussels, we make a radical shift from the past to the future. The extraordinary "Atomium"—theme structure of the 1958 Brussels World's Fair—displays a side of Belgium that some tourists never experience: the remarkable scientific and industrial resources of the country that introduced the industrial revolution to the continent of Europe. The Atomium may look like simply a flashy display from the world of show business—a molecule of iron magnified billions of times to contain a restaurant, exhibits, escalators and look-out platforms in the atomic balls of the structure—but it is an engineering achievement second to few, requiring the most demanding wind-tunnel and structural tests to achieve, and the efforts of a highly developed steel-and-iron industry to build. It is an indication, if you needed one, that Belgium is not simply ancient plazas, medieval churches, Flemish paintings and exquisite restaurants.

Compare the Atomium to the tired theme symbols of the recent World's Fairs and other great expositions of recent times. Those range rather wearily from the huge globe of the 1964 New York World's Fair to the huge globe of EPCOT in Florida, to the huge globe of the 1982 Knoxville World's Fair—a repeated failure of imagination in each instance. When Belgium planned a World's Fair, it dared to experiment in the most spectacular sense. When excited Brussels, heady with notions of how peaceful nuclear power could transform the World, prepared the theme symbol of that Fair, it turned to Belgium's structural engineers to create giant atoms and molecules capable of soaring virtually unsupported over the Fair buildings, completely round and enclosed without obvious apertures for intaking air or disposing of waste, yet capable of moving 4000 persons each hour into and through its exhibits, restaurants, snack bar, and panoramic viewing platform.

The 335-foot Atomium is considerably higher than the spire of Brussels' Town Hall, weighs many tens of thousands of tons, and rests primarily on one ground-level, center "atom", supported elsewhere by three, slanting pylons. The 10-foot-wide, metal tubes connecting the other eight "atoms", through which escalators and elevators run, are meant to represent the binding forces that attract atoms in the physical world. One of the clanking, sloping escalators on which you'll ride from exhibit to exhibit is among the longest in all the world, and the elevator that goes up the single vertical tube to the highest, restaurant-housing "atom" is the fastest in Europe, at 16.4 feet per second. Belgian engineer A. Waterkeys is the metal-genius who designed the "Atonium" and worked out the equations, on paper, that overcame serious obstacles to the construction of such a giant "tinkertoy" supporting such heavy weights and movements. Note how the use of thousands of small "triangles" of metal succeeded in creating ball-like atoms that seem, but obviously aren't, perfectly round.

Inside are tributes to the pioneers of atomic energy—Rutherford, Roentgen, Bohr, Curie, Planck, Einstein—and detailed exhibits, innocent in their fervor and belief, of how that energy could be applied to peaceful uses. Remember that this was 30 years ago! Other exhibits dealing with the potentials of solar energy are quite remarkable in their foresight—they perform the function that a World's Fair is supposed to perform, but often doesn't: exposing developments on the very frontiers of technology and science. More modern exhibits added in recent years, display cutaways of the American space shuttle and related devices for space exploration.

The Atomium occupies large, park-like grounds adjoining the King's own Royal Park of Laeken, affording partial glimpses of the palace-residence of King Baudoin and Queen Fabiola, and the fanciful Japanese and Chinese pavilions which his great-grandfather, the flamboyant Leopold II, assembled there. Nearer to the Atomium is a large, modern, merchandise mart where Belgian sellers and largely foreign buyers meet throughout the year in football-field-sized show-rooms to inspect every kind of retail product (furniture, textiles, shoes, gifts) and to contract for their purchase and shipment (primarily on Mondays, when 1200 stands are in operation, as against 400 on other days). If you have any sort of commercial calling card on your person and will show it to the guard, it will usually suffice to gain you free admission.

Meanwhile, the Atomium itself is open daily from 9:30 a.m. to 6 p.m. for an admission charge of 80 francs ($2.22). It is open in the evenings until 9 p.m., but for the "Panorama" viewing level only (50 francs, $1.39). To reach it, take the metro to: Heysel.

Opening in 1989 in the area immediately next to the Atomium: a 12-acre "leisure park" of permanent attractions: water sports, cinemas, an exhibit of Europe in miniature ("mini-Europe"). Known as "Brupark", it bids to become a major entertainment facility of Brussels, and adds one more reason for visiting the Atomium. Admission prices: 210 francs to "Mini-Europe" with its 400 faithfully-reproduced models of buildings, landscapes, roads and railways; 250 francs to the pools at the "Oceadium" water leisure center; 65 francs to the re-creation of Brussels as a medieval village; normal movie rates to the "Kinepolis" cinema complex. Obviously, *Brupark* is now a major added attraction of Brussels.

WATERLOO: Twenty minutes south of Brussels, at the bottom edge of the Forest of Soignes, are rolling farmlands so vast that they seem to have been chosen by a set designer for the drama that took place upon them. In one of those many eerie coincidences that seem to mark the event, England's Duke of Wellington had surveyed this site in 1814, more than a year before the Battle of Waterloo, and commented that if he ever had to fight in the Low Lands, he hoped it would be here. Yet it was Napoleon who then marched directly to the very same location, without prodding of any sort, and chose Waterloo for the clash that shaped the destiny of the world.

Here once again, as it can never be sufficiently emphasized,

Europe brings to you what you bring to it. To the unprepared tourist, Waterloo is simply a rather large expanse of ordinary farm-lands surrounding an immense, man-made memorial mound ("La Butte du Lion"), at the foot of which are seedy, carnival-type buildings containing creaky, nickelodeon-like films of the de-picted event, overblown "dioramas", wax models in mouldy cos-tumes of the early 1800s, a few stone farmhouses bearing bullet holes and plaques, worn memorials to long-forgotten regiments of hussars in handlebar moustaches. To the tourist instructed by history, it is this very lack of modern showmanship, the 19th-cen-tury absence of multi-media effects, the "as is" quality of Water-loo, that makes it unbearably exciting. Here, a great figure—the kind who comes along once in a thousand years—possessed of the energies and abilities of a dozen world leaders, whose achieve-ments in fields of government and law have endured to this day, but a man flawed by excesses, unable to stop, always overreaching —it was here that a great reforming figure was crushed by forces of reaction allied to stop him.

In 1812, Napoleon had made the fatal error of invading Rus-sia, where distance, climate and guerrilla attacks had largely de-stroyed his army of 600,000 men. Defeated for a second time in Central Europe, in 1814, he had been forced into exile on the Is-land of Elba by the allied powers of Austria, Prussia, England and Russia, who proceeded at the Congress of Vienna to negotiate the re-division and re-structuring of the traditional nations of Europe. And then, while the diplomats danced and dallied in Vienna, Na-poleon escaped from Elba to the south of France, and marched on Paris, from which the newly-installed King Louis XVII proceeded to flee—to Ghent, in Belgium. As the French rallied to their char-ismatic Emperor, the Allied armies—the English led by the Duke of Wellington, the Prussians by Marshal Blucher, the Dutch by Prince William of Orange—hastily regrouped their forces and marched to meet the inevitable attack by Napoleon upon their core divisions stationed—where else?—in Belgium. Beribboned marshals and generals, dukes and duchesses, noble thrill-seekers of all sorts, converged on Brussels in a festive mood, certain that they would soon witness the end of the upstart, at a battle expected to take place near the Belgian city of Mons. On June 15, 1815, in a mansion near the Royal Park of Brussels, they danced at a cele-brated party organized by the English Duchess of Richmond to honor the Duke of Wellington. As Lord Byron described the scene in his *Childe Harold:* "There was a sound of revelry by night/And Belgium's Capital had gathered then/Her Beauty and her Chivalry—and bright/The lamps shone o'er fair women and brave men".

Into the party came the chilling news: Napoleon was headed for Brussels, to split the English and Prussian armies. Officers in dress uniforms bid adieu to their female partners of the evening, and quietly stole away to join their regiments. To show his disdain and *sang-froid*, the Duke of Wellington calmly continued dancing till near the dawn. For two days, advancing spearheads of the two armies engaged in preliminary skirmishes. By the morning of June 18, 1815, they confronted each other—150,000 men in all—on the vast, rolling farmlands outside the village of Waterloo, just below Brussels.

It had rained heavily throughout the night. To permit the ground to dry and firm for the maneuvering of his cannon, Napoleon delayed the attack till late morning—a serious error, as it later transpired. It was this delayed start that allowed Prussian reinforcements, later in the day, to turn the tide of battle.

The battle began with a French attack on the farmhouse at Hougomont on the flank of the Allied lines, whose bullet-scarred walls you can still see from the top of the "Butte du Lion" (Lion's Mount), and to which you can walk along the crude road that passes through the exhibition area. As the gallant English defenders of Hougomont repelled charge after charge, the remainder of the French line gradually went over to the attack all along the front. In an approach that was totally unlike him, dispensing with the lightning-like feints and audacious "end runs" that had characterized his earlier battles, a surprisingly stolid Napoleon directed a straightforward, head-to-head pressure of brute force upon the opposing armies. Some say he was ill on the day of the battle, or exhausted from a lifetime of incessant struggle. Time after time, French cavalry charged upon British "squares"—infantry drawn up in box-like formations, opening periodically to permit gunners to run inside for protection while reloading their rifles. Time after time throughout the day, as thousands on each side died, the British "squares" held firm. Yet the valor of the French troops almost succeeded. "It was the nearest run thing you did ever see", said Britain's Duke of Wellington, who had throughout the day, impervious to the shot and shell falling about him, dashed on his grey charger along the line to rally his troops.

Had Napoleon possessed his entire army, he would undoubtedly have won. He had, instead, dispatched a portion of his force under Marshal Grouchy to pursue a Prussian army under Marshal Blucher. Frantic messages had been sent to Grouchy throughout the afternoon, to recall him to Waterloo. As the day came to an end, a cloud of dust on the horizon signalled the arrival of another army. French spirits soared. Was it Grouchy? It soon turned out to be Blucher. In a desperate last effort to crush the enemy before Blucher could arrive, Napoleon called up his last reserves, the elite Imperial Guard, the grey-haired, six-foot veterans of earlier Napoleonic triumphs, in huge bearskin hats. For one last time, they marched in review before Napoleon Bonaparte, shouting "Vive l'Empereur!" And then marched to their deaths. An English regiment, strangely out of line, found itself able to attack the flank of the French charge with withering gunfire. The Imperial Guard wavered, then fell back. A cry rang out: "La Garde recule! Sauve qui peut!" (The Guard is retreating! Every man for himself!) It was a brief instant of panic that quickly turned into frenzied, headlong retreat. While French generals in tattered uniforms and smoke-blackened faces sought to halt the retreat, the flight of the main French armies became a wholesale rout, sweeping all before it. Napoleon himself barely escaped. Weeks later, in a port on the channel coast where he was vainly attempting to sail to America, he surrendered to a frigate of the British navy, and was ignominiously sent with several loyal retainers to exile on the infamous isle of St. Helena where he died several years later. In Brussels throughout the battle, the sound of cannon convinced numerous English camp followers to flee for safety to Antwerp, sure that Napoleon would conquer. Now Brussels became the destination for thousands of British sightseers (including Lord Byron) anxious to see the nearby battlefield. Forty years later, Victor Hugo wandered upon the same fields to gather color and atmosphere for the Waterloo scenes in his *Les Misérables,* and wrote that the very ground of Waterloo "tremble encore d'avoir vu la fuite des géants" (still trembles from having seen the fall of giants).

Years later, hundreds of Belgian housewives carried repeated baskets of earth to that spot on the battlefield where Holland's Prince of Orange had been wounded, to create the one-hundred-yard-high, pyramid-like hill with steps and observation plateau that overlooks the battleground: the soaring "Butte du Lion" (bearing a bronze lion). When you yourself make the heart-pounding, 226-step, tiring ascent, free, to the top, you'll realize the scope of their accomplishment. The hillside staircase is available for use daily from 9:30 a.m. to 5 p.m.

At the foot of the Lion's Mount is the big, round building that houses a famous, 360-degree, diorama painting **("Panorama")** of the battle done in the late 1800s by French artist Louis Dumoulin, three other Frenchmen and one Belgian. A museum as well as a "Panorama" (you walk upstairs to a circular viewing platform to take in the dramatic mural, made lifelike through the addition of wax soldiers, horses and cannon), it evokes the event with dramatic, French flair. Note how, gradually, the chaos of the battle divides itself into two halves as you walk about the platform: the French attacking (and Napoleon in the distance on his white charger), on one side, the English squares being attacked by Marshal Ney (the Duke of Wellington and Prince of Orange far back) on the other. The **Museum of the Waterloo Panorama** is open daily from 9:30 a.m. to 6 p.m., for an admission of 60 francs. Alongside that circular structure is the tiny **"Wax Museum"** of the Battle of Waterloo (same hours, same 60 franc admission) displaying an amazingly-lifelike Napoleon, as well as other notable figures in their perfectly-preserved plumed hats, brocaded jackets with epaulets, white trousers with boots and swords. Nearby is a **Movie Theatre** (60 francs adults, 35 francs students) showing a marvelously-hokey, ancient, sepia-toned, half-hour, filmed re-creation of the extraordinary battle. And all around are souvenir shops filled almost entirely with busts and other tributes to Napoleon, with scarcely a trace of the victorious Wellington. I am told that British teenagers touring the grounds of Waterloo are usually convinced by the omnipresent aura of Napoleon, that it was he who won the battle! "Isn't it a shame" (pronounced shy-me), said one youngster from Liverpool.

The celebrated, farmhouse bastion of Hougomont (now a private farm) is about a kilometer down the cobblestoned road that runs along the side of the "Panorama" building. A plaque out front pays tribute to troops of the English "Royal Wagon Train" who held out against such furious and repeated French attacks (which needlessly wasted both time and several thousands of Frenchmen, say military historians).

The main building running alongside the battlefield goes to the village of **Waterloo** (five kilometers away) in one direction, to **"Le Caillou"**, the farmhouse headquarters of Napoleon on the night before the battle (five kilometers away) in the other direction. Less than a hundred yards past the "Lion's Mount" on the way to "Le Caillou", are monuments on both sides of the road to various figures of the battle (Sir Alexander Gordon, the young adjutant to the Duke of Wellington, killed in the battle; the Hanoverians who fought so valiantly); if you'll descend from your car at that point, you'll discover that the vast expanse is not at all flat, as it appears from the Lion's Mount, but deeply undulating and rolling; it's as if generals on both sides had conspired to choose the perfect battlefield in all the world. In the white brick farmhouse of "Le Caillou" (on the left of the highway as you drive towards it, and easily missed; look for a yellow lion rampant upon a dark blue backdrop), Napoleon's headquarters on June 14, 1815, a museum of Napoleonic relics and writings, including the bed where he slept, is well worth the visit and the admission charge of 20 francs (56¢).

The **Wellington Museum,** 147 Chaussée de Bruxelles, on the main street running through the small village of Waterloo, is the other key museum, and your best source for books and leaflets on the battle; consider purchasing the full-sized reproduction of the London Times of June 20, 1815, which contains Wellington's historic dispatch of the battle, an exultant editorial, news of unrest in Paris, all alongside genteel want-ads for "gentlemen butlers" and other Nicholas Nickleby-type employment. In this old inn where Wellington slept on the night before, and to which the wounded, young Gordon was later brought to die (his room and bed, and the letter of condolence immediately written by Wellington, are especially moving), paintings, maps and models of the great clash of arms will round out your knowledge of the event. It is open daily throughout the year, from 9:30 a.m. to 6:30 p.m. April through mid-November, and from 10:30 a.m. to 5 p.m. mid-November through March, for an admission charge of 60 francs. For a total of 270 francs ($8.10) you will have visited the Panorama (60 francs), the Wax Museum (60 francs), the Movie (60 francs), the "Musée Le Caillou" (20 francs), and the Wellington Museum (60 francs). The "Butte du Lion" is free.

You can reach the village of Waterloo (and its Wellington Museum) by train from the Gare du Midi (South Station), but the best way to see the battlefield (if you haven't a car) is by *bus* "W" from the Place Rouppe—it goes all the way to, and returns from, the "Butte du Lion." From the Bourse (Stock Exchange) a block or so from the Grand' Place, walk down the several, short blocks of the Rue du Midi, passing a score of stamp collection shops and coin dealers ("numismatists"), to the Place Rouppe (site, incidentally, of Brussels' sublime "Comme Chez Soi" restaurant). Just off the square is the starting place for orange buses with blue stripes and a big "W" (for Waterloo) designation above their front window— except on Sundays, when frequency slows somewhat, a cluster of them are always standing there preparing to depart. They leave every half hour to Waterloo and its battleground, take 40 minutes for the trip, and charge 66 francs ($1.83), one-way.

A BRUSSELS-BASED VISIT TO BRUGES, GHENT OR TOURNAI: The sixth and final "must-do" of your visit to Brussels is a day-trip to one of the older art cities of Flanders or Wallonia—Bruges, Ghent or Tournai—each less than an hour away. Not to have seen at least one of these is not really to have visited Belgium! Although travellers with more time will stay overnight and longer in the other major cities and attractions of Bel-

gium, travellers to Brussels alone should never, ever pass up the chance for a quick day-excursion to a city of the Middle Ages, all so easily reached by quick train or modern highway from Brussels.

Through the center of the inner city of Brussels runs a mainly-underground railway line serviced by three stations: the *Gare du Nord* (North Station) at the top, near the Place Rogier; the *Gare Centrale* (Central Station) in the middle, near the Grand' Place; and the *Gare du Midi* (South Station) at the bottom. Though the 22-track Gare du Midi is the largest, most important and most "international" of the three, you can reach any point in Belgium from any one of the three. If a train goes from the Gare du Midi to Ghent and Bruges (as all of them do), for instance, it has either originated at the Gare du Nord and then passed through the Gare Centrale on its way to the Gare du Midi, or else it can be boarded by taking a train from the Gare du Nord and Gare Centrale to connect at the Gare du Midi. The same applies in the other direction for trains departing from the Gare du Nord to other cities in Belgium. All trains passing through the Gare du Nord (North Station) are either coming from the Gare du Midi (South Station) or going to the Gare du Midi.

To virtually every major city of Belgium, trains depart hourly or even half-hourly from Brussels, and there is the same frequency of arrivals back to Brussels from those other cities. Smart tourists making a day excursion simply go to the Central Station (Gare Centrale) early in the morning, check the schedules and buy their tickets there, and then take the appropriate train or connecting train to Bruges, Ghent, Tournai or whatever. It costs no more— no supplement at all—to go anywhere from any of the three Brussels stations, all of which charge the very same price. At the Gare Centrale, trains on tracks 1, 3 or 5 go to the North Station, trains on tracks 2, 4, or 6 go to the South Station, and trains on track 1A go to the Airport. A typical schedule, requiring that you "translate" the 24-hour clock used by the Belgian Railways: leave Brussels (Midi Station) at 1300 (1 p.m.), arrive Ghent at 1331 (1:31 p.m.), arrive Bruges at 1357 (1:57 p.m.). From Ghent on the return trip, a particularly good daily train departs at 1855 (6:55 p.m.), arriving at Brussels' Midi Station a half hour later at 1925 (7:25 p.m.), amply in time for dinner in Brussels.

An oddity of Brussels' three-station system is that you cannot use the direction of your trip to determine the last station from which the train departs: trains proceeding *north* of Brussels (to Bruges, Ghent or Ostend, for instance) leave from the *South* station. Several trains going south or south-east from Brussels (to Liège, for instance) leave from the *North* Station. Finally, you must bear in mind that the large signboards in the station's waiting room often list only the last city to which a train goes. It's therefore helpful to know that all trains going from Brussels to Ostend stop first in Ghent and Bruges, although only the word "Ostend" is listed high up on the wall. And take heed of the pesky 24-hour clock: the departure time of "0300" refers to 3 *a.m.*, and not to 3 *p.m.*—the latter designated as "1500".

With these lessons absorbed, with not one but three stations available to you, and with the aid of that frequent, punctual, reliable Belgian rail system, a trip to Bruges, Ghent or Tournai is as easy as a subway ride in other capitals. And such an excursion is just as important: the "art cities" of Flanders and Wallonia are among the most glorious sights of *Brussels,* and at least one should be visited in the course of your Brussels stay. Skip now to our chapters on these cities (paying particular note to those days of the week in which most of the museums in them are closed)—and then make your choice!

THE SECONDARY SIGHTS

Though their designation as "secondary" will be violently disputed by the Brusselians, here now are the optional sights to be visited by tourists having a special interest in their subject matter or themes. They are listed in no particular order.

THE "CINQUANTENAIRE" MUSEUMS: These are "world-class" museums of long standing: "Cinquantenaire" means 50th Anniversary, and the massive Cinquantenaire Museums, in the "Parc du Cinquantenaire" ("Jubelpark"), were built in 1880 in a burst of pride to celebrate the 50th anniversary of the independence of Belgium; they flank a high and equally immense Triumphal Arch completed several years later, the entire, vast complex reflecting the extraordinary riches and expansive optimism of 19th century Belgium. You come here on Line 1 of the Metro (subway) in the direction of "Alma/Hermann-Debroux", getting on at, say, Brouckère or Gare Centrale, and getting off at Station Schuman. Approaching the Arch, with central Brussels at your back, the **Museums of Art and History** are in the giant structure to your right (enter at the end of the building), while the **Museum of the Army and Military History** is in the equally large structure to your left (enter at the middle).

Musées Royaux d'Art et d'Histoire

Despite their name, these are not museums of paintings, nor do they deal in any really major sense with Belgium—but rather relics and antiquities of the entire world, spanning all of time, are their subject matter: the Egyptian, Greek and Roman Civilizations, the Decorative Arts of Europe, the Civilizations of Pre-Columbian America and the Far East, European industrial art and popular traditions, some national archaeology, spread over scores of rooms and multiple floors that could take an entire day to view, and should be visited by persons of the highest tastes and intellectual outlook. A 15-yard-wide mock-up of the ancient city of Rome, viewed from an upper balcony, is alone worth the visit, and there is the full-scale reproduction of a Roman temple and mosaic floor to see, as well as ethereal Greek vases (whole acres of them), priceless tapestries and re-created rooms of exquisite, 17th-century furnishings, ravishing porcelain and glassware, even a spacious Gothic garden—one unexpected delight after another. Though the exhibits of antiquities are theoretically open on *even* days only, and the applied arts on *odd* days only, a great deal of overlapping occurs, and you'd be well-advised to come at any time: daily except Mondays, from 9:30 to 12:30 and from 1:30 to 4:45 on weekdays, continuously on weekends from 10 to 5, without admission charge. Don't ever confuse these "Musées Royaux d'Art and d'Histoire", as some do, with the "Musées Royaux des *Beaux Arts*" (the Ancient Art and Modern Art Museums in the center of town), or with the completely separate "*Palais* des Beaux Arts" nearby.

Musée Royal de l'Armée et d'Histoire Militaire

For more popular tastes, the Military Museum covers whole football fields (seemingly) with Belgium's martial history, and includes an aviation museum that would be large enough to stock several Jumbo Jets (and does display a dizzying array of warplanes from 1914 to date), as well as an outdoor tank museum (among the world's largest); since few signs lead to these latter, vast rooms, into which one sometimes pops unexpectedly via an unmarked door, ask. And if the large hall dealing with World War I is closed for repairs, as it often currently is, ask a guard to go in anyway (pleading that this is your only possible visit, from many thousands of miles away); as this is Belgium, he will usually succumb. Mark it high on your list: there are few museums of war as rich as this, supplying such an unforgettable record of our baser instincts and such a complete contrast to the exhibits of civilization across the way. "Since Adam and Eve first ate the apple," wrote Bertrand Russell in his 20-word *History of the World* illustrated by a mushroom cloud, "mankind has never refrained from any folly of which it was capable". Admission to the military museum is free, and the several different wings are open daily except Mondays from 9 to noon and 1 to 4:45 p.m. in summer, till only 4 p.m. in winter; avid army buffs will follow up a visit here with one to the medieval military collection in the Porte de Hal on the Boulevard de Waterloo at the start of the Rue Haute.

ARCHITECTURE OF "L'ART NOUVEAU": At the turn of the century, Brussels gave birth to a remarkable, new architectural style—"l'Art Nouveau"—that featured the almost complete elimination of the straight line. Its foremost practitioner was the Brussels architect Victor Horta (1861–1947). His foremost masterpiece is the townhouse **Hôtel Solvay** at 224 Avenue Louise (which can be visited only by appointment requested in writing), and the foremost work of his followers is the townhouse **Hôtel de St. Cyr,** at 11 Square Ambiorix near the E.E.C. Building (its facade of recessed circles and noodle-like window frames is like no other exterior on earth, and must be seen). Horta's own home has been made into the **Horta Museum,** 25 Rue Americaine (open daily except Mondays from 2 to 5:30 p.m., for an admission charge of 60 francs ($1.67); take tram 37, 81 or 93 to the close-in commune of St. Gilles)—a shrine to that style and to a much-underrated architect of increasingly-recognized stature—and it is there (or at the Brussels Tourist Office in the right-hand-side of the Town Hall on the Grand' Place) that you will be able to obtain a free, illustrated listing of the several other major Art Nouveau structures in Brussels. Among them is the rather important tavern/restaurant **"De Ultieme Hallucinatie"** (The Ultimate Nightmare), at 316 Rue Royale (a short walk behind the Botanical Garden and the Hyatt Regency Hotel), where a chic group of young professionals congregates to drink in a stunning setting of this style. If you have any interest at all in architecture, you won't want to miss the Horta Museum, and neither should you fail to see the Hôtel de St. Cyr (a townhouse, not a hotel) at 11 Square Ambiorix, a single, long block from the E.E.C. Building; it will tell you that human possibilities have not yet been exhausted, and that mankind will continue to create in fashions not yet dreamed of. Brussels is the world's capital of that swirling, twisting, cascading, spiraling, "Art Nouveau", which makes use of the normally-ugly industrial material of iron, and of earth colors and light flooding through large windows.

THE MUSEUM OF CENTRAL AFRICA: Chances are that whenever you pass a particularly grandiose, 19th-century structure, boulevard or park of Brussels—the Bourse, the Palais de Justice, the Cinquantenaire Museums, others—it was built or inspired by Belgium's second native ruler, King Leopold II (1835–1909). A man of inexhaustible drive, known today as the "builder-king" or the "capitalist-king", he refused to permit the small size of Belgium to limit his ambitions. "Un pays qui touche à la mer," he said, "n'est jamais petit" (A country which borders on the sea is never little). So what did he do when he observed that other European nations were acquiring colonies in Africa and Asia—a project beyond the capacity of the little Belgian State? He bought the African Congo, himself! From his own purse, employing the explorer Sir Henry Morton Stanley (of "Stanley and Livingstone" fame) as his surveyor, and as a purely personal investment, he purchased a rubber-rich area of Africa 80 times the size of Belgium, and renamed it the "Congo Free State". Later, following international protests over the harsh labor policies of Leopold's overseers there, it was annexed to Belgium as the "Belgian Congo", and is today the independent nation of Zaire, though it retains close commercial ties to Belgium.

The booty and baggage from Leopold's involvement in the Congo—lively African masks, dwellings, canoes and costumes, maps and mementoes of the Stanley and Livingstone expeditions, the most important ethnographical relics of a then-stone age civilization—were brought to Brussels, to a magnificent palace which Leopold had erected from 1904 to 1909 on the dream-like grounds of the park of Tervuren, a side extension of the Forest of Soignes (see below). It was designed in the style of Louis XVI to resemble the "Petit Palais" of the Champs Elysées of Paris, and is a fitting setting for the important collection it houses. Known initially as the "Museum of the Belgian Congo", but now the **Royal Museum of Central Africa,** 13 Leuvensesteenweg, it deals with both the physical sciences relating to Africa (geology, minerology, paleontology, zoology), the human sciences (anthropology, ethnography), and with the record of Belgium's presence in Africa; charges no admission; and is open from 9 to 5:30 from mid-March to mid-October, from 10 to 4:30 at all other times. From any underground station of Brussels, take the Metro to "Montgomery", and there change to Tram 44 (the "Tourist Tram") which follows a breathtaking itinerary through luxurious residential neighborhoods and ravishing woods and forests to the great Museum.

ART IN THE SUBWAYS: Along the escalators, ticket booths or tracks themselves, upon the ceilings or the walls beside them: a single vast work of modern art. It was a bold leap, beyond anything attempted elsewhere, and it has created a major, continuing, aesthetic experience for the riders of Brussels' modern subways, and a significant tourist attraction for the foreign visitor. When Brussels began construction of its subway system in 1969, it immediately set aside 2% of the awesome construction budget for Art—especially-commissioned, contemporary art that would adorn and "elevate" the majority of stations in the system. A farsighted and forceful connoisseur, Emile Langui, then succeeded in persuading the public authorities to permit the art world alone to select the creators of the works that would go into the walls or ceilings of underground stations. An autonomous, permanent commission, composed of persons so eminent that they would be free from all outside pressures, was established to make the selections. Artists, it was agreed, would be chosen solely by reputation among their peers, regardless of their politics (or anti-social behavior!). And once chosen, they would be given *carte blanche*. Working from the very outset with the engineers and architects who were planning the form and shape of each station, these top Belgian artists—ranging from the world-famous Paul Delvaux to the newest *enfant terrible* operating out of a shabby garret studio near the Gare du Midi—proceeded to create either murals (often on acryllic-treated metals) or sculptures or bas-reliefs that have given a sense of tingling aliveness to the tasteful and uncluttered subway stations of Brussels. Imagine starting the working day, every day, with exposure to modern art as you descend the escalator of your neighborhood subway stop! Brussels' subway stations are now such a celebration of life that suicides have virtually ceased within them—only nine since 1976. By contrast, one suicide per fortnight continues to occur in the Paris Metro.

Not every station yet possesses its work of art—33, or about 60% of the completed stations, do; and among the stations passed over to date is the important Place de Brouckère, surprisingly. But **Station Bourse** near the Grand' Place (which you'll undoubtedly be seeing) has two: "Nos Vieux Trams Bruxellois" (Our Old Brussels Trams), in oil, on panels, by the eminent Paul Delvaux (a night scene of bygone Brussels streetcars, but with atypically-clothed females alongside, and thus lacking the subconscious eroticism and terror of most Delvaux'; see our chapter on the Belgian Coast and its Delvaux Museum); and "Moving Ceiling", a cascade of stainless steel cylinders (some fixed, some mobile) falling from the roof, by the sarcastic Belgian artist, Pol Bury, who affixes electric motors to some of his oscillating works. And **Station Botanique** has three: "Les Voyageurs" (the travellers) by Pierre Caille (21 funny, wooden cutouts between panes of glass, of anxious commuters ceaselessly dashing to and fro, day-dreaming all the while);

"Tramification Fluide" (Smooth Tramways) by Emile Souply (giant, clustered clothes hangers in brilliant colors against white, a stunning image); and "The Last Migration" by Jean-Pierre Ghysels (a highly abstract flight of birds, in oxydized copper, meant to signify the antithesis of the unnatural, sun-excluding, closed life of the subway).

Among the remaining stations, the greatest of all works, in my view, is the **Station Hankar** ("Notre Temps" by Roger Somville, a 500-square-yard acryllic painting on concrete requiring two years to complete, of the violent movement and march of humanity for social justice, including motorcyclists retreating from their social obligations, war-like struggles, a caricature of the Chilean dictator Pinochet, all in frenzied streaks and daubs of red and yellow flame-colors that spread across the right angles of the station and visually eliminate those angles; the artist, in his words, has sought to create "an art that will make them scream in rage"). Outstanding, too, is **Station Merode** ("Ensor: Vive la Sociale", an oil mural by the exciting Roger Raveel; faceless humans in a social setting, next to an Adam and Eve copied from the Van Eycks' "Holy Lamb" in Ghent, all under a banner ceaselessly asking what 19th-century artist James Ensor had meant by his exclamation: "Vive la Sociale"; see our discussion of Ostend, home of Ensor, for more on this); **Station Porte de Namur** ("Het Uiteindelijk Verkeer" by Octave Landuyt, four massive, ceramic bas-reliefs of four stages of the human condition: apparently, birth, love, aging, death); **Station Montgomery** ("Themas" by famous Pol Mara, four pop-art collages devoted to sheer sensuality). The other locations of Brussels' "Art in the Subways" include: **Station Comte de Flandre** (Paul Van Hoeydonck's "Icarus"—small, sculpted astronauts flying overhead); **Station Parc** (Marc Mendelson's "Happy Metro to You"); **Station Aumale** (Jean-Paul Laenen's photo collage, "Metrorama '78); **Station Rogier** (Jan Cox' anti-war "The Fall of Troy"); **Station Anneessens** ("Sept Ecritures" by Pierre Alechinsky); **Station Arts-Loi** ("Isjtar" by Gilbert Dedock); **Station Vandervelde** ("La Grande Taupe" by Paul De Gobert); **Station Petillon** ("Que La Mer Epargne" by Lismonde); **Station Saint-Guidon** ("Wij Leven" by Frans Minnaert); **Station Gribaumont** ("Le Tropolitain" by Frans Nellens); **Station Roodebeek** ("Integration Roodebeek" by Luc Peire); **Station Thieffry** ("Sculptures" by Felix Roulin); **Station Gare de l'Ouest** ("Compositie" by Guy Vandenbranden); **Station Josephine Charlotte** ("La Fleur Unique" by Serge Vandercam); **Station Osseghem** ("Stop the Run" by D'Haese Reinhoud, and "Driehoek in Beweging" by Hilde Van Sumere); **Station Parc**

"La Ville", a mosaic mural by Roger Dudant); **Station Etangs Noirs** ("De Zwarte Vijvers" by Jan Burssens); **Station Herrmann-Debroux** ("L'Aviateur" by Roel D'Haese); and **Station Jacques Brel** ("Coming Up for Air" by Maurice Wyckaert).

To squeeze in the viewing of as many as ten of these on a single subway ride and for a single fare, simply go to the Metro station at the Gare Centrale (Central Station) and take Line 1 in the direction of "Alma/Demey". Stop at **Station Arts/Loi** (for viewing artwork 1), reboard and go to **Station Merode** (artwork 2, upstairs), then get back aboard a train going to Demey, stopping at **Station Thieffry** (3), **Station Petillon** (4), and **Station Hankar** (5). After viewing the extraordinary acryllic at Hankar, retrace your steps back to **Station Merode,** and reboard a train going to "Alma", stopping at **Station Montgomery** (6), **Station Josephine-Charlotte** (7), **Station Gribaumont** (8), **Station Roodebeek** (9), and **Station Vandervelde** (10); then return on the same line to the center of Brussels.

And if you're insatiable for "Art in the Subways", you can squeeze in six more by simply travelling on Line 1 in the other direction. From **Station Arts/Loi** (1), take a train in the direction of "Saint-Guidon", stopping at **Station Comte de Flandre** (2), **Station Etangs Noirs** (3), **Station Gare de l'Ouest** (4), **Station Jacques Brel** (5), **Station Aumale** (6), and **Station Saint-Guidon** (7). On still other trips and visits, you can make a point of seeing **Station Anneessens, Station Bourse, Station Rogier, Station Botanique, Station Osseghem,** and **Station Porte de Namur.**

Art in the subways! Though other cities may have inserted various "theme" exhibits into an odd terminus or two, as Paris has done with its Louvre Station, only Brussels among the cities of the world has flung the specially-commissioned works of its finest modern artists throughout virtually its entire transport system. Subways, usually the most monotonous of institutions, have here become vital and alive, through Art, in a city of Art and in a country of Art.

ROYAL BRUSSELS: Royal Brussels is that graceful, elegant assortment of government buildings and embassies surrounding the delightful "**Parc de Bruxelles**" at the side of the **Place Royale**; the best Metro stop for arriving there is "Parc", or else walk up the Mont des Arts from the Grand' Place, following the same instructions as for reaching the Museum of Ancient Art (see above), and then turn left at the Place Royal into the Park. The Royal Palace (which cannot be visited inside, other than in August) is at one end of the Park, the "Palais de la Nation", Belgium's Parliament (which can), is at the other. Go to the front of the Parliament building if you wish to view the art and furnishings of its many antechambers, go to the back (and bring your passport for identification) if you'd care to attend a session of the parliament or a regional council, held most days (especially Tuesdays, Wednesdays and Thursdays) starting at 2 p.m., from October through June or early July. Turn either left to the Senate, or right to the Chamber of Representatives, both of them with translator's boxes for simultaneous renderings from Dutch (Flemish) into French, and vice versa. The Palais de la Nation was completed in 1783 to house the Sovereign Council of Brabant, during those days when Belgium was under Austrian rule; and quickly became the national legislature after the declaration of Belgian independence in 1830.

THE JACQUES BREL FOUNDATION: The modern balladeer of Belgium, Jacques Brel (1933–1979) was a lyricist-poet and singer of such passion and intensity that next to him, all other performers seem mild and uninvolved. He was from Brussels, of a Flemish family, and began his career with relatively standard songs about naive, first love. "Quand on n'a que l'amour" was an international hit. In time, his lyrics grew bitter and ironical, anti-church, revolutionary, shocking the more stolid folk of his native land. His most famous anti-establishment song, "Les Bourgeois", flailed at middle class hypocrisy, insensitivity; it used crude words heard over Belgian radio for the first time, and resulted in efforts to ban or stop him. He moved for a time to Paris, and presented celebrated one-man concerts at the Olympia Music Hall. His songs were heard there by an American producer, who translated their message into the unusual, plotless musical, "Jacques Brel is Alive and Well"; it became one of the longest-running shows in Off-Broadway history, and is still presented all over the world in hundreds of productions each year. Though Brel hated injustice and inequalities, and excoriated their appearance in his own country, he loved Belgium. His song, "Le Plat Pays" (The Flat Land), is like a second national anthem. In it, he talks of a table-top country in which cathedrals serve the function of mountains—"des cathedrales pour uniques montagnes"—in "le plat pays qui est le mien" (the flat land that is my own). When the life of Don Quixote was set to music in "The Man of La Mancha", he translated its lyrics into French, and himself played the part of the idealistic old knight who sang "The Impossible Dream".

Ill and unable to perform for the last eight years of his life, Brel died of cancer in 1979. His daughter, France Brel, a petite but determined young woman in her 20s, resolved to perpetuate his memory, ideals and good works through the creation of the **"Foundation Internationale Jacques Brel"**. Fittingly, its head-quarters are next to a popular Brussels record shop, in a modern shopping arcade ("Passage 44") near the Place Rogier, at 44 Boulevard du Jardin Botanique (phone 218-26-75), open Tuesday through Saturday from 10 a.m. to 6 p.m. There one attends periodic mid-day and evening lectures open to members and non-members alike (in French) on a broad variety of subjects ("French Songs of the 20th Century", "The Right to Die in Dignity"); views paintings and sketches of social protest (and numerous photos of Jacques Brel); and is able to watch and hear videotaped recordings of the electrifying concert appearances of Jacques Brel, of which those at Paris' Olympia Music Hall will lift you out of your seat. In a sound-proofed room, wearing ear-phones and facing television monitors, you'll thrill to Brel's vibrant voice, the depth of his emotion, his pity for the poor and dispossessed, his anger at the unfeeling, as he sings with a Promethean force, his face bathed in sweat. You should precede your request to watch a Brel performance by either joining the Foundation (for 500 francs, $13.90) or by taking out a "day membership" (250 francs, $6.94), although the staff has been known to permit youthful non-members from abroad to make use of video facilities without charge. No one can fail to be inspired by this contact with a totally pure spirit, selfless and dedicated, who represents the very best aspect of Belgium. He wrote, in a quatrain that has become the Foundation's credo: "Sans avoir rien/Que la force d'aimer/Nous aurons dans nos mains/Amis le monde entier" (Having nothing other than the force of love, we will have in our hands Friends the world over).

THE CASTLE OF GAASBEEK: The chilling sight of a moat-surrounded, medieval castle is quite easily had in Belgium, in the center of Ghent (Castle of the Counts of Flanders, 12th century), near Ghent (Ooidonk or Laarne, 13th century), or in Bouillon (Godfrey the Crusader's, 11th century); but no castle is more easily accessible (by bus and then on foot) than **Gaasbeek,** seven miles to the southwest of Brussels. Go to the Place Rouppe in Brussels (see our instructions for Waterloo, above), and this time board a bus to Anderlecht ("LK"), asking the driver to let you off beyond that town at the road to Gaasbeek, about a half-hour out. From there it's a ten-minute walk down the highway to the village of Gaasbeek (where you can dine at several charming, farmstyle restaurants) and a further 20-minute walk uphill to the Castle (opposite the entrance to which are still further restaurants). Burned and pillaged by angry residents of Brussels following the murder of popular Everard t'Serclaes by the Lord of Gaasbeek in 1388, it was soon rebuilt in all its splendor and occupied for centuries and until quite recently by 35 other, successive Lords of Gaasbeek (of which one was the Count of Egmont beheaded by Philip II), who left priceless furnishings, suits of armor and tapestries within. You can visit inside from April through October, daily except Mondays and Fridays, from 10 a.m. to 5 p.m., but even in the winter time it's instructive simply to gaze upon the exterior of this imposing fortress/residence and to ponder the social organization that raised a few so high. Directly around the structure is countryside recognized from the paintings of Peter Breugel the Elder, especially his "Wedding Procession" now hanging in the Maison du Roi of Brussels' Grand' Place.

THE HOME OF ERASMUS: Though universally known by the above title, this really isn't the home of the 16th-century Dutch humanist, but that of a Flemish clergyman whom he visited here for several months, writing important and often reproduced letters from the same location, in 1520. (Erasmus lived for a much longer time, from 1517 to 1521, in nearby Louvain.) A beautifully-furnished and rather affluent dwelling of that time, it has now been made into a small museum dealing with the theologian and scholar who sought to introduce tolerant reason and common sense into the often strident and extreme Scholastic doctrines of the time, skirting so dangerously close to heresy that he lived the last years of his life in Protestant Basel (though he continued to oppose the views of Luther). The **"Home of Erasmus"**, at 31 Rue du Chapitre, Anderlecht (Brussels), is open daily except Tuesdays and Fridays from 10 to noon and 2 to 5, for an admission charge of 20 francs (56¢). Take the metro (subway) to St. Guidon, or take tram 103 and ask to be let off near the well-known site.

AUTOWORLD: The newest of Brussels' main attractions, **"Autoworld"**, occupies several floors of the "Palais Mondial" in the complex of museum buildings at the Parc du Cinquantenaire, the very same area that houses the Army and Military History Museum and the important "Musées Royaux d'Art et d'Histoire". There, on display, are the several hundred classic automobiles collected and restored for decades by a Ghent auto dealer named Ghislain Mahy. Though the somewhat-similar Harrah's auto exhibition in Las Vegas may outnumber Mahy's, the quality of the latter's collection is said to be the finest in the world, and any visitor to Brussels interested in the impact of automobiles upon our world will find "Autoworld" to be a fascinating visit. It's open daily from 10 a.m. to 5 p.m. (April through October until 6 p.m.) for an admission charge of 150 francs ($4.16).

THE BROWSING STREETS: Several pages from now, we'll be discussing the shopping opportunities of Brussels, and the distinct streets and areas in which they're found. Here we merely point out that browsing and window shopping at the unpressured, "laid back" mercantile establishments of Belgium's capital is a relaxing sightseeing activity regardless of whether you buy a thing. In Brussels, as unlike so many other cities, no one pressures you to buy, or discourages browsing—try it and see.

THE CATHEDRALS: The Gothic Cathedral of the Middle Ages, in all its exalted majesty and statement, is the outstanding achievement of nearly a dozen Belgian cities; and one of the greatest—the actual **Cathedral of St. Michael**—is in Brussels, on the hillside sloping upwards from the area of the Grand' Place. Unfortunately, nearly 80% of it is under reconstruction, and will remain closed to the public for years to come. What little you can see is a portion of the choir entered from the side of the edifice at the Place Ste. Gudule, and open daily except Sundays from 7:30 a.m. to 6 p.m., Sundays from 2 to 6 p.m. A soaring vaulted ceiling, perhaps the highest in Belgium, but partially obscured by netting; stained glass windows of immense size, and massive columns; black-and-white marble floors and chapel altars—all of these provide hint of the grandeur within, in a structure begun in the 1200s and then requiring 300 years to complete. Because of that, it reflects all major architectural styles, from the Romanesque-Transitional of the 1200s, through all stages of the Gothic, to the early Renaissance fashions of the days of Charles V. But scarcely any of this can really be seen until the work of reconstruction is complete, and for your own experience of the great Gothic churches, you must either travel to the other major cities of Belgium (and their cathedrals) described in the chapters ahead (Ghent, Bruges, Antwerp, Liège, Tournai, Mons), or else content yourself with the lovely but lesser "Notre Dame des Victoires du Sablon"—the **Church of the Sablon**—on the Place du Grand Sablon of Brussels.

The Church of the Sablon

In the 1300s, members of Brussels' Cross-Bowmen's Guild used the Place of the Grand Sablon as an archery range, later building a small chapel at the top of the field. According to legend, the

Virgin Mary was so touched by this tribute that she directed an Antwerp "beguine" (member of a secular convent), Beatrix Soetkens, to spirit away a small statue of the Madonna from the Antwerp Cathedral and to transport it to the Sablon chapel—a feat soon done. Upon the now-consecrated site, the religious of Brussels built the church of "Notre Dame au Sablon" in the 15th and 16th centuries, adorning its entrance facade with dozens of statuettes of medieval people: knights, court ladies clutching the folds of their long skirts. Gaze upon them, and you may be thrilled to realize that these are *contemporaneous* portrayals in stone of the society of that time. Though the church isn't of sufficient importance to warrant lengthy inspection, its stained glass and vaulting, its remarkably delicate chapels and statuary, are of considerable beauty, and will assist your introduction to the great cathedrals of other Belgian cities.

Place du Petit Sablon

Emerging from the church, you'll want to use the occasion to visit the adjoining "Petit Sablon" slightly up the hill, a delightful, 19th-century garden honoring the Counts of Egmont and Hornes, their arms about each others' shoulders, marching almost jauntily to their deaths at the hands of Philip II (in a well-known, epic statue at the top of the garden). They are flanked by Belgian notables of the 16th century, and the entire little square is surrounded by 48 famous bronze statues of the medieval guilds—it being an outdoor "parlor game" in Brussels to identify each ancient Guild by the clothing and tools of each statuette figure. The six at the very bottom of the Square, along the Rue de la Regence, are, from left to right (facing the square), a gunsmith, a plumber, a stonecutter, a laundryman, a coppersmith, a wheelmaker. Can you identify the others?

THE SPECIALISTS' MUSEUMS: Of these there are two score and more, but we'll content ourselves with ten of the broadest interest: **Museum of Musical Instruments,** 17 Place du Petit Sablon (celebrated collection going back several centuries, open only from 2:30 to 4:30 on Tuesdays, Thursdays, and Saturdays, 4 to 6 on Wednesdays, 10:30 to 12:30 on Sundays, otherwise closed); **Museum of Posts and Telecommunications,** 40 Place du Grand Sablon (of surprising interest and breadth, including vast postage stamp collections, open Tuesdays through Saturdays from 10 to 4, Sundays from 10 to 12:30 only); the **Bellevue Museum,** 7 Place des Palais (at the extreme right side of the Royal Palace as you face it; furniture and other objects of the royal family, open daily except Fridays, from 10 to 5 p.m., with mandatory guided visits at regular intervals, for which you must wait); **Museum of Chalcography,** 1 Place du Musée (displays old engravings and also sells them at moderate prices; open weekdays only, from 9 to noon and 2 to 5); **Wiertz Museum,** 62 Rue Vautier (paintings of a local master, daily except Mondays from 10 to 5); the **Chinese Pavilion,** on the Avenue Van Praet in the Royal Park of Laeken (daily except Mondays from 9:30 to 12:30 and 1:30 until 2:30 p.m.); the **Museum of Gueuze,** 56 Rue Gheude in Anderlecht (for consummate beer lovers, an actual brewery producing the local beer of Brussels, but open Saturdays only, from October 15 to May 15, 11 a.m. to 4 p.m., 60 francs); the **Theatre Museum,** 46 Rue de Flandre (in an awesomely lovely patrician home of the 17th century, near the Place Ste. Catherine, open weekdays only from 10 to noon and 2 to 5, and closed the month of July); and the **Locks Museum,** 70 Rue des Bouchers (on the restaurant street, off the Grand' Place, displaying locks and keys in infinite varieties, open on request only).

THE FOREST OF SOIGNES:

In a city of many, many parks, this is the largest, a wooded and velvety-green, 12,000-acre domain larger than the parks of nearly any other great capital (Berlin among the few exceptions). It starts at the far end of the broad and elegant Avenue Louise. In "haut de la ville" (upper Brussels), near the Brussels Hilton, the Place Louise is at the head of that 1¼ mile Avenue Louise, which ends at the playground-filled "Bois de la Cambre" (Cambre Woods), start of the giant **"Fôret de la Soignes"** (Forest of Soignes, pronounced "swan-yuh"). It extends all the way south to Waterloo. Inside its vast expanse are two racetracks ("hippodromes"), golf courses, boating lakes, restaurants (of course), riding and jogging trails, "arboretums" of several hundred tree species, the ruins of a former abbey ("Groenendael"), and the marvelously-maintained grounds and groves on gently-sloping hills filled with paths for pedestrians, cyclists and roller skaters. If it's a sunny day, you will want to inhale the ozone of perhaps the world's greatest park, and afterwards you'll exclaim, as did the English essayist and novelist Arnold Bennett in the 1890s: "Brussels—what boulevards, what parks, what palaces, what galleries, what cafes and restaurants!"

HEADQUARTERS OF THE EUROPEAN COMMUNITY:

It offers no program of touristic visits, and can be viewed inside only by groups making arrangements in advance (for whom a film is shown), and yet you will want at least to pass by the futuristic, 12-stories-high, glass-sided slabs, in the shape of an unequal, four-pronged star, that are Brussels headquarters of the European Community. When six nations—Belgium, France, West Germany, Italy, the Grand Duchy of Luxembourg, and the Netherlands —signed the Treaty of Rome in 1957 establishing the European Economic Community (the "Common Market"), they immediately thought of Brussels as a main site for administration of the organization. And Brussels just as quickly offered use of the several-square-block area known as the "Berlaimont", named after a convent once located there, next to the "Rond-Point Robert Schuman" honoring one of the four "fathers" of modern Europe (Jean Monnet of France, Alcide de Gaspari of Italy, and Paul-Henri Spaak of Belgium the others accorded that title). These were the statesmen who dreamed that the E.E.C. might provide the basis for an eventual political unification of Europe.

Britain, Ireland and Denmark joined in 1973, Greece in 1981, Spain and Portugal in 1986, and today in Brussels, the European Community has attracted several hundred other international organizations, chambers of commerce, and like bodies, including the important "Euratom" and the political council of N.A.T.O. Is Brussels the true capital of Europe? Well, within 170 miles of this crucially-central city are 72,000,000 citizens of Europe (London, Paris, Frankfurt, Amsterdam, among them). Within 170 miles of New York are only 22,000,000 persons, and decidedly less within the same distance from Washington, D.C.

The Rond-Point Robert Schuman and the Berlaimont Building are at the end of the Rue de la Loi in "upper Brussels" (the Metro stop is "Schuman"), just before the start of the Cinquantenaire Park. The Square Ambiorix, with its remarkable Art Nouveau building at no. 11 (see above), is one long block away, up the rue Archimede, and might be combined with a visit to the Berlaimont.

MEET THE BRUSSELIANS: Imagine, now, visiting any of the foregoing sights, or more like them, in the company of an English-speaking resident of Brussels, who either joins you on foot, or takes you to them in his or her car, and charges not a single penny for the service. In the chapters ahead, we've frequently used the word "friendly"—the most overworked term in tourist literature —to describe the population of Belgium, but here is a concrete example, an almost absurdly extreme example, of that quality. Amazing as it may seem, dozens of residents of Brussels have signed on with a program known as "Meet Brussels and Its Inhabitants" to provide either personally-conducted tours or an hour or two of conversation over a drink—totally free—to foreign tourists. On the entire continent of Europe, even in friendly Denmark, there does not exist a similar service—yet the shy Belgians have done nothing to publicize it abroad or even to boast at home that their extraordinary people have supported such an effort.

To "Meet a Brusselian", either phone the **Bus Bavard** ("Chatterbus" organization, see below, operator of the service) at 12 Rue des Thuyas (phone 673-1835 to request their list of hosts), or look for the explanatory leaflet distributed in three locations: at Bruxelles-Accueil, 6 Rue Tabors (behind the Stock Exchange), at Infor-Jeunes, 27 Rue Marché aux Herbes (close to the Grand' Place), or at any of the city's youth hostels—they are all stocked with copies. The leaflet resembles, superficially, a classified ad section of "personals"—"I am Flemish and crazy about music, literature and modern art", "I am a mother of five children, and would like to discover Brussels myself with other people fond of old stones with a history", "I like my city and enjoy meeting foreigners", "I will show you amusing, Brugelian, funny, out-of-heaven places"—and is accompanied by phone numbers for contacting the hosts directly, and the days or evenings when they are free to take you around; but as the writers usually take pains to emphasize their serious family status, any thoughts you may entertain of more-than-meeting the Brusselians should be banished forthwith. If you are a traveler who enjoys the company of new people, and an open exchange of views, and are not simply seeking a "free tour", then "Meet the Brusselians" will be a surprising highlight of your European stay.

BRUSSELS WITH THE "BABBELBUS":

Because my own preferences lie heavily with independent, do-it-yourself-type sightseeing, I've provided walking instructions, and subway stops, for most of the sights described above. If you'd prefer an escorted tour of the motorcoach variety, you'll find several companies offering them from locations around the Grand' Place, or on the "Grands Boulevards", of which **Autocars Henri de Boeck,** 8 Rue de la Colline (phone 513-7744), is as typical as any. It offers four departures daily (at 10 a.m., 11:30 a.m., 2 p.m., and 3 p.m.) of a two-hour city tour costing 550 francs ($15.28) as well as lengthier excursions to Waterloo, Ghent, Bruges and the Ardennes.

But you can also take the **"Babbelbus"**! Operated by a 30-year-old, multi-lingual veteran of Brussels' student travel world—he is the always enthusiastic, irrepressible Philippe Baeyens—it's another unique Belgian institution, a tour (so he claims) that reveals the bad as well as the good, the ugly as well as the attractive, the classic sights mixed with the life of the average resident; only Belgium, with its notorious sense of proportion, could possess such a tour.

The **"Babbelbus"** (Chatter bus; "Bus Bavard" in French), reached by phoning 673-1835, is an assortment of battered, 8-passenger vans that depart twice daily (from May through September), at 10 a.m. and 2 p.m., on the unique itineraries (the classic as well as the awful) described above, that last for almost three hours, cost 600 francs ($16.67), including the farewell drink described below, and are accompanied by a sophisticated, often politicized, commentary, both wise and witty. "That's the Royal Palace," notes Philippe, as the van passes the imposing edifice. "If the flag of Belgium is flying over it, it means the King is in residence. If a foreign flag is flying over it, it means we've been invaded again!" Babbelbus also operates a three-hour, morning **walking tour** departing daily except Mondays from April through September at 10 a.m. for only 220 francs ($6.11), including drink at the end; and an occasional evening visit to a **beer-serving tavern,** for which a 900 francs ($25) fee entitles you to taste nine separate glasses of the many different species of Belgian beer. Both the walking tour and the one by van end at a typical workingmen's tavern in the Marolles district, where you relax over a glass of unique Brussels beer (faro, gueuze or kriek, included in the price of the tour) for half an hour, while the grizzled denizens of the bar look upon *you* as a sightseeing attraction! It's all great fun, and highly recommended by me. The various offerings of the "Babbelbus" (Chatterbus) are booked by phoning its reservation number— 673-1835—and arranging to be picked up at the two or three starting points for the tours; the number is answered even in evenings and on weekends.

NIGHTLIFE AND ENTERTAINMENT: The evening cultural opportunities offered by Brussels are extraordinary for a city of only one million persons, which is half the size of the metropolitan population of say, Cleveland, or Liverpool, or Sydney, all with a minor fraction of the theatres maintained by Brussels. In addition to over *forty* playhouses presenting French or Flemish (Dutch)-language drama (of little interest to most tourists because of the language used), there is a major season of grand opera at the **Théâtre Royal de la Monnaie** on the Place de la Monnaie off the Rue Neuve; extensive offerings of ballet through much of the year at the **Cirque Royal,** at 81 Rue de l'Enseignement in "haut de la ville", or occasionally at the Théâtre Royal de la Monnaie; classical concerts, recitals, chamber opera and chamber music in various halls of the **Palais des Beaux Arts,** 23 Rue Ravenstein, and at numerous other concert halls throughout the city; evening circus at the **Place Flagey;** English-language theatre at the *Arts Centre* of the British School at 19 Steenweg op Leuven, and at the **Jacques Franck Cultural Centre,** 94 Chaussée de Waterloo; and, for the tourist anxious to see the classics, even though performed in French or Dutch, there are major productions of timeless plays at the historic and exquisite **Theatre Royal du Parc,** in the Park of Brussels at 3 Rue de la Loi (Strindberg, Shakespeare, Goldoni, Michel de Ghelderode, Tennessee Williams, in one recent season), at the **Théâtre du Rideau de Bruxelles** in the Palais des Beaux Arts at 23 Rue Ravenstein (Molière, Shakespeare), at the **Théâtre Molière,** 1 Rue du Bastion (Molière), and at the **Théâtre National** of the Centre Rogier at the Place Rogier (George Bernard Shaw, Jean-Paul Sartre, Friedrich Durrenmatt, in a recent season, all in French, as well as contemporary plays of stature from the New York or London stage); there is also considerable *avant garde* theatre in smaller playhouses throughout town. Brussels is the world's largest center of French-language theatre outside of Paris.

Complete listings of presentations for the coming week are most easily found in two supplements: **"What's On"** bound into every edition of the English-language magazine, *The Bulletin,* sold at all newstands and distributed in the Brussels tourist office on the Grand' Place, at the Town Hall; or in the **"L'Agenda des Loisirs"** section of the Thursday edition of the newspaper "Le Soir", again at all newsstands or the tourist office. You'll find additional listings and theatre leaflets (as well as a ticket-purchasing service) at the tourist office, and you ought also to visit the main lobby of the **Palais des Beaux Arts,** at 23 Rue Ravenstein, to obtain a clearer picture of their extensive and distinguished concert and theatre offerings; the latter is a Victor Horta-designed structure found within short walking distance uphill from the Grand' Place, full of all sorts of "Art Nouveau" touches, and a major cultural institution of Brussels.

And then there are the movies, the glory of Brussels! Because of the need to provide both French and Dutch translations in this bilingual city, foreign films are never dubbed, but rather sub-titled, and English-language films are heard in English! In addition to enjoying at least two dozen nightly choices in the cinemas of the **Avenue de la Toison d'Or** or **Avenue Louise** in "haut de la ville" (upper Brussels), and at least a dozen English films on the "Grands Boulevards" in the center, Brussels offers nightly classic films at remarkably low cost (30 francs, 83¢) in its outstanding **"Musée du Cinema"** (Cinema Museum), in the Palais des Beaux

Arts, this time using the entrance at 9 Rue Baron Horta. When in doubt over what to do for the evening, simply go to the "Musée du Cinema"—you will rarely be disappointed.

"Jazz"—a broad category comprising rock and roll, blues and the "boogie", in addition to what some know as "jazz"—is another major evening attraction of Brussels, heavily emphasized, and presented in a number of locales, of which the major one is the **Brussels Jazz Club,** at 13 Grand' Place, open most nights except Wednesdays and Sundays, with changing international acts. We haven't the space (or the inclination) to discuss the less impressive nightclubs or cabaret shows of Brussels, of which there are many.

A final advice is to make every effort to secure tickets for the **Ballet of La Monnaie** if the troupe is performing during the period of your stay in Brussels. It does so at periodic intervals throughout the year—sometimes at the Palais des Beaux Arts, in addition to the theatres listed above—and delivers a dance program of distinguished quality, always with those fresh balletic touches for which the group's choreographers are famed.

SHOPPING IN BRUSSELS: Though Brussels can't compare

in shopping opportunities to London, Paris or Rome, it enjoys one advantage they lack: extremely compact shopping areas, and therefore ease of shopping, the ability to effect one's purchases quickly and without traversing long distances. In a tight three blocks of the **Boulevard de Waterloo** (in "upper Brussels"), you find every great name in de luxe European apparel for gifts, from Giorgio Armani to Coco Chanel—the very summit of the clothing world. In three compact blocks of the nearby **Avenue Louise,** you then descend one category, almost effortlessly, to such less expensive but high quality names as Cacharel, Burberry's, Louis Vuitton. In a three-hundred-yard stroll along the **Rue Neuve,** you satisfy all your normal needs, at department stores and large shops stocking every popularly-priced item. And in the streets immediately around and off the **Grand' Place,** you buy souvenirs and lace without walking for more than five minutes. We'll quickly review the shopping areas, and then discuss a few individual stand-outs.

Lace and Souvenirs: the Grand' Place and L'Ilot Sacré

Hand-made lace manufactured by ladies seated at cushions dotted with a pattern of pins, is the item that almost all visitors seek to bring home. It sells here for as little as 150 francs ($4.17) for tiny handkerchiefs to as much as 25,000 francs ($695) for elaborate tablecloth-and-napkin sets; but in all price ranges and on all sorts of cloth—exquisite ladies' blouses, christening robes and wedding dresses, stylish evening apparel—it is always a value, priced surprisingly low for the work that obviously went into it, a unique Belgian bargain. **Louise Verschuren,** at 16 Rue Watteau near the Place du Grand Sablon, and **"Manufacture Belge des Dentelles",** at no. 8 in the enclosed St. Hubert Galleries off the Grand' Place, are typical of the better lace shops selling the highest quality goods at top prices; while **"Maison Antoine",** at 26 Grand' Place, is one of several shops selling popularly-priced lace directly on the Grand' Place; but a far less pressured setting for lace, at perhaps slightly cheaper prices, is along the lace-shop-lined rue Charles Buls which runs directly off the Grand' Place and becomes the Rue de l'Etuve as it nears the statue of the Mannekin Pis. As you browse along this street, passing successive lace shops (such as **Rose's Lace Boutique,** opposite the Amigo Hotel) interspersed among souvenir shops, you will eventually come to a large but unnamed souvenir store at **26 Rue de l'Etuve** (a short block before the Mannekin Pis) which carries, to my mind, the most tasteful assortment of low-priced souvenirs and cheap gift items in all of Brussels—if you have to buy this sort of item, you might as well do it at No. 26! Owned by the proprietors of the **Semal Lace Shop,** across the street at No. 43, it sells not simply copper statues of the Mannekin Pis—the ubiquitous souvenir around here—but small items of Val St. Lambert crystal (from the famous glassmakers of Belgium's Liège district): small plates and ashtrays for as little as 350 francs ($9.72), a box of six Val St. Lambert ashtrays etched with birds for 1760 francs ($49), a box of four for 1330 francs ($37), "Bergkristall" silver necklaces for 1400 francs ($39), a lace tablecloth with four lace napkins for 1395 francs ($38.75), and of course the Mannekin Pis for 60 francs ($1.67).

Art and reproductions, stamps and coins: Rue du Midi and elsewhere

A second specialty of Brussels are the paintings and collections listed above, found in numerous areas, but especially on the **rue du Midi,** starting at the Bourse and running parallel to the "Grands Boulevards". Here are stamp collections and velvet cases of coins so numerous and varied—at least twenty specialized stores, continuing for three blocks—that they could have been lifted from a small boy's dreams (but the scenes inside are of old men smoking pipes and using tweezers to display a rare specimen to another small boy grown old). **Belgasafe,** at 24 Rue du Midi, is one of the largest of the stamp-and-coin stores, with an impressive inventory; but a smaller, one-proprietor shop, of which there are many, may prove more congenial to you; those gentlemen, in the traditions of their trade, speak nearly every major language.

Amid all the coins and stamps is the wondrous reproductions shop of **G. Arekens,** at No. 15 Rue du Midi, specializing in the Flemish Primitives! Of the dozens of such reproductions stores in Brussels, all possessing their favorite themes, only Arekens will unhesitatingly pull forth the Portinari Altarpiece of Hugo van der Goes, already in a gilded frame, and selling for 2150 francs ($60), or Memling's Virgin with Child and Apple, already framed, for 2300 francs ($64), or smaller reproductions of masterworks of the 1400s, in simpler frames, for as little as 1500 francs ($42). . . . Walk down the Rue du Midi after your visit to Arekens, this time to No. 35, and you'll discover an inexpensive and quite unpretentious antiques shop that somehow completes the relaxing visit to the old fashioned world of the Rue du Midi.

For authentic prints and engravings of past centuries— scenes of the Grand' Place and the Grand Sablon, posters of Napoleon, ancient maps and etchings of Belgian scenes—the vast, cluttered floors of the **Galerie Appolo,** on the Place Ste. Gudule opposite the side entrance of the Cathedral of St. Michael and Ste. Gudule, are the place to browse; it offers one of the broadest assortments of prints in Brussels, some selling for as little as 250 francs ($6.94), and although it is only one of many such stores (found around the Mont des Arts, in L'Ilot Sacré, and off the Place du Grand Sablon), its serious atmosphere and warmth have a special appeal to me.

Original art? The **Falkner Gallery,** at 9 Rue des Sablons (on the Place du Grand Sablon), and **De Jonckheere,** 55 Boulevard de Waterloo, display actual works of the 16th and 17th centuries for sale; while **Isy Bracho,** at 62a Avenue Louise, is the great Brussels gallery of contemporary art, selling works by Paul Delvaux, René Magritte, others. Prices are high.

Antiques: the Place du Grand Sablon

In addition to the items displayed at its weekend market, outdoors in the center of the square, antiques of extraordinary variety and in every price range are sold in numerous large stores directly on the stately Place du Grand Sablon, and in the streets running directly off it. The especially-large, two-floor, **Antique Center "Anne de Beaujeu",** at 7 Rue des Sablons, is especially interesting, moderately-priced—and non-intimidating. You stroll without pressure or interruption through warehouse-sized premises, in a structure that is itself like an old antique. Like most of the establishments around the Sablon, this one closes on Mondays, and has short Sunday hours, from 10 to 2. Far more expensive, but with museum-quality pieces (17th-century Brussels tapestries, Louis XIV cabinets and commodes), is **Jean Tollemans,** at 15 Rue des Sablons—atypically expensive in an area of quite reasonably-priced antiques.

Once-in-a-lifetime-shopping: the "Boulevard de Waterloo"

Apart from tourists, residents and other ordinary folk, Brussels is full of high-living diplomats—three different (and often duplicating) corps of foreign envoys accredited separately to the E.E.C., N.A.T.O., and the Kingdom of Belgium. Their number, already unusually large, is then augmented by executives of the many hundreds of multi-national corporations headquartered here, and the grand result is an army of the affluent-attracting shops made just for them. So, if you've yearned all your life for a classic Chanel woman's suit ($1000), or a white sable coat costing more than a car, or a velvety-soft, leather notepad from "Hermes of Paris", you've come to the right place! In that area of Brussels known as "haut de la ville" (upper Brussels), in a three-hundred-yard stretch of stately shops on the **Boulevard de Waterloo,** starting just below the Brussels Hilton near the Palais de Justice, is every gold-plated name in de luxe, European shopping, almost as if those haughty types had collectively agreed to squeeze themselves onto the same segment of street. To name just a few, there are: **Gucci,** at 66 Boulevard de Waterloo (selling even light-weight ladies suits for $500); **Chanel,** at No. 63 (her classic, coarse-textured outfits priced at $1000 and up); **Janine Lecomte,** at No. 58 (boutique dresses from $300 to $500); **Marcel Lasca,** at No. 57 (Rolex watches); **Hermes of Paris,** at No. 58 (exquisite gift items of top quality); **J & F Schlachmuylder,** at No. 46 (the Belgian furrier of such high renown, with white sables and fur-lined raincoats); **Cartier** and **Givenchy** within the Hilton; **Harry de Vlaminck,** at No. 32 (elegant men's clothing); **Giorgio Armani,** at No. 13; **Yves St. Laurent,** at No. 12; **Guy Laroche,** at No. 4; numerous others designed for stratospheric incomes only. Rarely will you find such a de luxe selection in cities of a similar size.

The "upper middle class": Avenue Louise and Avenue de la Toison d'Or

Just below the very top category, less expensive but still of top quality, are the shops and stores of the **Avenue Louise,** running perpendicular to that broad, "upper Brussels" throughfare known as the "Boulevard de Waterloo" on one side, and "Avenue de la

Toison d'Or" (Avenue of the Golden Fleece) on the other. Avenue Louise shops—more than fifty of them—are chic, trendy, somewhat expensive (especially as you walk further away from the Boulevard de Waterloo), but not unreasonably so; and a typical selection would include **Dean's,** at No. 50 Avenue Louise (Pierre Cardin men's suits for $400); **Bouvy,** at No. 4 (youthful ladies dresses for $250 to $350); **Bogner,** at No. 164 (a much cheaper boutique, in the $150 to $200 range for dresses); **Scarpine,** at no. 3 (far-out fanciful shoes and leather items); **Burberry's** at no. 7 ($200 women's suits, $150 to $200 rainproof coats); **Louis Vuitton,** at No. 25 (suitcases); **Caroline,** at No. 37 (imitations of the classic Chanel suit, for only $400); **Edouard,** at No. 21 (fur coats); **Christoffel,** at No. 40 (jewelry and watches); **Dujardin,** at No. 8 (children's fashions).

Returning now to the Boulevard de Waterloo, note that the other side of that remarkably wide roadway is called the "Avenue de la Toison d'Or". On it are additional shops of the Avenue Louise category: **Delvaux,** at No. 24 Avenue de la Toison d'Or (Belgium's own artist of leather, selling ladies purses of futuristic design), and **Studiohaus,** at No. 236 Avenue de la Toison d'Or (Rosenthal china), are outstanding.

Back in the area of the Grand'Place, the **Royal St. Hubert Arcades** ("Galeries Royales St. Hubert"), built in 1847 as the first covered walkway in Europe, is a trove of superb purchases in the high quality field. Its **"Monsel",** at No. 4 Galerie de la Reine (one of the three sections of the Arcades) houses the world's chic-est umbrellas, a store-full of them selling for as little as 500 francs, $14 (and as much as 1950 francs, $54); the selection is so large, and so tasteful, as to defy comparison from any other city; while the much smaller **Ganterei Italienne,** across the hall at No. 3, offers elegant, rather conservative Italian gloves for as little as 1000 francs ($28) for washable suede. **Church's English Shoes,** at No. 11 Galerie du Prince (again in the Arcades), is where men shop for the classic styles, at prices ranging from 5000 to 6000 francs ($139 to $167). In a city filled with shopping arcades—18 of them—Saint Hubert is historic, and as much of a sightseeing attraction as a shopping area, with its cinema, repertory theatre, restaurants, cafes, and "chocolatiers". Main entrance is just off the top of the Rue du Marché aux Herbes, a short block from the Grand' Place. How modern and advanced it must have seemed to the people of 1847—and how graceful it still is!

BRUSSELS MISCELLANY: Because most museums in Brussels are closed on Mondays, it's best to use Monday for that excursion to Bruges (where everything is open that day) or to Ghent (where a great deal is open on Mondays—the key exception being the latter's Museum of Fine Arts). . . . Brussels' best exchange rate for foreign currency is provided, in my experience, by the exchange desk of the elegant **Crédit-Générale** at No. 5 Grand' Place ("bottom" of the Square; enter and walk all the way to the end, then down a short flight of stairs), and when that's closed, at the exchange office on the Rue de la Colline, No. 2, directly off the Grand' Place. Never change your money at a Brussels hotel, or for that matter at any of the Brussels railroad stations, where rates are poor. And while we're on the subject, two other activities are never to be practiced in or from a hotel (anywhere): making long distance phone calls, or sending out your laundry. . . . Brussels' utterly legal, closely supervised, and rather expansive red-light district, where ladies ply their trade from behind crimson-lit windows, is clustered on the Rue du Marché and Rue Matheus to the west of the Place Rogier. . . . Taxi fares appearing on meters in Brussels are already inclusive of both service charge and tax, and it is unnecessary to add anything other than small change to the amount charged, a welcome discovery. . . . The proximity of Brussels to all other major Belgian cities is a point that can never be sufficiently stressed, and will be repeated here. Brussels is only 46 kilometers (about 29 miles) from Antwerp, only 53 kilometers (33 miles) from Ghent, the same 53 kilometers from Charleroi, 79 kilometers from Tournai, 96 kilometers (59 miles) from Bruges or Liège. One should never pass up the opportunity to visit at least one other Belgian city—on a trip to Brussels.

EXCURSION TO LEUVEN:
Which brings us to Leuven (Louvain in French), only 26 kilometers (16 miles) from Brussels. Though now primarily known as the quiet site of Belgium's oldest university, it was a rival of Brussels in the 13th and 14th centuries, the capital then of Brabant, and a richly impressive city of the Middle Ages, which it still is. Its gingerbread-like Town Hall of the 15th century, adorned with stone tracery, statuary and patterns to an almost unimaginable extent; its medieval Market Square; its peaceful Beguinage at the bottom of the hill descending from the central town area; and especially its Gothic Church of St. Peter, with its riveting triptych of the "Last Supper" by 15th-century "primitive" Dirck Bouts—one that stops you in your tracks, and alone justifies the trip—all make for an enthralling visit so easily accomplished from Brussels. Simply drive there on motorway E5, or take the proper train headed for Liège and stopping in Louvain, short minutes away.

BRUSSELS

Too many travelers confine their stays to Brussels, enjoying only a small segment—however rich it is—of the masterpiece called Belgium. The remaining sights of this compact, easily-travelled nation are second to none in Europe—however extreme that statement may appear. To prove it, we ask only that you accompany us now—to Bruges.

CHAPTER V

BRUGES THE MAGNIFICENT

□ □ □

. . . Where Time Stopped

BRUGES
DAMME

When we first wander through it, astonished and silent, we try to rein in our excitement. After all, on our travels through Europe before visiting Bruges, we have seen other perfectly preserved medieval communities: Carcassonne, Siena, Avila, Rothenburg. But those were mere villages, small, secondary towns; Bruges is a medieval *city* perfectly preserved, a giant, sprawling, ancient metropolis once of world significance, and yet today almost unaltered in its former splendor, its awesome beauty and size. Suddenly, those people of the Middle Ages cease, in our minds, to appear a quaint and backward species, to be patronized. All at once we realize, if we hadn't before, that people have nearly always had aspirations and achievements equivalent to ours. And if we were born, as I was, an American, optimistic and arrogant, rarely looking back, believing in the constant upward progress of human civilization, we feel shaken by Bruges; we learn decisively that mankind has both advanced and declined, that aspects of the past were perhaps superior to the present, that an age nearly 700 years ago, and later reviled as "dark", enjoyed artistic, commercial and physical prowess of a sort that many later eras and nations have still to attain.

BRUGES!

A city arrested in time. A Pompeii or a Brigadoon. An urban portrait caught as if by stop-frame photography, of a community that died while it was still young. The most heavily-visited touristic site in all of Belgium, it is the victim of one of the strangest natural events of history—the "silting of the Zwin"—which snuffed out its commercial life in the late Middle Ages, caused it to miss the Industrial Revolution, and thus paradoxically saved its unique medieval legacy from the wreckers' ball. If only more ancient cities had suffered such misfortune!

Bruges, in medieval times, was the greatest trading center in northern Europe, a multi-national marketplace for importing and exporting, storing and displaying, cloths and spices, herrings and wine, every variety of goods. Along its canals and in central squares, dozens of wealthy foreign merchants maintained exotic commercial palaces (these, unfortunately, have not survived), virtual embassies of their countries in which they lavishly entertained and dealt with the thousands of traders who flocked to a city renowned for its glitter and importance.

The focus of all this movement, the vital access road, was the "Zwin", a waterway, an estuary that connected Bruges to the North Sea. In the mid-1300s, at the height of Bruges' renown, and for reasons still not fully understood, the Zwin began to "silt up", to fill with sand denying passage to deep-draft ships. Only slightly dismayed, the city moved its port area to suburban Damme, on a less affected segment of the Zwin four miles away, and Damme grew to the size of 60,000 residents (it now has 1,500!). But relief was only temporary. In the 1400s, and while Bruges continued to enjoy unparalleled prosperity (as well as all the attendant artistic activity that comes with such prosperity), the Zwin outside Damme proceeded to silt up, becoming clogged and impassable within a few short years.

And Bruges died. Literally died. With the ending of ship traffic, commercial activity virtually ceased, and large portions of the population—some estimate as many as half—left to seek employment in Antwerp and other cities, abandoning their stunning homes, their commercial palaces, their magnificent squares. For most of the remaining residents, poverty set in. While other factors also contributed to the dizzying decline of Bruges—the outmoded and overly-restrictive commercial practices of the long-established merchants and guilds of Bruges, the eventual preference shown by Burgundian dukes for the eastern cities of Brabant, the unsuccessful rebellion of Bruges against the arrival of Maximilian of Austria as the first Hapsburg ruler of Flanders—it was that congealing, thickening, solidifying Zwin that dealt the death

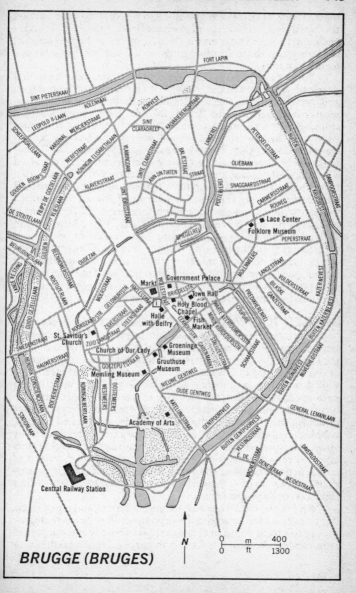

BRUGGE (BRUGES)

blow. Today, at that point on the Zwin where ships once entered the North Sea, outside the glamorous Belgian resort of Knokke-het-Zoute, you can walk on the Zwin, romp up and down upon it, scattering crumbs to strolling birds on the wet but firm land of a former waterway.

But not everything ended in Bruges, nor was its architectural development frozen in the 1400s. With the onset of religious wars and persecutions in the late 1500s, Catholic nuns and priests, monks and friars, fled to Bruges for safety, building additional churches and accommodations for themselves. Those structures survive to this day. In the 16th century, various wealthy philanthropists dotted the city with almshouses ("godshuizen") built for the poor; they, too, survive. In the 17th century there occurred a weak revival of sorts, and gabled, 17th-century houses and structures, in fair quantity, remain from that era. But Bruges remained a backwater, dozing through the 18th and 19th centuries until a Belgian writer, Georges Rodenbach, inadvertently broadcast its charms to the world in a novel called "Bruges La Morte" (Dead Bruges) and set off a wave of tourism. Soon thereafter, wise minds forbade any further tampering with the facades of Bruges, and the city embarked on its second career, this time as a monumental European tourist destination. I have often felt that if the international airport of Belgium were located outside Bruges, rather than Brussels, overseas tourism to Belgium would triple!

BRUGES TODAY: It is a city of dreams, where every walk brings reveries, every stroll results in unexpected discoveries of beauty. You walk behind a gate, and there is a ravishing courtyard, the kind you'd imagine from the last scene of Cyrano de Bergerac, or one you'd find in a monastery cloister, peaceful and green. You walk down a lane, and there is a canal and regal swans upon it. You gaze up at buildings, and there are exquisite, carved-stone emblems of the guilds or functions they once served. Everywhere are canals (in this "Venice of the North") and small, arched bridges, cobblestoned streets, ranks of aged medieval structures covered by vines, interspersed with trees—for there are large, flowering trees everywhere—guardians of peaceful repose and quiet, except of course in the majestic main squares where towering belfries, cathedrals, market halls—themselves supreme works of art—draw sightseers to gaze upon them.

And the homes! They all have pointed roofs, and are of brick, but brick used for an aesthetic purpose, set in patterns that draw the eye to a focal point, or create designs of beauty and purpose in even modest dwellings, bricks set in curved, archway fashion, or bricks set aslant, or bricks that criss-cross upon themselves to make the architect's statement. Whole books have been written about the brick facades of Bruges, about the placement of windows, the shaping of roofs and gables that permits one to discern the century of a building's construction; just as Italy, in the Middle Ages, excelled in marble, and France in stone, so medieval Bruges was the creator of brickwork never again equalled in its variety and charm. Compare even the modest commercial structures of Bruges with the mindless and squat, vapid rectangles that constitute the retail architecture of most cities in North America!

ORIENTATION AND GETTING AROUND: The great inner city of Bruges, the original Bruges, is shaped like a slightly-lopsided egg, surrounded almost entirely by a broad waterway that bears no name (it is a Ring Canal) except for the broader, southern, off-shoots of it known as the **"Lake of Love"** (Minnewater, or "Lac d'Amour"). This was the port of Bruges in the Middle Ages; flanked today by sloping, grass lawns, it is the ideal site for a picnic in Bruges; and the narrow park areas that almost continually line the remainder of the Ring Canal are the place to jog in Bruges, or to enjoy a lengthy and always delightful stroll along almost-pastoral scenes of sheer beauty.

The railroad station is just to the side of the "Lake of Love" (Minnewater), while the best arrival point for motorists is a giant, elongated square known as **" 't Zand"**, several hundred yards up from the Station, slightly within the "egg". 'T Zand is site of a mammoth underground parking garage, where motorists should immediately park, leave, and forget, their cars; it is surrounded by hotels, and is within easy walking distance of the "Grote Markt" (Market Square)—down either the Noordzandstraat into the Sint-Amandstraat, or down the Zuidzandstraat into the Steenstraat. You will not want to drive your cars within Bruges; you do violence to the atmosphere by doing so (in addition to discovering only limited, and one-way, streets down which you can drive). Except for the initial use of a taxi from the Station to your hotel (rarely more than a $4 ride), you then walk, for all purposes, in Bruges. Walking is what Bruges is all about, in a touristic area where distances are short and pleasantly covered, and only the residents use, or even know about, the buses that go to outlying neighborhoods.

The center of Bruges is the **"Grote Markt"** (Market Square) with its renowned Belfry of Bruges, almost in the very center of the "egg", and no more than five to ten minutes from the most tightly clustered grouping of important attractions of any city: the overpowering Memling Museum of the Hospital of St. John, the Chapel of the Holy Blood, the "Hall of the Flemish Primitives" in the Groeninge Museum, the spectacular medieval home of Louis de Gruuthuse, the cathedrals, the canals, the swans, the canal boats —it makes you wish you were without luggage, and able to rush there right away! But there are practical needs to be considered, which we impatiently discuss while awaiting the glories of Bruges!

LODGING IN A CITY OF THE PAST: Who would spoil the mood of Bruges by seeking rooms in a modern high-rise? Fortunately, there are none. Nor are there hotels that distract the visitor from the humbling lessons of history. None of the hotels of Bruges is both large and de luxe, and travellers demanding world-class rooms or amenities should stay in Brussels and commute to Bruges. Having said that, it's important to add that the hotels of Bruges are delightful lodgings of architectural distinction (even the Holiday Inn occupies a period building!) and far more numerous than in most other Belgian cities. They are also small, intimate and refined. Of the 76 hotels of Bruges, only 11 have more than 25 rooms, and the giant among them possesses exactly 128—roughly half the size of most road-side motels.

Perhaps the best of the Bruges hotels is the 18-room **Hotel "De Orangerie"** at 10 Kartuizerinnestraat (phone 050-34-16-49), in a central position along a canal. Outside is the facade of a 16th-century building; inside the eclectic furnishings of an affluent country house selected by a brilliant interior decorator. Rooms, which are large and with modern beds, look onto a garden courtyard or at the canal, and you can also breakfast in good weather on a terrace overlooking the passing canal boats. Travelers of the finest tastes choose this elegant, four-star lodging, and pay from 4000 to 7000 francs ($111 to $194) per double room (there are no singles), depending on size and location, including breakfast, service and tax.

Comparing quite respectably is the 17-room **Oud Huis Amsterdam** at 3 Spiegelrei (phone 050-34-18-10), again on a centrally-situated canal, and around a courtyard of tables and plants; its antique bar is a popular favorite among a trendy set of Bruges residents. This time the house is a 17th-century "gentlemen's" residence, with heavy, Flemish-style furnishings, but the lightest and brightest of guest rooms: beamed ceilings and good, wide beds with firm mattresses, well-cared-for by an unusually friendly management solicitous of your welfare. Rooms range from 2500 to 5000 francs ($69 to $139), single or double, including breakfast, service and tax. To complete the amenities, a horse-drawn "caleche" picks up guests of the hotel and transports them to the owner's restaurant—"De Burgoensche Cruyce", highly reputed among the nation's gourmets—in another section of town; and the same caleche is available for other free trips of the guests' choosing.

Two older, and longer-maintained, hotels of Bruges deserve the term "exquisite" as their adjective. They are the 18-room **Pandhotel,** at 16 Pandreitje (phone 34-06-66), and the 9-room **Duc de Bourgogne,** at 12 Huidenvettersplein (phone 33-20-38), the former in a white-stone townhouse on the elegant street called Pandreitje in the very center of Bruges. Queen Anne furnishings, lace-covered tables in your bedroom, velvet-covered chairs in public areas, old-fashioned beds but gleamingly-new bedroom fixtures—those are the features of this genre of small hotel, typical of many more in Bruges, and offering an experience akin to staying in someone's elegant but old-fashioned home, not quite as comfortable as stretching out on the airfield-sized hard mattresses of a Hyatt Regency or Hilton. In compensation, you pay a moderate 2950 francs ($81.95) for a twin-bedded room at this topnotch Pandhotel of Bruges, including continental breakfast, service and tax; 2400 francs ($67) single. Two blocks away, the even-more-elegant Duc de Bourgogne in a landmark building of the 15th century, stunningly furnished with museum-quality antiques, and better known for its luxury restaurant, is somewhat on the same order, but with larger rooms of brocaded, gold-colored curtains, masses of old furniture, beds with silk coverlets, bedrooms with crystal chandeliers, dressing tables with ruffles of embroidered cloth, original art on the walls. It is an experience staying here, directly on a stunning canal, at the more logical (but still reasonable) cost of 3750 francs ($104) for a twin-bedded room, breakfast, service and taxes included. Diagonally across the canal from the back of the Duc de Bourgogne, on an enchanting and secluded little canal-side square, the 12-room **Hotel Bourgoensch Hof,** at 39 Wollestraat (phone 33-16-45) offers slightly more modern facilities at a high season charge of $118, including breakfast for two, for a double room.

If both the Pandhotel and Duc de Bourgogne are full, then phone the 48-room **Sablon,** at 21 Noordzandstraat (phone 33-39-02), of quality and prices similar to those of the Pandhotel, as is the elegant but more modern, 28-room **Hotel Europ,** at 18 Augustijnenrei (phone 33-79-75).

The most modern hotel of Bruges, amazingly enough, is the 128-room **Holiday Inn-Pullman,** at 2 Boeveriestraat (phone 34-09-71), at the top of 't Zand, that gigantic square that's now the major parking area of Bruges (underground). Its 17th-century exterior, a combination of several adjoining buildings, is obviously like no Holiday Inn you've ever seen, but inside the mood turns modern, though relatively tasteful (with exposed brick walls), and the large and sunny rooms are everything we weary travellers crave: two queen-sized beds with modern, hard mattresses; every other hotel facility; large indoor swimming pool and sauna on the ground floor. Though lacking the charm, historical quality and remarkable medieval settings of our earlier choices, it is—by purely physical standards—among the best hotels of Bruges, yet it charges only 4200 francs ($117) for a twin with two breakfasts, service and tax, 3300 francs ($92) for a single. If the Holiday Inn-Pullman is full, walk up the street to the smaller (80 rooms), modern **Park Hotel**, at 5 Vrijdagmarkt (phone 33-33-64), still on 't Zand, with functional modern rooms (tv, radio, mini-bar), one notch down in quality from the Holiday Inn. Three thousand francs ($90) per twin, not including breakfast; 2500 francs ($69) single, without breakfast.

The hotels named thus far are all in the inner city. Because I don't mind the short extra walk, the hotel at which I stay in Bruges (as did the beauteous French film star, Catherine Deneuve, on a recent visit; she left a signed photo, now proudly displayed) is the 21-room **Pannenhuis**, at 2 Zandstraat (phone 31-19-07), on the far side of the Ring Canal, about 10 minutes on foot from 't Zand. A rambling, lodge-like, early-20th-century home on small grounds of its own, a garden in back, it is managed by a charming young couple who work long hours to merit their high quality rating and the renown of their equally-important ground-floor restaurant that looks out on the garden. Rooms are furnished in a hodge-podge of styles, including art deco; most are fairly large; magazines are piled on the stairway landing for your use (there is no elevator); parking out front is free and available; and rates are a reasonable 2800 to 3400 francs ($78 to $94) twin, 2300 to 2800 francs ($64 to $78) single, including continental breakfast, service and tax, and always for the warmest personal attentions by the highly solicitous hosts. A high recommendation.

Bruges' low-cost standouts

A popular, moderately-priced hotel of Bruges, located where three canals meet, is the **Uilenspiegel**, 2 Langestraat (phone 33-85-16), charging only 1500 francs ($42) single, 2000 francs ($56) double, including service, tax, and a generous breakfast served in a dining room made picturesque with curios and antiques; Daniel Puype is the gracious host. Alternately, try the **Grand Hotel du Sablon**, well located at 21 Noordzandstraat (phone 33-39-02), whose rooms with private bath rent for 1450 francs ($40) single, 2200 francs ($61) double, including breakfast, service and tax.

And for even less

The best of the cheapest? They're found on the second and upper floors of the restaurants lining the east side of 't Zand, where rooms without private bath or shower, but with hot and cold running water, and with continental breakfast included, are priced at ultra-low rates: 650 to 750 francs ($18 to $21) single, 1000 to 1300 francs ($28 to $36) double, at the **Graaf van Vlanderen** (Count of Flanders), 19 't Zand (phone 33-28-80); the **Gouden Aap,** 18 't Zand (phone 33-31-50); and **Hotel Leopold,** 25 't Zand (phone 33-51-29). Youth hostels? The largest, with 216 beds, is the **Europa-Jeugdherberg,** at 143 Baron Ruzettelaan (phone 35-26-79), charging from 280 to 350 francs ($7.78 to $9.72) per bunk per night, depending on various factors. An alternate choice for about the same: the **Bauhaus International Youth Hotel,** at 135 Langestraat (phone 34-10-93).

In a city so largely devoted to tourism, the hotels are heavily booked on weekends, much more lightly occupied from Monday through Thursday (a pattern opposite to that of Brussels)—you'll want to plan and act accordingly. But every night of the week, there's heavy patronage of Bruges' celebrated restaurants:

THE REMARKABLE RESTAURANTS OF BRUGES: Can

a tourist-dominated city produce great cuisine? Most food critics say No; they argue that restaurants achieve greatness only when they each possess a stable, talented clientele capable of demanding and then recognizing great feats of the kitchen (and that definition excludes most tourists). Yet despite the fact that it is flooded with tourists—at times inundated with tourists—Bruges is acknowledged by every major observer to be among the two premier food cities of Belgium, comparable to Brussels. While it possesses no single restaurant of three-star greatness (of which Brussels has several), it offers a dozen standouts in the weighty categories just below; and in Bruges, of course, meals take on an added dimension from the breathtaking medieval settings in which they're served.

Again by common acknowledgment, the three top establishments of Bruges ($60 to $70 the average meal, including wine) are **De Snippe,** at 53 Nieuwe Gentweg (phone 33-70-70), closed Sunday evenings and Mondays; **Restaurant Weinebrugge,** at 242 Koning Albertlaan (phone 31-44-40), in Bruges/St. Michiels, housed in a white-washed, chateau-type structure with grounds, closed Wednesdays, Thursdays and the months of September and February; and **Manderley,** at 13 Kruisstraat (phone 27-80-51) in Bruges/Hertsberge, closed Sunday evenings and Mondays; the latter two restaurants located in suburban areas accessible comfortably only by car. As for the renowned De Snippe, it's a patrician, step-gabled home of the 16th century, with fairly limited seating, usually requiring reservations, often sold out, and somewhat of a walk from where you'll usually be.

Four, special, quality restaurants

Therefore, you'd do best to seek out your own memorable experience of *la haute cuisine* in four only-slightly-less-distinguished, centrally located, and also somewhat less expensive restaurants, situated so close to one another that if one is full, you have only to stroll to another. All four are strikingly attractive, and three are located near the most popular outdoor site of Bruges—the Rozenhoedkaai—where tourists, dazzled by the view, take photographs of a particularly lovely vista of intersecting canals and stately canalside structures. Off the Rozenhoedkaai runs a short but unusually elegant street called Pandreitje, a minor "Park Avenue" of Bruges, and it is here at the end of Pandreitje, at opposite sides of the street, that two busy restaurants are patronized not simply by tourists, but by considerable numbers of Bruges-ites, those Venetians of the North, themselves!

Restaurant Den Braamberg, 11 Pandreitje (phone 33-73-70), and **Restaurant 't Pandreitje,** 6 Pandreitje (phone 31-11-90), both occupy ground floors of two Renaissance-period homes whose interiors have been furnished in modern, but sumptuous, refined style, fitting settings for a "nouvelle cuisine" approach—lighter, less richly-sauced—to the classic dishes of the Belgian table. Den Braamberg is the cheaper, charging 1200 francs ($33) for a multi-course lunch, 1700 francs ($47) for a grander dinner including wine (and with service charge always included, as it is everywhere in Belgium). Closed Sunday evenings and Thursdays. 't Pandreitje serves an elaborate 1850 franc ($51) meal of four courses, each course containing several choices, but also offers a strictly prescribed but wonderfully tasty 1300 ($36) "Menu Classique" (lunch only) of four courses fixed to provide: *terrine de lapereau* (paté of young rabbit) to begin, *le bouillon aux jeunes légumes* (broth with fresh vegetables) as your soup, *le cochon de lait aux grains de moutarde* (roast suckling pig with mustard sauce) as a main course, then *le choix de desserts* (a choice of desserts) from a multi-level, silver trolley of fruit tarts, puddings and light, fluffy cakes. At $36 including service, in a sumptuous setting and prepared by a serious chef, that's a rare value. 't Pandreitje is closed Sundays.

Le Duc de Bourgogne, at 12 Huidenvettersplein (phone 33-20-38), back at the Rozenhoedkaai and only 50 yards from it, occupies the most stunning location in all of Bruges, in the equally stunning, medieval hotel-structure of the same name overlooking a dream-like section of ancient canals topped by gracefully-floating swans and illuminated at night. The dining rooms that enjoy this view are large, classic, luxurious and candle-lit, like Empire drawing rooms, with brocaded curtains, pastel paintings of medieval scenes, velvet chairs, waiters in the most formal evening clothes—yet, in summer, consistent with the tolerance of Belgium, some guests enter and dine in open collars and sweaters. They choose from an immensely varied à la carte menu of every classic dish, and what comes from the kitchen are large portions of traditional haute cuisine accompanied by all the classic sauces, all presented in traditional style; you will not find here the exotica (fruits with meats, red cabbage leaves wrapped around crabmeat souffles) of the nouvelle cuisine, which occasionally turn up at den Braamberg and 't Pandreitje. Dishes are priced to total around $50 for a three-course dinner, less if you are very cautious about your selections, and the restaurant is closed Mondays and throughout most of July.

Restaurant Den Gouden Harynck ("the Golden Herring"), at 25 Groeninge (phone 33-76-37), is again in this very same picturesque area; from the Rozenhoedkaai simply walk down the "Dijver" along the canal, till you pass Groeninge Street on your left, and turn down that street for 50 yards. Here is the most inventive of all our choices, a kitchen peopled with Belgian surrealists who serve such novelties as goose livers roasted with raspberries, oysters topped with black caviar, all the fanciful, novel but perfectly harmonious concoctions of nouvelle cuisine chefs that are best taken (but only if you haven't eaten all day) in a six-course, 2600 franc ($72) "menu de degustation" (tasting menu, or, better translated, "sampling menu") consisting of small-portioned, daily-changing items that have best attracted the chef's attention in his market shopping that morning; and including wine in the $72 price. More sensible: a 1300-franc ($36), four-course lunch; or à la carte appetizers (averaging 700 and 720 francs) and main courses (from 820 to 920 francs) chosen separately, for a $42-or-so complete meal. Exquisite setting of local antiques; closed Sunday evenings and Mondays.

Less costly, equally picturesque

Because you won't always crave such a grand meal, at such substantial cost, it is exciting to discover a far less costly Bruges standout in a setting that will keep you dreaming. **Restaurant "ter Reie"** (along the Canal), at 9 Nieuwstraat (phone 33-61-38), directly opposite the Gruuthuse Museum a short walk from the Rozenhoedkaai, is a big, rambling cottage alongside the canal, with row-boat dock and other picturesque touches, and an old, old interior that seats nearly 120 persons—the "poor man's Duc de Bourgogne". I've eaten there on three occasions, choosing from three different menus in ascending order of cost. The first time, feeling casual, the simple "Menu de Jour" for 650 francs ($18), a measly four courses of simple, non-celestial items: soup, a tiny bowl of pink-fresh Belgian shrimp flavored with lemon ("crevettes"), then a grilled "loup de mer" (a sea fish served with a steamed stalk of buttered broccoli), a choice of desserts. The second time, feeling flush, the four-course "Menu Régional" for 850 francs ($24): a plate of cooked endives au gratin, a piping hot "shrimp bisque" soup, a classic rabbit stew with pearl onions and tiny carrots, a moist, baked pear in white, confectionary sauce. The third occasion, throwing caution to the winds, the "Menu de Poisson" (fish banquet), for 1500 francs ($42), *including* a half bottle per person of a dry Chablis: salmon mousse to begin, whipped by a Cuisinart into cloud-like foam, then broiled lobster with endives, a melon-flavored sorbet to clear the palate, a plate of baked turbot (resembling our scrod), with small yellow asparagus, cheeses for dessert, a bit of Kirsch-flavored fruit as a surprise bonus —and remember that the wine, an excellent Chablis, is included in the $42 price.

Facing the Belfry ($11 to $15)

Let's now descend to the level of $11 to $15 for a three-course meal tastily-prepared, delightfully flavorsome, but un-elaborate, quickly-served, and easily reached in a central setting. In other cities, you'd invariably find such values by shunning the areas where tourists gather and heading instead into the neighborhoods; in Bruges, you do exactly the opposite—you march without hesitation into the tourist-crammed Market Square ("Grote Markt"), walk to the side of the Square opposite the mighty Belfry, and quickly seat yourself at the sidewalk tables (or inside the rustic, wood-lined interiors) of ten—exactly ten— workaday, middle-class restaurants occupying the gabled and gilded medieval buildings that form a continuous line opposite the Belfry. Those ten little wonders compete a bit raucously for the tourist trade with colorful, tourist-attracting placards and black-boards proclaiming all manner of sensational prices for table d'hôte feasts; yet they cater to sufficient Belgians, at the same time, to stay sensitive and alert to the high-quality preparation of these moderately-priced meals. And thus, if you'll order the 525-franc ($14.60) four-course "menu" of **Restaurant Belfort,** at 32 Markt —my own favorite among the ten—you'll be mildly surprised to receive an exceptional, delicately-flavored, fresh asparagus soup to begin, little chunks of the costly vegetable floating on top; then a plate of young, fresh Dutch herring as tender as butter, and covered with finely-chopped onions; then a quarter roast chicken, moist and topped with a brown sauce; and fresh fruit salad for dessert. Similar meals, but of only three courses, are priced at 455 francs ($12.64), at **De Sneeuwberg,** another of the ten, and for only 375 francs ($10.40) at **De Vier Winden,** cheapest of the ten. At the last named, that $10.40 brings you a spicy fish soup, then a chicken Waterzooi or mushroom omelette, with ice cream for dessert—and, of course, with service charges and taxes included.

Cheaper still ($6 to $8)

Now look to an adjoining side of the same, great Market Square, housing a remarkable "charcuterie" (delicatessen), the **Vandenhende Gastronomie,** whose displays of rainbow-colored appetizers, patés and cheeses in dozens of subtly-different varieties will awaken your appetite, no matter how recently you've eaten, and inspire you to plan a picnic meal along the Lake of Love—it is one of the finest charcuteries of Belgium. Off the side of this shop runs **St. Amand's Street** ("Sint-Amandstraat"), which widens, after 75 yards, into a little square housing the remarkable **Ristorante le Due Venezie.** There, for only 250 francs ($7), in normal, sit-down surroundings, you enjoy a three-course meal (service included) of minestrone, then veal cutlet Milanese or Cannelloni or Lasagne, then ice cream or fruit salad for dessert (and, for 330 francs, you substitute a Florence-style steak for the veal cutlet). Or you simply order "Spaghetti Fruits de Mer" (spaghetti with a seafood sauce of chopped clams, shrimps and the like) for 180 francs ($5), spaghetti Bolognaise (with meat sauce) for 150 francs ($4.17).

Fifty yards further up St. Amand's Street: a restaurant curiosity that proves strangely satisfying after a day or two of exotic, multi-course meals in Bruges. The **Chicken Inn,** at 31 St. Amandstraat, features one item: half a magnificently-roasted chicken, along which are ranged three different sauces into which you dip each tasty morsel. Together with the chicken, you receive two large chunks of bread, and the entire, three-sauced dish, which causes me to dream even as I type these words, costs only 180 francs ($5).

Rock-bottom (under $5)

"The People" eat at the Simon Stevin Square ("Simon Stevin Plein", named after a renowned Belgian mathematician), off the Steenstraat, the latter an important shopping street that runs from the Market Square to St. Saviour's Cathedral ("Sint Salvator"); the always-bustling little square, with its outdoor fountains, sidewalk tables and benches, is a block before the Cathedral, and houses a giant, permanently-mounted, waffles-and-french-fries stand selling Belgian fries covered with the sauce of a beef stew ("Frieten met Stoofvlees") for 160 francs ($4.44), french fries alone for 45 francs ($1.25), with mayonnaise an extra 10 francs. Alongside the stand: an early 17th-century building housing Bruges' version of **Pizza Hut,** perhaps the world's only Pizza Hut to sell accompanying glasses of red wine for 45 Belgian francs ($1.25), in addition to those standard pizzas. One mammoth variety, made for four persons, and known as a "Pizza Margherita" (but simply with tomatoes and mozzarella cheese), sells for 335 francs ($9.30)— that's $2.35 a person. Back on the Steenstraat, just before the Cathedral, the cafeteria of the **Sarma Department Store** is the major cheap eating place of Bruges, charging 165 francs ($4.58) for its large, daily, one-plate specials ("dagschotels"), only 130 francs ($3.61) for spaghetti bolognaise, only 35 francs (97¢) for beer, a Belgian record of some sorts! It remains open during normal department store hours, offers a wide selection of plates, and is heavily frequented by the craftier, cost-conscious citizens of Bruges.

A light snack

   · Civilized is what we'd call this last establishment. An almost unique Bruges tradition is the operation of small tea-shops in bookstores, and the upstairs tea-shop of **De Nieuwe Raaklijn,** at 3 Geldmundstraat (which runs off the "Eiermarkt" (Egg Market) at the edge of the "Grote Markt" (Market Square), is an outstanding example of this wonderfully cultivated approach to literature and life. Downstairs are the standard international magazines, newspapers, and Dutch and French-language books. Upstairs is an especially large display of English-language Penguin paperbacks, the famed English line of both modern and ancient classics, and adjoining the books is a quiet counter and tables frequented by the most appealing residents of Bruges, quiet, modest, unassuming, intelligent. You select a Penguin book—say, Aldous Huxley's *Point Counter Point;* then sit at the counter to enjoy moderately-priced light sandwiches and tea, salads, or—as I recently did—a two-egg "uitsmijter" with ham (bread, topped with ham, topped with two fried eggs, garnished with pickles and lettuce, a light meal) for 80 francs ($2.22), accompanied by beer for 35 francs (97¢); and you read the Penguin book while munching, all the while enjoying soft breezes that stir through curtained-windows into the delightfully-silent tea shop/bookstore. Bruges at its best! And whether you then buy the book—is up to you.

THE TREASURES OF BRUGES

You are now about to take a short walk—short in distance, but important in depth, a stroll that passes institutions housing at least a dozen of the world's greatest masterpieces, from Memling to Michelangelo (yes, Michelangelo), all presented in a setting of ethereal architectural beauty, all capable of being seen in a day or less. It starts at the Market Square ("Grote Markt"), goes on to the Burg, proceeds to the Rozenhoedkaai (where you digress a bit for a canal boat tour), and then heads up the world's most concentrated Museum Street, the canal-lined "Dijver". The experience reaches a form of crescendo at the Groeninge Museum (for the "Hall of the Flemish Primitives"), then attains an Apocalyptic Climax at the Hospital of St. John (Memling!), after which it's emotionally downhill to the Church of Our Lady (Notre Dame) and the Cathedral of St. Saviour (Sint Salvator)—places that anywhere else would be regarded as sights of surpassing importance. There is a largely-untranslatable French word—"bouleversé" (roughly, "turned upside down", "shaken up", "made dizzy")—which alone can describe my own emotions on the day when I first took the Classic Walk of Bruges.

THE "GROTE MARKT" (MARKET SQUARE):

> *"In the marketplace of Bruges stands the Belfry*
> *Old and brown;*
> *Thrice consumed and thrice rebuilded, still it*
> *Watches 'oer the Town"*
>
> —Henry Wadsworth Longfellow,
> *"The Belfry of Bruges"*

We begin at the great Market Square ("Grote Markt") of Bruges, where a lively open market once did take place every Saturday morning until 1 p.m. At one side of the Square: the awesome **Belfry of Bruges,** built in the 1200s, in one of those perfectly proportioned shapes that makes a breath-catching masterpiece out of a simple tower (the tower of the Palazzo della Signoria in Florence comes to mind as yet another such example). This one is mammoth in width and depth, yet "as delicate as a vase", its summit a crown celebrating the ancient liberties and privileges of Bruges. Inside: the world-famous carillon bells that chime briefly every quarter hour, and were heard by Memling and Van Eyck just as you are hearing them now. (Hour-long carillon concerts are presented weekly, on designated evenings in summer, at mid-day on weekends and Wednesdays all other times.) You can glimpse the carillons by attempting the exhausting, 366-step, circular climb to the top of the Belfry Tower (50 francs), from which most of Flanders, and even the sea, are spread out before you.

The American poet, Henry Wadsworth Longfellow, climbed there before you, on a dark, winter morning more than a century ago, and the sound of the bells of Bruges "seemed like a heart of iron beating in the ancient tower," causing visions of a glorious past to cross his mind as he gazed down upon the square below:

> *"I beheld the pageants splendid, that adorned those days of old;*
> *Stately dames, like queens attended, Knights who bore the Fleece of Gold,*
> *Lombard and Venetian merchants, with deep laden argosies,*
> *Ministers from twenty nations, more than royal pomp and ease*
> *I beheld the Flemish weavers, with Namur and Juliers bold*
> *Marching homeward from the bloody battle of the Spurs of Gold*
> *Hours had passed away like minutes, and before I was aware*
> *Lo! The shadow of the Belfry crossed the sun illumined square."*

The building from which the Belfry soars is the **Halles** (literally, "Halls"), equally distinguished, almost fully as old (late 1200s), once used for various trading and commercial purposes, now the home of the Bruges tourist information office in its right-hand wing (as you face it). Around the remainder of the square are buildings from every century of the late Middle Ages, but the most imposing of them—the Provincial Palace, housing government offices of West Flanders—is a trompe l'oeil disappointment, a neo-Gothic structure built towards the end of the 19th century, and unable, for reasons that one might ponder, to match the majesty and strength of such medieval works as the Halles and the Belfry. Still, the effect of the entire square is overwhelming, unforgettable, fit witness to the power, color and excitement of a mighty medieval city. Of particular interest is the little, castle-like building called the "Cranenburg" on the corner of Sint Amandstraat, where Maximilian of Austria—first of the Hapsburgs in Flanders—was kept prisoner for a time in the late 1400s. An unpopular foreigner following the death of his wife, Mary of Burgundy, in a hunting accident, Maximilian sought to quarter German troops in Bruges, and otherwise seemed to threaten the independence, privileges and pocketbooks of the city. Its citizens locked him in the Cranenburg, where they forced him to watch the trials and executions of numerous of his followers (including a servant named Peter Lanchals) taking place directly in the Square. When Maximilian, after much complex negotiation, was finally released and restored to power, he required that Bruges show its penance for the murder of poor Lanchals by maintaining swans, for all posterity, in the canals of Bruges!

> *"I beheld poor Maximilian kneeling humbly on the*
> *ground,*
> *I beheld the gentle Mary, hunting with her hawk and*
> *hound."*

In the middle of the Square: the statues of butcher Jan Breydel and weaver Pieter de Coninck, who inspired the uprising in 1302 by artisan-workmen of the Guilds against the French-supporting, wealthy patricians and merchants who hitherto had dominated the Guilds. In the event known as the "Matines of Bruges" (pictured in a bas-relief at the base of the joint statue), these patricians were awakened early in the morning (hence, "matines") and murdered; two months later, the same enraged artisans went off to defeat the knights of France at the Battle of the Golden Spurs near Courtrai (Kortrijk), and the return of the troops of Bruges from that battle is also portrayed in a bas-relief at the base of the statue. Violence and beauty, swans and golden spurs—the "Grote Markt" of Bruges!

THE BURG: From the dazzling Market Square, one walks down the single-block-long **Breidelstraat** (lined, on the right, with lace shops) to the second major and majestic square of Bruges, the **Burg.** It was to this historic location that, in 827, the very first Count of Flanders, a Frankish adventurer named Baldwin of the Iron Arm ("Bras de Fer"), brought his 20-year-old bride, Judith, whom he had abducted from her father, the King of France. Enraged, the King had pursued the newlyweds, hounded and excommunicated them, then reluctantly accepted the marriage when he feared that his son-in-law might ally himself with the fearsome Viking invaders of Northern Europe. Accordingly, he invited Baldwin and Judith to check the Viking advance by taking up residence and a "fiefdom" at a waterside "landing stage" (a "brygghia") that the Vikings had already established on marshy lands near the North Sea. This "brygghia" became Bruges, and Baldwin established a fortified castle (which no longer exists) as the centerpiece of what then became a populated area—a "Burg"—in the Brygghia. In later years, the Carolingian-style St. Donatian Cathedral also arose on the Burg; it was destroyed, dismantled brick by brick, by religion-hating zealots of the French Revolution during the annexation of Flanders to France in the 1790s.

What does remain on the Burg is equally important: the Town Hall of Bruges, the Basilica of the Holy Blood, the Palace of Justice.

The Town Hall of Bruges

Oldest town hall in Belgium (1376), it is certainly one of the most beautiful, a Gothic wedding cake of pointed spires and elaborate statuary adorning the stone facade in uniform rows, the effect marred only by the fact that most of the statues were removed from their niches and destroyed by those soldiers of the French Revolution in 1795—they have not been replaced, though plans are constantly announced to do so. Inside, you wander about through lobby and halls till you see the evocative painting of the Burgomaster receiving Napoleon on his visit to Bruges, then return to the lobby and immediately head up the red-carpeted stone staircase to your left to the immense, scarlet-colored **Gotische Zaal** ("Gothic Room"), with its stalactite-like ceiling completed in 1402. The immense pride of medieval people in their civic institutions, the majesty and might of medieval cities, literally resounds from the lavish detailing and decor of the walls, ceiling and floor of this richly-ornamented chamber. Have you ever seen a latter-day civic room, or a meeting room anywhere, to equal it?

A much later addition to the splendor of the Gothic Room are its dozen wall murals completed in 1895; imagine them as bearing consecutive numbers starting near the chimney piece, and you'll enjoy a mini-course in the history of Bruges by perusing: 3 (Derek of Alsace, Count of Flanders, arriving with the Relic of the Holy Blood in 1150); 6 (Philip of Alsace, a later Count of Flanders, granting a charter to Bruges in 1190); 1 (The Triumphant return of the troops of Bruges from the Battle of the Golden Spurs in 1302); 4 (Lodewijk of Male, Count of Flanders, laying the cornerstone of the Town Hall in 1376); 5 (A burgomaster of Bruges visiting the studio of Jan van Eyck in 1433). Later, in the mid-1400s, the highly cultivated, art-loving Burgundian Dukes thought enough of this room to choose it for their most important "States General"—parliamentary-like advisory councils—of the Low Countries (Belgium and Holland), and their regard for this resplendent room has been maintained by every subsequent ruler and civil body of Bruges. Your 30-franc entrance fee admits you also to an adjoining small, civic museum where a painting on the far wall depicts the Burg in the days before St. Donatian's Cathedral was destroyed.

The Basilica of the Holy Blood

Next door: an equally remarkable structure, equally famed for what it contains: which is nothing less than the purported substance of Divinity.

A holy Relic. When knights returned from the Crusades, they often returned with Relics—a fragment of the True Cross, a tiny branch from the Crown of Thorns. But when Derek of Alsace, Count of Flanders, returned to Bruges in 1150 from the Second Crusade, he brought back the Relic that staggered all of Europe: a cloth allegedly soaked with the blood of Christ. It was immediately placed in the Burg, in the Chapel of St. Basil, now the "Basilica of the Holy Blood", where it is displayed to the public every Friday morning throughout the year from 8:30 a.m. to 11:45 a.m.

The awesome artifact is kept today in a small glass vial, in an open container of gold that is placed, on those Fridays, on an elevated side altar in the Upper Chapel, behind which sits a priest flanked by an armed city policeman and a member of the 40-person, centuries-old "Confraternity of the Holy Blood", ultimate guardian of the Relic. Solemnly, the faithful line up to view and kiss the vial, after first depositing 10 francs in a coin collection box nearby. After each kiss, the priest carefully wipes dry the vial. "Why don't you go up to see it?" suggested the devout lady guide who first showed me through. "But I'm not a Catholic", I protested. "Oh, everyone goes to see it," she responded with typical Belgian tolerance. And after making my 10 franc offering, I ascended the stairs, stooped down to view (without kissing) the glass-enclosed brown stain of blood on the fragment of cloth, and passed on without protest from policeman, priest or guardian. You, too, can do the same.

The Basilica, built in the 1100s, was once a thoroughly Romanesque structure, and its downstairs interior still is—probably the purest example of Romanesque architecture you will see in Belgium, with its distinctive rounded arches and heavy pillars, its squat and horizontal lines, its gloomy, stone interior with poignant statues of the crucified Jesus. Upstairs everything changes! Now the Basilica becomes a green-and-yellow fairyland of emeralds and gilt, of rich panelling, paintings, striped ornaments of every sort, a dazzling display of both Gothic and Renaissance elements that, in later centuries, completely transformed the formerly-Romanesque facade and upper story of the building into a Venetian-like palace-of-a-church. A wide stone staircase worn by the feet of millions of pilgrims leads both to the upper story (where admission is free) and adjoining museums (20 francs) housing the ornately-figured reliquaries—golden containers or casques—associated with the Relic.

If you are lucky enough to be in Bruges on Ascension Day (May 4, 1989; May 24, 1990), you can see the 1½-hour "Procession of the Holy Blood" honoring the Relic, as it winds through the streets of Bruges past tens-of-thousands of spectators, re-creating—in marching tableaux—both Old and New Testament epics preceding the death of Christ. Adam and Eve, Abraham and Isaac, Roman centurions on horseback, Christian disciples, all depicted by citizens of Bruges in authentic costumes, singing, miming and declaiming the Biblical events as they pass before you, presenting in effect a yearly Passion Play on the streets of Bruges, uncovering that intense strain of Catholic belief in Northern Flanders.

For at least one week prior to the Procession (and often for a longer time in May), the Relic of the Holy Blood is on continuous display in the Upper Basilica; it is then carried through the streets of Bruges at the end of the Procession, attended by a Bishop of the Church. A Great Event of Europe, this is only one of those many colorful festivals, processions, joyous gatherings and celebrations that make up the very fabric of Belgium, the glittering nation of color and pageantry.

The Palace of Justice

Recommended to the lawyers among our readers, for the opportunity it provides to witness Belgian court proceedings. You need only enter the Palace quietly, and proceed to the audience section of several courtrooms where you'll hear oral arguments (in Dutch) presented to a trio of questioning judges by lawyers attired in the distinctive black gowns and long, white collars of the bar of Bruges. Or, for a courtroom that witnesses actual civil and criminal trials, look for the outdoor sign pointing to the "Museum of the Brugse Vrije" to the right of the main entrance (as you face it), where a fascinating glimpse of proceedings—the defendant flanked by two armed policemen, undergoing questioning directly from a bench of judges—can often be had. At the back of this latter courtroom is then the door to the "Alderman's Room" of Bruges with its world-famous **Chimney Piece** built for Charles V in 1529—this should be seen. Further along this side of the square: the **"Provost's House"** (Deanery), formerly housing officials of the now-destroyed St. Donatian's Cathedral, and the stunning **"Old Recorder's House"** built in the 1500s, complete the major structures of the peaceful Burg, whose ghosts date back to the birth of Bruges!

ROZENHOEDKAAI: From the Burg, walk down the little, archway-covered **"Blinde Ezelstraat"** ("Blind Donkey Street", after the blindfolded beast that marched on a treadmill to grind grain in the Middle Ages) and turn sharp right past the Building of the Fishermen's Guild (see the crossed fishes in front) into the tiny Huidenvettersplein Square, site of the interesting Tanners' Guild House. If you had turned left instead, you would have walked to the stone counters and colonnades of the Bruges fish market, where you can consume one of those marvelous, fresh, raw Dutch herrings from neighboring Holland, covered with grated onions, for only 60 francs ($1.67).

A canal-boat tour

Here at the Huidenvettersplein one encounters the first of the several boat-dock departure points for a deservedly-famous, not-to-be-missed canal cruise of Bruges. The company called **"Venetie van het Noorden"** (Venice of the North) is one of five such firms clustered in the area, all of which charge 110 francs ($3.05) for a virtually identical, 40-minute cruise of the spectacular vistas afforded to visitors by the peaceful, dream-like canals of Bruges; another such firm departs from a landing on the Rozenhoedkaai a few yards away. Depending on the time of day and your schedule, you'll either want to interrupt your Classic Walk for an immediate cruise, or return at a later time for what is an indispensable activity on your first visit to Bruges; the boats depart not at set times, but simply whenever sufficient people cluster to fill one boat, and the degree of imminence of such a departure —which you can judge on the spot—might also affect the timing of your cruise. Whatever you decide, you'll soon be floating past swans and ducks, viewing ancient brick and trailing vines, gracefully drooping trees, and the almost unique alternation of architectural styles that is a treasure of Bruges: the Middle Ages, the late Gothic period of that time, the Burgundian era, the northern Renaissance, the frivolous Baroque of the Counter-Reformation, the 17th century—and almost nothing of a later time! You return to your departure point at the Huidenvettersplein (from which you then walk a few yards to the Rozenhoedkaai) or to Rozenhoedkaai direct (if you started from there). At the Rozenhoedkaai, where camera enthusiasts react frenziedly to the enthralling sight of intersecting, medieval canals, you look to one side and discover the canal and street called the **"Dijver"** (pronounced "diver"), flanked further up by a narrow park on which antiques are displayed for sale every Saturday morning. You Have Arrived—at the Street of Museums!

THE DIJVER—"MUSEUM STREET": The Groeninge Museum, the Arents Museum, the Gruuthuse—you'll pass them in quick order as you walk up the Dijver, along the canal, towards the Church of Our Lady, which you will see in the distance. Reaching Mariastraat, you then turn left and find the 12th century Hospital of St. John, with its Memling Museum, across the street. If you plan to visit all four museums (and you should), buy a "Combination Ticket" for 200 francs ($5.56) at the first museum you visit, permitting you to visit all four; otherwise you'll pay 80 francs per museum.

The Groeninge Museum

One of the two sublime museum experiences of Bruges (the other is the Memling), this is the home, the shrine, the ark, of the Flemish Primitives. Though the "primitives" are displayed in museums and churches all over Belgium, nowhere else are so many major 15th century works (a full thirty of them) clustered as here. Everyone except Dirck Bouts is represented: Van Eyck and Memling, Rogier Van der Weyden, Hugo van der Goes, Petrus Christus, Gerard David, Hieronymous Bosch, and the various anonymous "Masters" of various schools and subjects. Here are the bright and luminous tones resulting from the world's first use of pigments mixed with oil (see Chapter III), the photographic realism and exquisite precision, the magnificent grouping of figures, the pure and unquestioning religious belief of "the Age of Faith", the painstaking devotion of long months and indeed years to a single painting, with which the Flemish greats of the 1400s so stunned the artistic world of that time.

The museum itself (open daily from 9:30 a.m. to 6 p.m. from April through September; open daily except Tuesday the remainder of the year, this time from 9:30 a.m. to noon, and from 2 to 5 p.m., always for an admission charge of 80 francs) is a smallish place, like a simple, one-story-high convent in style, its contents compressed into exactly 15 small, whitewashed rooms bearing consecutive numbers, through which you should walk consecutively—and therefore chronologically. Rooms 1 through 5 house the "primitives", while the higher-numbered rooms then trace the development of Belgian painting (especially from the area of Bruges) into modern times.

Rooms 1 through 5: The supreme work (room 1) is Jan Van Eyck's **Madonna with Canon Joris van der Paele** (1436) commissioned for the now-destroyed St. Donatian Cathedral in Bruges by the eminent, white-chaliced churchman shown kneeling in the painting as he is presented to Mary and the baby Jesus by a hat-tipping St. George, his patron saint, while a magnificently-garbed St. Donatian looks on. The five figures, and especially the textures of the clothes and chain-mail they wear, are caught as if by a camera, while the expression on Canon van der Paele's face is an unforgettable combination of strain, awe and overwhelming emotion; how else would such a figure react upon being presented to the Divinity he had served all his life? Nearby: the only surviving secular painting by Van Eyck (as best I know)—a brutally honest portrait, blemishes and all, of his wife, Margaret. It carries its original frame, on which is written in Latin: "My husband Jan finished me in the year 1439 on June 17—my age was thirty-three." Note that a portrait of Christ in the same room is characterized as being "Naar van Eyck"—"after" Van Eyck—the word "naar" indicating, as it does of several other paintings in the Groeninge, that the work is a copy, not the original, of an artist's masterpiece, or else is done in the style of the master.

Nine other works are standouts in the "Hall of the 15th Century Flemish Primitives" (rooms 1 through 5): Rogier van der Weyden's **St. Luke Painting the Virgin** (1435) (since Luke was Patron Saint of the Painter's Guild, the "biographer" of Mary is here portrayed as creating a portrait of her; note the two, interesting secular figures in the background who gaze out on an almost-abstract, white-capped waterway that flows alongside a Flemish town); the "modern" and mildly-abstract **Isabel of Portugal with St. Elizabeth** by Petrus Christus (1457), thought to be the left panel of a triptych commissioned by Isabel; Gerard David's "diptych" (two paintings) known as **The Judgment of Cambyses** (1498) (showing the conviction and punishment of a corrupt Persian judge, condemned to be skinned alive; I confess I find it impossible to look at the judge in his awful agony portrayed through his by-then catatonic face; the painting hung for centuries in the Town Hall of Bruges as an admonition to the politicians of Bruges); David's **Baptism of Christ** (1499?) (a rich combination of graceful figures, landscapes, flowers and embroidered cloths, and famed as much for the exquisite grouping of little girls, daughters of the donors, shown in the right-hand panel, as you face it; cup your hand about your eye to blot out all but the little girls, and see what an enchanting tableau results); Hugo van der Goes' **Death of the Virgin** (1480) (the apostles gathered in despair about the deathbed of Mary, the whole suffused with an unusual and unforgettable bluish-white light; this was van der Goes' last picture, painted shortly before he died of melancholia); Hans Memling's **Moreel Triptych** (1484) (commemorating the two, serene, brown-garbed saints shown in scenes of paradise in the center panel, which is flanked by panels of the donor (a Bruges alderman named William Moreel) and his wife, both shown with their respective patron saints, sons and daughters; nearby, two independent panels of angels done for another triptych in hues of grey—so-called "grisailles" (gray wings, or panels)—are also by Memling); the terrifying, surrealistic **Last Judgment** by Hieronymus Bosch (1499?) (fire and brimstone approaches from afar to engulf the world); the 10-panel **Ursula Legend** by an unknown master (1482) (obviously influenced by Memling, whose masterpiece—the Shrine of St. Ursula—and the underlying Ursula legend, are discussed in our description of the Memling Museum, later in this chapter); and the strong portrait of **Louis de Gruuthuse** by still another unknown master (1472) (depicting the powerful Lord of the Gruuthuse mansion that we'll be visiting, a few feet up from the Groeninge; the emblem of the Order of the Golden Fleece, founded by Philip the Good, Duke of Burgundy, hangs from a chain around his neck).

Rooms 6 and 7: Flemish painters of the 16th century, of which Pieter Pourbus was incontestably the most important (see, in particular, his portraits of Jan van Eyewerve and Jacquemyne Buuck as they stand before the same window looking out on a scene of Bruges). **Room 8:** Flemish painting of the 17th century (Jacob van Oost the Elder the most important, a portraitist who mirrors the movement of that age from purely religious to strictly secular concerns; see his superb **Portrait of a Bruges Family** (1645) strolling in the sun, and catch the little boy in the bottom right-hand corner, a copy of his tall, stout father). Nicolaas Maes, an important Dutch painter of the 1600s, is also found in Room 8. **Rooms 9 and 10:** Flemish painters of the 18th century, especially Jan Garemijn of Bruges, whose **Digging of the Ghent Canal** (between Bruges and Ghent) (1752) is an important, panoramic *tour de force*. Room 10 contains a freely-translated, white marble copy by Jean-Robert Calloigne of Michelangelo's **Madonna and Child** in Bruges' Church of our Lady (discussed later in this chapter), interesting mainly for the opportunity it provides to gauge the vastly superior artistic genius of Michelangelo (when, later in your Bruges stay, you see the real thing). **Rooms 11 and 12:** Belgian art of the 19th century, among which Edmund van Hove's **Life's Sunset** is, to some, particularly moving. **Rooms 13, 14 and 15:** Modern Belgian art of the 20th century—including Servaes, Permeke, Magritte, Delvaux; there are better examples of these modern masters in other Belgian museums. But as you walk into the Groeninge's concluding room, 15, excitement mounts again with the Pop Art of the highly contemporary Roger Raveel (he of the

Brussels subway—see our Brussels chapter), with the vibrant Raoul de Keyser, with Pol Mara, and especially with the sculpture of an amazingly-lifelike young woman seated on the museum's floor gazing pensively at scattered photos—Jacques Verduyn's **Kate and her Photos** (1978).

To your bemused surprise, you exit Room 15 just 10 feet away from where you entered Room 1—the "Hall of the Flemish Primitives". In an hour or so, you have traced the entire course of Belgian Art from the Virgin Mary of Van Eyck's **Madonna with Canon van der Paele** to **Kate and her Photos,** all at a museum ranked high, with great reason, among the riches of Belgium. The Groeninge!

The Arents Museum

Up the street, again alongside the Dijver: the rather minor **Arents Museum** ("Ärentshuis"), in the rich, patrician home of the Bruges family of that name, displaying impressive oil paintings of various historical phases of Bruges, but far less interesting examples of chinaware, silver and pewter, and several upstairs rooms of ink sketches and paintings by an English painter of the second rank, Frank Brangwyn—he bequeathed them to Bruges. Although the Arents can be skipped if you're short of time, you will at least want to dart inside the courtyard for a free look at a glassed-in carriage museum of Bruges attached to the main house. Visiting hours for both are 9:30 to noon and 2 to 6, closed Tuesdays in winter; admission 80 francs to the main exhibit.

The Gruuthuse

A few steps further up the Dijver, and we are back—unmistakably—to a major sight: the **Palace of Gruuthuse.** In the brilliant Belgian era of the Dukes of Burgundy (1388 to 1477), then the richest sovereigns of Europe, more wealthy than the kings of France, the most powerful of the Flemish nobles serving those Dukes were the Gruuthuse clan. This is their home, appropriately splendid. Here lived Louis de Gruuthuse, vigorous into his 80s, when he served as stand-in for Maximilian of Austria in the proxy marriage to Maria of Burgundy, daughter of the last Burgundian duke, Charles the Bold. Glitter and size, glorious artifacts of those days, await you within. And if you'd care to glimpse the gulf that separated such a man as Louis de Gruuthuse from the ordinary citizens of Bruges, walk immediately to Room 17 upstairs. This was the Gruuthuse private chapel, its windows cut into the wall of the immense, adjoining Church of Our Lady, so that Louis and the Gruuthuses could witness and attend services from their own home, unsullied by the presence of common folk! The gall of it all!

Two thousand three hundred fifty-nine numbered household and decorative items of antiquity are displayed in the labyrinth of rooms and winding stone staircases that make up the Gruuthuse, including paintings by various minor masters of Bruges (Nos. 1 to 72), illustrated panels of wood and wood sculpture (Nos. 100 to 282), stone sculpture (Nos. 300 to 438), 15th- to 18th-century furniture (Nos. 500 to 632), textiles, tapestries, embroidery and lace (Nos. 1150 to 1260; rooms 18 and 19 are extraordinary in their displays of lace), weapons (Nos. 1900 to 1969), and musical instruments (Nos. 2250 to 2311, in rooms 11 and 12, an especially important collection), not to mention cooking utensils and tools of past centuries, plaques, glassware, ceramics, iron chains, shackles; the purchase of a 5-franc, English-language catalogue of exhibits, sold at the entrance, is a must. Though most items postdate the actual time of the Gruuthuses, enough relates to the 15th and 16th centuries to provide you with a sense of the manner in which such over-privileged nobility lived. And there still remains, boldly painted, carved and etched, constantly re-appearing in the entrance hall and throughout the building, Louis of Gruuthuse's challenging motto: "Plus est en vous", "Plus est en vous"— "More is in you", "You are better than you think", the proud and confident exhortation of a soldier/diplomat/patron of the arts who left his mark on Bruges. If you will wander relaxed through the Gruuthuse, pausing at leisure to fantasize about those times, you will enjoy an indelible experience of history. The Gruuthuse is open 9:30 to noon and 2 to 6, daily in spring and summer, daily except Tuesdays at all other times. Admission is 80 francs.

The Hospital of St. John (and Memling Museum)

Though there is more to come, nevertheless the heart-pounding climax of your walk through Bruges is the **Hospital of St. John,** with its remarkable **Memling Museum,** both reached by turning left at the Mariastraat, at the end of the Dijver. Built in the 12th century and magnificently preserved, this was (and partially is) a working, charitable hospital of the Middle Ages, one of whose wards is depicted in an ancient painting hung near the main entrance: there you see the very same large room of arches, pillars and brick walls that now stands before you, but lined in those days with compact, wooden, sleeping cubicles in which two and more patients would be crammed for warmth; the painting shows it all. To the side of the main entrance is the picturesque and fully-furnished Apothecary Room of those ancient days, which also should be seen, but the primary reason you are here is the **Museum of Hans Memling,** the painter who belongs as much to Bruges as Brueghel belongs to Brussels, Van Eyck to Ghent, Rubens to

Antwerp. He arrived here in the 1450s to study at the studio of Rogier van der Weyden (by whom he was greatly influenced), stayed on in a city whose cultural life had soared under the Dukes of Burgundy, and soon became the leading painter of Bruges. His museum here, itself a 13th-century sick ward, consists of one, large, high-ceilinged room containing only six of his works, but they are enough, more than enough; they alone overwhelm the senses. And they include Memling's incomparable **Shrine of St. Ursula,** which experts have named as one of the Seven Wonders of Belgium. We'll discuss it last.

The St. John Altarpiece: As I write these words, I have on my desk a five-panel, stand-up postcard-reproduction sold at the Memling Museum of Memling's great triptych/altarpiece, the **Mystic Marriage of St. Catherine** (1479), one of the six works displayed. Tiny as it is, it acts like a steely magnet, throbs with vibrant color, invites a never-tiring study. On a richly-brocaded throne atop an oriental rug so real you could touch it, sits the Virgin Mary engrossed in a book held by an angel. On her lap the Baby Jesus; on one side, St. Catherine of Alexandria in a red-velvet blouse with white tunic, a brocaded skirt of gold and black; on the other, St. Barbara in rich green and brown. Everyone is reading, or staring into the distance, while a red-haired harpist plays in the background; no one seems aware that the baby Jesus is placing a ring of betrothal on Catherine's finger. The scene is silent, motionless, mystical, endlessly puzzling but unforgettable.

In the story drawn from the Golden Legend of saints, passed on through the re-telling of it throughout Medieval Europe, Catherine of Alexandria was a young woman of noble birth who lived in the 4th century, and was famous for her intellect, beauty and fierce chastity; she yearned never to be touched by unholy hands, had visions of being married to the one worthier suitor, the Son of God. She converted the wife of a Roman emperor and numerous followers to Christianity, causing the emperor to convene an assembly of 50 pagan philosophers to debate and convert her—instead, they were confuted and converted by Catherine (and instantly executed). Catherine was herself sentenced to be slashed to death by a wheel bearing sharp razors on its rim; as the whirling blades approached her, the wheel exploded, killing numerous bystanders. Catherine was then decapitated in the normal manner. At the instant of her death, a voice called from heaven: "Come join me, my beloved bride", and Catherine achieved her divine betrothal. Angels bore her body to the top of Mt. Sinai (where today's St. Catherine's Monastery commemorates the event), and Catherine became the much acclaimed patron saint of unmarried women, philosophers, schools, colleges; the "Catherine wheel" a much depicted symbol (it appears at the bottom of Catherine's cloak in the "Mystic Marriage" painting). Spinsters in the Middle Ages prayed to St. Catherine, as did Julie Andrews in a memorable scene from the musical, "Camelot".

Memling's response to the Catherine legend, the reaction of an artist full of love and goodness, a gentle man, was to create of Catherine, of Saint Barbara, of even the shiny-faced harpist, young women of an almost blinding inner beauty, princesses so pure, females so ideal and unworldly, as to constitute a milestone in art; stare closely upon them, and see if you agree. In the panel at the right of the Mystic Marriage scene: the vision of St. John the Evangelist on Patmos, dreaming of God on His throne, against a panoply of war; by itself, this is a supreme painting. In the left-hand panel: the martyrdom of St. John the Baptist, including a tiny vignette of the demand for his death, at upper left. And then there are the almost monochromatic outer panels of the work, portraying the friars and nursing nuns who commissioned the work and made themselves immortal.

Again by Memling: And in the very same room—the twin-painting "diptych" of burgher **Martin van Nieuwenhove** alongside the magnificently-composed **Virgin with Child and Apple;** the so-called **Floreins Altarpiece** donated to the Hospital by Jean Floreins (the gentleman with open Bible, at left) and depicting the Adoration of the Magi; the sensual, full-lipped painting of the blond **Sybylla,** her face partially covered by a diaphanous veil requiring unimaginable artistry and technique to portray; a small **Descent from the Cross.** But all else pales before the **Shrine to St. Ursula.** To appreciate it best requires that you know something of the story it depicts:

Ursula—the legend itself: No story so captivated the medieval mind as did the tale of St. Ursula and the 11,000 Virgins, a history seemingly corroborated by the discovery in the 12th century of a Cologne ossuary containing hundreds of female bones. Ursula was the ravishingly-beautiful daughter of a king of Brittany in the 4th century, whose hand was desired by the son of a pagan British king. To put him off, the deeply-Christian Ursula agreed to the marriage only if she could first make a three-year-long pilgrimage to Rome attended by ten maidens, each of whom would be further accompanied by a thousand virgins; and only if her suitor would also go to Rome to be baptized. The small female army traveled there via Cologne and Basle, in the first of which Ursula was advised by an angel of her coming martyrdom. In Rome, the devout group so charmed the Pope that he offered them his protection and impulsively decided to accompany the group on the return trip (perhaps sensing and desiring his own martyrdom).

Arriving in Cologne, they blundered into the armies of Attila the Hun, which proceeded to slaughter all but Ursula. Struck by her beauty, Attila offered to spare her if she would marry him; Ursula, steadfast as ever, refused and was killed. A terrible retribution was instantly visited upon the Huns by the citizens of Cologne.

The story, first transcribed by a monk of the Abbey at St. Omer in 975, swept across Europe, resulting in basilicas, monuments, devotions, paintings to Ursula, her mention in all the martyrologies, the increasing veneration of relics (skulls, ankles, shanks of hair) ascribed to her and her multitude of companions. When Christopher Columbus, sailing the Caribbean in 1493, espied a seeming multitude of small islands, he named them after "las once mil virgines"—the Virgin Islands! It was with this legend that Hans Memling was asked to decorate a small reliquary casque by two sisters, nuns, of the St. John Hospital in 1489. For nearly 350 years thereafter, the casque was stored away in the Hospital and exhibited to the public only on feast days. When that happened in the late 1500s, the painter Peter Pourbus would sit and gaze upon it for hours. Today, following the revival of interest in the long-neglected Hans Memling, it has been named one of the Seven Marvels of Belgium.

The Shrine to St. Ursula: The small box, less than three feet in length, is shaped like a small Gothic cathedral, gilded throughout, its major illustrations appearing in the arched spaces on both sides and ends. At one end: St. Ursula, like a giantess, spreads a protecting cloak around her ten main companions, all the while grasping the arrow with which she was killed. At the other end: the oft-repeated theme of the Virgin Mary offering an apple to the Baby Jesus, while at her feet the two nuns who had commissioned the work kneel in prayer. At one side: **Panel One** depicts the arrival at the dock in Cologne—the city's buildings portrayed exactly as they were. In the window of one, an angel foretells the coming tragedy to Ursula. At the right, one particular maiden wears her hair in pony-tail style; Ursula's is braided about her ears. **Panel Two:** the disembarking at Basle, and at the upper right, the young virgins, with walking sticks and warm scarves, proceed to cross the Alps. **Panel Three:** arrival in Rome, where the young ladies are received by a magnificently attired Pope, while male converts are baptized in a large stone basin.

On the other side: **Panel Four** shows the embarkation for Cologne, as the Pope and other churchmen join the group for the return trip. The sky is darkening. **Panel Five:** the surprise ambush upon arrival in Cologne! Barbarian swordsmen and archers proceed to the slaughter. **Panel Six:** Ursula is offered her life, but disdains the advances of the pagan leader, and is killed.

You may now recall in the Groeninge Museum, earlier visited, a much larger, nine-panel work by an unknown **Master of the Ursula legend,** also painted in the 1400s, tells the same story, in much greater detail and elaboration, with more numerous instances of *genre* — little scenes of commercial activity, the comings and goings of people within a cathedral. But in the scant space available to him, Memling has wrought an exquisite miracle. In each of six tiny panels, he has portrayed multiple scenes that unfold in a time sequence within each panel; he has made a magnificent whole of an odd-shaped box; recreated an entire medieval world of commerce, religion and war; conveyed a message of idealistic commitment; drawn faces, bodies and buildings of haunting loveliness within the space of a few centimeters. In the Hospital of St. John, near the enchanting canals of Bruges: the single greatest masterpiece in a city of artistic wonders.

The Church of Our Lady

Emerging from the Memling Museum and its ancient Hospital, you need only cross the street to visit the soaring, Gothic **Church of Our Lady** ("Onze-Lieve-Vrouwekerk", "Notre Dame"), built as early as the 12th century, and renowned, among other attributes, for its 360-foot-high, spiked, spire, highest in Flanders, and also because it serves as display case for the only statue by Michelangelo—"Madonna and Child", in carrara white marble—to have permanently departed from Italian soil. Purchased from the Italian genius by a wealthy Flemish merchant, it is perhaps one of his minor works, but a masterpiece nevertheless, which juxtaposes a delightfully human, cherubic and slightly pudgy, five-year-old Jesus, touchingly clinging to his mother's thumb for security and standing on the folds of her robe, with a more abstract and other-worldly Mary, obviously troubled by the eventual fate of her son; the statue is found in the right-hand apse of the church, behind a protective shield of glass. Half-way down the nave, a particularly glorious oak pulpit and canopy (designed by the same Jan Garemijn whose 18th-century **Digging of the Ghent Canal** we've admired in the Groeninge Museum) seems to be supported, improbably, on the right toes of the two angels flanking the pulpit. The massive, several-ton work is in fact suspended from the metallic sunburst above the canopy, a detail among hundreds that one might note in a church that surely must be ranked among the most impressive of Belgium's scores of Gothic churches and cathedrals, and contains numerous other outstanding paintings and features. Its most chilling possessions are in the choir; lying side by side, the two massive mausoleum tombs, topped by reclining bronze effigies, of Mary of Burgundy and her father, Charles the Bold, Duke of Burgundy, beneath which a portion of the church floor has been cut away, replaced by a thick pane of glass, and spotlighted, to reveal the actual simple coffin which recent studies have apparently shown to contain the actual remains of Mary of Burgundy (and a container with the heart of her son). Her own heart is in the tomb of her mother in the Antwerp cathedral. The floodlit coffin, displayed for all to see: was it the long Spanish occupation of Belgium that implanted this occasional taste for the morbid, the grisly, in the rituals of Flanders? Note how this particular display seems so better suited to the religious observances of Spain than to the tastes of the modern Low Countries. Overlooking all: the second story balcony of the Gruuthuse home, built into the wall of the church ambulatory (to the left as you face the mausoleums), from which Louis de Gruuthuse and family participated somewhat aloofly in the Masses observed downstairs. Beneath the windows through which they gazed, their motto confronted the worshipers below: "Plus est en vous". Entrance to the mausoleum area is from 10 to 11:30 a.m. and from 2 to 6 p.m., for an admission charge of 30 francs (83¢).

St. Saviour's Cathedral

From the Church of Our Lady, the 13th-century **Cathedral of St. Saviour** ("Sint Salvator", "Saint Saveur") is a two-minute walk up the Mariastraat into the Heilige Geeststraat. Already, you've undoubtedly glimpsed this great Gothic headquarters of the Bishop of Bruges; its extraordinary tower is topped by a strange, later, neo-Romanesque construction of several turrets, spires, multiple, columned buildings standing in the sky—the effect that of a little celestial city, yet utterly appropriate to its setting, and an example of how the mixture of architectural styles can nevertheless create impact and beauty. Inside, we are back to the Gothic, with numerous decorations from a later age, and with a particularly beautiful choir area of 48 stalls overhung with magnificent tapestries and surmounted with the coats of arms of members of the Order of the Golden Fleece, who met here in 1478. The highlight is a seven-room museum immediately to the right of the nave as you enter, where numerous reliquaries, displays of vestments, and paintings, include two important triptychs: Dirck Bouts' graphic **Martyrdom of St. Hippolytus** (1470) and Peter Pourbus' **Last Supper** (1599). The work by Bouts is a particular masterpiece from the age of the Flemish primitives, its central panel depicting the saint as he is about to be rent asunder by horses tied to each of his arms and legs, while the left-hand panel is of the donors of the painting, the right-hand one of a pagan emperor vainly attempting to persuade Hippolytus to renounce his faith. If only to see it, you'll want to add St. Saviour's to your itinerary through Bruges. The cathedral museum is open 2 to 5 p.m. (and also from 10 a.m. to noon in summer), daily except Wednesdays, for an admission fee of 30 francs (83¢).

The Beguinage and other sights

Important as it is, the Classic Walk of Bruges is only one of several recommended strolls, and dedicated sightseers will derive pleasure from simply walking at random in ever widening circles around the inner city areas somewhat further from the Grote Markt and the Burg; there, every one of a hundred medieval streets, many hundreds of ancient homes, nearly a dozen other major churches and chapels, throw off a continuing spell, and a full list of the additional museums, city gates, guild headquarters and convents of the city, would require many pages of this book. At least see the 13th-century **Beguinage,** where widows and spinsters of Bruges retreating from the pressures of city life went to live, in a walled-off, giant, grassy square surrounded by dignified small homes, calm and repose; there they conducted themselves almost as nuns, but without taking vows and with occasional contacts to the outside world. The Beguinage (inhabited today by Benedictine nuns) is near the Lake of Love, just north of the Minnewater Park; from St. Saviour's Cathedral, walk down the Heilige Geeststraat into the Katelijnestraat, and turn right at the Wijngaardstraat, soon crossing a tiny bridge over a canal to the Beguinage entrance. It stays open until 7 p.m. daily, one or two hours later than the museums of Bruges, and is a fitting cap to the end of day.

NIGHTLIFE AND EVENING ENTERTAINMENT: When twilight descends on the glitter and beauty of Bruges, most visitors simply enjoy long, lazy dinners, then wander along illuminated canals, then go to bed. Though there are Flemish-language theatres, a rich daily assortment of recitals and classic concerts (which culminate in the "Festival of Flanders" presenting noted artists and groups in churches and on concert stages around town during the first two weeks of August), an opera-presenting **Marionette Theatre** at 36 St. Jacobsstraat (phone 33-47-60; it performs late June to early-October only), and occasional splashy evening events at the 85-acre **Boudewijn Park,** Belgium's largest outdoor amusement complex found two kilometers outside the city at Bruges/St. Michiels, there is little nightlife of the sort meant for tourists, not even a red-light district (you go to Antwerp or Brussels for that!). Tourists with cars often head at night to the ultra-near Belgian Coast (20 minutes away), either for dinner or to gamble until morning at the elegant Casino of Knokke (see our chapter on the Belgian Coast), and more sensible tourists take in English-language films (presented without dubbing, as they always are in Flanders) at the several movie houses of Bruges, of which the ones with multiple showings (at least two different films each night) are the **Cine Memling**, at 19 Hoogstraat (phone 33-06-60); the **Cine Kennedy**, at 14 Zilverstraat (phone 33-20-70); and the **Komplex 't Gulden Vlies**, at 23 Kuiperstraat (phone 33-45-12). Most features begin at 8 and 10:30 p.m. Obviously, you can't expect to carouse until dawn, or enjoy bacchanals, in the city of the Holy Blood!

SHOPPING IN BRUGES: Lace is the classic tourist purchase,

but shopping opportunities of all sorts are surprisingly abundant. If you will simply stroll the several hundred yards of the **Steenstraat,** starting at the Market Square ("Grote Markt") and continuing to the area of St. Saviour's Cathedral, you'll pass dozens of reasonably-priced boutiques, chic shoe stores, all with state-of-the-art fashions, all displaying consistent good taste (as you'd expect in Bruges), and all crammed into that relatively short stretch of street. The **Zilverpand,** at the end of the Steenstraat off the Zilverstraat (again near the Cathedral), is then a multi-building shopping complex, modern but cleverly simulated to resemble ancient times, where high-quality merchandise of every sort is attractively presented.

The renowned lace-shops of Bruges are found all over the city, but clustered on the Breidelstraat leading off from the Market Square. **Huis Selection,** at 8 Breidelstraat, **Bobbin Lace Palace,** at 20 Breidelstraat, and **Oud Brugge,** at 22 Breidelstraat, are among the lace specialists, their choices ranging from an astonishing $8 for small handkerchiefs to several hundreds of dollars for richly-elaborate lace dresses or tablecloth sets; within the $20 to $40 area, you'll find dozens of coveted gift items whose Bruges label or packaging is guaranteed to thrill the recipient. How an exquisite, hand-made product can be sold so cheaply is a subject of continuing puzzlement to me. One establishment, the **"Little Lace Shop",** at 32 Wijngaardstraat (phone 33-64-06) near the Beguinage, actually guarantees the presence during shopping hours of an actual lace maker. From 9 to 6 on weekdays and Saturdays, from 10 to 1 and 2 to 5 on Sundays, except when she's in the back kitchen making coffee, the skilled artisan sits at a chair and large pin-cushion, utterly absorbed, her fingers flying like those of an enraptured pianist, the wooden spools clicking and clacking, the lace taking form before your eyes, a virtual miracle of complex construction. What emerges is exactly like the elaborate lace collars and cuffs on the strolling, 17th-century Bruges couple portrayed by Jacob van Oost the Elder in Room 8 of the Groeninge Museum.

Lace-making was a leading industry of Bruges in the city's poverty-stricken 1700s, when church-sponsored employment projects discovered a market for the highly-desired "Binche" or "Point de Fée" (Fairy Queen Stitch) components of Bruges-made lace. The direct descendant of lace-making convents and schools once maintained and taught by the Apostoline Sisters, is today's state-sponsored **Lace Center** ("Kantcentrum") of Bruges, at 3 Peperstraat (phone 33-00-72), where children as well as adults, foreigners as well as Belgians, are taught the art of lace-making in both full-time and part-time courses at tuition costs almost nominal in size. Although you may occasionally pass lace-making ladies seated at the doors of their homes in Bruges, this—and the "Little Lace Shop" earlier described—provides a guaranteed opportunity to witness the fascinating hand-crafting of lace. Like the carillons of the Belfry tower, lace is a Pride of Flanders.

BRUGES MISCELLANY: Despite all the wondrous cultural attractions of Bruges, it's hard not to revert eventually to the subject of food. And although I've earlier warned about the difficulty of obtaining a reservation at the renowned **De Snippe,** I can't resist telling about the seven-course "menu surprise" devoured there on my last visit: a small plate of tissue-thin and palely-pink smoked salmon covered with strawberry-flavored vinegar and spiced with red-and-yellow peppercorns, all of it like a tiny abstract painting; a salad of cold veal brains and strips of delicately-spiced roast chicken on a bed of clover and radicchio; then a bowl of tender, boiled scallops in a fish-stock soup; a tray of tiny, steamed "langoustines"—little crabs—which one sucked to extract their delectable meat; then a several-bite serving of assorted fish, shrimps and prawns broiled in an oil so hot that it continued to spit as it was set on the table; then the main course of rare roast duck and stuffed potato oozing with cream, scallions and chives; and the selection of any number of sweet fruit tarts and chocolate eclairs from a giant trolley. Total cost, including a bottle of young red Beaujolais (Villages), and coffee at the end: precisely 2600 francs ($72) per person, service included . . . Apart from obtaining them at the train station, bicycle rentals can be had in the center of Bruges, in the basement of **4 Hallestraat** at the side of the Bruges Tourist Office on the Market Square ("Grote Market") . . . Since times immemorial, walking on one's own two feet has been the preferred method of touring Bruges; yet amazingly, there's now (since 1983) a daily, 2¾ hour, escorted motorcoach tour of Bruges and vicinity that mainly concentrates on the sights outside the city gates: the Castle of Male, suburban Damme, the harbor of Zeebrugge, Dudzele, Lissewege, the barn of Ter Doest. It leaves twice a day (at 10 a.m. and 3 p.m.) from the Beursplein near 't Zand, costs 350 francs ($9.72) for adults, 175 francs ($4.86) for children under 12, and can be booked either at the departure point, at the Tourist Office (phone 33-07-11), or by phoning the motorcoach company, **Reiswijs,** at 35-83-08. . . . If, on a more traditional walking tour, you'd care to be accompanied by an experienced, personal guide, phone either the **Koninklijke Gidsenbond** (Royal Guide Association), at 38-40-06, or the **Westflaamse Gidsenkring,** at 82-32-02. Both charge $24 for two hours, $12 per hour thereafter, for the services of a dedicated resident and art historian of Bruges, some descended from the very people whose homes, paintings and tombs you'll be viewing.

INTO THE OUTSKIRTS

From all the many nearby sights of Bruges, we've chosen as your final visit:

AN EXCURSION TO DAMME: The young man heading the small tourist office of Damme gazed out from its Gothic main square onto the flat, green, polderland that stretches for miles to meet an almost limitless sky, the grassy expanse bisected by a straight canal heading towards the spires of Bruges, and involuntarily, as if I were not there, he gasped aloud: "It is a place to love!" Damme, the ancient port of Bruges, four miles from its outskirts, is a tiny replica of Bruges set in a rural scene so beautiful that one talks in whispers as one drives along the thin line of leaning poplars that flank its roads. It is an example of how medieval Europeans endowed even the smaller towns with architectural glory. The Gothic city hall of Damme, one-twentieth the size of Brussels', is an exquisite gem. The main market square, one-tenth the size of Antwerp's, is a ravishing space. The council chamber of Damme, one-sixth the size of Bruges' Gothic Room, compares respectably to it!

Damme (so named after "De Dam"—the dike—built here on the waterway serving Bruges) purchased its civic freedom from a Count of Flanders more than 800 years ago (in 1180, to be exact) and reached its peak of importance in the 14th and early 15th centuries as the bustling port of Bruges—as Bruges went, so went Damme. Ships actually sailed on the Zwin to a point just in back of the present city hall, where they discharged their wares into a vaulted, ground-floor market warehouse ("halles"), still partially existing today, of that same town hall. Because Damme also possessed the right of the "staple" over wine and herring—various medieval powers of inspection and taxation relating to those goods—its commercial importance was immense, its name renowned (the world's maritime laws of the sea were actually called the "zeerecht van Damme", "droit maritime de Damme"), and merchants all over northern Europe purchased their "Muscadeele" wines, their "Bourgoengen", from famous wine wholesalers located in Damme—yes, Damme! How fleeting is the quality of fame! Regularly pillaged and burned to the ground by various invaders, especially the French, it rebuilt each time and maintained its commercial vigor until the mid-15th century when the continued silting of the Zwin caused ship traffic to cease. Thereafter, its population drifting away, Damme became a garrison town for various invading armies. In 1810, the latest in its line of rulers, none other than Napoleon Bonaparte, himself conceived the idea of a new canal that would link Damme (and therefore Bruges) to the River Scheldt leading to the North Sea, enabling France to bypass the English blockade of the North Sea and Channel ports further to the west. But by the fall of Napoleon at Waterloo in 1815, that canal had been completed only as far as the small Dutch town of Sluis, across the border, and Damme was ever after condemned to lead a touristic, not a commercial, existence.

It is on that straight-as-an-arrow **Napoleon Canal** (the "Damse Vaart") that one most pleasurably makes the trip from Bruges to Damme today, floating for 35 minutes through a most typical and ethereally beautiful Flemish landscape of flat, green "polderland" (land once under water) until you see the giant windmill and white-washed, 18th-century farmhouse of St. Christopher (what a hotel it would make!) that heralds the start of Damme. The Bruges-to-Damme ferry, the **"Lamme Goedzak"**, makes the trip daily from April 1 to October 1 from the Noorweegse Kaai no. 31, leaving Bruges at 10 a.m., noon, 2 p.m., 4 p.m. and 6 p.m.; returning from Damme to Bruges at 9 a.m., 11 a.m., 1 p.m., 3 p.m. and 5 p.m.; by timing things right, you can spend one-to-five hours in Damme, either for a quick stroll-through, a leisurely lunch, or a thorough look. One-way fare is 100 francs ($2.78) for adults, 60 francs ($1.67) for children under 12. Or, you can rent a bicycle at the train station or in town (see "Bruges Miscellany", earlier) for the easily accomplished ride through pure country air on land flat as a board, or you can drive there or take a taxi (a maximum of $12, one way). If you do drive, make a detour first to the stately, 13th-century Abbey ("Abdij") of Male (St. Trudo) in Bruges/St. Kruis, a former castle of the Counts of Flanders six kilometers from Bruges, to see the controversial black-and-white paintings of the Passion of Christ by an early 20th century Belgian master, Albert Servaes, that cover one wall of the church; a nun will let you in when you ring the bell.

The residents of Bruges, those supreme gourmets, regard Damme as a culinary capital, and flock there at lunch and dinner to patronize no fewer than 22 restaurants in the tiny town, most of them clustered around the Market Square and on the street that then continues off the Market Square, the Kerkstraat. I like the big **Bij Lamme Goedzak,** at 13 Kerkstraat (closed weekdays in winter), the much smaller, costlier **Restaurant de Lieve,** at 10 Jacob van Maerlantstraat behind the Town Hall (closed Monday evenings and Tuesdays). Simply shop the window menus to select a restaurant in your own price range. The outstanding restaurant of the Damme area (you'll need a car), trembling on the brink of receiving its third star from the *Guide Michelin,* is Pierre Fonteyne's **Restaurant Bruegel,** at 26 Damsevaart Zuid (phone 050-50-03-46), three-or-so kilometers from Damme, seven-or-so kilometers from the sea, on the way to Oostkerke. Here, in a stunning one-room farmhouse surrounded by green fields and straight lines of trees, one of Belgium's great chefs offers a pencilled menu of classic local specialties, but at prices among the highest in the land, especially for his six-course "Menu 'Colibri' ". The latter contains such stunners as two contrasting, creamy patés ("les deux foies gras") to begin, broiled lobster flavored to resemble none you've previously had and accompanied by a delicate, cream-sauced spinach, lamb of the countryside with thyme sauce, more. The Bruegel is closed Tuesdays, Wednesdays, January and February, and you'll need a phoned reservation. The low-cost, "mass volume" restaurant of the Damme area, is a larger, multi-room farmhouse called **De Sifon,** near a road-crossing hamlet named Sifon, again on the way to Oostkerke, into whose windows I've peered on a day when it was closed, but haven't yet tried. Closed Tuesdays.

No one stays overnight in Damme; it has but one tiny hotel, the **Gasthof de Gulden Kogge,** on the Napoleon Canal at the entrance to town (phone 35-42-17), charging 1320 francs ($37) for a bathless double room; and the **Hungenaert** family, at 31 Kerkstraat (phone 35-33-56) takes in bed-and-breakfast guests for about 600 francs ($17) per person in a double room. Rather, after dining at one of the crowds of restaurants and drinking their visual fill of the extraordinary rural setting, most visitors quickly wander the eye-popping sights of the Gothic main square; they visit the magnificently-restored, mid-15th century Town Hall, successor to the earlier market hall built in 1241, and tour its Aldermen's Room and museum (ask someone to point out a "goedendag"— those vicious spiked balls used to such effect by the medieval soldiers of Flanders); they also gaze and visit at the two, extraordinary, 15th-century patrician homes jointly known as **"De Grote Sterre"** (the Great Star), diagonally across from the south corner of the City Hall—it later housed the Spanish military governor in the 17th century; they see the **Wyts House,** at the end of the Jacob van Maerlantstraat behind the Town Hall (with museum inside) that provided the romantic setting for the wedding in 1468 of Charles the Bold (last, major Duke of Burgundy) and Margaret of York (sister of the English king)—their statues adorn the two last niches on the right side of the Town Hall (as you face it); they walk several hundred peaceful steps to the quiet setting of the **Church of Our Lady,** parts of which were built in the 13th century, and also view its thoroughly 13th-century ruined tower, which seems to symbolize the decline and fall of Damme—astonishingly, that tower and its adjoining transept were deliberately demolished by church trustees in the early 1700s to conform the size of the church to the pitifully-reduced population of Damme; the transept arches are a magnificent specimen of the very earliest Gothic style, the main church is like an early Gothic poem, and contains, among many other furnishings and works, the miraculous "Cross of Damme" found floating in the sea by 13th-century fishermen and carried through the streets of Bruges each year thereafter in the Procession of the Holy Blood; after viewing the church, our hypothetical visitors wander the star-shaped dirt **ramparts** of the city which replaced its former walls in the early 1600s when military men considered the mound-shaped fortifications to afford better protection; they visit the remarkable, three-room museum of antiquities in the ancient **Hospital of St. John** (9:30 to noon and 2 to 6:30 p.m., but closed on Sunday mornings)—its central facade was built in 1250; they stand at the statue of 13th-century **Jacob van Maerlant,** "father of Dutch Poetry", in the Town Hall Square —he was born and buried in Damme; but mainly they return to the homes on the Market Square known as "De Grote Sterre" to visit the **Museum of Tijl Ulenspiegel,** on the second floor, just above the tourist office of Damme:

The Legend of Tijl Ulenspiegel

> *"A Damme, en Flandre, quand Mai ouvrit leurs fleurs aux aubépines, naquit Ulenspiegel, fits de Claes. . . ."*
> (At Damme, in Flanders, when May opened hawthorn blossoms to the sun, there came into this world Ulenspiegel, son of Claus)

With those immortal words, the Belgian novelist Charles de Coster opened his epic *Adventures of Tijl Ulenspiegel* (1867) set largely in Damme. An updated version of the story of a witty young man of Flanders that had been published in Europe as early as the late 1400s, de Coster's Tijl Ulenspiegel took as its main theme the revolt of the Netherlands against the 16th-century occupation and inquisition of Philip II of Spain, and cast the youthful rogue, Tijl Ulenspiegel, as a sort of ancient Lanny Budd or Captain Victor Henry, appearing everywhere, experiencing everything, of the struggle of the Lowlands against Spain. As befits a man of then-maritime Damme, Tijl Ulenspiegel even joins the "Sea Beggars"—the rebel Dutch/Flemish navy—in the latter stages of the war. Earlier, he had experienced the execution of his father as a heretic, burned at the stake; had undergone cruel tortures himself; yet relentlessly and undeterred, but keeping the good humor and sense of proportion of the typical Belgian, he had persevered in the fight for independence, in a novel variously known today as "the Bible of Flanders", the "breviary of freedom".

After each adventure, Tijl returned to Damme; and Damme today honors its native revolutionary with this interesting upstairs museum of the countless books, operas, symphonies, poems and works of art inspired by the pre-de Coster legend and the post-de Coster reaction, the latter to a book that gave a certain national consciousness to Belgium and pointed a new and more confident course to Belgian literature. The museum is open winter weekdays from 9 to noon and 2 to 6, winter weekends from 2 to 6 only; and then, in late spring, summer and early fall from 9 to noon and 2 to 6 on weekdays, 10 to noon and 2 to 6 on weekends. Admission is 20 francs.

CODA: If you will find a friendly official on your visit to the Town Hall of Damme, he or she may permit you to climb an interior or wooden staircase/ladder to the mechanism that works the clock of the belfry tower and rings its ancient bells. A massive and wonderfully complex machine of black iron shaped into intricate forms, utilizing pulleys and levers of every type, it will appear to you like a product of the Industrial Revolution, may even seem like machines of the current day. Then look at the inscription embossed in iron: it was built in 1459! How accomplished were these underrated people of the Middle Ages, how gifted and determined! In the sleepy, dreamy, softly beautiful sights of Bruges and Damme, we've gained a first glimpse of the events, achievements and outlook of that time; in powerful, turbulent Ghent—to which we next turn—we derive a wholly different and contrasting view that some visitors find even more edifying and of greater excitement.

CHAPTER VI

TURBULENT, SEETHING GHENT

□ □ □

. . . Where Medieval Europeans First Rose Against Privilege and Power

A lion rampant, shrieking out an angry challenge, on a giant, silken banner of scarlet and gold hung from a gilded Belfry tower. Ghent! From its medieval flag, still displayed throughout the city, ancient Ghent reveals itself in a single image. Ghent, the roaring lion of Flanders! Ghent, the throbbing, pounding Mill City of the Middle Ages, where tens of thousands of weavers, fullers and dyers periodically emerged from pitched battles against each other, bloody riots and wars against their rulers and would-be rulers, tumultuous protests and demonstrations, to manufacture the heavy Flemish cloth worn in every ancient land of Europe (and today preserved in paintings by Flemish masters found in museums around the world).

The largest city of medieval northern Europe except for Paris, a monumental place by the standards of those times, with a 13th-century population of over 60,000 souls, performing an almost unique (for then) mass-volume manufacturing activity, Ghent did everything to size: its unbroken line of centuries-old canal houses on the enchanting **Graslei** ("herb canal"), which we'll soon be viewing, are three times as large as ordinary canal structures of that age; its 15th-century **Butchers' Hall** ("het groot Vleeshuis") still extends for a full city block; the bell on its Cathedral tower weighs 12,000 pounds; its supreme masterpiece, the Van Eycks' **Adoration of the Mystic Lamb,** consists of no fewer than 24 panels!

But awesome as it is, aged as it is, Ghent is a living city, not simply an urban museum. Because its development continued well beyond the architecturally graceful Middle Ages and into the often inelegant 19th and 20th centuries, it is not always a "pretty" town, is occasionally dark and begrimed, somber and stark in spots. And today's Ghent is an active, commercial city, fourth largest in Belgium (after Brussels, Antwerp, Liège), a place of bustling crowds who rush to and fro, shopping and chatting, in seeming indifference to the brooding, ancient structures that dot the streets and stand out among more modern buildings. It is rather the tourist, less jaded, who is repeatedly jolted by the discovery of these brilliant, historic artifacts that date from every key age of post-Roman times, these structures of successive ages that make Ghent into a veritable history book of Europe. For everything is here. In the Crypt of Ghent's Cathedral of St. Bavo are remnants of the Carolingians. In Ghent's Castle of the Counts of Flanders—itself built in 1180—are foundations of earlier forts dating to the 900s. Along the ravishing "Graslei" of Ghent is a mammoth grain hall of the 1200s. Nearby is the Belfry dating from the 1300s, a Town Hall built mainly in the 1400s and 1500s (with later additions), the shops of the Veldstraat with homes of the 1700s housing an American delegation negotiating with the British in 1814, a French king fleeing from Napoleon in 1815. Ghent has seen everything, done everything, enjoyed or suffered every European triumph or defeat, and—in the period of its greatest eminence, in the 1200s and 1300s—dramatically witnessed the very industrial, labor and class conflicts that have so troubled the world in modern times. Ghent is thus a travel adventure that enlarges the understanding and consciousness of those visitors who come prepared for it.

THE BUBBLING CAULDRON OF EUROPE: Long before

there was an industrial revolution, Ghent possessed many of the attributes of an industrial city. Long before the era of capitalism, Ghent enjoyed a form of capitalist organization. Evolving from an Abbey ("Abdij") founded by St. Amand in the 600s at the meeting place of the Scheldt and Leie Rivers, Ghent developed in the 1200s into Europe's largest producer of cloth from wool, employing upwards of 30,000 persons—all organized in strictly delineated Guilds—to weave and finish and dye the yarn they imported from England.

At the start of their story, in the 1200s, these cloth workers were relatively subdued, dominated by a rich group of merchants and land-owning patricians who ruled the city through a 39-member Council of Aldermen. In 1302, the underdogs—and their counterparts from Bruges, Ypres and Courtrai—rose up in a series of bloody, labor-related conflicts that continued, at least in Ghent, for 200 years. They defeated the French at the Battle of the Golden Spurs. They seized power from the Merchant Class and transferred it to the Guilds. They immediately invested themselves with privileges and protections. When farmers in the countryside sought to weave cloth, the Guilds of Ghent marched into the farms and destroyed the farmers' looms. When Bruges sought to build a canal to the Scheldt, the men of Ghent marched to that canal and violently stopped its construction. When corn from northern France passed through Ghent on the River Leie, the Guilds of Ghent exercised their right of the "Staple", requiring that the produce be warehoused first in the Grain House still standing on the "Graslei", then transshipped on by the Guild of the Free Boatmen, whose proud headquarters also still stands on that same awesome stretch of center-city canal. Lashing out against everyone around them, lacking a clear political or economic philosophy that might give coherence to their actions or produce results, sensing themselves poor and oppressed, yearning to eliminate the middlemen who stood between their cloth and the ultimate user, these medieval figures provided the world with a foretaste of the future, a testing ground for economic conflict.

Their vanguard were the weavers—suspicious, angry, volatile, violent weavers. Their field of agitation and battle was Ghent's **"Friday Market"** ("Vrijdagmarkt"), the immense square that we'll be visiting in later pages, where, periodically, weavers would engage in savage battles with fullers or other Guilds, or would themselves be defeated and executed by soldiers of the Count of Flanders or the King of France. Their greatest leader was **Jacob van Artevelde,** whose statue now occupies the hallowed central position in today's Friday Market. Himself a wealthy landowner, he became one of the world's first labor leaders, seeking better conditions for the working population of Ghent, and a continuing source of raw materials for their looms. When the King of France ordered his medieval vassal, the Count of Flanders, to cease importing wool from England, threatening ruin for Ghent, van Artevelde did the unthinkable. In 1340, he invited the English king, Edward III, to the Friday Market, and there proclaimed him King of France! Several years later, sensing that van Artevelde's courtship of England was producing insufficient results, a faction in Ghent brought about the murder of van Artevelde.

In effect, the roiling, boiling, 14th- and 15th-century population of Ghent made their city into a City-State. They championed the cause of urban independence. They opposed, in their turn, every ruler who passed through Belgium. Whoever, whatever, wherever—Ghent was Against. On successive occasions in the 1300s, they fought the Count of Flanders. In the late 1300s, they battled the Duke of Burgundy. In 1453, angered by a tax on salt (and thus perhaps providing inspiration to a later Mohandas K. Ghandi), they rose up against the greatest of the Burgundians, Philip the Good, and maintained a revolutionary government for several years until the inevitable capitulation, when the town fathers were made to kneel in hair shirts and beg forgiveness. Undaunted, they rebelled next against the great Charles V, refusing to pay taxes for the upkeep of Hapsburg armies. In 1540, Charles returned to his birthplace, coldly sentenced the town to immense penalties for their lèse majesté, and again forced dozens of town elders to kneel for their pardon, this time wearing nooses around their necks.

Were they simply hotheads, these ancient people of Ghent? Or were they perhaps the forerunners of those great figures in history—the Thomas Jeffersons and the Simón Bolivars—who struggled for democratic liberties and against absolute tyrants? Imagine yourself living in an age when a handful of kings, counts, princes and emperors possessed, through an accident of birth, the unlimited right to control your destiny, to force you to beg them for life. Other cities and nations acceded rather easily to such authority, but never the 14th- and 15th-century people of Ghent. Is it not possible that, like the nuclear protestors of a later day, they saw the world with greater lucidity and sensitivity than their placid neighbors? Is it not possible that *they* were the sane elements living in a world of madness?

Sadly, their days of surpassing glory, and those of Ghent, were soon over. The punishment meted out by Charles V simply capped a decline that had already begun in the earlier 1500s. Instead of exporting their wool to Ghent, the merchants of England began to manufacture their own cloth from it, at home, throwing thousands out of work in Ghent. The restrictive practices of the Guilds of Ghent themselves enabled other more modern cities to surge ahead. The religious wars of the late 16th century resulted in the emigration of highly enterprising Calvinists from Ghent to Holland, to England, and from there to North America. The later depredations of Louis XIV, the excesses (and occupation of Ghent) by the French Revolution, took their toll. And soon, the city that was once the second largest in all of northern Europe, became simply one among many other substantial European cities of commerce and light industry (its population today about 250,000 persons, double that of Bruges), and certainly not a behemoth. And the people of Ghent, those quick-tempered stalwarts of the Guilds, ceased to have the characteristics of a perpetually angry mob. Today, in fact, the population of Ghent is rather conservative. They vote in just about the same fashion as other large cities of Flanders, and their "Friday Market" no longer seethes with surging crowds of violent weavers.

But I confess to harboring a sneaking admiration for those turbulent, fickle, explosive, riotous, scheming, ancient citizens of Ghent. What a city they left behind them! What monuments of architecture and art! What examples and traditions! And most of their legacy is superbly preserved to edify, enchant and excite the visitor of today.

AN ORIENTATION TO GHENT: Although it is a sprawling place of several square miles, its most important sights form a relatively compact medieval core in the very center of town, easily covered on foot once you have arrived at the center of the city. The main **St. Pieter's Railroad Station** is *not* central, nor within easy walking distance of the center, although connected by convenient streetcars to the area where you'll want to be. Tourists arriving by train should simply board any streetcar marked "Korenmarkt" or "Centrum", while visitors with cars should push deeper into the center, to the area just behind St. Bavo's Cathedral where, sooner or later, you will eventually find a parking spot. If you don't, then drive to the "Friday Market" ("Vrijdagmarkt") where a large underground parking garage lies beneath the mammoth square.

Where exactly is the center of Ghent? Unlike many other Belgian towns, it has no single "Grote Markt" (Market Square) where all the major buildings—Town Hall, Belfry, Cathedral—are concentrated. Although the Korenmarkt ("Corn Market") Square—site of the 19th century, neo-Gothic post office, two department stores and major streetcar terminal—is technically referred to as the "Centrum", the major, medieval sights and buildings are actually scattered within a much larger, but less-than-half-mile-square area shaped like a slightly lopsided rectangle, in which the Korenmarkt occupies a position near the bottom left-hand corner.

The four points of the "Golden Rectangle of Ghent" (my own invention) are St. Bavo's Cathedral, the Friday Market ("Vrijdagmarkt"), the Castle of the Counts of Flanders, and St. Michael's Bridge. The bottom, south side of the rectangle is lined by the "Three Towers" of Ghent, all in a straight row—St. Bavo's, the Belfry, and St. Nicholas' Church—and all pointing, roughly, to St. Michael's Bridge. The left-hand, west side of the rectangle is lined by the River Leie, which splits in two, near the top, into a "Y" whose branches roughly encircle the Castle of the Counts of Flanders. The stem of the "Y", along the Leie, is where you'll find the enchanting "Graslei". You can begin your touring at any one of the four points of the rectangle, although I'll be recommending that you start at the Cathedral of St. Bavo, later in this chapter. The entire rectangle can be covered quite easily on foot, and should only be traversed on foot.

Again at the bottom, south side of the rectangle, near St. Nicholas' Church, there starts the main shopping street of Ghent —the Veldstraat—which plunges southwards, changing names along the way, until it reaches St. Pieter's Railway Station about 1¾ miles south of the "Rectangle". It is in this same general area that you'll find the Citadel Park and its important Museum of Fine Arts; and streetcar lines charging 24 francs each way provide the link between the two areas.

Ghent was once crisscrossed by a number of rivers and canals, of which only a few remain today, but they are sufficient in size to provide you with remarkable opportunities for sightseeing boat cruises of the city (described later in this chapter). The narrow River Leie winds and twists through the city, eventually meeting the equally narrow (in Ghent) River Scheldt, and two major canals— the Ketelvest and the Lieve (not to be confused with the Leie)— form connecting branches or offshoots of the two rivers. You will not, on a short visit, grow familiar with the complex pattern of these waterways, but you should grasp two immediate points about the "Rectangle". First, it is a wonder. It contains not merely a dozen major attractions, but two particular sights that can be rated among the world's most important: a painting (the "Adoration of the Mystic Lamb") that is one of the greatest in the history of art, a series of structures (along the "Graslei") that are among the greatest in the history of architecture. Second: it is not where you will probably be staying in Ghent. Apart from a handful of choices, the hotels of Ghent are located outside and sometimes a mile and more from the area of the remarkable "Rectangle".

OVERNIGHT IN GHENT: Because Ghent is so very near to Brussels, less than 40 minutes away by car or train, the same distance from popular Bruges in the other direction, most overseas visitors commute to it from Brussels, or pause for but a short while on their way from Brussels to Bruges. It goes without saying that such visitors are misguided and deprive themselves of much pleasure and insight by scheduling too short a time in a city that deserves an overnight stay and two days of touring.

That bit of advice, valid in the past, has been made more valid still by the recent emergence (all within the past two and three years) of several fine new hotels in Ghent that satisfy the budget needs of every category of traveller.

The city's top hotel is now the two-year-old **Novotel Centrum** at 5 Goudenleeuwenplein (phone 24-22-30), in the very center of the historic inner city. It's a rather spectacular renovation of a 14th-century building whose facade remains untouched, but whose interior has blossomed with a glass-topped, greenhouse-like lounge, swimming pool, luxurious modern furnishings against exposed-brick walls, and much else. Comfortable rooms with broad beds and firm mattresses rent for 3100 francs ($86) single, 3675 francs ($102) double, including tax and service, but not a $9 buffet breakfast available downstairs. Equally elegant, but a less thorough renovation of an historic, period (1865), building, is the 30-room **Hotel Gravensteen** at 35 Jan Breydelstraat (phone 25-11-50), across from the Castle of the Counts of Flanders. Four-star luxury here is sold for 2650 francs ($73.60) single, 3700 francs ($102.77) double, this time including breakfast. Add the new **Alfa Flanders Hotel,** 121 Koning Albertlaan (phone 22-60-65), as still another, gleaming, new, deluxe hotel of Ghent, charging a top, summer rate of 4800 francs ($133) single, 5900 francs ($164) double, including breakfast, service and tax.

Not new, but modern, and extremely serviceable, are three motel-type structures (although fairly elaborate ones) located rather far from the center and mainly suitable for travelers with cars. These are: the slickly-modern and strictly functional **Holiday Inn,** at 600 Ottergemsesteenweg (phone 091-22-58-85), at the junction of the two major motorways on the edge of Ghent, a five-story, concrete-and-glass block of large, Holiday-Inn-standard rooms, with indoor swimming pool, sauna, tennis court and children's garden. Each of its 120 rooms has two large comfortable beds, color TV and all the contemporary amenities, and rents for a reasonable 3400 francs ($94) single, 4300 francs ($120) double, including continental breakfast, service and tax. Next, the almost-identically-modern, but smaller (40 rooms) **Europahotel,** at 59 Gordunakaai (phone 091-22-60-71), away from the center in a fresh and open, green, new suburb known as the "Blaarmeersen", but not far from St. Pieter's Station. For similarly modern rooms with giant windows and color TV sets, you'll pay only 1900 francs ($53) single, 2250 francs ($62.50) double, including breakfast, service and tax. Slightly cheaper rates, roughly similar amenities, are offered in the functional brick building of the **Hotel Ascona,** at 105 Voskenslaan (phone 091-21-27-56), five hundred yards from the Station in the direction of the motorways.

An in-city stand-out of Ghent is the colorful **St. Jorishof (Cour St. Georges),** opposite the Town Hall at 1 Botermarkt (phone 091-24-24-24), claiming to be the oldest hotel of Europe. In a building dating from the year 1288, which now sports a 16th century, step-gabled facade, the hotel operates 70 traditionally-styled rooms, renting for 1825 to 3400 francs ($51 to $94) single, from 2350 to 3500 francs ($65 to $97) double, but mainly within the lower range in both categories. All rates include continental breakfast, service and tax. Frightened to stay in a hotel built in 1288? You needn't be. The majority of rooms are in a much later annex in the unseen, inner courtyard where construction isn't regulated by National Monument laws preventing modern improvements; rooms are pleasant and perfectly comfortable, although public facilities are virtually nil because of the celebrated restaurant (see our later discussion) that fills the ground floor. The historic setting and atmosphere of your accommodations (which once housed Napoleon Bonaparte), the superb location just two blocks from St. Bavo's Cathedral in the center of everything, makes this a top hotel selection of Ghent.

Two more-moderately-priced choices have also opened in the last two years to change the hotel picture in Ghent. The 134-room **Arcade Hotel,** 24 Nederkouter (phone 25-07-07), is a typical member of the well-known European chain of modern but strictly-utilitarian hotels. Fifteen hundred forty francs ($43) for singles, 1810 francs ($50) for doubles, 1985 francs ($55) for triples, but not including an optional breakfast (160 francs) and television (155 francs). The just-opened **Ibis Hotel** is planned to be just as modern, just as utilitarian, but perhaps a touch cheaper in price than the Arcade.

Near the train station

Apart from a number of extremely cheap (but entirely proper) small lodgings places located up staircases above downtown restaurants in the historic center—we'll be discussing those later —the majority of Ghent's remaining hotels are clustered near St. Pieter's Railroad Station about a mile and three-quarters from the medieval heart of town; and the best of these, a hundred yards up a pleasant side-street heading off the station square, is the modern, glass-fronted, six-story **Hotel Carlton,** at 62 Blvd. Koningin

Astridlaan (phone 091-22-88-36), twenty-five rooms with private bath, firm modern beds and TV, yet renting for a low 1375 to 1750 francs ($38 to $49) double, only 1100 to 1475 francs ($31 to $41) single, with breakfast, service and tax included. A drive-in garage, next to the lobby, provides convenient parking space.

Other station area hotels—and the station in Ghent occupies an entirely respectable, residential-style area—include the rather simple **Castel,** at 9 Koningin Maria-Hendrickaplein (phone 091-21-17-43; $42 for a twin with shower), and the **Claridge,** at 36 Koningin Maria-Hendrickaplein (phone 091-22-25-87; $30 twin); and there are quite a few more, all similarly priced.

In the very center, but rock-bottom-priced

The most cost-conscious of travellers to Ghent, those adventurers willing to skip the frills, are paradoxically the people who will be able to stay in the very center of the city; they can have their cake and eat it, too! Along St. Bavo's Square ("St. Baafsplein") in front of the great cathedral, along the Golden Lion Square ("Goudenleeuwplein") in front of the nearby Belfry ("Belfort"), and along the Corn Market Square ("Korenmarkt") in front of the great St. Nicholas' Church, are strings of restaurants and cafes that each possess a tiny and extremely inexpensive pension-type lodging on top! You'll want to try: the **Hotel Du Progres,** at 9 Korenmarkt (phone 091-25-17-16), charging 750 francs ($21) for a bathless double room and breakfast; **'t Vosken,** at 19 Baafsplein (phone 091-25-73-61), pricing bathless twins at 1000 francs ($28) with breakfast included, bathless singles at only 600 francs ($17); the slightly better, historic **De Fonteyne,** at 7 Goudenleeuwplein (phone 091-25-48-71), yet with rates of only 870 francs ($24) for a double with bath, only 800 francs ($22) for a bathless double, and 470 francs ($13) for its solitary single room, again with bath down the hall. At rates like these, why not stay in Ghent and commute to Brussels?

RESTAURANTS AND CAFES, WATERZOOI AND SUCH: Except for the stately, parkside townhouse known as "Apicius", which all food critics rank among the 10 best of Belgium, Ghent is not an area dotted with celebrated restaurants—the city is too work-a-day in its outlook, too fast-paced, down-to-earth. But the lack of such standouts—which in any other city would spell disaster for dedicated gourmets—simply means that most of your meals in Ghent, instead of being memorable, will be merely superb; such are the generally high food standards of Belgium—and Ghent. And the afore-mentioned **Apicius,** at 43

Koning Leopold II Laan (phone 22-46-00), off the Citadel Park, will fully compare with any other great "name" restaurant of Belgium serving French cuisine, for diners willing to spend $75 per three-course meal, including wine. Apicius is closed at lunchtime on Saturdays, all day Sunday, and from mid-July to early August. Its closest competitor is the oddly-named, smaller, cheaper ($45, without wine) **Horse Shoe,** at 12 Lievekaai (phone 23-54-62), shut for lunch on Saturdays, all day Sundays, and the month of July.

For more normal dining, you'll want to consider the following (in descending order of cost):

Elegant dining, at $21 plus wine

In the finest location in all of Ghent, at the immediate end of St. Michael's Bridge gazing across the River Leie onto the enchanting Graslei, the **Graaf van Egmond** (Count of Egmond), 21 Sint-Michielshelling (phone 25-07-27), is a weather-blackened, old stone mansion of the 1200s, as hard as that may be to comprehend, whose facade upon the river (but not upon the street) was refaced by builders of the 1600s with red brick, in step-gabled, Renaissance style; the Count of Egmond, Philip II, William the Silent, all passed through the elegant townhouse on various missions. (From it you can see three of the celebrated towers of Ghent, straight in a row.) The building today is a so-called "gastronomic complex" whose ground-floor "Gastronomisch Restaurant" offers a high-quality meal of three courses for only 750 francs ($21), to which the addition of wine (a good vintage even) will result in a $25 dinner, service included! In a gracious setting of brown/yellow, satiny wallpaper, copper chandeliers, casement windows looking out onto the ravishing scene, you begin with either sparkling-hot snails, herring or "Bouchée à la Reine", choose one of six different main courses—I enjoyed the beef tongue with lemon sauce, and end with a chef's dessert, all for that remarkably low, 750-franc ($21), plus wine, cost. For 1200 francs ($33), you choose from a vastly expanded selection among four courses: Lobster Bisque with an Armagnac flavor, or a creamy, asparagus soup, to begin; then a second appetizer of scotch salmon or a serving of broiled lobster, eels or paté mousse; followed by turkey with apricots, or pigeon with raisin sauce, or hot sweetbreads in strawberry sauce, several others, as your main course; a platter of cheeses or choice of desserts, to end.

(If you haven't the time for a full meal, but still crave the view of the Graaf van Egmond, you can go upstairs to a plainer grill room, where an all-you-can-eat, serve-yourself, cold buffet, is only

300 francs—$8.33—accompanied by all the wine you can drink for an additional 120 francs—$3.33. Both restaurants are open seven days a week.)

Meals at a medium price ($12 to $20)

Back in the very center of Ghent, two blocks from St. Bavo's Cathedral, and across the street from the resplendent Town Hall, the always-reliable, medium-priced restaurant of Ghent is that of the 13th-century **Hotel St. Jorishof (Cour St. Georges),** at 2 Botermarkt (phone 24-24-24), whose lodgings we've already discussed in the section above. To the list of its famous room guests, add an endless stream of celebrated diners! In 1477, ambassadors of the Hapsburg emperor were banqueted here on the occasion of their visit proposing the marriage of Maximilian of Austria to Maria of Burgundy, in the very same, high-ceilinged, balconied, Gothic hall (on two levels) of dark mahogany walls and stained glass windows, in which you'll now be eating—it's been marvelously preserved except for a tasteless forest of Kiwanis Club pennants hung from the ceiling of the elevated room. The 725-franc ($20), four-course menu (there are no à la carte selections) includes service charge, brings you a flavorful, hot soup to begin, then a choice of appetizers so giant in portion as to make a full meal (my "filets de harengs Niçoise" filled a dinner plate with three, six-inch-long slabs of Dutch herring, diced onions, and an entire, sliced beefsteak tomato), then rare lamb chops or even rarer steak or light veal cutlet or roast chicken or broiled fish, and dessert (chosen from a large selection), all prepared with such skillful touch that it is utterly unnecessary to consider the 875-franc ($24) "Menu Charles Quint" (eels with green sauce, or fresh shrimps on toast, then chicken Waterzooi à la Gantoise—see our description of this famous Ghent specialty, below, then flaming Crepes Paysanne), or the gigantic, 925-franc ($26), four-course menu offering a choice of 38 different appetizers and 19 separate main dishes, including veal kidneys "Pompadour", duckling "à l'orange", Scotch salmon "Florentine", "Sole Walewska", filet mignon "Grand Veneur", rabbit "à la Flamande". Talk about Belgian excesses! The large restaurant, open every day of the week, is closed only for the Christmas period, from December 18 to January 3.

If St. Jorishof is full, and you haven't a reservation, then simply walk down the street to the smaller **Central au Paris,** at 9 Botermarkt, closed Tuesdays and Wednesdays, which prides itself on the Gallic flavor of its dishes (but also features Waterzooi!). It offers three set courses for 450 francs ($12.50) and 550 francs ($15), four courses and coffee for 800 francs ($22), charges only

50 francs for soup, 330 francs ($9) for elaborate French appetizers, 450 francs ($12.50) for separate meat main courses; the moderately-priced set "menus" are obviously the better choice.

Finally, a restaurant oddity in Ghent is the surprisingly accomplished, surprisingly genteel restaurant of St. Pieter's Railroad Station, the **Buffet Station Gent St. Pieters,** at Koningin Maria-Henrickaplein, open seven days a week. If you're passing nearby, or staying in a hotel alongside, you'll want to wander through the extraordinary, high-ceilinged, station-style rooms with historic walls murals, brown tiles, wooden-panelling and tuxedoed waiters serving a special four-courses-and-coffee for a total of 600 francs ($17), individual plates for 350 and 375 francs ($9.72 and $10.40), all of high quality. What railway stations elsewhere do the same?

Slightly cheaper ($15)

Back on St. Bavo's Square (St. Baafsplein) in front of the Cathedral in this central area of Ghent, the huge and considerably cheaper **Raadskelder Restaurant,** in the 15th-century cellar/crypt of the building adjoining the Belfry, is a colorful underground hall of vaulted arches and dirndl-clad waitresses, inexpensive, but recommended only with hesitation: it is a mass-volume operation catering to busloads of tourists visiting Ghent, and not even the management, in my humble view, would claim to match the tastiness and careful preparation of what you'll usually find in Ghent. Still, it is quite remarkably cheap (a four-course "tourist menu" for 550 francs, $15.20; a three-course "regional menu"— eels in green sauce, chicken Waterzooi and dessert—for 525 francs, $14.60; half a roast chicken, with french fries and salad, for 300 francs, $8.33; spaghetti Bolognaise with giant meatball, enough for a family, 240 francs, $6.67—and it is open every day, throughout the day, from 9:30 a.m. to 10 p.m.; but don't expect meals of the quality available for a few dollars more at previous selections. Four other tourist-style restaurants on St. Bavo's Square, this time with sidewalk tables, are similarly-priced, and one of them—**'t Vosken,** at 19 St. Baafsplein—charges 280 francs ($7.77) for a simple, filling bowl of chicken Waterzooi, only 210 francs ($5.83) for a daily-changing meat dish ("dagschotel") with those incomparable Belgian french fries.

Waterzooi—*vat is it?* And now that we've repeatedly mentioned this specialty of Ghent, which is pronounced "vahter-zoi", and is made either with chicken or fish, we should advise that "Waterzooi" is a lightly-creamed broth filled with large chunks of chicken or fish. To make a reasonable facsimile of it at home, boil the white meat of a chicken—and only the white—in water (using, say, four large pieces), then add carrots and celery (never onion), and at the end beat in the yolk of two eggs and ¼ cup of heavy cream. Waterzooi! To match the tastier restaurant versions of Waterzooi, use chicken stock to cook the chicken, then add two or three tablespoons of flour, a diced leek and celery, sprinkle in parsley, nutmeg, lemon juice, a bit of butter; and throw in two or three tiny boiled potatoes to bulk up the serving. For fish Waterzooi, substitute carp or pike for the chicken, and use fish stock. What results is a rather bland, but smooth and soothing, easy-on-the-stomach cross between a soup and a stew—Ghent's favorite dish (but available in other cities, too). And be forewarned: although you must try Waterzooi at some point of your stay, don't expect the first sip to set off bells, or to cause flights of angels to pass overhead. (To experience the latter phenomena, you must eat at Villa Lorraine in Brussels, or drink a glass of any Belgian Trappist beer, or dine on fish smothered in this nation's classic white wine sauce.) Waterzooi à la Gantoise, Gentse Waterzooi, is simply an uncomplicated, pleasant, peasants' dish that provides a calming contrast to the richer meals you've had and an example of the broad variety of Belgium's cuisine.

A banquet with ever-flowing wine for $10.70

Four courses plus all the wine (or beer) you can drink, for 385 francs ($10.70), including service charge! That's the flamboyant offer of the large and interesting **De Leiepoort,** at 166 Kortrijksepoortstraat (phone 25-31-14), on a narrow, streetcar-bearing shopping street about two-thirds of the way from the city center to the Museum of Fine Arts; it's a brisk, but manageable, walk, an even easier streetcar ride—Kortrijksepoortstraat being an extension of the Nederkouter which is itself an extension of the Veldstraat, the thronged main shopping street of Ghent. If you'll make the effort and the trip, you'll find yourself in a labyrinth of old wooden rooms looking out on the picturesque River Leie, patronized by a youthful and intellectual crowd of "Gentenaars" drawn to the cheapest banquet in town (soup, then choice of such appetizers as a cassoulet of fish au gratin or fondu parmesan, then main course (many of which carry supplements of 40 or 50 francs), a dame blanche (vanilla ice cream with hot chocolate sauce) or fruit salad or fruit mousse for dessert, and that unlimited red, white or rosé wine or beer—à volonté, as they say. Closed Wednesdays, and on weekdays during the second half of August.

The meals for under $7

A member of Belgium's cheapest retail chain, the **Sarma Department Store,** on the bustling, central Korenmarkt Square, diagonally across from the main post office, is the predictable site for Ghent's most heavily patronized self-service cafeteria and adjoining grocery store (the latter for picnic ingredients); both are on the third floor. At the cafeteria, spaghetti with meat sauce and meatballs for 95 francs ($2.64); "vol au vent"—a form of chicken pot pie—for 125 francs ($3.47); half a roast chicken and Belgian fried potatoes for 150 francs ($4.17); rumpsteak for 195 francs ($5.40); and a small pitcher of red wine for 30 francs (83¢), all easily permit the assembly of a filling, under-$7 meal. And if that's too much for your budget, then hie to the side of the **Butchers Hall,** near the Castle of the Counts of Flanders, where two outdoor stands—one familiar, one frightening—open for business at noon and 5:30 p.m., respectively. The traditional one is simply a *frituur* selling heavenly, Belgian french fries; but ask that your chips be covered not only with mayonnaise but with "stoverij saus"—shredded remnants of a beef stew and gravy—and for a total of 65 francs ($1.80), you'll have a memorably-filling meal of carbohydrates and protein. The second stand sells the Belgian version of escargots—fat and spicy *welks,* five times the size of a snail, and already extracted from the shell. If it's your first experience with welks, you'll shut your eyes as you pop the ghastly creatures into your mouth, utter a prayer, begin chewing, and . . . come alive to still another Belgian food delight! For less than a dollar, you've added a tangy seafood course to your penurious feast of french fries, worthy of an Escoffier!

300 different beers

Beer is yet another of the city's most sensual treats. Though they may have grown mellow in recent centuries, the contemporary people of Ghent ("Gentenaars") support an unusual number of those odd Belgian bars that serve upwards of 300 varieties of beer, some brands even bearing the year when they were bottled (imagine ordering a Heineken '81 or a Carlsberg '79!). And while an occasional tavern of this sort is perhaps unsuitable for the more timid or fastidious tourist, others are like teahouses, genteel teahouses; an example is the **Oud Middelhus** occupying a 17th-century building at 6 Graslei, no less. It lists 300 beers, including 8 draft beers, and if you'll start with one of its monk-brewed Trappist variety, you'll be a devotee of Belgian beer for life. Elsewhere in Ghent, a mere 250 varieties are stocked by the larger, somewhat rowdier (only by a little bit) **"Dulle Griet",** at 250 Vrijdagmarkt ("Friday Market"), but those include "alle Trappist en Abdijbieren" (all Trappist and Abbey-produced beers) and eight different types of Gueuze. And then there's the intimate **De Templier** tavern at that point just off the bridge near the same Friday Market where the "Dulle Griet" cannon (see our sightseeing discussion) is situated; it's known throughout Ghent for stocking a "Ridder" beer having an alcoholic content of 23%. Since persons imbibing such a fiery brew have been known to stagger off with the elaborate goblet (and wooden holder) in which Ridder is served, the bar posts a notice reading "schoen af" (shoes off) next to its sign for "Ridder". The stricture is seriously meant. Ordering the beer, you're immediately asked to present a single shoe to the bartender as a hostage for return of the goblet!

Colorful taverns, waterzooi and walks—these pale, however, before the actual sights of Ghent concentrated in its medieval core.

TOURING THE "GOLDEN RECTANGLE" OF GHENT

For an immediate foretaste of what's ahead, you can, if you wish, rush straight to St. Michael's Bridge—southwest point of the rectangle—and there enjoy an extraordinary view of the highlights of Ghent. From the center of the Bridge, the entire Graslei presents itself, and beyond that, the turrets of the Castle of the Counts of Flanders. In another direction you see the "Three Towers" of Ghent, and still other ancient structures at other turns. But by far the wisest course for a first-time visitor to Ghent is to start at St. Bavo's Cathedral at the southeast corner. By doing so, you assure yourself of viewing the supreme masterwork of Ghent (and one of the Seven Wonders of Belgium): the "Adoration of the Mystic Lamb", by the brothers Van Eyck. By starting elsewhere, you run the risk of mis-judging the time, missing the viewing hours, or encountering a crowd or other mishap that might prevent you from experiencing a magical, multi-panel painting that influenced the art of all subsequent time.

ST. BAVO'S CATHEDRAL, SITE OF THE "MYSTIC LAMB": Viewed from afar, its white stone turned brown by the passage of time, it is not among the more impressive cathedrals of Belgium, and its tower of four spires placed in a square is in fact rather unimaginative. But inside! Inside it is breath-taking, perhaps the most lavishly decorated of Belgium, flinging black and white marble in intricate Baroque patterns and shapes against the often unadorned facades of the Gothic era, covering every inch of its two dozen chapels with priceless paintings and statuary, tomb carvings and screens, inscriptions, memorials and remembrances.

St. Bavo's was largely built in the 14th and 15th centuries atop the site of the 12th-century Church of St. John, a part of which still survives in the central section of the Cathedral's remarkable Crypt. Ravaged by Protestant iconoclasts in the 16th century, who destroyed noted stained-glass windows, statuary and paintings (the "Mystic Lamb" was successfully hidden from them, in an attic), it was largely redecorated through the efforts and funds of a wealthy, 17th-century Bishop of the Church, Anthony Triest. It is therefore appropriate that one of the several sculptural masterworks of the Cathedral is Bishop Triest's own tomb, up the steps and to the left side of the high altar, done by the son of the great Jerome de Quesnoy who sculpted the delightful Mannekin Pis in Brussels. Bishop Triest in magnificent vestments with lace cuffs made striking by the white marble in which they are carved, lies half-reclining atop his sarcophagus, propped up by an elbow, his gaze relaxed, confident, kindly, dignified, calmly awaiting redemption. At his head and feet, Mary and Jesus, respectively; below and atop his effigy, cherubic angels. The second, striking, sculptural masterpiece of St. Bavo's is surely its 18th-century pulpit, halfway down the nave, of white marble actually entwined with oak. At its foot sits an old man, Time, his sleep disturbed by the horn-blowing angel above him. He awakes and lifts a cloak from his eyes to see a young maiden pointing to a text of the Gospel: "Awake to the teachings of Christ". Such exalted art, done with such fervor and care, serves as prelude to the supreme sight of the "Bavo": the Ghent Altarpiece, otherwise known as:

The Adoration of the Mystic Lamb (1432)

It awaits you less than fifty yards from the small chapel of the Vijd family for which it was designed, where it was hung more than 500 years ago, attracting the likes of Philip II of Spain (who nearly spirited it away) and Hermann Goering of the Third Reich (who did), along with most other major rulers of Europe, most celebrated artists and art critics, and millions of others before you who have walked the corridors of time into the presence of this consummate work. A dazzling 24 panels requiring, it is believed, at least 12 years to complete, its monumental theme is nothing less than the summarized State of Mankind following the sacrifice of Christ, its achievement a synthesis of the natural sciences, the culture and the social structure of the early 1400s, its subject matter all the major groupings of people, divine and secular, who participated in the biblical story and the later spread and support of Christianity. And when you have stared at it for a time, you will suddenly realize that although the painting deals with religion, it is also occupied with people, and proudly so. For the first time, ordinary mortals mix on an equal basis with angels and saints, are portrayed to the same dramatic extent, are magnificently garbed, are creatures worthy of respect. The ultimate redemption of man is now in progress, the painting seems to say, and a great beautiful world has emerged, wondrous to behold and enjoy, a model to be served with high ideals and fervor. In Ghent, the medieval city of questing, striving, turbulent people, an artistic affirmation of the worth of humanity, of people, has taken place.

On the glittering central panels, which loom before you when the more subdued, reddish-brown outer paintings are swung back on their hinges to reveal the major theme, the world is portrayed as a vast, sloping lawn of grass dotted with hundreds of daisies and other exquisite flowers, encircled by shrubbery and trees behind which are cathedral towers and the shining cities of the time. Horticulturists who have examined the tiny plants with magnifying glasses have found each of them scientifically exact, have even affirmed that the flowers found growing in shadows are only those species that could in fact blossom without light.

In the center foreground of the lawn is a graceful Fountain of Life; behind it, on a scarlet altar, is the Holy Lamb spouting blood into a goblet, the very symbol of the sacrifice of Christ, surrounded by angels praying. Around the central figures are multiple groups in perfect symmetry, all engaged in adoration of the Lamb. To the immediate left of the fountain, in the foreground: kneeling prophets of the Old Testament, ecstatic, along which, standing, are a cross-section of both pagans and ordinary medieval burghers, some still doubting, some pouting, puzzled or awed; among them is the poet Vergil. To the right of the fountain, the 12 apostles, kneeling; beside them, standing, all the great officers of a triumphant Catholic faith: Popes, Bishops, saints, all magnificently attired in jewel-bearing chasubles, adorned with magnificent crowns. To the immediate left of the Lamb, the Holy Martyrs of the church, in church garments, emerging as if in a procession from a grove of oranges. To the immediate right of the Lamb, the Holy Women—among them, St. Ursula, carrying the arrow that killed her—dressed in pastel gowns, with roses in their hair. Above them all is the sky of dawn. To the left of the main, center, bottom panel are two vertical panels, of which the farthest left is of the Righteous Judges, flanking a panel of Christian Knights on horseback; stare, if you will, at the details of the armor and cloth of the youthful knight in the foreground, a garland about his head, a holy banner on a red pole clutched in his hand. To the right of the main, center, bottom panel: two flanking panels of common people, of hermits and pilgrims led by an out-sized St. Christopher, some walking barefoot to pay homage to the Lamb.

Above the five, bottom, central panels is then an upper row of seven extraordinary portraits, the center one of a benevolent, kindly God bestowing His blessing, the Holy Mary to His left, John the Baptist to His right. At the extreme ends, a naked Adam and a naked Eve, two ungainly, scraggly-haired creatures who could have emerged from a jungle, and stand in marked contrast to the more cultivated human beings of a later time portrayed below. (These starkly realistic portraits so shocked Joseph II of Austria, one of the interminable line of Belgium's often insufferable foreign rulers, that he had substitute panels made of an Adam and Eve clothed in animal skins; the bogus, clothed portraits now hang just inside the west entrance to St. Bavo's Cathedral, the Van Eycks' nude originals having been restored to their proper place with the "Lamb".) Finally, two exquisite female groups next to Adam and Eve respectively: the Singing Angels, their foreheads furrowed, their cheeks bulging with sound, to the left; the Performing Angels, their leader pressing firmly with slender, feminine fingers on the tiny keys of an organ whose silver pipes and grainy wood are astonishing in their realism. Has anything more beautiful been painted than the hands of that angel?

When you first walk into the viewing room, you will find the scenes just described to be covered with "introductory" outer panels of red, brown and yellow, dealing with the Annunciation by the Angel Gabriel to the Holy Virgin: "Hail, Mary, full of grace, the Lord is with you". The words emit from him in their Latin form and are written on the painting. Mary's response— "Ecce ancilla Domini" (Behold the Handmaid of the Lord)—are in reverse lettering as they are directed back to Gabriel. Behind the windows of this holy scene are secular buildings and street views of the ancient city of Ghent.

Below the Annunciation are the striking, red-garbed figures of the childless couple who financed and donated the work, and in whose family chapel it hangs: a rich alderman of Ghent named Joos Vijd, and his equally affluent wife, Elisabeth Borluut. Between them, framed as are the donors in a row of Gothic niches, are unusual painted statues of St. John the Baptist holding the Lamb, and of St. John the Evangelist, whose vision of a day when "all nations and kindreds and peoples and tongues stood before the throne and before the Lamb" (Revelations vii, 2–12) undoubtedly provided inspiration for the work. At the very top, prophets and sybils who forecast the coming of Christ, and the Redemption of Man portrayed in the inner panels. When these outer panels are opened, they reveal the stunning panorama of the Lamb and its religious and temporal adorants.

It is generally believed that the work was conceived and begun by Hubert van Eyck in 1420, and completed, on Hubert's death in 1426, by Jan van Eyck by 1432, and this traditional explanation is thought to be supported by the partially-indecipherable and perhaps-forged Latin inscription on the frame of the painting:

> ". . . ubertus eyck maior quo nemo repertus
> incepit pondusq johannes arte secundus
> . . . iodici vyd prece fretus
> uersu sexta mai vos collocat acta tueri"

which translates to (with speculation filling in the gaps):

> "Hubert van Eyck, than whom there was no greater
> Began this work; his brother Jan, second in art,
> Completed it at the request of Joos Vijd;
> He invites you, by these words,
> This 6th day of May /1432/ to gaze upon it."

But if each brother worked on parts of the painting, then who did what? Most scholars can find no discernible difference in technique between any two scenes or figures. One art historian has suggested that Hubert van Eyck (of whom no other work survives) was a sculptor, not a painter, who began work on a never-completed, great stone Gothic frame in which the panels done by his brother would have appeared in recessed form to better advantage and perspective; there is some slight evidence to support the theory. However it came about, the masterpiece promoted both the genius and the methods of these great Flemish "primitives" who first perfected the use of translucent oils placed layer upon layer, on a base of oak wood, to produce the depth and shimmering colors of this surpassing work. Every fact and figure on it, every petal of every flower, every centimeter of cloth, is portrayed with scientific exactitude. It is as if the brothers had established a laboratory, through this work, to present the flora and fauna of their time in a fashion designed to encourage a delight in nature and mankind. It can be viewed for hours without exhausting the variety and detail of it. And it was instantly acclaimed, soon squabbled over, even robbed of two of its panels as recently as 1934. While one was soon recovered, the thief died before revealing the location of the second—that of the Righteous Judges—which is today perhaps buried in a Flemish field or lost in the clutter of a rural attic; a copy has been used in its place. "At the end of time," wrote a Belgian poet, "masterpieces like this will be taken into paradise; not only the painting itself, but the lost panel as well."

Behind the Cathedral of St. Bavo, fifty yards or so away, stands a bronze monument to the brothers van Eyck. The two men are shown simply seated upon a bench, wearing laurel wreaths about their heads, receiving the homage of a grateful, adoring Ghent.

The "Mystic Lamb" is shown on weekdays and Saturdays from 9:30 to noon and from 2 to 6 p.m., on Sundays from 1 to 6 p.m., for an admission fee of 40 francs ($1.11), which provides entrance as well to the Crypt of St. Bavo's.

Rubens in St. Bavo, and Justus of Ghent

At the other end of the Cathedral, along the ambulatory, is the "Rubens chapel"—an unexpected treat! In a city where no other major canvas of Peter Paul Rubens is kept, St. Bavo's displays his important "Conversion of St. Bavo", a typically monumental work by the Antwerp master done in response to a direct request by the Cathedral in 1624. St. Bavo, before his religious rebirth, was an 8th-century Count, dissolute, drunken, money-crazed. Here he presents himself at the monastery as a candidate for admission, looking up with beseeching joy into the eyes of the Abbot of the monastery and St. Amand; the bearded face of the Count, soon to become St. Bavo, is a self-portrait of Rubens. Beneath him are the fleshy, curvaceous women he will now be leaving: his wife, and a companion. A servant distributes his wealth to the poor. In this composition are all the artistic elements to which you'll thrill when later you stroll among a sea of Rubens paintings in Antwerp: dynamic action, dramatic force, not the other-worldly stillness and mysticism of the early Flemish primitives, but intense passion, human-scaled. In the tradition of the Baroque, for which he was the greatest exemplar, the painting is of movement and energy. Yet note how Rubens also remains a Flemish realist: the cloaks of the priests, the armor of St. Bavo, are precise to the last detail. (More about Rubens in our next chapter.)

Only the limitations of space prevent reference to dozens of other treasures of St. Bavo's, among which the 15th-century "Triptych of the Calvary" by Justus of Ghent (the popular name for Joos van Wassenhove) is another widely-acknowledged masterpiece, glowing with extraordinary color; it is currently displayed in a chapel of the Crypt. You will respond to a wide variety of works in this immensely rich cathedral, but you must take care not to miss the five major subsidiary sights to the "Mystic Lamb": the earlier-described Tomb of Bishop Triest, the Pulpit, Rubens' "Conversion of St. Bavo", the "Calvary" of Justus of Ghent—and now, the Crypt:

The Crypt

As important as the Cathedral is its giant Romanesque Crypt, largest in Belgium, for which your ticket to the "Mystic Lamb" admits you without additional charge. It is a vaulted and well-lighted (but extremely chilly) underground sanctuary, whose central portion dates from the 12th century. Crude religious frescoes of the 1400s cover many of the pillars, tombs of Bishops and rich patricians fill many of the 15 chapels lining every side of the mammoth room (itself the size of the actual sanctuary upstairs), and museum display cases and other areas show off church vestments as old as the 16th century, gold and silver reliquaries (of which the sculpted silver casket containing relics of St. Macharius will cause you to catch your breath), church sculpture and paintings, and more than a score of ancient manuscripts, of which one in particular—the 9th-century "Evangelarium" (Gospel Book) of St. Livinus—is riveting. Laboriously written and illustrated by one man, probably a monk working for years from dawn to dusk in a Carolingian monastery, it is one of those celebrated "illuminated manuscripts" by which the Church kept alive the light of learning in one of mankind's darkest periods. And thus, with the exhibits of its Crypt, the Cathedral of St. Bavo completes its exposition of an 800-year segment of human history: from Carolingian times and the Romanesque era, through the Gothic age and 15th-century art, to the period of the Counter-Reformation and the Baroque—the latter represented by a dizzying forest of white marble sculptures and decor, and by the power of a magnificent Rubens painting.

THE BELFRY, THE CLOTH HALL, AND "ROLAND":

> ". . . Till the Bell of Ghent responded
> Oer lagoon and dike of sand,
> 'I am Roland! I am Roland!
> There is Victory in the land!'"
> —Henry Wadsworth Longfellow

Across St. Bavo's Square from the entrance to the Cathedral is the second of the three mighty towers of Ghent, the 14th-century **Belfry** ("Belfort"), which rises from the ancient Cloth Hall ("Lakenhalle"). From the 1300s until 1540, it was the home of two inanimate objects endowed almost with personality, the breath of life, by the medieval burghers of Ghent. One was an iron chest containing the written "Privileges", or charters, of Ghent, exacted over the centuries from the Counts of Flanders. People then believed that if these papers were lost, the Privileges would be lost; on several noted occasions, rowdy crowds forced guardians of the Belfry to open the chest and extract other less admired

papers—such as treaties or proclamations reducing the Privileges
—which they tore into shreds, or ate!

The other was **"Roland"**, the great alarm bell of Ghent cast in
1314, which rang to advise of invading armies, to call out the town
militia, to inspire uprisings and defiance. The people called it "Roland" after the classic, 8th-century, Carolingian epic, "Les Chan-
sons de Roland", which told of a wounded soldier of Charlemagne, a certain Roland, who with his dying breath, in a remote
clearing, blew a horn to warn and save the great king from danger.
The bell named Roland became a similar hero to the feisty weavers
and other folk of Ghent. "Mijn naam is Roeland" (My name is Roland), went their cocky warning. "'k kleppe brand, En luide storm
in Vlaanderland" (When I make noise, there is a Storm in Flanders!).

In 1540, when Charles V rode grimly into Ghent to punish
the city for its defiance of him, his earliest act was to sentence Roland to be removed from the Belfry and destroyed. In later years,
the missing Roland was replaced by an equally enormous
"Triumphante". In the 20th century, the latter cracked and had to
be removed when human bell-ringers were replaced by a faulty
electric mechanism to sound its awesome tones. You can see the
unhappy "Triumphante", and thus gain an idea of Roland's size,
by simply walking to the square directly in front of the Belfry—
the Burgomaster Braunplein—where it sits under all weather in a
grassy nook on a ground-level pedestal. In 1948, a new Roland
bearing the proud inscription "Als mense luyd es storme int lant"
(When I ring, there's a storm in the land) was hoisted into the Belfry to accompany 51 smaller bells that sound throughout the day.
You can see the bells, and enjoy an exhilarating, panoramic view of
Ghent, on those unpredictable days and periods when the city
opens and operates its lift to the viewing gallery of the famous
tower.

Ghent's unique, indoor "Sound and Light"

On every day throughout the year, and usually throughout
that day, the city does present a pint-sized, but surprisingly-
effective, 20-minute "Sound and Light" show on a period of its
history, that of "Ghent and Charles V", all dramatically produced
by special media effects on the second floor of the Cloth Hall
("Lakenhalle") adjoining the Belfry (ascend the stone steps outside). In cities like Rome, or Athens, or Cairo, "Sound and Light"
consists of giant spotlights stabbing through the night at epic
stone ruins, while the voice of Orson Welles or Sir John Gielgud
ponderously intones a commentary backed by symphony orches-

tras. In Ghent, the lights are cast upon a large, tabletop, miniature model of 16th-century Ghent, and successive portions of the city or key buildings are lit in colors evoking various emotions, as a commentator against a musical background tells of the love/hate affair between Ghent and its most famous native son. You see the Cathedral of St. Bavo in its setting of the 1500s, the Belfry, the hundreds of small medieval homes, and numerous buildings later destroyed—the lavish Prinsenhof where Charles was born, the Abbey of St. Bavo which Charles dismantled and replaced with a "Spaniard's Castle" designed to dominate the unruly city. It is all quite fascinating, useful to your understanding of Ghent as you later tour the city on foot, well-worth the nominal admission charge of 15 francs (41¢). And although the Ghent tourist office would never refer to the presentation as a "Sound and Light" as I have (they call it, more modestly, an "Audio-Visual Play"), it stirs the adrenalin in the way a "Sound and Light" should. "You are most heartily welcomed to Ghent", booms the English-language announcer, as the music swells. "Enjoy the many treasures from a hard but illustrious past!"

The 20-minute "Audio-Visual Play" is presented continually throughout the day in several alternating languages: in spring, summer and fall from 9 to 12:30 and from 1:30 p.m. to 5:30 p.m., in winter until only 3:30 p.m., daily except *Mondays,* but you may have to wait for the conclusion of a French-language or Dutch-language presentation of it; there are no fixed English-language schedules, and the attendant simply puts on such tapes as the needs of his audience require—if you and your companions are the only persons about, as often happens, he will instantly turn the dial to English. While the importance of this show is not great enough to warrant a long wait, wasting your limited time in Ghent, it warrants ascending the stairs to learn if you've been lucky enough to arrive near the time of an English-language show. You usually have been.

Later, as you emerge blinking into daylight from the darkened upstairs theatre, look up at the spire that crowns the top of the Belfry. On it is a fierce copper dragon ("De Draek") several feet long but looking tiny at that height. It was allegedly brought to the city of Bruges by a crusader who had acquired it in the Middle East, then stolen from Bruges by Ghent and placed atop Ghent's Belfry. In 1500, upon the birth of Charles V in Ghent, the overjoyed people of Ghent shot cascading fireworks from the mouth of that Dragon to celebrate the fact that here at last would be a strong, native-born ruler who could devote himself single-mindedly to the problems of the country he controlled—namely Belgium. Charles, through no fault of his own, proceeded in a few short years to inherit not simply a few additional countries requiring his attention, but almost the entire world. And Belgium again became simply a pawn in larger struggles.

THE TOWN HALL OF GHENT: Now from the Belfry, we make a short detour to view the 15th-/16th-century Town Hall ("Stadhuis") of Ghent before continuing on our walk to the last of the Three Towers. Leaving the Belfry, turn sharp right down the Botermarkt for less than a hundred yards, and you'll find the extraordinary structure at the corner of Botermarkt and Hoogpoort, where it appears to be two-buildings-in-one: a fairly simple Renaissance facade along most of the Botermarkt side, an immensely ornate Gothic pattern of stone lacework and statuary, Gothic stone embroidery, Gothic curlicues and filigreed columns along the remainder of the Botermarkt and most of the Hoogpoort side. Some visitors conclude that architectural tastes changed during the period of its construction; a more cynical explanation infers that the city ran short of funds following its severe punishment by Charles V, and was forced to adopt a cheaper style of adornment on the sections as yet unfinished.

Groups visiting Ghent, and making application in advance, can visit the historic, imposing "Pacificatiezaal" (Pacification Room) inside the Town Hall, where the provinces of the Low Countries (Belgium and Holland) signed the epochal "Pacification of Ghent" in 1567—the high point of the revolt against Philip II of Spain. William of Orange had made a victorious entrance into Ghent; the Spanish seemed on the run. In a move that anticipated and pre-dated the French Revolution and American Declaration of Independence by at least 200 years, the delegates virtually ruptured their ties with the Spanish Hapsburg ruler of the Netherlands, declaring that he had forfeited his right to their unquestioning allegiance by tyrannical acts. And equally important, they declared that all groups in the provinces would henceforth respect the religious consciences of the others, abandoning the pursuit of heretics, enabling Catholics and Protestants alike to live and worship in peace. It didn't work—at least in Ghent. Within months, Ghent became a rather repressive Calvinist republic, and soon Catholic friars were being burned at the stake on the Sint-Veerleplein Square. Several years later, Spain regained control of Ghent and the other southern provinces, and Catholic rule returned to the area that is now Belgium. But what a magnificent declaration of tolerance, so historically premature, had earlier been made at the Town Hall of Ghent!

ST. NICHOLAS' CHURCH, ST. MICHAEL'S BRIDGE —AND THE GRASLEI!: Return now to the Belfry, and look

for the third tower, that of St. Nicholas' Church ("St. Niklaaskerk"), which we use as a guide post for finding St. Michael's Bridge just beyond the Church. St. Nicholas', a large part of which was built by the year 1250, is the oldest of the structures we've discussed so far, a classic example of the simple and stolid "Scheldt Gothic" style using sharp-pointed cones in place of pyramid-like spires. But recent reconstruction of its interior has required such heavy scaffolding and labor that it will remain closed to the public for several more years.

The Graslei

A thoroughfare called "Cataloniestraat" runs along the south side of the church directly into St. Michael's Bridge, after first passing the large and busy Korenmarkt Square. Upon reaching the Bridge, cross to the center and turn to the right. The canal you see was the ancient harbor of Ghent. On your left: the graceful Koornlei; on your right, the ravishing, unforgettable quay of the **Graslei,** an unbroken line of giant, glamorous Guild Houses of the 1200s to the 1600s, Romanesque, Gothic and Renaissance, rivaling the Grand' Place of Brussels in beauty and impact. Looking like a color-coordinated stage set of ornate orange, coral, yellow and reddish-brown gingerbread houses of massive size, they impress you with the power of the Guilds; cause a dizzying recognition of the once-staggering importance of this medieval city; provoke you to picture in your imagination the comings and goings of colorfully-dressed merchants in brown velvet knickers and bright yellow jerkins, in flowing lace and buckled shoes, wearing flamboyant scarlet hats, who once strode into and out of these commercial headquarters; and they instill in you a hushed reverence for age and for the past. In the order of their appearance starting near the Bridge and continuing up the Graslei, the large headquarters buildings are (1) The House of the Free Boatmen (1500s), who enjoyed superior shipping privileges to all the rest, (2) The Annex House of the Grain Measurers (1600s), (3) The tiny House of the Receiver of the Staple (1600s), a sort of customs house, (4) The Staple Warehouse (1200s!), a wide and squat Romanesque survivor of seven hundred years, (5) The Main House of the Grain Measurers (1500s), (6) The House of the Free Masons (1500s)—from whence we get: Freemasons—those renowned builders of houses who possessed all the jealously-guarded secrets of building handed down from father to son. Across the canal, the less impressive Koornlei of 17th-century structures is mainly notable for its Baroque/French Regency "House of the Un-Free Boatmen" at No. 7 on the quay—a junior guild living off the leavings of the favored Free Boatmen. When the cloth trade of Ghent declined, shipping and the collection of customs duties on grain provided much of the city's commercial income. Yet from such crass, prosaic activities, there emerged, in the form of this canalside street called Graslei, an architectural masterpiece. It leaves you weak.

Canal-boat sightseeing cruises

At the end of the Graslei, a short walk up the canal, are the embarkation docks for the two major canal-boat sightseeing companies of Ghent. They are: the **"Benelux"** company, which operates the large, glass-enclosed boats; the **De Hooiaard"** company, which operates the lower, smaller, open boats, capable of passing under a number of lower bridges that "Benelux" can't negotiate (and thus able to traverse a greater length of canal); the latter also usually omit the multiple translations of commentary necessary on the larger boats. But when it's raining outside, you'll want to be in a "Benelux"! Both companies charge 100 francs ($2.77) for adults, 60 francs ($1.67) for children 3 through 12, for their 30-minute cruises departing every 20-minutes-or-so, 10 a.m. until 6 or 7 p.m., from Easter until the end of September. As you return to the dock—having passed such unique sights as a 13th-century Dominican monastery, a medieval industrial slum, the ramparts of the Castle of the Counts, the city's only ancient home to preserve its wooden facade—the loudspeaker on your boat emits the strains of a Bach quartet, or "Eine Kleine Nachtmusik". Syrupy as it sounds, you're impressed. And you must now decide whether you have the time for such a boat-ride, or must first rush along to the Castle of the Counts of Flanders.

SIGHTS ON THE WAY TO THE CASTLE: From the end of the Graslei (a crossing called the "Grasbrug"), you continue to follow the waters of the Leie past the gigantic, gabled **Butchers Hall** ("groot Vleeshuis") of the 1400s, to a second bridge (the "Vleeshuisburg") where you turn left into the St. Veerleplein Square and the awesome Castle. But if you have the time, you'll continue on the street along the Leie called the **Kraanlei** (not to be confused with the earlier-mentioned Koornlei), which is also lined with fascinating structures—this time with fanciful, 17th-century homes ("The Seven Works of Mercy" at No. 77, "The Flying Deer" at No. 79), whose names are explained by the bas-reliefs on their facades. And if you'll proceed to No. 65 Kraanlei, you'll descend into deep architectural antiquity, consisting of 18 connected almshouses ("god-shuizen") for the poor, of which 8 were built in 1363; they now lodge the **Folklore Museum of Ghent** (admission 40 francs) devoted to exhibiting the actual "model rooms" and other realistic settings of the people and craftsmen of Ghent in the relatively modern times of 1890–1910. Apart from the one in Liège ("Musée de la Vie Wallonne"), which towers over all the rest, this is one of the better of the many folklore museums of Belgium; and an idea of its interesting contents emerges from the names of its larger exhibits: the 19th-century Grocery, the Domestic Weaver, the Cooper's Workshop, the Cobbler's Attic, Clog-Maker's Workshop, Hat and Milliner's Shop, Pipes and Tobacco, Printing Works, Baker's and Cake Shop, Barber, Chemist's Shop, Druggist, Wood-Turner, Stairmaker, Chandler, Pewterer, Almsman's House, Estaminet (Tavern), Games and Recreation, Ghent Marionette Theatre (at which the museum stages actual performances every Wednesday at 2:30 p.m., every Saturday at 3 p.m.), Lace Makers, Folk Religion and Art, Corporate Life, Photographers, Brushmakers and Basket Weavers. Your own interest in old-fashioned times will determine whether you make the detour and allocation of time for the Folklore Museum (closed Mondays in winter), which is also known as the Alyn Children's Hospice ("Kindren Halyns Hospitaal") for reasons too complex to tell here. Lacking such interest, you'll backtrack along the Kraanlei to the Vleeshuis (Butchers Hall) Bridge and cross it to the:

CASTLE OF THE COUNTS OF FLANDERS ("GRAVENSTEEN"):
MCLXXX. 1180. The Roman numerals carved into stone at the gateway entrance to the keep and the "donjon" cause as much of a chill as the grey and foreboding 12th-century bulk that looms before you. It was designed to intimidate and impress, by Philip of Alsace, Count of Flanders, who had returned to Ghent from the Crusades and built it to resemble a Crusaders' castle he had seen in Syria. Imagine the subliminal fear that burghers of Ghent carried with them as they passed this symbol of power on their daily rounds; imagine the courage it took to storm the castle, as people of Ghent repeatedly did in the 1300s. Endowed with six-foot-thick walls, drawbridges and encircling moats, battlements, turrets, firing holes and towers, it was nearly impregnable; inside were spacious underground storage areas and deep water wells (which you can view), "oubliettes" (sinister holes in the cellar floor) for disposing of recalcitrants, armories and penal chambers, high-ceilinged audience halls for receiving petitioners, separate upstairs apartments and narrow, Romanesque, arched windows for the Countess, a labyrinth of damp

stone passages and stairwells through which you, today, can clamber and climb, in a structure far more complex, and larger, than at first appears. It is important to ascend the ramparts of the donjon, the high central building, for a panoramic view of the ancient roofs and towers of Ghent; on the way upstairs through the residence of the Counts, you'll pass the even more important torture rooms and quite remarkable torture museum displaying instruments of coercion and punishment used long beyond the reign of the Counts and into recent centuries (as late as the times just before the French Revolution abolished the use of torture in Belgium in the 1790s) when the Castle served as law courts and prison for the authorities of that time. That's why you'll see a small guillotine, in addition to ornate decapitation swords, spiked iron collars (whose sharp ends you escaped only by keeping your neck in the very center of the collar for many, many sleepless hours), thumb screws, human branding irons, racks, and a form of pitchfork for preventing persons being burned at the stake from escaping the flames. (We have progressed since those days, but have we, in a time when politicians still clamor for capital punishment, progressed very far?) Incidentally, elements of the foundations of the Castle are believed to date from construction done by Baldwin of the Iron Arm in the 800s, and in recent years, coins and other relics of even earlier Gallo-Roman times have been unearthed in excavations still in progress. But the main structure was completed, as the inscription he placed on the gateway entrance tells you, by Philip of Alsace in 1180. MCLXXX!

Admission to the Castle of the Counts is 50 francs ($1.39). For 60 francs ($1.67) more, you can gain entrance to a modern theatre housed within a Castle building of the 1100s, where the City of Ghent presents a stirring, multi-screen, multi-projector, 30-minute film on the history and culture of Ghent ("Ghent in Multi-Vision", the "Ghent Experience") every day from 9:20 a.m. to 5:10 p.m., from April 1 to October 2; the English-language version is presented twice daily at 10 a.m. and 1:50 p.m. Should those particular times prove inconvenient, you ought nevertheless to consider sitting through a French, Dutch or German presentation, because (a) the ticket counter will provide you with a written, English language summary of the narration, in any event; and (b) the narration accounts for only about a third of the running time of the film, the rest occurring with musical background only. Having, by this time, personally viewed most of the sights of the "Golden Rectangle of Ghent", you'll enjoy repeating and absorbing the experience through the eyes of skilled camera people.

The Castle of the Counts of Flanders (the "Gravensteen")

does not follow traditional museum schedules of Ghent, but is open every day of the week from 9 a.m. until 5:15 p.m. in spring, summer and fall, until 3:15 p.m. only from October 2 through March 31.

THE FRIDAY MARKET ("VRIJDAGMARKT"): The
gateway entrance to the Castle of the Counts looks out on the St. Veerle Square (St. Veerleplein), where medieval prisoners from the Castle were taken for their public executions. If you will re-cross the River Leie at this point and turn left on the Langemunt, you will soon reach the giant Friday Market Square ("Vrijdagmarkt") whose entrance is marked by a massive cannon, **Dulle Griet** (Mad Meg), used by the armies of the Dukes of Burgundy in the mid-1400s, and now found on a small "Kanonplein" (Cannon Square) of its own, a short block from the larger square. Dulle Griet was able to hurl a cannon ball weighing several thousands of pounds.

When people have organized, rebelled, rioted or otherwise protested in Ghent, they have generally done so in the Friday Market Square. They did so in the 1300s under the leadership of Jacob van Artevelde, whose statue now stands there on a granite base bearing the colorful shields of the 52 guilds—those associations of craftsmen controlling all economic life in medieval Ghent. They did so in the late 1800s under Edward Anseele, noted founder of the Socialist Party of Belgium, who came from Ghent. Scan the buildings surrounding the Square until you view a turn-of-the-century, office-type structure bearing the strangely proud inscription, "Ons Huis" (Our House). Above it, again inscribed in stone and in Dutch, are the words "Werklieden aller Landen, Vereenigt U" (Workers of all nations, unite!). This is Ghent head-quarters for one of Belgium's three major political groupings, the Socialist Workers Party.

In the year 1800, after centuries of economic decline, mass-scale manufacturing activity had returned to Ghent when a prominent citizen named Lieven Bauwens stole the British "spinning jenny" (a pioneering, cloth-making machine) from one of its factory locations in Manchester, spirited it piecemeal across the Channel to Ghent, and brought along several workers from Manchester to teach their Flemish counterparts to use it. He was soon operating a prosperous linen factory in an abandoned Abbey, and thousands of persons soon flocked to Ghent to seek work in cloth-making plants soon sprouting like mushrooms. In their wake came urban slums, a sharp decline in living standards, child labor and other classic industrial conditions of the late 1800s that caused Anseele to rail and thunder. If, on your earlier visit to the

Castle of the Counts of Flanders, you climbed to one of the high vantage points atop the walls, you were able to see the 19th-century factory smokestacks and their surrounding working quarters that marked this era of Ghent's history. It is in the Friday Market Square that one now most poignantly feels the hard-fought rise of "syndicalism" (unionism) in Belgium that soon took on a political character and led to the formation by Anseele of a Socialist party that won seats in the Belgian parliament as early as 1894—twelve years before the British Labor Party did the same in England. From this beginning sprang a comprehensive Belgian system of welfare, and regulation of working conditions, that provided an early example for much of the rest of Europe.

SIGHTS OUTSIDE THE "GOLDEN TRIANGLE"—MUSEUM OF FINE ARTS, AND THE "BIJLOKE": No
one with a serious interest in art and/or antiquities will leave Ghent without first visiting two final, major institutions a mile south of the Rectangle. To reach both, go to the "Korenmarkt" (Corn Market Square), the so-called "centrum" of Ghent, and there board any streetcar going to St. Pieter's Station—they bear a "St. Pieter's" sign, charge 24 francs (67¢), and head south along the major shopping street of Ghent whose name changes from Veldstraat to Nederkouter to Kortrijksepoortstraat. Get off at the intersecting Charles de Kerchovelaan, near the Citadel Park. To your left, walking uphill for several hundred yards along the Park, is the Museum of Fine Arts; to your right for a slightly shorter distance along the Ijzerlaan to the Bijlokekaai, is the Bijloke Museum.

Ghent's Museum of Fine Arts
You'll find it in the Park, at the end of the Park, a somewhat incongruous Greek temple of reddish limestone and brick, adorned with winged statues, fronted by Doric columns, a Belgian flag on top. It is not a large museum, and it attempts, in somewhat schizoid fashion, to divide its viewing space precisely in half to show Ancient Art (on your right) and Modern Art (on your left). But it is wonderfully lit by large sky-lights cut into the roof, and it presents a select group of masterworks in quantities small enough to be savored at leisure; they do not overwhelm you with choice. And though several rather secondary (but quite worthy) 15th-century "Primitives" are dutifully displayed in Room 1, the highlights are from the 16th century consisting of two renowned classics by Hieronymus Bosch in Room 3, and three by Peter Bruegel the Younger (son of the towering, early 16th-century figure) in Room 6.

Bosch's **"Christ Carrying the Cross"**, found here, is his last-known painting, and a sharp divergence from the jumbled, fantastical panoramas of grotesque little people impaled on spikes or emerging from cracked eggs while fishes dropping bombs fly overhead, for which this earliest (1450–1516) of the Belgian surrealists is famed. But though the mood is less visionary, less nightmarish, it is nonetheless impassioned. The painting consists simply of 18 heads, of which 16 are bestial, uncaring individuals of all sorts who mock or decry or disregard the idealist, here Christ carrying the Cross. The Flemish/Dutch Bosch, who particularly disliked members of religious orders, took pains to include a crazed, tonsured monk at upper right, then counter-balanced that figure by the head of St. Veronica at bottom left, carrying her handkerchief with the image of Christ. The composition, especially the diagonal of the cross, is breathtaking, the painting so modern it could have been done in 1989. The other great Bosch in Ghent's Museum of Fine Arts is **"De Heilige St. Jerome"** (the Holy St. Jerome), a similar departure from numerous earlier works in which Bosch had repeatedly dwelt on the worldly or erotic temptations that beset the holy man seeking the Godhead through intense prayer or contemplation. Here, in a calmer painting undoubtedly done towards the end of Bosch's life (like all his works, it is undated), and containing no "temptations", an emaciated St. Jerome simply lies outstretched upon a rock, praying to a crucifix, in a strange glen of discarded stone objects, one perhaps a tablet of the commandments, far from a peaceful green world in the background. It portrays an individual who has seemingly achieved peace and calm understanding, which one hopes was also then the state of the once-agitated Bosch.

The three, much-reproduced masterpieces by Pieter Brueghel the Younger (known as "Hell" Brueghel; he is the profligate and somewhat less prolific of the two sons of the elder Peter Brueghel) are in a totally different mood of playful affection, love of the common folk, gentle needling of human attitudes and poses; and they are the son's own paintings, not copies of his father's greater scenes (as is the case with much of the younger Brueghel's work in Brussels' Museum of Ancient Art); they alone justify a visit to Ghent's Museum of Fine Arts. **Wedding Feast** ("Boerenbruiloft") is that classic composition (found on restaurant place settings all over Belgium) of two, aproned, volunteer waiters emerging on the run from the unseen kitchen of a barn with heavy planks supporting wooden bowls of warm pudding (or is it mush, or pancakes?) to the guests at a long table. The bride is easily spotted; she sits under an identifying object tacked against a cloth on the wall of the barn. But where is the groom? Or is this a pre-wedding reception when guests traditionally brought gifts of money to the bride, in the absence of the groom? **Village Wedding** ("Dorpsbruiloft") portrays the unbridled revelry of guests after the ceremony: couples dancing to a bagpiper, one man with bulging codpiece; couples kissing; a guest urinating against the wall (upper left), others in a dalliance (at upper right), the bride (apparently) at center rear underneath a basket tacked to a hanging cloth. **"The Lawyer of Bad Things"** ("Advocaat van Schlechte Zaken") is a stinging portrait of apprehensive and obsequious peasants waiting in line to confer with a smug and unbearably arrogant lawyer, his office so strewn with papers as to highlight his less-than-useful role in society. Other commentators (perhaps lawyers) have appended the far-less-satisfying title of "The Paying of the Tithes" to this sardonic commentary on foolish pomposity, but I for one can't find the basis for the latter name.

Other highlights of the "ancient art" section of Ghent's Museum of Fine Arts include a number of small sketches and tentatives by Peter Paul Rubens in Rooms 1 and 7 (his **"De Geseling Christi"**, the "Flagellation of Christ", is especially noteworthy); other 17th-century works by Anthony van Dyck; as well as the great **Familieportret** ("Portrait of a Family") by Cornelis de Vos (1585–1651), the superb **Heads of Two Men** by Jacob Jordaens (1593–1678), all in Room 7; the **Bejaarde Dame** ("Portrait of an Elderly Lady") by Frans Hals in Room 11; and various other Dutch/Flemish masters (Nicolaes Maes and Govaert Flinck) in Rooms 10 and 11. A Tintoretto is found in Room 12!

The modern section of Ghent's Museum of Fine Arts is administered by a separate **Museum of Contemporary Art,** whose supporters have sought for years to house their increasingly-important collection in a separate building to be someday found or erected in Ghent (it would then become the second major museum wholly devoted to modern art in Belgium, after Brussels'). Because their 400-or-so paintings and other objects are far too many for the space allotted to them here, the works must be constantly rotated between warehouse and display area, in ever-changing exhibitions, but the paintings that are *always* displayed include: James Ensor's (1860–1949) monumental achievement of the 19th century, **Lady with Masks** ("De Oude met Maskers"), in which that period's most eminent Belgian master created a new world of modern art; Georges Rouault's **The Holy Face,** a similar breakthrough in abstraction; works by Yves de Smet; the utopian aircraft of a Belgian fantasist named Panamarenko; paintings by Pol Mara of Antwerp; and dozens of other extremely exciting experiments by Belgian men and women working on the frontiers of art. But much as I would like to discuss them (especially Roger Raveel, he of the Brussels subway), I can't guarantee that specific works will be on display at the time of your visit. Go instead to see a contemporary general collection of the highest order.

Ghent's **Museum of Fine Arts** ("Museum voor Schone Kunsten"), incorporating the Museum of Contemporary Art, is open daily except Mondays from 9 to 12:30 and from 1:30 to 5:30 p.m., and charges admission of 40 francs ($1.11). Its address, in Citadel Park, is 3 Nicolaas de Liemaeckereplein.

The Bijloke Museum

Well past the other end of Citadel Park, but not far, is a final "should see" attraction of Ghent. It houses the richest collection of antiquities in all of Belgium, displayed in a remarkable Abbey attached to a medieval hospital, of which parts were built in the 13th century, others in the 14th century. For several ensuing centuries, the Abbey of Bijloke, at 2 Godshuizenlaan, lodged an order of Cistercian Nuns until it became, in recent times, the "Museum of Antiquities". It is one of nine major abbeys, monasteries, convents and beguinages in Ghent that somehow survived, and coexisted with, the strong secular strains of the city's history. Two other abbeys—that of St. Bavo on the Gandastraat, and St. Peter's Abbey on St. Pietersplein—are also open to the public, the former mainly for its outer ruins, but it is in this Bijloke Abbey and museum that one gains the best impression of medieval monastic life, in addition to viewing a remarkable exhibit of the treasures of the city of Ghent itself.

GHENT'S EVENING ENTERTAINMENT: In addition to a lively, seven-member group of Flemish-language theatres, where you won't understand a word, Ghent maintains an impressive, 19th-century musical theatre, the **Royal Opera** ("Koninklijke Opera"), at 3 Schouwburgstraat, presenting operas in their original languages (Italian, French, German) on Fridays, Saturdays, Sundays (matinee only) and Tuesdays from October until mid-June. It presents classics of the spoken theatre (Hamlet and the like) at the large and traditional **Royal Flemish Theatre,** at 7 St. Baafsplein, just in front of the entrance to St. Bavo's Cathedral, on Fridays, Saturdays, Sundays (matinee only), Mondays and Thursdays, attracting some theatre buffs among non-Dutch-speaking tourists already familiar with those classics. And it presents pantomime theatre causing no trouble at all, on Saturday and Sunday evenings at the **Hoste-Sabbatini Theatre,** at 23 Burgstraat (phone 25-25-15).

The **"Festival of Flanders"** in Ghent, of celebrated international musical performers, runs from late August to mid-September, and is presented not simply in the standard theatres, but in enchanting special settings: the Town Hall, the Castle of the Counts, St. Bavo's Cathedral. Tickets are sold, commencing June 1, at Info-Toerisme, 37 Graaf van Vlaanderenplein, Ghent, while a schedule of performances can be had at an earlier time from Festival van Vlaanderen, 18 Eugeen Flageyplein, Brussels.

Beyond those opportunities, it warrants re-mentioning that movies in Flemish cities such as Ghent are always presented in their original languages, never dubbed. For many tourists surfeited with culture, the most pleasant evening activity is simply a relaxing film. And after the repeated blows to your solar plexus from the greatest sights of Ghent—the Mystic Lamb! the Castle of the Counts! the Graslei!—a little mindless evening relaxation, at a cinema and following a leisurely Belgian meal, isn't such a bad idea. The theatres showing multiple films each night include **Calypso 1, 2 and 3**, at St. Michielshelling (phone 23-35-03), **Studio Skoop I and II**, at 63 Jacob van Arteveldeplein (phone 23-49-48), and **Majestic Club 2000**, at 56 Veldstraat (phone 24-20-06); there are others.

SHOPPING IN GHENT: Antiques and art are the items that most foreign shoppers seek out in Ghent. The antiquarians are clustered on the Onderbergen (where there's **Van Hoecke**, at No. 6, **Beyst**, at No. 40, **'t Gouden Pand**, at No. 66), on the Bagattenstraat (**Antica**, at No. 163 and **Buyle**, at No. 154), and on the more easily found, but often more expensive, Koornlei (**Coorevits**, at No. 1, **Verhaeghe**, at No. 2) and Kraanlei (**Rosa Roos**, at No. 13, **Meirlaen**, at No. 17). Despite the current exchange rate for the Belgian franc, you can often discover remarkable values, especially for the smaller pieces that you can carry back with you. The art galleries selling originals of contemporary Gentenaars are most easily found on that important shopping street, the Nederkouter (**Gallery Vyncke-Van Eyck**, at No. 37, **Kaleidoskoop**, at No. 45), which then becomes Kortrijksepoortstraat (**Gallery Aktuee**, at No. 61), which in turn intersects with the De Kerchovelaan (**Lavuum**, at No. 45) about a mile from the center. Again you'll find prices considerably lower than you're accustomed to pay for art at home.

The cheapest of the large variety stores, good for a whole host of mundane wants, is the **Sarma**, on the central Korenmarkt (Corn Market) Square. Needing an extra suitcase to carry back overflow purchases and clothes, I recently bought a serviceable cardboard variety there for the equivalent of $12. The standard stores are on the city's major shopping street, the **Veldstraat**, running southwards off the sightseeing area near St. Nicholas' Church. There's a big **Inno** department store there, as well as every other well-known chain and boutique; it is on the site of "Inno" that John Quincy Adams (6th President of the United States), Henry Clay and Albert Gallatin lived for six months in 1814 while negotiating the Treaty of Ghent that ended the U.S. war with England. Several steps further along, at No. 55 Veldstraat, is the **"House of the Hundred Days"** (the 18th-century, rococo mansion of the "d'Hane-Steenhuyse"), so called because Louis XVIII of France, fleeing from Paris, lived here and entertained lavishly during the period between Napoleon's escape from Elba, and Waterloo; its ballroom possesses the world's most extraordinary parquet floor, five years in the making, and proudly signed by the expert carpenter who made it—ask an attendant to pull back the carpet to show you. (Pardon the digression, but even on a shopping excursion, one cannot escape the eventful history of Ghent!) Suffice to say that every variety of European merchandise and Belgian wares are available on the Veldstraat, its sidestreets, and its extension.

MISCELLANY OF GHENT: Desiderius Erasmus said it best:
"I do not think that in all Christendom there is a city that compares with Ghent in majesty and might". . . . Starting your sightseeing at the "Audio-Visual Play" on the second floor of the Cloth Hall next to the Belfry, you can save nearly a dollar per person by purchasing a "Combination Ticket" for 175 francs adults, 120 francs children, that admits you to the "Audio-Visual Play", the Mystic Lamb and Crypt at St. Bavo's, the Gravensteen (Count's Castle) and "Ghent in Multi-Vision" show, and on a boat trip of the Leie. I'd still begin at St. Bavo's. . . . Though the several more important institutions (St. Bavo's, the Castle, others) are open daily, most museums in Ghent are closed on Mondays, and that might be taken into account in scheduling your visit. Museums are otherwise open from 9 to 12:30 and from 1:30 to 5:30 p.m. . . . If you're staying near the railroad station of Ghent, you can treat yourself by strolling to **Vandenbouhede,** at 153 Blvd. Koningin Astridlaan, just off the station square. This is a perfectly ordinary Belgian bakery, no different tham many others, and therefore all the more astonishing in revealing the heights to which Belgian bakeries aspire and reach. Walk inside and splurge 20 francs (56¢) on an elaborate, fresh fruit tart, or a feathery chocolate eclair; simply to smell the merchandise is to swoon! . . . Maurice Maeterlinck (1862–1949), the mystical, anti-naturalist, Nobel Prize-winning playwright, who sought to penetrate beyond reality, deep into the inner life of both people and the universe, in

such plays as *The Intruder, Pelleas et Melisande, The Blue Bird,* was born in Ghent and educated at its University. Students of theatre have puzzled over his slogan, "Within me there is more", obviously inspired by the "Plus est en vous" motto of Louis de Gruuthuse in nearby Bruges. . . . Speaking of Bruges, remember that it was a trading city of medieval times, while Ghent was a manufacturing city. . . . Surely, that reddish brown building on the Graslei, and the adjoining one in tones of yellow and light orange, are both among the greatest architectural feats of all time. . . . Walking in a reverse direction from the touring itinerary earlier recommended, one passes alongside the Kraanlei enraptured at the sight, thinking nothing could be more beautiful. But the best is yet to come, at the Koornlei facing the remarkable **Graslei** of Ghent.

CASTLES ON THE OUTSKIRTS: St. Niklaas, Den-

dermonde, Aalst and Oudenaarde are the chief satellite cities of Ghent about 18 to 20 miles away, each with stunning Gothic town halls and market places lined by step-gabled homes and headquarters, all easily reached if you have a car for roaming through "East Flanders". Along the way, you can stop at or pass by two celebrated 14th-century castles: magnificent **Ooidonk,** off the road to Deinze (past Deurle) in the direction of Kortrijk (but this one, being still inhabited, can be visited inside only on Sundays in July, August and the first half of September; all other times, you simply drive around the grounds), and stately **Laarne,** which can be visited thoroughly, inside and out, for a 50-franc admission fee, daily except Mondays (and even on Mondays in crowded July and August) from 10 to noon and 2 to 6; take the highway towards Ostende and turn off towards Destelbergen. Among the best-preserved medieval castles of Europe, Laarne is today furnished with 17th-century pieces, but your own imagination will quickly conjure up the look of earlier times. That's because you've now been to Ghent!

Ghent—the Lion of Flanders, a cross about its neck, a crown upon its head! Though other Flemish cities use a similar symbol, Ghent deserves it best! In this vital metropolis and through its remarkable history, Belgium teaches a lesson about the unquenchable human urge for liberty, progress and justice.

CHAPTER VII

ANTWERP AND ITS DIAMONDS

□ □ □

ANTWERP
MECHELEN
LIER

They shimmer, they sparkle, they illumine and glow, almost to the same degree as the actual diamonds flooding into its sprawling, world-famous "bourse" (market) of precious stones. Imagine a city literally studded with diamonds, structural gems, so resplendent and glittering that "diamond" is the only suitable image that springs to your mind as you dream-walk through Antwerp. Diamonds? The glamorous, 17th-century home of Rubens is an Antwerp diamond, radiant with the spirit of genius. The tiny Museum Mayer van den Bergh, with its burnished woods and colored marble, its priceless Bruegels, is a diamond. The awesome and classic Antwerp Museum of Fine Arts is a diamond "as big as the Ritz". And that strange-sounding Plantin-Moretus of Antwerp, a luxurious "factory" of 16th-century books, in textured stone and embossed-leather walls—it, too, is quite simply a diamond, as all of them are, as precious and treasured as the blue-white gems that make up the city's most famous industry.

ANTWERP, THE CITY THAT SUCCEEDED

In purely material terms, Antwerp is perhaps the richest city of Belgium. Its giant port (third largest in the world), host to thousands of ships each year, throbs with energy and movement; while its elegant, main, shopping thoroughfare—the **Meir**—supports large, bustling stores of the most modern appearance. Its highly cosmopolitan nightlife section extends over a considerable area and remains brightly-lit and active until late, late at night. Its population, including suburbs and such, is approaching 1,000,000, rivalling Brussels.

But it is in the quality of its urban life, in urban services, as a liveable city, and not simply in terms of high income (for Dallas and Houston have that, too), that Antwerp is, in the ultimate sense, "successful", impressing city planners from around the world. It is one of the few large cities to have preserved the attractive ancient architecture and traditions of its central area without sacrificing commercial progress or becoming a "dead city". Its entire, large inner portion extending from the River Scheldt to the intermediate ring avenues of the Frankrijklei and Italielei contain scarcely a single skyscraper, and none of the blight associated with office projects. People live, in large numbers, in the central city, and leaven the commerce of that area with their presence. They enjoy parks and numerous open spaces. The poor live not in dehumanized, high-rise rectangles, but in graceful structures resulting from the single most innovative approach to repairing war-damage, or replacing slum decay, in Europe: neo-medieval, four-story townhouses along winding, ancient lanes, all of the most modern construction, but of abstract design approximating the styles of the Middle Ages. In the project known as "Onze Woning" in the area of the **Butchers Hall** (the "Vleeshuis") near the Market Square, you'll be goggle-eyed at the unusual "social housing" (subsidized, low-income housing) that replaced the devastation caused by German V-1 and V-2 rocket attacks in World War II.

THE CITY OF NEW IDEAS—A HISTORY: In thus approaching its modern, urban problems, Antwerp has shown the same freshness of attitude that characterized its commercial policies in the Middle Ages. While other Flemish cities became increasingly mired in the restrictive rules of the Guilds, in ancient "privileges" and stultifying practices, Antwerp was daring to follow a more modern course. It simplified commercial systems, threw open whole business areas to persons outside of the Guilds, narrowed the veto powers of Guild leaders, organized factories as a means of production, opened one of the earliest Stock Exchanges. Medieval merchants soon began pouring into Antwerp, breaking their links with other cities; at the same time, Antwerp's chief commercial rival, Bruges, suffered that terminal blow: the silting of the Zwin Estuary (see our Bruges chapter), blocking Bruges' access to the sea, causing transport to shift to Antwerp.

As Bruges declined, Antwerp soared. From its key position on the broad River Scheldt, enjoying harbors of breathtaking size and direct, easy access to the sea, it became a trading center without compare. By the early 1500s, with Bruges eclipsed, Antwerp emerged as the most powerful commercial city of the world, and a place of resplendent appearance and culture.

Of all the ancient "art cities" of Belgium, it is therefore the "newest" and most "modern". Whereas Tournai reached its peak of influence in the 1100s, Bruges and Ghent in the 1200s and 1300s, Brussels in the 1400s, Antwerp enjoyed its headiest period in the 1500s, and saw itself as the prophet of a New Age. When city fathers began construction of a new Town Hall in 1565, they scorned the notion of designing it in medieval Gothic style, in the manner of the great town halls of Brussels or Louvain. Rather, they turned to the architecture of the Renaissance, in which form you see that structure today on the Market Square.

Early origins

Deep water, a natural port on the right bank of the River Scheldt, caused Antwerp to be a Gallo-Roman settlement as early as the 2d century A.D., and probably accounts for the city's name: "aan-de-werpen" (on the wharves), or "anda" (opposite) the "werpen" (waterway). Invaded and populated by Salic Franks from Germany in the 5th century, it soon developed a towering, stone fortress along the riverside (whose successor—the impressive, 13th-century "Steen"—stands beside the water today, housing the National Maritime Museum), became a municipality/county of the Holy Roman (German) Empire in the 900s, passed to the Dukes of Brabant (vassals of the Holy Roman Emperor) in the 1100s. As you cruise upon the River Scheldt in the course of your own stay, conjure in your mind that the far, opposite, Left Bank was once enemy territory belonging to the French-allied Counts of Flanders, while the city on the Right Bank remained loyal to the loosely-German-supporting Dukes of Brabant. In 1357 the city was seized by the Count of Flanders, then passed in the 1400s (as did both the Low Countries) to the Dukes of Burgundy, and then in the 1500s to the Hapsburgs (Charles V), under whom Antwerp enjoyed its greatest prosperity.

And later development

In the religious upheavals of the late 1500s, culminating in the revolt of the Netherlands against Philip II of Spain, commercial Antwerp was—as you'd expect—a Protestant stronghold, the actual headquarters of William the Silent. On November 4, 1576, it suffered terrible retribution in the form of the "Spanish Fury", as unpaid troops of the Duke of Alva slaughtered eight thousand citizens, destroyed a thousand buildings, plundered and tortured to the cry of *"Santiago! España! A sangre, a carne, a fuego, a sacco!"* (St. James! Spain! To blood, to flesh, to fire, to sack!) Later occupied by Spain, and brought firmly back to the southern camp, it suffered a second blow from the victorious Dutch in the north: they closed the Scheldt, which runs mainly through Dutch territory for most of its upper length, blocking Antwerp's access to the sea for the next two hundred years. But though Antwerp suffered a major decline, it remained a strong commercial center, becoming also a capital for the Catholic Counter Reformation in the 1600s, as well as a burgeoning artistic and intellectual center graced by its renowned Peter Paul Rubens and Anthony van Dyck.

In 1800, Napoleon Bonaparte strides upon the scene. The French at long last have reopened the Scheldt to Antwerp, and the visionary Emperor sees Antwerp as "un pistolet braqué sur le coeur d'Angleterre" (a pistol aimed at the heart of England). Giant new docks are begun, seagoing commerce is revived, and the port of Antwerp grows to a 20th-century size only slightly smaller than that of Rotterdam or New York. In World War II it serves as a chief supply harbor for the Allied armies, undergoing vicious bombardment by self-propelled German rockets. Today, prosperous and progressive, but often too self-confident to trumpet its attractions abroad, it is the most underrated tourist city in all of Europe—a treasure house of extraordinary riches, of fine dining and entertainment, vital and alive.

ORIENTATION AND GETTING AROUND: It is also the easiest city in Belgium for tourists to wander, because it possesses one continuous thoroughfare (under different names, but one major one) that cuts across the city from west to east along or near a great many of the sights of tourist interest.

A street called Meir

Most of Antwerp occupies the right bank of the River Scheldt ("Schelde" in Dutch, "L'Escaut" in French). Imagine the Scheldt running north-and-south (it is actually slightly angled here—but no matter). From the very mid-point of that central river area, near the turreted fortress of the "Steen" and the place from which "Flandria" sightseeing boats leave for their excursions on the river, is the first section of the "tourists' street"—the quaint *Suikerrui* ("Sugar Quay") lined with budget restaurants and inexpensive cafes.

From the river, the Suikerrui proceeds, in two tiny blocks, to emerge into the vast **Market Square** of Antwerp, a subdued and less fanciful rival of Brussels' Grand' Place, with its Renaissance Town Hall, 16th-century Guild Houses, and famous statue of the Roman centurion Brabo—he seems hauntingly alive, in eternal motion—flinging the amputated hand of the evil giant Druon into the Scheldt. Prior to Brabo's victory in the ancient legend, Druon had exacted cruel tributes from boatmen passing on the river, cutting off the hands of those unable to pay. Now he suffers the same fate, inadvertently providing the alternate (but totally specious) explanation of the city's name, from "ant" (hand) "werpen" (to throw): Antwerp.

A tiny block from the "top" of the Market Square (opposite the Town Hall), and you are at the great **Antwerp Cathedral,** to which we'll be returning later. Along the right-hand side of the Cathedral (as you face it), a bit further up, is a mammoth, elongated square lined with the sidewalk tables of cheery cafes surrounding the statue of Peter Paul Rubens: it is called the **Groenplaats.** At the top, wide side of the same square, going in the same direction, are then two curving streets—"Eiermarkt" and "Schoenmarkt" —that both emerge into the **Meir.** And now you are home free. For the "Meir" (pronounced "mare", as in "old grey mare") is the broad, main, shopping boulevard of Antwerp, traversing much of the inner city and lined with every major store. Halfway along it, to your right, is the garden promenade called the "Wapperstraat" housing the Home of Rubens, main attraction of Antwerp (you'll see it immediately).

Along the Meir is the recently-erected statue-memorial to Rubens' student, Anthony van Dyck, so spanking white in its newly-cut stone that residents call it "the ice cream cone". As it nears the main railroad station, the Meir almost imperceptibly changes its name to **Leysstraat** for a one-block stretch, and then becomes the important, broad **De Keyserlei.**

The "Keyserlei" is the major movie-theatre street of Antwerp, and serves as a border of the vast entertainment district of several square blocks immediately to the north. In a short while, the "Keyserlei" ends at the **railroad station.** The **"diamond district"** is to the immediate right of the station, along and between the Pelikaanstraat and Vestingstraat. The wondrous zoo of Antwerp —in the heart of the city!—is to the immediate left of the station (as you face it).

From the river to the railroad station: the Suikerrui, Market Square, Cathedral, Groenplaats, Meir ("swamp" or "lowland") and De Keyserlei. Because they all flow in one direction, as almost a single artery, I like to call them all by the name of their longest stretch: Meir—a street called Meir. You can walk the entire distance in a brisk half-hour. You can also take a streetcar along the entire route (30 francs) between the railroad station and the Groenplaats, plunging underground along the Meir and De Keyserlei.

A few pages from here, we'll be returning to the sights found near the Suikkerui and the Meir. Before we do, we'll treat briefly with the hotels and restaurants of Antwerp.

HOTELS OF ANTWERP: Belgium's richest city possesses the nation's richest city hotel: **Le Rosier,** 21 Rosier (phone 231-2497), a glamorous, satin-walled townhouse of plushly-decorated rooms, all in scarlet red, or in brown or lavender, like out of the Arabian nights—a child's dream of luxury, almost too-obviously-designed by a three-man partnership (two decorators and an antiques dealer) for honeymooning couples or wealthy executives on a spree. If satiny, boudoir living is your cup of tea, and you're able to pay from 5500 to 6500 francs ($153 to $181) per room, depending on size, you'll make long-in-advance reservations for this "stately pleasure dome", where high tea is served downstairs for 350 francs ($9.72) per person, next to French windows, floor-to-ceiling, looking out onto an exquisite garden.

Coming down from that level, the city's top first class hotels, in large modern buildings, are mainly located on the outskirts of the inner city, usually at the turn-offs from modern motorways, and therefore more suitable for busy, business travellers possessing their own cars, than for tourists. Because you're well familiar with this rather standard type of functional, modern, slab-sided, high-rise hotel, we'll mention only that their rates average 4100 francs ($114) per double room, 3300 francs ($92) single, with breakfast, service and tax included, and that their names are **Crest Hotel,** 10 G. Legrellelaan (phone 237-2900) (300 rooms); and **Quality Inn,** 66b Luit. Lippenslaan (phone 235-9191) (180 rooms). Nearby, a tiny bit closer to town, the 220-room **Pullman-Park** at 94 Desguinlei (phone 216-4800), is even tonier than the first two, a thoroughly deluxe and quite stunning structure with marble throughout and atrium-high water sculpture in the lobby—it could have been built for Dallas. But double rooms are 5400 francs ($150), singles a more moderate 2900 francs ($81), including buffet breakfast, and the taxi ride to the Central Station, say, or to centrally-located sightseeing, is at least 240 francs ($6.67), each way. The modern, 120-room **Novotel,** 6 Luithagen-haven (phone 542-0320), is also on the outskirts, but a notch down in category, charging only 2850 francs ($79) for a double room with breakfast, service and tax.

In the touristically-important, inner city of Antwerp (the area between the train station and the river), the city's top hotel (after the Rosier; it, too, is central) is also its newest: the 95-room, four-star **Hotel Carlton** at 25 Quinten Matsijslei (phone 231-1515), within easy walking distance of everything important, and completed in 1988. A refined and distinguished hotel, but modern in style and with well-equipped rooms, its rates are fairly moderate for its category (at least in its first year of operation—they'll undoubtedly ascend): 2900 francs ($81) for a standard single, 3700 francs ($103) for a standard double, 3400 francs ($94) for a superior single, 4200 francs ($117) for a superior double, always including continental breakfast. Weekends (Friday and Saturday nights), the charge drops to 2900 francs ($81) for either a single or double superior room.

Runner-up to the Carlton is the equally-modern, 120-room **Hotel De Keyser,** 66 De Keyserlei (phone 234-0135), a block from the train station, and itself a seven-story "block" of glass and stainless steel, with black marble lobby, dark subdued lighting—you get the picture. Rooms are modern, functional, of reasonable comfort, but otherwise undistinguished, and rent for a high (by Belgian standards) 5340 francs ($148) double, in high season, with breakfast and all else, 4180 francs ($116) single with breakfast. De Keyser belongs to the Alfa International chain which operates three other, spanking-new, gleamingly-modern, strictly-functional hotels in the center of Antwerp: the small **Empire Hotel,** 13 Appelmansstraat (phone 231-4755), in the diamond district, marred only by the entrance to a parking garage next door, but with attractive rooms (4500 francs ($125) in high season for most double rooms, with breakfast, service and tax); the impressive, glass-sided **Theatre Hotel,** 30 Arenbergstraat (phone 231-1720) (3540 to 4120 francs, $98 to $114, double with breakfast); and the slightly larger, slightly more modest **Congress Hotel** at

136 Plantin en Moretuslei (phone 235-3000) (2860 francs, $79, per double room, breakfast included, 2530 francs, $70, single). On a lovely, leafy boulevard just beyond the commerce but within easy walking distance of it, the somewhat older **Hotel Plaza,** 43 Charlottalei (phone 239-5970), with its big picture windows, its elegant but modern comforts, is ranked close to the Carlton and De Keyser, but charges less than 4000 francs ($111) for most of its double rooms (with breakfast).

In the moderately-priced category ($80 or so for a double room), the Congress Hotel named above is your leading specimen, and about the only suitable choice in the central city area. From there one descends to the budget category, where Antwerp shines. For at the large (150 rooms), modern **Hotel Arcade,** 39 Meistraat (phone 231-8830), on the well-located Theater Plein (Square), double rooms rent for only 1850 francs ($51), singles for 1575 francs ($44), including service and tax, and the outlay brings you a brand-new accommodation in a recently-completed building with elevator, snack-room and bar. Its arrival on the scene provides Antwerp with reliable, medium-level lodging.

For a lesser sum, I like the rooms with private bath renting for only 1100 francs ($31) double, 800 francs ($22) single, this time including breakfast, at the 50-room **Billiard Palace Hotel,** 40 Koningin Astriplein (phone 233-4455). A block from the train station, near the bright lights of the entertainment district, "Billiard Palace" owes its name to the championship billiards tournaments played on its sweeping, second floor expanse of 26 billiards and pool tables (largest such room in Europe); yet upstairs and within, all is ladylike proper, and there are even correct young women behind the reception desk to point the way to rooms that are old-fashioned, but this time equipped with private bath at those 1100-franc levels.

The most pleasant of the city's youth hostels (open to all ages), charging 270 francs ($7.50) per person, with breakfast, is the **"Boomerang"** at 58 Volkstraat (phone 238-4782), open all year, and excitingly located on a semi-residential street only a single block from Antwerp's Royal Museum of Fine Arts. A 60-bed townhouse built in 1878 for a wealthy Antwerp family, it preserves all sorts of charming period touches, including wrought iron fireplaces and a heavy, polished, mahogany staircase leading upstairs to rooms, some of which are doubles, others 6-bedded dorms. Downstairs, off a marble lobby suitable to the in-town mansion this once was, two-course dinners are served in the evening for 210 francs ($5.83). Hostel cards are not needed, and curfews are not imposed. Alternates, at a sometimes higher price (say,

400 francs, $11.11, per person), include the **"New International Youth Pension"** at 256 Provinciestraat (phone 230-0522) and **"Square Sleep-Inn"** at 1 Bolivarplaats (phone 237-3748).

Because Antwerp is only half-an-hour by train from Brussels, surprisingly close, a great many tourists commute there from the capital, returning each night. This can be done, provided only that you allot at least two days to this attraction-packed city; and because two days are a bare minimum for enjoying Antwerp, you'd be better advised to stay overnight for a day—or two!

RESTAURANTS OF ANTWERP: From almost as many restaurant choices as Brussels offers, we can do no more than attempt a brief sampling:

The "top three" (1700 to 2200 francs, $47 to $61, plus wine)

About the very best of Antwerp's restaurants, no one is in doubt or disagreement: they are (a) the lovingly-restored, directors' room of a mercantile structure of the 16th/17th century; (b) a boat; and (c) a shrine to modern, suburban elegance.

Sir Anthony van Dijk, upstairs at 16 Oude Koornmarkt Vlaaikensgang (phone 231-61-70), no more than one hundred yards from the Town Hall, is the "centerpiece" of Antwerp's most ancient quarter, the mercantile structure described above, surrounded by exquisite antique shops in houses perfectly maintained in their former style. Upstairs in a large, stately room of dark, brown, beamed ceilings against cream-colored walls, the latter hung with oil paintings and tapestries, a rising young chef named Mark Paesbrugghe—assisted by only four others in the cooking staff—is building here a nationwide reputation for his highly-advanced, lightly-sauced, non-fattening, nouvelle cuisine; yet you can eat (with great care) for as little as 1600 francs ($44) plus the cost of wine, although you ought really to attempt the 2200 francs ($61) "menu de dégustation" (tasting menu), not including wine. Like all the great Belgian restaurants, this one offers that increasingly familiar froth of puréed chicken and duck livers ("mousse de foies") among its appetizers, but then proceeds to its own, utterly unique "mosselsoep met witloof" (a creamed broth of mussels and endives, mixing in a perfect match), and a dozen, elaborately-constructed, highly inventive main courses, all fascinating, which include veal kidneys marinated in a Trappist beer ("le rognon de veau aux petits oignons, poireaux et à la bière de Rodenbach"), baked goose liver in aged cheese and wine ("le foie d'oie poêlé au Sauternes et au Roquefort"), the latter a particularly renowned specialty. Closed Sundays, closed Saturdays for lunch, and closed the first half of August.

Restaurant La Perouse, on the Steen dock (phone 232-35-28), is a boat, one of the Flandria sightseeing fleet, that remains (usually) fixed to its mooring point on the River Scheldt almost directly in front of the Suikkerui. Though it then disappears from that mooring from late May to late September (presumably to enter sightseeing service), it sits during fall, winter and spring in the shiniest splendor—its brass and steel polished to a mirror-like gleam—performing the least-expected function of any "boat" since the S.S. France: teaching the rest of us to eat! Chefs Hugo Kermans and André Pauwels have won stars, every sort of accolade, for a thoroughly Belgian menu ("salade de crevettes grises", "waterzooi de poussin") supplemented by a very few French specialties of the classic sort, on a list in which appetizers *average* 600-or-so ($16.70) francs, main courses 850 francs ($23.60)—meaning that you will eat for just under 1900 or 2000 francs ($53 or $56), depending on whether you have dessert, but plus the cost of wine. Closed Sundays and Mondays, and of course closed all through the summer.

Restaurant de Bellefleur, 768 Kapelsesteenweg (phone 664-67-19), near park-like, zoological gardens in the area to the north of Antwerp known variously as "Ekeren" or "Kapelle", is the third "laureate" of Antwerp, best for tourists with cars, who will be repaid for the effort with a serious approach to cuisine at prices below what they'd pay for so famed a restaurant in Brussels; de Bellefleur will cost around 1700 francs ($47.20) per person, plus wine, for a grand repast prepared by its bearded young chief, Jan Buytaert. Try his "zeetong met witloof", which presents a lightly-steamed fish filet bearing a "polish" of white wine sauce, all atop a bed of endives almost "melted" into unrecognizable shape by a process known only to Mr. Buytaert. His de Bellefleur is open only on weekdays, and is closed in July.

Elegant dining for 1275 to 1500 francs ($35 to $42), plus wine

Restaurant Belon, at 3 Vestingstraat, in the heart of the entertainment district, is my own personal favorite in Antwerp, for the kindness of its maitre d' (Luc Ramael) and the genius of its chef, his wife (Liesbet Ramael)—that's a reversal of the normal roles in most high quality Belgian restaurants. Though their à la carte rates are veddy-veddy expensive, they serve a remarkable, four-course prix fixe dinner for 1500 francs ($42) all-in, which starts with six Belon oysters topped with caviar, and then goes on to scallops, next grilled duckling with accompaniments, and finally luscious dessert. All in a gleaming setting of elegance. Closed for lunch on Saturdays, and closed all day Sundays.

Neuze Neuze, 19 Wijngaardstraat (phone 232-57-83), is the trendiest of the Antwerp names, a smartly-furnished, two-story room of the most modern decor set squarely beneath the beamed ceilings and arches of an ancient structure two blocks from the Antwerp Cathedral in the oldest section of town. A quartet of chefs whose cartoon images grace the menu labor away at a highly inventive menu; their exotica includes "gebraden kwartels met mats et aardbeienazijn"—roast quail with corn and strawberry vinegar; "warme ganzelever met een honingsausje"—butter-fried goose liver with a sauce of honey; "gesmoorde kreeft met passievruchten"—stewed lobster with passion fruits; "lamsribgebraad met mostaardzaadjes en roomsaus"—roast lamb chops with mustard sauce of Meavy. The results always excite and sometimes astonish—are never dull, always fun. And because nearly all appetizers (hot and cold) are priced around 525 francs ($15), most main courses for 750 francs ($21), you'll nearly always spend 1275 francs ($35), plus wine, for a two-course meal of a very special quality. Closed Sundays, for lunch on Saturdays, and the latter half of August.

Traditional dining for 1000 francs ($28) to 1500 francs ($42), plus wine

Het Vermoeide Model ("The Bored Model"), 2 Lijnwaadmarkt (phone 233-52-61), occupying all three stories of a 16th century structure whose interior brickwork is exposed, leans against the side of the Antwerp Cathedral—the back wall is the cathedral's wall—in the fashion in which that ancient Gothic edifice was once surrounded by homes, shops, and cowsheds leaning up against it; most have now been removed. You can walk onto the top floor terrace of the "Bored Model" to glimpse still other sections of the Cathedral. Fresh fish is the specialty here, priced at 600 francs. Appetizers are mainly 250 francs, a great many desserts 150 francs. And the three courses total just under 1000 francs ($28), not including wine, for a refreshing meal in an unusual setting among a chic clientele. Open seven days a week.

Tasty, Belgian dining for 500 to 700 francs ($14 to $19), plus wine

Panaché, 17 Statiestraat, is the spacious, modern room behind Antwerp's large "charcuterie" (delicatessen) of the same name, perhaps the city's largest and busiest restaurant, as modern as anything to be seen in London, New York or Los Angeles, and located just a short block to the side of De Keyserlei; as you near the railroad station on that main thoroughfare, simply turn left for one block on either the Anneessensstraat or Briedelstraat, and there you'll be. Open until 1:30 a.m. every day of the week (but closed the entire month of August), it offers a vast selection of every conceivable dish, from "vol au vent" to spaghetti bolognaise, from eels in green sauce to chicken croquettes or rumpsteaks, all so numerous that numbers (running into the hundreds) are affixed to each menu item to facilitate easy ordering. For soup, you'll pay from 100 to 135 francs ($2.78 to $3.75), for half a roast chicken 260 francs ($7), for steaks of eight different varieties 450 francs ($12.50), for veal cutlets 375 francs ($10.40). It is difficult to spend more than $15 or $16, sometimes including wine or other beverage; and to insure you don't, order the three-course tourist menu for 475 francs ($13).

In **de Schaduw van de Kathedraal** ("A l'Ombre de la Cathedrale", In the Shadow of the Cathedral), 17 Handschoenmarkt (phone 232-40-14), directly on the picturesque little square in front of the Antwerp Cathedral, and brilliantly named, is cheaper than most others around here, with soups and appetizers for 95 to 200 francs ($2.64 to $5.56), chicken or pork dishes with potatoes for 350 and 375 francs ($9.72 and $10.40), steaks for 450 francs ($12.50). A nice-sized room with banquettes and mirrors, it adds a certain flourish to its standard Belgian dishes (which include several varieties of mussels and eels), and yet easily permits dining for under 700 francs ($19.45)—costliest in this category—but this time including wine.

De Peerdestal, 8 Wijngaardstraat (phone 231-95-03), two blocks from the Cathedral, with its large bar where you can eat speedily, or while alone, or while reading, seats 150 persons, and stays open daily except Sundays until midnight; here are high-quality dishes in fast food style! Soup for 90 francs ($2.50), mixed salad 145 francs ($4), chicken for 295 ($8.19), steaks with salad for 395 francs ($11), with fish the only pricey item. Order steak, chicken or cod-fish, and the total, with soup, will amount to about 500 francs ($14). Closed Sundays.

Standard meals for 500 francs ($15), including wine

Viskeuken, 10 Korte Koepoortstraat, near the main square and the Cathedral, is outstanding for fish—which is nearly all it serves—at moderate prices resulting, perhaps, from its large and exceedingly-plain setting. Order "raie", "kabeljauw" or "truite" (trout) at the reasonable prices (for fish dishes) of 250 to 380 francs, and avoid the costlier "lotte", "sole", "saumon" and "turbot". Or, better yet, order the special, table d'hôte lunch—fish soup, then main course, then dessert—for 450 francs ($12.50), *including* a glass of white wine.

China West, at 12 Statiestraat (phone 233-65-52), in the railroad station area one block off De Keyserlei, stays open daily until 5 *a.m.* because of the popularity of its two, four-course Chinese feasts: one at 375 francs ($10.40) for soup, eggroll ("loempia"), chicken curry and dessert, the other at 495 francs ($13.75) for a larger selection of exotic dishes, all in a large and exotically-designed restaurant.

Hearty meals from 250 to 400 francs ($7 to $11.11), including beer

For meals at this level, you go to the eight, tourist-attracting, maritime-style restaurants of paper tablecloths and hand-lettered menus on large, posted signs (but with fresh flowers on each table!) of the Suikkerui ("Sugar Quay") leading to the River Scheldt and the sightseeing boats just off the Market Square ("Grote Markt"). Golden french fries with creamy, molten innards! Steamed mussels! Roast chicken! "Carbonades" or "Stoofcarbonades" (beef stew simmered in beer)! Those are the gustatory delights of the popularly-priced "peoples' Belgium", devoured here with an appetite born of the sparkling air of the broad River Scheldt! At **Restaurant 't Steen,** 1 Suikerrui, soup followed by a half roast chicken or pork chop or "carbonades", with french fries and vegetable, total all of 300 francs ($8.33). Steamed mussels with french fries "à volonté" (as many as you wish) are 350 francs ($9.72), spaghetti 150 francs ($4.17), an omelette 90 francs ($2.50). At **Restaurant Overzetboot,** 8 Suikerrui, mussels with french fries are 320 francs ($8.88), half a chicken with fries and salad only 250 francs ($6.94), brook trout with fries 300 francs ($8.33). And values are much the same at **Restaurant "De Schelde",** 1 Suikerrui, and **Restaurant Pegasus,** 11 Suikerrui.

Meals for under 200 francs ($5.50)

Return now to that big **Restaurant Panaché** at 17 Statiestraat (a block to the left of De Keyserlei, facing the station), but this time to the front, delicatessen portion of it, which displays surely the largest selection of sandwich ingredients in Belgium. At least 50 are served, on long, hard rolls, for from 70 to 80 francs ($1.95 to $2.22) apiece for most, the species ranging from "leverpastei" (liver paste, 70 francs) to "filet American" (raw hamburger, 75 francs) to matjes herring (85 francs) to "kaas" (cheese, 58 francs)—each an adequate meal with coffee, tasty and refreshing. And Panaché is open every day of the week until late, except in the month of August.

Restaurant Inno on the 4th floor of the Inno Department Store at 82 Meir—Antwerp's main shopping street—is for your standard, self-service cafeteria meals that can total (with some effort) to under 200 francs ($5.55). It's open all shopping days from 9 to 6.

Marina's Tavern, at 19 Wapper, is next door to the Rubens House—a visit you'll definitely make—and is both cozier and more attractive inside than would seem from without. It also serves a two-course menu each day for a flat 200 francs ($5.55), which brings you a giant plate (tasty, too) of meat with french fries, preceded by a large bowl of soup. Recommended.

And finally, **Coucou** at 33 Breidelstraat, is for those occasions when all you crave is a spicy, roast chicken. That's all it serves, at 55 francs ($1.53) for a quarter chicken, 105 francs ($2.91) for half a chicken, 195 francs ($5.42) for a whole one; three-course meals, with chicken as the main course, are 350 francs ($9.72). And Breidelstraat is an easily-located sidestreet of the important De Keyserlei, to the left, one block before you reach the Central Station.

The Ethnic, Late Night and Sunday Restaurants

In a city so cosmopolitan, the variety of dining choices is what you'd expect—stunning. Simply walk up De Keyserlei in the direction of the station, and turn left along any of its side-streets: Van Ertbornstraat, Anneessensstraat, Breidelstraat. You'll be entering the neon-lit movie and entertainment district of Antwerp, and there too are to be found every sort of foreign restaurant—Cambodian, Turkish, Italian, Thai—their windows full of appealing dishes, their hours late, their days of operation virtually continuous. It is especially on the Breidelstraat and Statiestraat in this district that restaurants are open until early in the morning, and on Sundays (when most other restaurants in Antwerp are closed). For both Belgian dishes and the ethnic brand, the dozens of entertainment-district restaurants to the left of De Keyserlei (as you approach the Station) will never let you down.

. . . And the Beer

Like every major Belgian city, Antwerp has several of those unique-to-Belgium cafes serving as many as 300 brands of beer. At the sophisticated and rather luxurious **"Kulminator",** 32

Vleminckveld (phone 232-45-38), which is near both the Museum Mayer van den Bergh and the Hotel Rosier, you'll be stunned to see a glass-enclosed section displaying beers in the same fashion as wine cellars are often displayed; some bottles are as costly as 165 francs ($4.58). The strong German beer known as "Kulminator", featured here, is itself 105 francs ($2.91) per bottle, but a heavenly flask of "Orval" from the monastery discussed later in this book is only 70 francs ($1.94), and "kriek" (that Asti Spumante of beer) and others among the hundreds displayed are cheaper still. The cafe, which should be visited by every lover of beer, is open from 11 a.m. to 1 a.m., Saturdays and Mondays from 5 p.m. to 1 a.m., closed Sundays. If you can find Lange Gasthuisstraat, you'll find Vleminckveld, which runs roughly parallel to it . . . Not nearly as posh, but with a greater selection of beers (perhaps a thousand, largest in the world), is **Bierland** at 28 Korte Nieuwstraat near the Cathedral; it, too, deserves a place among the must-see attractions of Antwerp.

THE SIGHTS OF ANTWERP: And now we arrive at the "Diamonds", those "collections" of Antwerp that literally sparkle with the radiance of intellect and exalted human endeavor—there is no other way to describe them. They are, or are in: (1) The Home of Rubens, (2) The Home of Plantin-Moretus, (3) The Museum Mayer van den Bergh, (4) The Vleeshuis (Butchers' Hall), (5) The Antwerp Cathedral, (6) The Royal Museum of Fine Arts. Beyond the six are other popular sights and activities—the "Steen" and its Maritime Museum, the cruises along the Scheldt of the staggering port of Antwerp, the actual Diamond District and Diamond Industry, the Zoo—but it is the six "Diamonds" which must be seen before all else. Three of them—the great Residence that multitudes flock here to visit, and the monumental panels and canvases of the Cathedral and the Royal Museum—are associated with one man, whose very name now stands for Antwerp.

Introducing Peter Paul Rubens (1577–1640)

He was the son of a Lutheran, his father an Antwerp lawyer who had taken the family to religious safety in Germany and there displayed the lust and daring he so obviously passed on to his son by seducing the estranged wife of William the Silent, leader of the revolt of the Netherlands against Spain. Imprisoned for the act, Rubens' father was later released in response to pleas from his strong-willed but forgiving wife. Upon his death, Rubens' mother returned with her son to Antwerp, converted with him to Catholicism, and apprenticed him to a series of noted Flemish artists, from whose ateliers he emerged as one of the most accomplished painters of all time.

His success was meteoric. At the age of 32, having further matured his art through eight years of travel through Italy, he was already in demand by every royal court and patron. His fame was Europe-wide, his paintings copied by etchers and distributed throughout the known world. No one doubted his genius, which influenced an entire age, and other noted artists agreed without hesitation to fill in the colors on a painting Rubens had sketched or to laboriously add the details for which the Master had no time. So massive was his work load, so monumental the works he agreed to do—whole ceilings of state buildings, giant altarpieces, multiple decorative portrayals of various eminent lives, the facades of churches, the adornment of the streets of Antwerp for various royal visits—that he was compelled to establish, in his regal home off the Meir, a veritable factory of painting in which others mixed the paints, cleaned and laid out brushes for his swift use, completed the swirling shapes and forms emerging from the inexhaustible invention of a titan-like mind.

He was the Prince of the Baroque—that art style of exuberant curlicues and rounded forms, of curvaceous extravagance and movement, that made the assertive statements of the Catholic Counter-Reformation. The figures he depicted bulged with straining muscles or fleshy curves and fat, his women exuded sensuality and rosy, dewy flesh. His compositions danced with life, seemed to move, were caught in moments of the most extraordinary drama, endowed with a lust for life, clothed in the richest raiment. Everything in them is larger than life, yet they are all painted in perfect proportion and with that camera-like realism applied to human features and material objects that has always been the glory of Flemish art.

He was a thoroughly happy man who believed in the assumed verities of his time. In addition to achieving unprecedented material success at an early age—fame and prosperity that never left him—he enjoyed two successful marriages, to the attractive, impish Isabella Brandt until her death in 1626, then to the buxom, 16-year-old blonde daughter of a family friend, Helene Fourment, whom he married in 1630 at the age of 53, and whom he immortalized in numerous sensual portraits in every pose and costume. He never doubted the social structure of his time, or the rights of royalty—those sources of such riches and adulation heaped upon him. In depicting so simple a scene as Queen-Mother Marie de Medici arriving by boat at a port, he portrays the very waters, the fish, mermaids, Neptune himself, dancing with delight, erupting from the waves, at her safe homecoming. He not only painted, he served as a diplomat for various thrones, attempting at one point to persuade the errant Dutch to come rejoin the Catholic Empire of Spain. Though a pagan in his unabashed love for the human form and classic mythologies, he was a total religious Believer whose paintings exalt the Christian faith with unequalled force.

Because his thinking is so out-of-step with prevailing modern attitudes, and because he has been so widely imitated by lesser talents, his paintings are not always immediately appreciated by persons happening on them for the first time. It is repeated viewing that trains our eye to see, that gradually reveals to us the genius and talent that makes his work unique, that ends by astonishing us with the rich range of his mind, and brings the sheerest pleasure to a communion with his paintings. He created with speed, and tirelessly—over a thousand major works—and his paintings are found all over Belgium. But they are clustered especially in his own home city, in the rich churches, museums and homes of prosperous Antwerp.

The Home of Rubens

Start first with Antwerp's major attraction, the rich, patrician **Home of Rubens** on the broad promenade known as the "Wapper" (formerly a canal) that juts off a mid-point of the city's main street, the Meir. Rubens built it in 1610 when he was 33 years old, awash in the wealth his genius had brought him, and anxious to live surrounded by those symbols of the Roman civilization, and classic mythologies, that had become familiar and intimate from his eight-year sojourn in Italy. As you pass from outside, into a courtyard lined by a Baroque portico that then opens onto a large, patterned garden, you will be struck by the sculpture and friezes that cover the facade of Rubens' giant studio to your right. Here is Seneca the Stoic, in a place of honor; Marcus Aurelius; the gods Mars, Jupiter, Juno and Vesta; a satyr, a faun, Pan and Silenus; the Greeks—Plato, Socrates, Sophocles; scenes from the legends of Agamemnon, Silenus, Vulcan and Venus. As you then pass into the living quarters to your left, the scene changes to a classic Flemish home, brought to perfection by exquisite taste (and prodigious wealth): the parlor (now containing an engraving of the home as it appeared in 1692), the kitchen, the dining room with gilded leather walls and a black-and-white marble floor copied throughout the world, the "art room", and off that latter area, a recessed, semi-circular "apsidal" sculpture gallery in which Rubens displayed his most precious possessions. When celebrated visitors waited to see the Master, while he and his assistants labored away in the mammoth studio, those visitors were usually ushered by a servant into the art and sculpture gallery, there to be absorbed and entranced by Rubens' own collection.

In every room of the Rubens house are 16th- and 17th-century works of lesser (but important) Flemings—Jacob Jordaens, Adam van Noort, Jan ("Velvet") Bruegel, Cornelis de Vos—some of which are believed to be from Rubens' own collection, once numbering over 300 pieces. But there is also an occasional Rubens, most notably his rakish self-portrait at the age of 47, in the dining room, and several in the giant, two-story-high studio: "The Annunciation" (1628), an "Adam and Eve" painted by the as-yet undeveloped master at the age of 23 (in 1600), prior to his stay in Italy, "Cimon and Pero", "The Ethiopian Magus", and fragments of an altarpiece prepared for a Brussels church. Not by Rubens, but fascinating, is the painting in Rubens' "art room" by William van Haecht (1593–1637) of another famed collection of that time, "The Art Room of Cornelis van der Geest", some of whose pieces have survived only through their appearance in miniature within these frames. Don't miss it. And in the "apsidal" sculpture gallery, note the bust of Rubens' favorite, Seneca. It appears, almost as if photographed, in Rubens' "The Four Philosophers" hanging in the Pitti Palace of Florence; a photograph of that painting, enabling you to check Rubens' precise rendering of the bust, appears at the side of the sculpture gallery here.

Upstairs is the large bedroom in which Rubens died (not now furnished as a bedroom, however), two smaller bedrooms, a linen room, the living room with giant hearth and portraits of Rubens' grandparents, several small studios in which Rubens or his pupils sketched models or worked on smaller pieces, and the tapestry-adorned landing from which one walks downstairs into the lofty, main studio. Throughout are paintings, furnishings and detail to absorb you for hours, in this combination home-workshop that provided a fitting setting for the artistic magnificence emerging from it. It is the most heavily visited site in Antwerp, and is open every day of the week from 10 a.m. to 5 p.m., for an admission of 50 francs ($1.39) for adults, 20 francs (56¢) for students or young persons 12 to 19, free for children under 12. By purchasing a combined ticket to three Antwerp museums (including the Rubens House) for 100 francs ($2.78), adults reduce the single admission cost.

Rubens in the Antwerp Cathedral

Antwerp's soaring Cathedral of "Our Lady", largest Gothic church in Belgium and indeed one of the largest in the world, emerged only recently (1983) from years of reconstruction into radiant, sand-blasted, white-stone, interior glory (although a small portion of that interior remains blocked off). Some visitors go to view its classic Gothic forms, its unusually wide nave lined with six parallel arches, but most come to see one of the Seven Marvels of Belgium, the giant triptych, Rubens' **"Descent from the Cross"**, to the right of the main altar as you face it. It was painted in 1612 on commission from the Guild of the Gunsmiths, when Rubens was at the very height of his fame and ability, and in it he soared to sheer lyrical perfection, achieving a major leap beyond his powerful, but less fluid, less gentle, "Raising of the Cross" which also hangs in the Antwerp Cathedral, nearby. Here, the body of the lifeless Jesus, his foot grazing the shoulder of Mary Magdalene, is tenderly lowered from the cross by loving friends and followers grouped with Him into a diagonal of figures which dazzles with its virtuosity. The Mary Magdalene, with her rosy pink complexion, is one of the most beautiful portraits of Woman ever done. The Virgin Mary, in blue, is dry-eyed but grief stricken, beyond consolation. The streak of color against dark background tones, the red of the cloak of Saint Joseph leaning back to support the body in his arms, the faintly bluish tint of the tragic but athletic Jesus, all combine into an unforgettable image, larger than life, but bursting with life, though depicting a tragic death. The two side panels deal, as does the central panel, with the "carrying" of Jesus. In the left-hand panel, the pregnant Mary, accompanied by Joseph, arrives at the rich home of relatives Elizabeth and Zacharias: this is the "Visitation" described by Luke. In the right-hand panel, Mary presents the babe to Simeon, in a richly-adorned temple, while Joseph kneels beside her; Simeon lifts his eyes skyward in gratitude to God. The infant, presented in spectacular perspective, is bathed in light, as is the brocaded gold cloak of Simeon upon which His head lies.

Behind the altar of Antwerp's Cathedral is Rubens' "Ascension of Mary"; elsewhere, in areas which tend to change from time to time (as of the date of this writing) is the dramatic "Raising of the Cross" by Rubens. But it is in "Descent from the Cross" that his talent fully erupted into an act of genius. As parishioners of the Antwerp Cathedral sit calmly at an ordinary mass, alongside this work, I sometimes wonder how they can keep their attention from straying to it. What a boon is theirs, to have enjoyed nearly 400 years of proximity to such a masterpiece!

The Cathedral of Our Lady, to which a visitor's admission of 30 francs (83¢) is charged, is open weekdays from noon to 5 p.m. (in winter from 2 to 5 p.m.), Saturdays from noon to 3 p.m., Sundays from 1 to 4 p.m.

Rubens in the Royal Museum of Fine Arts

The world's largest collection of major works by Peter Paul Rubens is found on the second floor—in two grandly impressive rooms at the very head of the stairs—of Antwerp's resplendent **Royal Museum of Fine Arts** on the Leopold de Waelplaats. A word about that institution is appropriate, before we turn to Rubens.

In the number of its masterworks, the depth of its collection of various Flemish schools, its representative sampling from every Flemish period, Antwerp's Museum of Fine Arts ranks with Brussels' Musée de l'Art Ancien as one of the two outstanding museums of Belgium. It is a fit witness to the power of Antwerp, for only a rich and confident city could have gathered such an array. Some consider it superior to the great gallery of Brussels.

You approach its Greek/Roman facade thinking you should be in a chariot, so flamboyant and startling are the classic horses, goddesses and columns of its marbled entrance. Inside, by contrast, all is functional. An easily-followed, spacious ground floor contains the Belgian "moderns" from 1830 on: an entire room (no. 21) of James Ensor, in all his styles and moods; haunting scenes of Flemish interiors by the important Henri de Braekeleer (rooms 19 and 27); the angry Constant Permeke and the mystic Albert Servaes (rooms 13, 14, 15); Delvaux and Magritte (room 8); the contemporary Roger Raveel of Brussels (in room 7); every other noteworthy Belgian of the 19th and 20th century; and one room only (no. 23) for the foreigners: Degas, Utrillo, Roualt, Chagall, Modigliani, Vlaminck, which is as it should be.

Upstairs are the ancients, and here one passes from one world-class masterpiece to another. To the left are the heart-stopping, dazzling works of the Flemish "primitives": Jan van Eyck's **"The Holy Barbara"** reading philosophy in front of the tower built by her jealous father to imprison her—a tiny monochromatic work of sheer perfection (Room Q); Roger van der Weyden's triptych of **The Seven Sacraments** illustrating the uses of the ancient cathedral; works by Dirck Bouts and Hans Memling, in all their other-worldly, yet brightly-colored, stillness (these, too, are in that remarkable Room Q); Jean Fouquet's **Mary and Child** in Room S, a highlight of the museum, portraying a hairless Virgin of abstract face and perfectly globular, exposed breasts bathed in strange shades of yellow, like the maiden from an outer-planetary episode of Star Trek, astonishingly sensual for an artist who lived from 1415 to 1480. In Room N: Hans Memling's giant triptych of **Christ Among the Singing Angels,** remarkably similar to a segment of the Van Eycks' "Mystic Lamb" in Ghent (the same straining choristers, the same head of God). In Room T: the life of medieval peasants in the villages of Flanders, as captured for all time by the sons of Pieter Bruegel, some copying works by their father. Room L: the original **"Wedding Dance"** by Pieter Bruegel the Elder. Rooms O and P: Metsijs and De Vos, and nearby, almost as if by afterthought, the later works of Rembrandt and Hals.

But all this is seen after first viewing Rubens—more Rubens than in any other location on earth—in Rooms J and I. The more modest antechamber (Room J) contains smaller drawings and oils of the master, primarily sketches in gold and brown in preparation for a larger work. The larger (and indeed massive) room (Room I), topped by a skylight that floods it with light, provides the reason for your visit: monumental works of that epic Peter Paul Rubens, done with an imagination and pictorial invention that endows familiar religious scenes with unforgettable drama. Here in Antwerp's Fine Arts Museum is the brilliantly-composed **"Last Communion of St. Francis"** as the legendary figure, here a real man, is carried to the altar and to the host in the dying moments of his life, a beseeching but beatific gaze to his face. Here we see the oft-reproduced **"Jesus and the Three Kings"**, with an unforgettable Moorish servant providing both the central focus of the painting and its most exotic contrasts; cup your hand about your eye to blot out all but the Moor, and see what an extraordinary portrait results. See, too, the playful Baby, reacting to the incense holder like a toy. Then turn to "Venus Frigida", the lush portrait of a chilly goddess. Then to see **Christ Lanced;** then to **"Christus Op het Stro"**, perhaps the most realistic portrait of that event ever set to canvas, blood flowing from his nostrils, blood on his arms and waist, his body turning bluish. We experience here the apotheosis of Rubens' art, and it is appropriate we do so in the public gallery of his own city, to which he brought such fame.

A visit to Antwerp's **Royal Museum of Fine Arts**—and especially to its second floor, where there are no minor works at all out of dozens displayed—is made without admission charge of any sort (a remarkable gesture on the part of Antwerp), daily except Mondays, from 10 a.m. to 5 p.m.

RUBENS CAN ALSO BE SEEN: In **St. Paul's Church,** 20 Sint-Paulusstraat (16th-century Gothic, with three major works by Rubens, including his important "Adoration of the Shepherds"; viewed daily except Sundays and Mondays from 9 to noon and 2 to 5, mornings only in winter); and in **St. James Church,** 73 Lange Nieuwstraat (Rubens' own parish church, in which he now lies buried under an intensely lyrical work from his late period—"Our Lady with Christ-Child on the Arm"—selected by him almost immediately before his death to adorn his burial chapel; open daily except Sundays from 2 to 5 p.m., for an admission charge of 30 francs (83¢).

The Plantin-Moretus Museum

The art which poured forth from the Antwerp studio of Peter Paul Rubens was accompanied during the very same year by a flood of books from the massive workshop-home of the Antwerp family known as **"Plantin-Moretus";** they can be said to have had an equal impact upon the intellectual outlook of the world of that time. Publishers as well as printers, upholding the most rigorous standards of scholarship, they created the world's first Atlas, the first newspaper, the first printed anatomy, disseminated the works of humanists in quantities never before dreamed of, printed multilanguage versions of the classics and the Bible (some illustrated by Rubens), provided a congenial home for men of intellect, including their contemporary and friend, Mercator. And they did all this from a structure so grand, with contents so carefully preserved, that it already became famous in their own time. In the mid-1600s, the town clerk of Antwerp wrote that future generations would visit the city to marvel at two homes: that of Rubens—and of Plantin-Moretus.

From the two wings then existing of the rich patrician mansion at 22 Vrijdagmarkt, Christoffle Plantin in the late 1500s raised the standards of printing to levels never attained before— or since. It was here that the type styles of Claude Garamond (1561) and Robert Granjon (1570) were most fully developed and duplicated for widespread use. And then most lovingly used. Gaze at the books in the display cases of the Plantin-Moretus and ask whether you have ever seen their equal. Plantin's grandson, Balthasar Moretus, the contemporary and friend of Rubens, succeeded to the "Officina Plantiniana" (by then the most renowned printing plant in the world) in 1610, added wings to make an enclosed rectangle of the sombre workshop-home, hired learned professors as proofreaders, drove himself to make an intellectual powerhouse of what then became known as the "Plantin-Moretus". As you walk through the first rooms of the dark, university-like structure, impressive in the 400 years of its age, you will first see portraits by Rubens of all family members, against walls in gilded Flemish leather, entering then into the rich living quarters of an affluent group that lived in the grand comforts earned from their eminence. Yet immediately alongside are the ancient workrooms, presses, type fonts, proofreading chambers, libraries of completed works, from which they were never more than a step away. Perusing the books and Baroque engravings of this lofty age—of which the five-language "Biblia Polyglotta" set in parallel columns of Hebrew, Aramaic, Greek, Dutch and French is surely Plantin's towering masterpiece—makes for an enthralling interlude, a highlight of your visit to Antwerp.

The **Museum Plantin-Moretus,** on the Vrijdagmarkt (Friday Market), is open every day of the year (except on major holidays) from 10 a.m. to 5 p.m., for an admission charge of 50 francs ($1.39) to adults, 20 francs (60¢) to juniors, or for one of the three stubs of a three-museum, combined ticket costing 100 francs ($2.78).

Museum Mayer van den Bergh

And still there are Diamonds to see. The **Museum Mayer van den Bergh,** 19 Lange Gasthuisstraat (phone 232-4237), is yet another glittering, richly furnished, but this time simulated home of the 16th century, built without consideration of cost in the year 1904 by the mother of Antwerp's most celebrated "collector", Fritz Mayer van den Bergh, who had died a bachelor at the age of 41. It was the world's first museum specially designed to display an existing private collection amassed by a man of such unerring taste that the word "connoisseur" could have been coined simply to apply to him. Though he was the son of a wealthy and titled Antwerp financier, he parlayed a strictly limited fortune into a collection worth several times as much, by buying and selling, casting off pieces of lesser importance to purchase masterworks. His eye was imbued with magical insight. At a lackluster auction of art in Cologne, he spotted a painting by a 16th-century Flemish artist unknown to the bidders, scarcely desired. He purchased it, then rushed to antiquarian books to find some mention of it. Its name? "Dulle Griet" (Mad Meg) by Pieter Bruegel the Elder, now the crowning highlight of the Museum of Mayer van den Bergh, on its second floor.

With its gilded leather walls and oil-polished maple cabinets, its sparkling miniatures of art and sculpture, its retables and radiant triptychs, the Museum Mayer van den Bergh is a shimmering diamond of 2000 facets (the works on display), which reveal themselves first on the ground floor in two poignant, full-length portraits by Cornelis de Vos (1600s) of wistful-eyed children, and include Quentin Metsijs' (1465–1530) important triptych of the Calvary, portraying Jerusalem as a Flemish town. Upstairs, in the library, are a world-acclaimed set of 60, bas-relief, lead "plaquettes" of biblical scenes ("Bathsheba bathing" is one) by a German master of the early 1500s, and there are low glass cases of exquisite Carolingian bas-reliefs in porcelain dating from the 9th century. There are several poorly-done but historically interesting copies by Pieter Bruegel the Younger of his father's "Census at

Bethlehem" and "Winter Landscape". But mainly, there is the work that attracts all eyes: "Dulle Griet" (Mad Meg).

No one knows exactly what it means. The 17th-century Flemish art historian, Carel van Mander, provided the only contemporary mention of it in 1604, referring in an aside to Bruegel's painting of "Dulle Griet, who loots at the mouth of hell". Some modern art analysts have concluded it is an allegory on human madness. My own instant reaction on first seeing "Dulle Griet" was to view it as Bruegel's anguished, bellowing comment on the ugly insanity of war. A giantess, Mad Meg, goes roaming a flame-ravaged battlefield, her eyes demented, driven insane by the destruction of her dearest ones, herself followed by an army of anguished women, all mindlessly collecting up the detritus and booty of war, in the wake of destruction of their families and way of life. Alongside this flaming statement is, incongruously, and on the same wall, Bruegel's gentle spoof of humanity's ever-repeated **"Proverbs":** "casting pearls before swine", "locking the barn after the horse has escaped", "throwing out the baby with the bath water", 12 parables illustrated in clearly-identifiable, oval sketches. To think that the young Fritz Mayer van den Bergh snatched up these medieval masterworks from bored auctioneers, or from bins of discarded, worthless oils!

The enchanting Museum Mayer van den Bergh is open daily except Mondays from 10 a.m. to 5 p.m., for an admission charge of 50 francs ($1.39) to adults, 20 francs (56¢) for children under 18 and students, and can be visited as one of three museums viewed on a 100-franc ($2.78) combination ticket.

The "Vleeshuis" (Butchers' Hall)

Gothic cathedrals have survived, but very few Gothic secular structures have; the **"Vleeshuis"**—Antwerp's 16th-century "Butchers' Hall"—is one of the few exceptions. It comes down to us in its precise, original appearance, magnificently restored, a tall structure of six-sided towers, with colorful, "striped" facade of alternating red brick and white stone, amazingly grand for such a prosaic function: the marketing of meat from ground floor stalls, by members of the powerful Butchers' Guild, who had their headquarters upstairs. Maintained today as a museum of medieval artifacts and archaeology, it displays armor and furnishings, ancient musical instruments and sculpture, the great altarpiece/"retable" (bas-relief sculpture) of the Abbey of Averbode (1514), other occasional paintings (among which "The Spanish Fury" depicting the sacking of Antwerp during the religious troubles of 1576, is riveting), all in a rich interior of strong vertical lines leading to high Gothic vaults, another "diamond" of Antwerp. Don't neglect to visit the cellars containing stone relics, or to climb the winding steps upstairs to still other exhibition halls. The Vleeshuis Museum, at 38 Vleeshouwersstraat, only the briefest walk from the Town Hall, is open daily except Mondays from 10 a.m. to 5 p.m., for an admission charge of 50 francs ($1.39) to adults, 20 francs (56¢) for children under 18 or students, less for adults if you purchase a 100-franc ($2.78) combined admission to three museums, of which the Vleeshuis is one.

Actual Diamonds

Finally, the diamond district of Antwerp, largest in the world, is directly to the right of the train station, as you face it; its drab appearance will initially come as a shock. But as you walk deeper into its streets, you'll realize that behind these ordinary, retail storefronts and modest, commerical buildings is a rather glamorous industry of immense world importance. Many of the workrooms, "stone"-cutters, jewelry mounters, and wholesale diamond merchants post signs inviting you to step inside for browsing or to shop; their prices are honest ones for high quality, and probably among the lowest in the world for comparable diamonds —but diamonds don't come cheap. In late 1988, a **Diamond Museum** ("Nieuw Provinciaal Diamantmuseum") opened on the Lange Herentalsstraat, with free entrance; a brillantly designed show room—the glittering **Diamondland**—is also a must to visit.

ANTWERP—THE SECONDARY SIGHTS: Overshadowed only by the brilliance of its main sights are 19 other museums of Antwerp, and the following:

First, the **"Steen"**, the omnipresent, 12th-century castle-fortress of Antwerp, which stands alongside the River Scheldt to the side of the Suikerrui, marking the spot where the city began. Even in Roman times there was a fortress here, then one destroyed by Vikings in 863, then the impressive, turreted battlement of the Middle Ages looming there now. In it is Antwerp's important **National Maritime Museum** of 12 major viewing halls, each dealing with a separate nautical theme: arts and crafts of the waterfront, people of the sea, yachting, shipbuilding, inland navigation, the history of shipping in different centuries, the mysticism and magic of the sea, all profusely illustrated by meticulously-crafted models, displays, and actual ship equipment, instructive even to the casual visitor, but of intense appeal to persons with special interest in the sea. The Maritime Museum of the "Steen" is open every day of the year except on six important holidays, and charges admission of 50 francs ($1.39) to adults, 20 francs (56¢) to juniors. It also participates in the scheme allowing you to purchase a 100-franc ($2.78) admission to three different museums of Antwerp, lowering the cost of entrance here to about 33 francs (92¢).

The **Antwerp Zoo,** 26 Koningin Astridplein, among the most extensive of Europe, is found just behind the Central Railroad Station, its entrance to the left of the Station (as you face it). Stocked with exotic species of fish, fowl and beast, brilliantly presented, it makes for a pleasant but rather expensive visit costing 260 francs ($7.23) for adults, 160 francs ($4.45) for children, and is available to you every day of the year from 8:30 a.m. to 5 or 6:30 p.m. (depending on season). Dolphins are shown at 11:30 a.m., 2:30 and 3:30 p.m.

Flandria sightseeing boat cruises are a must, departing from the Steenplein at the bottom of the Suikkerui every half-hour, daily, from Easter till the end of September, on a 170-franc ($4.73), 50-minute trip of that portion of the River that flows through the city itself. On the city side of the River in ancient times was the Duchy of Brabant. On the other side: the County of Flanders—enemy territory. As it flowed south, the Scheldt remained the border with Flanders, and continues all the way to Ghent and beyond. If you have time to spare, you'll find the most instructive Flandria cruise to be the 3-hour variety proceeding much farther along the River into the great industrial port of Antwerp, and departing in season at 10:10 a.m. and 2:20 p.m. (except on Saturdays, when only the afternoon trip operates), for a charge of 300 francs ($8.33) to adults, 180 francs ($5) for children 3 to 12. Though Antwerp ranks behind New York and Rotterdam in tonnage handled, it argues that *its* harbors deal with far more complex materials than theirs, and not with the bulk oil in which Rotterdam specializes; it also boasts the world's fastest turnaround time for the unloading and dispatching of ships. For miles on end, you'll see cranes and railway marshalling yards, extraordinary plants for processing the sea-shipped chemicals and petrochemicals that provide the city's prosperity, auto assembly lines and other factories that have found it best to locate themselves where materials are picked up and delivered. If you are also a motorist, and have at least two to three hours for an alternative view, you can drive along the port area by following instructions provided by the Antwerp Tourist Office at 9 Gildekamersstraat (phone 232-0103), carefully watching for the hexagonal signs along the 40-mile-long **"Havenroute"** (Port Route) that starts at the Steen Castle and stretches as far as the Dutch border.

Other worthwhile visits are to: the **Rockox House,** 10 Keizersstraat (16th-century home of Nicolaas Rockox, 1560–1649, famous burgomaster of Antwerp, noted humanist, and friend and patron of Rubens; it is furnished in classic Flemish style, and contains numerous important paintings, including two by Rubens; open daily except Mondays, admission free); **Ridder Smidt van Gelder Museum,** 91 Belgiëlei (this time a patrician home of the 18th century, richly-furnished in the French-dominated style of that age; open daily except Mondays for a 50-franc charge, but presently closed for repairs until mid-1989); **St. Charles Borromeo's Church,** 12 Hendrik Conscienceplein (the magnificently Baroque, 17th-century church of Antwerp, whose sculpture-adorned facade was largely designed by Rubens; but open only from 2 to 4 p.m. on Wednesdays, from 5 to 6 p.m. on Fridays); **Open-Air Sculpture Museum of Middelheim** (Rodin, Zadkine and Moore) in Middelheim Park (admission free, and usually open till 7, 8 or 9 p.m., depending on date, in spring, summer and fall); the **Museum of Regional Ethnology,** 2 Gildekamersstraat (folklore of Flanders, the life of ordinary people; open daily except Mondays from 10 to 5, for admission of 50 francs to adults, 20 francs to juniors, but presently closed for repairs until mid-1989); **Museum Maagdenhuis,** 33 Lange Gasthuisstraat (near the Museum Mayer van den Bergh, and easily combined with it) (a 16th-century home for young orphan girls, called "maagden" or maidens, open weekdays only from 8:30 a.m. to 4:30 p.m., entrance free); many more.

ANTWERP—NIGHTLIFE AND ENTERTAINMENT: As

many as forty theatres and concert halls—for opera, ballet, drama, cabaret, concerts, puppets—provide a rich array of evening choices, but in Flemish, which is Dutch, and for the usual tourist might just as well be Greek. As the unofficial capital of "Flanders", the northern half of Belgium, Antwerp gives staunch support to the Flemish culture, and it is here that one finds the **Royal Flanders Ballet** directed by the talented Robert Denvers, a student of Béjart, the **Royal Flemish Theatre** ("Koninklijke Nederlandse Schouwburg" in a modern complex on the Schouwburgplein), the **Royal Flemish Opera** ("Opera voor Vlaanderen", so noted for its performances of Wagner that some call it the "Flemish Bayreuth"), the **Flemish Chamber Opera** ("Vlaamse Kameropera"), the **Royal Flemish Conservatory** ("Koninklijk Vlaams Conservatorium"), and other major stages for the performing arts —all vocalizing in Flemish (Dutch). For at least the musical or dance theatre, which you'll enjoy despite the language problem, you'll find listings in all the papers, or in hand-outs at the tourist office, and you'll be thrilled to find most tickets—even those for the opera—selling for well under 500 francs ($14). The 2000-seat

Queen Elisabeth Hall at 26 Koningin Astridplein, is the city's most prestigious venue for celebrated concert artists, and ballets.

When it comes to movies, Antwerp leaves them in their original language, and appends both Dutch and French subtitles underneath, which spells heaven for the English-speaking tourist. The movies are spotted up and down De Keyserlei, and on the sidestreets in both directions, and they range from high art to softcore porn—this being a cosmopolitan city, remember. Movies provide a welcome respite for the hard-driving tourist. In the same brightly-lit district, this time almost entirely in the several streets to the left of De Keyserlei (as you face the station), are Antwerp's most numerous complement of disco bars, striptease bars, "hostess" cafes and taverns, of varying degrees of toughness, from the family-style to the highly elegant to the frank purveyors of sleaze, all easily judged by simply glancing inside. The red-light district, interesting to tour, is in the riverside and near-the-river streets just north of the "Steen" (Antwerp's fortress-castle on the River Scheldt). A second district of perfectly proper disco bars, heavily patronized by Antwerp's young population, is in the streets between the Market Square ("Grote Markt") and the Cathedral. And then there are simply those cafe-restaurants up and down De Keyserlei, where people converse and sip coffee until well past midnight, in a vitally alive city that enjoys the night.

SHOPS AND STORES: Diamond-buying is the major draw for tourists to Antwerp (see our discussion, above, of the diamond district), but all else is available in a richly-varied shopping district centering on the city's main street, the Meir: every major name, all the great department stores, dozens of specialty shops and boutiques. For souvenirs and lace, art reproductions, posters and books on Rubens and Van Dyck, you go the shops in the streets immediately surrounding the Antwerp Cathedral. **Galeries Petro Paulo Rubens** at 22 Groenplein, is especially well stocked with lace in the form of collars or cuffs on ladies' blouses, or for hand-crocheted, lace-like evening jackets. On any large purchase, keep always in mind the possibility of recovering 19% of what you've paid by having the appropriate customs declaration stamped upon your departure from Belgium; and always request the forms, and a receipt, on purchasing any substantial article.

ANTWERP MISCELLANY: The possessors of so thriving and attractive a city, the Antwerpers are understandably a bit cocky, and will claim in unguarded moments that they move faster than other Belgians. In the Spanish-dominated century of the

1500s, they called themselves "signoren" ("gentlemen" or "gentry"), referring to their cosmopolitan ways . . . If you haven't the resources (or the reservation!) for dining at Sir Anthony van Dijk, you ought nevertheless to wander about the dreamy, cobblestoned **courtyards** that surround its location **at 16 Koornmarkt,** on the small alley known as the Vlaeykensgang. When threatened with demolition for a parking lot, the entire complex of ancient structures here was purchased by Antwerp antique dealer Axel Vervoordt (among the most famous in Europe), and restored; his own antique shop here reflects the unerring taste of a master, and should be seen . . . Every Monday evening in summer (mid-June to mid-September), from 9 to 10 p.m., **carillon concerts** from the spire of the Cathedral draw large crowds to the inner city of Antwerp . . . On Mondays, when so much is closed in Brussels, the following are open in Antwerp: the homes of Rubens and Plantin-Moretus, the zoo and the Diamond Industry, the Steen and its Maritime Museum, the shops, and all Flandria boat trips on the Scheldt. Thus Antwerp joins Bruges as the place to be on Mondays . . . A **flea market** of sorts takes place every Wednesday and Friday morning until 1 p.m. on the Vrijdagmarkt (Friday Market), easily combinable with your visit to the Plantin-Moretus Museum. This is for second-hand goods of every description, similar to the wares at Brussels' daily flea market in the Marolles. A large **"Vogelenmarkt"** (Birds' Market) of live birds and animals, flowers and plants, draws crowds every Sunday morning from 8:30 a.m. to 1 p.m., near the City Theatre . . . And though you can easily wander the city yourself, on foot, bear in mind that **two-hour motorcoach tours** of Antwerp depart from the Market Square ("Grote Markt"), corner of Wisselstraat, at 2:30 p.m. on weekends in April, May, June and September, daily in July and August, for a charge of 275 francs ($7.64) to adults, 150 francs to children 12 years and younger. Inquire at the City Tourist Office, 9 Gildekamersstraat . . . Is there any doubt that Antwerp is the single most underrated city of Europe? . . . Trains from Brussels to Antwerp leave every 16 minutes throughout the day, departing from track 5 of the Gare Centrale and passing through the Gare du Nord on the way there; they require only 35 minutes for the trip. You have *no excuse* not to go to Antwerp!

MECHELEN AND LIER

Fifteen miles from Antwerp, no more, is **Mechelen** (Malines), a medieval gem of a city (pop.: 66,000), with glorious Gothic cathedral (the 13th-century St. Rombout's) and other churches; Gothic town hall; a world-renowned Carillon school, which also presents concerts in the Cathedral; ancient homes (including the resplendent, 16th-century palace of Margaret of Austria); and 14th-century Aldermen's House; in addition to art and sculpture almost without compare. A museum of tapestry—tapestry is still produced in the city—is a particular stand-out, as are the triptychs of Rubens found in the Church of St. John and the Church of Our Lady-over-the-Dijle. I haven't the space for further description, but you will definitely want to schedule a visit if you have the time. Nine miles from Mechelen: the ancient town of **Lier,** with its world-renowned Astronomical Clock that will set you to day-dreaming about time and the universe. See it, too, in addition to the town's dreamy "Beguinage"—an almshouse for poor women of the 15th and 16th centuries.

CHAPTER VIII

THE BELGIAN COAST

□ □ □

DE PANNE

OOSTDUINKERKE

OSTEND

KNOKKE

It goes on, and it goes on, and it goes on and . . . an almost endless expanse of beach, among the widest in the world, and almost continuously lined (except when intersected by port areas) with bathing-suited revelers enjoying the classic pleasures of the sea, and with hotels, holiday apartments, strolling promenades, saunas and sea-treatment centers, recreational facilities, restaurants—and intermittent casinos (four of them—at Ostend, Knokke, Blankenberge and Middelkerke). In all of Northern Europe, there is nothing quite like the Belgian Coast. Though only 65 kilometers long, and entirely within the small province of West Flanders, it is the longest, concentrated area of major beachside resort facilities along the Channel and the North Sea, its appeal so strong that it attracts the English, French, Germans and Dutch to almost the same extent that it draws Belgians!

THE CARNIVAL OF FLANDERS—SEASIDE STYLE:
The delights begin with the air itself—brisk, salt-laden air carrying the health-giving sting of iodine; with constant breezes deflected from sun-bathers by gaily-striped or curlicued windbreakers in the form of big, colorful umbrellas laid to their side, or

actual canvas wall shields, or wicker-type sedan chairs. The wind sweeps over a near-continuous and remarkably broad sand beach that, at points, and at low tide, reaches a width of as much as 500 yards. It slopes so gently, resulting in water so shallow, that you can wade in for another one-to-two hundred yards without the sea's reaching your thighs. The result is the world's safest beach for family vacationers: young children can play almost unattended without fear of wading in over their heads, and whole years can go by without the entire Belgian beach suffering a single drowning.

The beach is so very spacious, so uncrowded and clear, that you enjoy unusual freedom on it. In some sections, you see dozens of wind-driven sail-carts swooping along the sand; massed ranks of pedal-driven autos and bicycles-built-for-two; giant sandcastles in various stages of construction, adorned with sea shells; hikers climbing onto massive sand dunes resembling the Sahara; others wandering through adjoining bird and nature sanctuaries, or digging for shells. But those are the smaller pleasures of the Belgian coast. Alongside its more important sea-bathing and casino gambling are three other major distractions: the "Belgian surrealists", shopping—and food. We'll be visiting major seaside exhibits of painters Ensor, Magritte and Delvaux. We'll be going to shopping districts that rival those of Mayfair or Palm Beach. And we'll be surrounded throughout by the element that gives the Belgian coast its especial glitter: superb restaurants, in all price categories, that make every meal an occasion for which you wait expectantly.

You first choose a resort location from which to seek these joys. From the town of De Panne on the French border, to Knokke-le-Zoute on the Dutch border, are a dozen seaside communities almost evenly spaced, each catering to a different composition of tourists, each with a slightly different appeal. From West to East, they are **De Panne** (lower-middle and middle class, a widely-varied (French, English, Dutch, German, Luxembourg) international clientele, most of them from France across the border), **St. Idesbald, Koksijde, Oostduinkerke** (middle class, a great many Germans, in addition to Belgians), **Nieuwpoort, Westende, Middelkerke, Ostend** (the English are at least 60% of its clientele), **De Haan, Blankenberge** (lower income English and Belgians), **Heist** (families), **Knokke** (elegant), and **Le Zoute** (hyper elegant). The casinos, as noted before, are at **Ostend** (the largest), **Middelkerke, Blankenberge** and **Knokke** (most elegant). Depending on your own craving for sightseeing, shopping or gambling, you as an overseas visitor will probably be happiest at Oostduinkerke (sightseeing and art) or Knokke (shopping and gambling); the sea-bathing facilities are fairly even quality throughout the long expanse.

GETTING THERE: From Brussels, trains to the sea (two hours away) leave with great frequency, heading to Ghent, and from there to De Panne; or proceeding to Bruges, and splitting off from there to either Ostend, Blankenberge, Zeebrugge or Knokke. From Bruges to Ostend is only 18 minutes by express, only 24 minutes by local, for a one-way fare of 80 francs ($2.22). From Bruges to Knokke is 26 minutes by local train, for the same 80 francs ($2.22). The trip from Brussels/Midi all the way to Ostend lasts all of one hour and 24 minutes (for a one-way fare of 325 francs ($9.02), from Brussels/Midi to Knokke one hour and 32 minutes, again for 325 francs ($9.02), one way; while from Brussels to De Panne takes nearly two hours, for a one-way fare of 390 francs ($10.83). You should stay overnight (or longer) at the coastal locations you choose (especially if you plan to visit the casinos), but if you don't, you reduce your transportation cost, from June 1 to September 30, by purchasing a one-day, round-trip excursion fare called "Une journée à la Mer" or "Een Dag aan Zee" (A day at the Sea); the latter brings you a 50% discount off the normal price and converts the one-way cost into a round-trip fare. For such a small expense, you are a foolish tourist indeed if you pass up a glimpse of the Belgian Coast on your visit to Brussels, Bruges or Ghent! And, of course, you can drive to any of these resorts on excellent roads.

Once arrived at De Panne, Ostend, Blankenberge or Knokke, you reach all other coastal towns either by bus, or by simply hopping aboard the quite remarkable electric tram (variously called the "Tourist Tram", or the "Tram de la Côte") that goes up and down the entire, 65-kilometer length of the beach on "La Route Royale" ("De Koninklijke Baan")—the succession of streets lying one block-or-so in from the seaside promenades. It runs every quarter of an hour in summer, half-hourly in winter, goes all the way between De Panne and Knokke (a two-hour ride, if you stay on for the entire distance), makes the same trip in the other direction, and charges 189 francs ($5.25) for, say, the ride from De Panne to Ostend, 232 francs ($6.44) for that hypothetical trambuff who would stay on all the way from De Panne to Knokke. Most visitors to the Coast use it at least once for darting to an adjoining town or two.

Anything more to be added, by way of introduction? Only that this is Europe's next-to-the-cheapest beach area (after Spain and Portugal), far less costly than the French or Italian Rivieras, less expensive than those occasional resort communities on the

Dutch, German and Scandinavian coasts. We'll assume you want to see it all, from west to east, starting at the very first city on the map:

DE PANNE

The French tourists who come here in heavy numbers from just across the border, a simple 40-minute walk along beach or street, call it "La Panne", as did an insensitive Winston Churchill in his war memoirs. But *De* Panne is a city of 10,000 Flemings, bustling and active, filled with carnival-type events and activities, a bit honky-tonk near the beach, but charming and attractive in its outer areas where the landscaping of homes and parks is manicured and graceful. It grows to a population of 60,000 in peak season (July and August), maintains nearly a hundred restaurants for them, has the very widest beach on the Belgian Coast (500 meters at low tide), and enjoys two other natural phenomena: a huge area of sand dunes (340 hectares), constituting one-third of all the dunes on the Belgian Coast (these are found immediately to the west of the town) and an adjoining, wooded, nature reserve of 65 hectares, through both of which one leaps and tramps with delight, viewing plants and growths, sea shells and weird, twisted sea wood, of great and exotic variety. Again on the west side of the beach, fleets of sail-equipped wind-carts go careening along the sand at considerable speeds, both in racing competitions and for thrill-seeking tourists who book a seat. Along the beach are 5,000 furnished flats for rental (and hotels, too; see below), while in the city is an extensive shopping area along the main street called "Zeelaan", and a leisure park called "Meli" about a mile from the center. As the closest Belgian city to England, De Panne's television sets receive four English channels (BBC1, BBC2, ITV and Channel 4), as well as 3 from France, 2 from Germany, 2 from Holland and 4 from Belgium! If one ever needed an example of the cross-cultural influences flowing over Belgium, one finds it in De Panne.

'DE ROOMS OF DE PANNE: Forty-five hotels and pensions are available for short stays (and a great many more apartment houses and other kitchenette-equipped lodgings—including the sprawling, 60-bungalow **Strand Motel**, on the beach, phone 058/41-11-96—handle the weekly and monthly rentals). With the exception of the modern (but small) **Sea Horse Hotel**, at 7 Toeristenlaan (phone 058/41-27-47), the **Sparrenhof**, at 26 Koninginnelaan, and the **Val Joli**, at 55 Barkenlaan, none of them is first class in quality, or new, but most are of a comfortable and charmingly old-fashioned style (of 1930s construction)—De

Panne having been developed in the first half of this century. And all are amazingly cheap, appealing to a cost-conscious, middle-class, family clientele.

Disagreeing with the official ratings, I find the 36-room **Hotel des Princes,** at 46 Nieuwpoortlaan (phone 058/41-10-91), with its homey, middle-class elegance and large, airy rooms, to be the most pleasant of De Panne's hotels; it is a block from the beach behind a tiny, triangular park, and charges only 1550 francs ($43.05) for a twin room with bath and breakfast, only 1600 francs ($44.44) per person for room and all three meals each day. And I like, in second position, the large, Tudor-style farmhouse-with-outdoor-swimming-pool known as the **Hotel du Val Joli,** at 55 Barkenlaan (phone 058/41-25-19), in a quiet residential setting six blocks from the sea (2000 francs, $56, for a twin with bath and breakfast). The officially-top-rated hotels of De Panne are the newly-refurbished **Gai Sejour,** above the restaurant of the same name at 42 Nieuwpoortlaan (phone 058/41-13-03), one block from the sea, charging 1800 to 3000 francs ($50 to $83) twin; and the more modern and relatively large (55 rooms) **Hotel Terlinck,** at 175 Zeelaan (phone 058/41-26-21), a block from the sea (1900 francs, $53, per twin). If neither has vacancies, then try the attractive, quiet **Hotel Les Ambassadeurs,** at 43 Duinkerkelaan (phone 058/41-16-12), forty yards from the beach, and with pleasant garden (as well as parking). At the latter, double rooms are 1600 francs ($44.44), breakfast for two included.

Cheaper (1200 francs, $33.33, for double rooms *without* private bath), almost as pleasant: the **Hotel de la Grand' Place,** 60 Zeelaan (phone 058/41-12-79); and **Hotel Francais,** over the restaurant of the same name, at 31 Kasteelstraat (phone 058/41-17-39).

Private homes

And then there are the families renting rooms in their private homes—a way to "meet the De Panners" on your Belgian trip, and to save considerable sums of money: few charge more than 1000 francs ($27.78) for a double room, often less, including breakfast for two. Try the **Devos',** 6 Duínenstraat (phone 058/41-36-69); the **Dewickes,** 37 Duinhoekstraat (phone 058/41-15-31); the **Serreyns,** 2 Kerstraat (phone 058/41-12-20); the **Vermoeres,** 8 Astridlaan (phone 058/41-45-21); the **Vanbillemonts,** 31 St. Elisabethlaan (phone 058/41-21-37); or the **Deleus',** 87 Ambachtstraat (phone 058/41-17-10).

MEALS AT THE SEA: In the separate little town of Adinkerke, 3 kilometers to the south of De Panne, reigns the areas's most distinguished restaurant, **"La Souricière"** ("De Muizevalle" in Dutch), at 28 Duinkerkeiweg (phone 058/41-16-00), to which dedicated gourmets will make a trip (closed Tuesday evenings and Wednesdays); but a near-equivalent and cheaper **Restaurant L'Avenue** is only one block from the sea, at 56 Nieuwpoortlaan (phone 058/41-13-70), on the so-called "Route Royale" or "Koninklijke Baan"; some prefer it to La Souricière. In an unpretentious setting for food of this quality (simple red tablecloths, cloth-covered hanging lamps), it offers a three-course meal—say, lobster bisque flavored with sherry, an unusual roast quail with fresh rhubarb, an assortment of dessert pastries—for as little as 700 francs ($19.50), a more exciting, five-course "Carte Blanche au Chef" (namely, whatever he decides to serve you) for 1000 francs ($28). The two other "name" restaurants of De Panne are **"Le Fox"**, 2 Walckierstraat (phone 058/41-28-55) (try their "Salade de poissons chauds au chêvre rôti au thym"); and **La Bonne Auberge**, on the beach at 3 Zeedijk (phone 058/41-13-98). The latter charges 750 and 900 francs ($20.83 and $25) for the average, three-course "menu". The restaurant of the earlier-named **Hotel Gai Sejour**, at 42 Nieuwpoortlaan (phone 058/41-13-03), a block from the beach near the very center of town, is also high in quality, but charges only 650 francs ($18) for a three-course "Menu Touristique", 1050 francs ($29) for a four-course "Menu Gastronomique".

   For the cheaper meals in De Panne, you go directly onto the beach promenade, the **Zeedijk**, where a long string of restaurants charge a standard 400 francs ($11.11) for three-courses invariably consisting of soup ("potage") to begin, then well-flavored chicken or side of pork with heavenly french fries, with salad or apple sauce ("compote"), and dessert. At that price, it's hard to complain. In the same restaurants, or at the "fritures" (fry houses) up and down the Nieuwpoortlaan (at Nos. 4, 15, 27, 29 and 35), mussels with french fries are a uniform 280 francs ($7.77), spaghetti 180 francs ($5). In an area of such gastronomic renown, where you'll be having at least one multi-course dinner of gourmet-level exotica per day, it might be well to limit the other meal to just such a simple plate of spaghetti, or mussels ("les moules") and french fries!

MISCELLANY OF DE PANNE: The celebrated Flemish mathematician of more than 400 years ago, Simon Stevin, was the first to see the possibilities of racing wind-driven sail-carts on the beaches of De Panne. He designed a military sail-cart that carried four, heavily-armored medieval soldiers on their patrols up and down the coast; you'll occasionally see etchings of the bulky device in literature on De Panne. . . . The 21st of July to the 15th of

August is the most heavily booked period in De Panne; try staying at another time. . . . Most shops close here on Tuesdays (except during high season) but are open both weekend days. . . . King Albert I, and wife Queen Elizabeth, lived throughout World War I in De Panne, from which he commanded the Belgian army clinging to that small piece of in-Belgium front at Ypres. A visit to nearby Ypres and Diksmuide brings you to trenches, memorials and other evidences of World War I.

THE DRAMA OF NEARBY DUNKIRK: From any point along the beach of De Panne, you may glance to the west and see the faraway cranes and other port structures of famous Dunkirk (in French, "Dunkerque") across the French border. On the 12-kilometer beach between France's Dunkirk and Belgium's De Panne, the British Army effected its almost miraculous evacuation to England in the dark days of late May and early June, 1940, a great many of them embarking from makeshift piers (of trucks driven into the sea) outside of De Panne (which made De Panne a target for ceaseless attack by German Stuka dive bombers). It was also in De Panne that Lord Gort, commander of the British Expeditionary Force, maintained his headquarters. Yet though De Panne got the bombs, Dunkirk got the glory! Which seems to be the age-old story of Belgium! (In fairness, Dunkirk was also completely destroyed during the evacuation.) Which of us has ever heard of De Panne in connection with the great evacuation from the beaches *between* Dunkirk and De Panne?

On May 10 of 1940, the German army had invaded Belgium, the Netherlands, France and Luxembourg. Though a 340,000-man British Army was sent to aid their continental allies, they and all others were quickly overwhelmed by the German Blitzkrieg. The British Army, whose capture by the Germans would have been devastating to England's ability to continue the war, was ordered to retreat to the port of Dunkirk and there attempt to escape to England. But Dunkirk's harbor was soon made particularly unusable by massive German bombardment, and a large part of the evacuation was forced to board smaller ships picking up the troops as they waded out from the beaches.

In a dramatic, near-desperate appeal, a call went to every marina, dock, river port, yachting club, in England: send any and every vessel you have—pleasure boats, sailing ships, motorized lifeboats, tugs and yachts—to the beaches between Dunkirk and De Panne! Hundreds of ships, hundreds of part-time sailors, accountants-turned-skippers, retired owners of small motorboats, fishermen in their small craft, converged on the coast of the French-Belgian border. As the "Mosquito Armada" reached the area of evacuation, they were viciously bombed by the German Luftwaffe, whose commander—Reichsmarshal Goering—had assured Hitler that air power alone could destroy the beachhead and prevent the escape. Unwisely, Hitler accepted the argument and diverted several of his attacking armored divisions to other portions of the front. Each day for eight consecutive days commencing May 27, as the Royal Air Force blunted much of the German air attack, tens of thousands of French and British troops were successfully plucked from the beaches and returned to England. At the start, British strategists had predicted they would rescue 50,000 men. In the end, they took out 338,000 men, losing hundreds of ships and sailors in the process to German bombs. The beaches from Dunkirk to De Panne were littered with the trucks and tanks of the British Army. But the Army itself had been saved. And a defiant Winston Churchill appeared before Parliament on June 4, when the last soldier had been boarded, to tell the story of the Dunkirk beaches. "We must be very careful," he said "not to assign to this deliverance the attributes of a victory. Wars are not won by evacuations."

But: "We got the Army away. . . . [Now] we shall not flag or fail. We shall go on to the end, we shall fight in France, we shall fight in the seas and oceans, we shall fight with growing confidence and growing strength in the air, we shall defend our island, whatever the cost may be, we shall fight on the beaches, we shall fight on the landing-grounds, we shall fight in the fields, and in the streets, we shall fight in the hills; we shall never surrender . . ."

You will not want to walk all the way to Dunkirk (though you can do so along the beach), but you will want to walk for a part of the way, treading upon sand made historic by a great victory over evil.

OOSTDUINKERKE

Except for the new Delvaux Museum in St. Idesbald, a short excursion from Oostduinkerke, there is little of major interest to detain the overseas tourist in the area between De Panne and Oostduinkerke.

Oostduinkerke itself is another matter. Scenically beautiful, a wide and immense beach adjoining a 350-acre nature reserve (the "Doornpanne") of protected sand dunes, including the highest dune (33 meters) in all of Belgium ("De Hoge Blekker"), Oostduinkerke is also a notch higher in standard than its immediate neighbors, somewhat less commercial and bustling, yet possessed of all the facilities and activities you'd want—they are simply presented in more refined fashion. A large open-air swimming pool of heated sea water is found in the center of the beach, allowing bathing on even chilly days; "sail-carts" are available for rental; and there's a particular emphasis here on horseback riding from several schools. Belgians and Germans make up nearly 95% of the guests in residence. They come not merely for sea-bathing and sunning, but for the area's especially high level of cuisine (and its renowned shrimp specialties; see below); for its many folkloric events (including its near-daily "horse-fishing"; see below); and for a broad array of serious museums and attractions nearby (see below). Though Oostduinkerke looks smaller than De Panne or Blankenberge, and has far fewer hotels and holiday apartments, its permanent population is actually 50% greater than De Panne's, and almost the same as Blankenberge's; they live in attractive homes scattered along the green "polders" (land reclaimed from the sea) to the immediate south of the bathing district.

OOSTDUINKERKE'S FAMED "FISHERMEN ON HORSEBACK":
Daily except Sunday, several sturdy old gentlemen—most are cafe owners—cover themselves with yellow slickers and heavy boots, climb upon horses as massive as Clydesdales (they weigh a ton), and set out on a colorful, one-and-half-hour trek through the shallow surf of Oostduinkerke, a hard and tedious "march" that has brought fame to the city and become one of the great touristic sights of Belgium. Man-and-horse against the sea! You'll see the scene reproduced on paintings, postcards and the stained-glass windows of churches, on posters hanging in every Oostduinkerke pub and café. The straining, giant horse, urged-on by its heavy-set, yellow-garbed owner, is dragging a large net through the shallow, foaming waters from Oostduinkerke all the way to Nieuwpoort. The object: shrimp ("crevettes", "garnalen"), tiny grey crustaceans feeding on the sealife and floor of these waters, shrimp cherished as the "Caviar of the North Sea". Periodically, the nets are emptied of their catch into large wicker baskets hanging from each side of the saddle; on an average day, the horse-fishermen will each bring in from 10 to 15 kilos (although extraordinary "takes" of more than a hundred kilos have been known). Most of the men bring their catch to their own cafes or pubs, where they immediately salt and boil the tiny delicacies, and sell them out almost as fast to a few waiting housewives and restaurant chefs serving them for lunch. One such pub is **"De Peerdevisser"**, on the grounds of the National Fishing Museum (see below), whose horseback-fishing-owner will sell you a small sack of the freshly-boiled shrimp if you catch him at the right time. The horse-fishermen start out about half an hour before low tide, and that can be anywhere between 5:30 a.m. and noon (ask your hotel).

The tradition of horseback-fishing began in the late 1400s, and is attributed to elderly men who devised the method when they were no longer able to endure the rigors of normal fishing from boats on the high seas. The tradition continues to exist only at Oostduinkerke, and there is considerable trepidation about whether successors will be found to continue the practice when the present small group retires from it. In 1983, each of them was received at the Palace in Brussels, and given an award by King Baudouin.

What is it that makes us so thrill to the view of the horsefishermen? The courage, strength—or subjugation—of the horse? Man and horse against nature? The glory of work? The age-old contribution made by the horse to man's survival in life and battle? The extraction of food from nature? At the beach of Oostduinkerke at low tide: a dramatic view of man and horse at work.

HOTELS OF OOSTDUINKERKE: A few paragraphs from here, we'll talk about actually enjoying those delectable shrimp—the preeminent food specialty of Oostduinkerke. For your prior, overnight needs, the **Hotel Artan,** on the Ijslandplein, 6 Zeedijk (phone 058/51-59-08), is a first recommendation, which literally towers above the others in every way. A modern high-rise directly on the beach (and not on the promenade above it), its units consist of large suite-like rooms with separate kitchenettes, yet rent for a top of 2940 francs ($81.67) double, and can quite easily accommodate families of four. The slick and functional hotel has indoor swimming pool, sauna and exercise facilities, cafeteria, coffee shop, bar, and in-room television sets receiving 15 international channels! Almost next door, again directly on the sand overlooking the sea, the somewhat similar, several-stories-high **Westland Hotel,** at 9 Zeedijk-West (phone 058/51-31-97), offers less elaborate rooms, but for a much less costly 1425 francs ($40) per twin, including breakfast for two. It, too, is relatively modern, in sharp contrast to the statelier, traditional hotels in town.

The beachside promenade of Oostduinkerke is the "Zeedijk", and running perpendicular to it is the long, broad, sweeping, Leopold II Laan. On that latter, highly impressive boulevard, the 75-room **Hotel Gauquie,** at 251 Leopold II Laan (phone 51-10-88), a short block from the sea, is a big but refined and old-fashioned tourist-class hotel with whitewashed facade, decorative tower, rooms with private bath or shower, yet it charges only 1500 francs ($42) for a twin-bedded room with private bath and breakfast, only 1000 francs ($28) per person for room and two meals a day, only 700 francs ($20) for children on the same demi-pension basis. How remarkably cheap is the Belgian coast! On the sea itself, you should like the small **Hotel Flandria,** at 24 Zeedijk (phone 058/51-17-83), over the restaurant of the same name (1550 francs, $43, twin, because of the seaside location), and the nearby **Pension Britannia,** at 21 Zeedijk (phone 058/51-11-77), somewhat on the same order (simple, tourist class) and close to the same price. If you'd prefer a better hotel of near-first class standard, try the adjoining town of Koksijde and either its **Hotel le Regent,** at 10 A. Bliecklaan (phone 058/51-12-10) (2700 francs, $75, double; there's also a highly-regarded restaurant here), or **Hotel Florian,** at 32 A. Bliecklaan (phone 058/51-69-82) (2000 francs, $55.56, twin).

Cheaper accommodations in Oostduinkerke, without private bath, are available at the **Pension Beau Site,** 71 Leopold II Laan (phone 058/51-12-36) (960 francs, $27, twin); the **Pension Edelweiss,** 276 Leopold II Laan (phone 058/51-23-78) (940 francs, $26 twin); or, best yet, at the **Pension M. Vanneuville,** 109 Albert I Laan (same as "La Route Royale") (phone 058/51-26-20); the last-named gentleman is the one who rents those 4-person bicycles you see whizzing around the town. The Youth Hostel of Oostduinkerke is the **Huis Duinenrand,** at 6 Koksijdesteenweg (phone 058/51-10-54).

SHRIMPS . . . AND STILL MORE SHRIMPS: Though

every other dish is served, the restaurant specialties of Oostduinkerke are shrimps prepared in every conceivable way—to such an extent that certain similar dishes made elsewhere in Belgium are called "in the style of Oostduinkerke" ("à l'Oostduinkerquoise"). Nowhere will you taste these shrimp in more succulent form than at the unusual home-restaurant of Oostduinkerke's wandering-chef-returned-home, André Goossens. A laureate of the local hotel school, who then cooked in locations ranging from the Ritz in Madrid to the grand country inns of France, he returned with his wife and three young children to create a shrine to the shrimp in the precincts of his own modest home in a residential district of Oostduinkerke. The **Restaurant Bécassine,** at 20 Rozenlaan (phone 058/51-20-13), is the bric-a-brac-filled living room and adjoining parlors of the cozy residence, art covering the walls, soft classical music playing in the background, the decor homey and middle class, without the elegance you'd expect in what could be (but isn't) a pretentious setting. Mr. Goossens, in white toque and apron, stands in full view at the stone fireplace of the living room alongside a small table of fish and meats, and before your very eyes he grills the main features of your meal. His wife, Marie-Claire (French), stands in the small nearby kitchen preparing the vegetables and other plates. From his own fireplace post, he virtually reaches over to place all emerging creations on your plate, and what emerges is sublime—especially when made with the small, fresh shrimp caught by the fishermen-on-horseback that morning. Without asking, you're first served small tubular fish cakes, their interiors almost liquidy, and with only the most subtle taste of fish; or you're given a few, cooked, grey "crevettes" (shrimp) in fresh large mushrooms. The real appetizer (although it will fill you up) is Mr. Goossens' famous "Pomme de Terre farcie aux Crevettes" (350 francs, $9.72)—a crackling hot, open baked potato stuffed with the equally famous hot shrimp, and covered with an extraordinary hot white sauce. That a simple baked potato can be made to taste like this is a source of continuing astonishment! You go on to choose from an extensive menu of other creative dishes, both fish and meat, and dine quite easily for less than $30—indeed, there are three-course "menus" for 750 and 1000 francs ($21 and $28)—including the hot shrimps in baked potato, covered by that secret sauce. The renowned Belgian painter Paul Delvaux makes a point of eating here.

Imagine the dedication required to have created a nationally-known, indeed celebrated, restaurant in the living room of your own, fairly simple home, while three children play upstairs! Something of the character of Mr. Goossens emerges from his English-language dedication to a book of recipes: "When a nation has lost its love for good cooking, it has no longer any literature, no civilized wit, no social intercourse, no social unity. Only good cooking can avoid banality." Don't miss this reasonably-priced oddity, which is closed Thursdays and the first three weeks of October. Phone first.

Just as residents flock to Mr. Goossens' living room for baked potato with shrimp, they head a bit further from the sea to a large villa known as the **Restaurant Beukenhof,** 10 Alois Boudrijstraat (phone 058/51-27-10), for its renowned "Bouillabaisse de la mer du Nord" at 700 francs ($21), easily a complete meal. The garden-side setting is a striking one, the villa tastefully furnished, and three-course "menus" are available for 900 francs ($25). Closed Tuesdays.

In a more normal setting at the side of the sea, the **Restaurant Flandria,** of the Hotel Flandria at 24 Zeedijk (phone 058/51-17-83), is an Ardennes-style inn, in appearance, smoked hams hanging from the ceiling, but its extensive à la carte menu lists all the local seafood specialties at exceptionally moderate prices, and offers four quite innovative, four-course menus for only 500, 700, 800 and 1000 francs ($14, $20, $22 and $28). Even the cheapest of those meals, for 500 francs, is quite respectable in choice: it starts, as you'd guess, with "tomates aux crevettes" (a whole tomato stuffed with the boiled local shrimp, the whole covered by a mayonnaise-like sauce), goes on to soup of the day, is followed either by trout cooked with almonds or beef stew brewed in beer ("carbonades flamandes"), and ends with cheese, ice cream, or a mousse au chocolat, all for 500 francs ($14), service included.

Cheaper, three-course tourist menus (again featuring shrimp) for only 450 francs ($12.50) are found at the **Restaurant Santa Marta,** 58 Zeedijk, or on the street parallel to the beach promenade at the **Restaurant Christoph,** 43 Albert I Laan ("La Route Royale" or "Koninklijke Baan"), path of the electric tram scooting up and down the Belgian coast. **Mosselhuis André,** at 84 Albert I Laan, is the simple "friture" where you go for Oostduinkerke's best mussels and fries, prepared with a skill decades in the making.

ON SURREALISM AND THE SEA: Apart from the horse-fisherman, whom you should definitely try to see, the major sights of Oostduinkerke and vicinity are two quite remarkable museums:

The National Museum of Fishing

Though most of us eat copious quantities of fish, how often do we think of the arduous and often dangerous work needed to gather them in from the high seas? From the towns of Nieuwpoort (adjoining Oostduinkerke to the east), Ostend and Zeebrugge on the Belgian coast, large Belgian fishing fleets depart each day on trips ranging from two days (from Nieuwpoort) to two weeks (from Ostend and Zeebrugge), and to fishing areas as far as Iceland. This museum—the **"National Visserijmuseum",** at 4 Pastoor Schmitzstraat in a small park just behind the Town Hall (center of Oostduinkerke)—tells their story and their history over the past several hundred years. Many never return, and as you enter the grounds, you pass memorial stones bearing the names of hundreds of Flemish fishermen lost at sea, some as recently as the 1970s. "Ils ont offert leur jeune vie à la mer" (they have offered their young lives to the sea), says an engraved inscription. "Seul, leurs noms sont restés. Ils resteront pour toujours gravés dans ces pierres" (Only their names have survived. They will survive forever, engraved on these stones).

Inside the museum are instructive maps of where the fleets go to provide fish for the restaurant tables of Brussels and elsewhere; remarkable models (made by the curator) of the ships they use and have used; celebrated paintings of fishermen (including the horse-fishermen) and of the sea itself (the latter by Louis Artan, an artist of high rank, after whom the city's leading hotel was named), old fashioned photos of them, all manner of fishing implements, and too many other items to name. Part of the museum complex is a reconstructed, typical fishermen's house of the area, with its furnishings of the late 1800s, this one the "fermette" of a horse-fisherman who gathered shrimp at low tide, then used the same horse in the fields for ploughing, all in between expeditions by boat. Outside are actual wooden fishing boats, their large "paddles" used for casting nets, and alongside is the "estaminet" (old cafe) **"In de Peerdevisscher"**, whose horse-fisherman-owner will serve you a beer—and that morning's catch of shrimp. The Fishing Museum, only one of its kind in Belgium, is a delightfully modern, one-story building with floor-to-ceiling windows (on one side) that create a sparkling atmosphere for your visit. And your visit, if you're a traveller open to new ideas and subject matter, will be a memorable one. The museum is open daily throughout the year from 10 to noon and 2 to 6 for an admission charge of only 30 francs (83¢).

The Museum of Paul Delvaux

The sight that literally dictates a stop or a stay in Oostduinkerke is a major, new museum devoted to the *oeuvre* of one artist: the Belgian surrealist Paul Delvaux. To view in one place nearly one hundred paintings by this important figure is to undergo an emotional battering, to arouse instincts and memories suppressed since childhood, to engage in an act of self-discovery.

Paul Delvaux, born in Brussels in 1897, still produces as many as four large paintings a year from his atelier in Veurne; he plans soon to move to a chalet on the grounds of the museum. For nearly fifty of his vigorous 91 years, he has struggled with an obsession that leaps vividly from every one of his striking and masterfully-done canvases, yet almost defies the effort to define it in words. The obsession relates to the female form, the nude or partially nude female in most instances, women unbearably beautiful, erotic, yet silent, impassive and alone, divorced from contact with men and with each other, absorbed in their own femininity. In a rare exception to the usually static theme, one makes love to a male statue. Though occasional men intrude, some fully clothed in professorial garb, others young men or boys totally nude, no man pays the slightest heed to the women.

The women are placed in an endless variety of patterns and poses, but mainly against three recurring settings: a deserted train station or trolley platform at night; a plaza of ancient Greece flanked by classic temples, columns, steps and arched facades; a chaise lounge or canopied bed on the portico of a Victorian home with ornamental iron decorations. Through numerous paintings wander skeletons, the most expressive skeletons in all the history of art, looking as if they still inhabited the bodies from which they came, human and alive in the stances they assume, the emotions they convey.

What does it all mean? Every one of us knows precisely what these paintings mean, because we experience a strong and distinct impact from each one, and yet are unable to articulate that experience in words; the reaction is an inner one and stems from our tempestuous sub-conscious. You may read a dozen learned treatises on Delvaux—one theory holds that he is repeatedly portraying his mother, who is therefore untouchable—and you may read Delvaux' own interviews on the work, and you will conclude that, like music, art of a certain level should never be interpreted with words, else why should its meaning have been conveyed through a painting?

It is fascinating, in the Museum of Paul Delvaux, to see earlier works of his before the obsession took hold. One is a superb, fiery, factory painting of the industrial revolution, evidence of his technical mastery; and it is perhaps sad that he has not applied those obvious gifts to broader themes. Yet like the memorable character in "One Hundred Years of Solitude", who sculpts one golden fish after another, only to melt each down and begin anew, he either seeks perfection or has found it in a simple, recurring image. And like Picasso or Matisse, who painted into their 90s, he is continuing to work and cannot stop. Though you will see at least one Delvaux in every major Belgian museum, and murals by him at the University of Liège, Brussels Convention Center, and Ostend Casino (only rare paintings by Delvaux have left Belgium), you will find no other grouping of his works, than there, capable of revealing his most extraordinary talent. Though he has painted incessantly for more than 60 years, Delvaux' output consists of only 370 paintings, each of epic quality.

"Le Musée Paul Delvaux", operated by the painter's nephew, Charles van Deun, is in a Flemish farmhouse called the "Vlierhof", marvelously modernized to show off each of the 100 works in displays. It is at 42 Kabouterweg (phone 058/51-19-94) in the town of St. Idesbald adjoining Oostduinkerke, and is open from April 1 to September 30 from 11 a.m. to 7 p.m.; in October, November and December on weekends only, from noon to 6 p.m. Admission is 80 francs ($2.22) for adults, 50 francs ($1.38) for students, artists, or the elderly, free to children under 10. Posters of Delvaux' work are sold, and a pleasant cafeteria provides snacks. To find the museum in the maze of streets that constitute St. Idesbald: from the Zeedijk that runs along the sea, turn down the main street of town, which is the Strandlaan. Drive down the

Strandlaan until you pass the A. Nazy Laan on your right, turn right into that street and proceed for two blocks, at which point you turn left for one block to the Kabouterlaan. Or, drive further down the Strandlaan, pass the P. P. Rubenslaan on your right, and turn right at the next intersection into what eventually is the Kabouterlaan. Surrounded by trees and bushes, the museum is scarcely visible from the street. Persevere.

OSTEND

Through a narrow channel cut through its beach, scores of ships of every variety and kind—including "P. & O. ferries" and "P. & O. jetfoils" from Dover and Folkestone in England—pass in and out of Ostend each day, docking at a large inner harbor at one side of the city. Ostend is not simply a resort community, it is a city of 70,000 residents, yet it also maintains a long and wide beach attracting vacationers who plan to sun and doze in the sea-side air. Because it is a city, active all year, a great many tourists give it preference (along with Knokke) in the late fall, winter and early spring months when smaller North Sea resorts calm down considerably and close a great many of their facilities. Ostend rarely ever closes anything—including its late-night restaurants, cafes, night-spots and Casino!

The wide Ostend Beach goes on for more than six kilometers, its most active section lying between the **Casino** ("Kursaal") at one end and the large **Thermae Palace Hotel** at the other. An elevated walkway above the beach—the Albert I Promenade—runs for its entire length, lined with modern apartment houses and hotels. Because Ostend was heavily bombed in World War II, and restored over the years by unthinking modernists, it no longer features the grandly-ornate, traditional rococo seafront facades that earned it the title, around the turn of the century, of "King of Resorts", "Resort of Kings". These are now contemporary, glass-fronted—and heavily controversial, disputed—buildings of several stories. Sixty years ago, at the start of similar debates in cities all over the world, the great Ostend painter, James Ensor, protested indignantly over such tinkering with the historic: "Unmask the moldy schemes of the improvement-mad!" he shouted. "Blast those who are filling in our wonderful docks! Public flogging for those who are leveling the gentle curves of our sand dunes!" Matters improve considerably in the several-block-square area just below the beach, entirely transformed in recent years into a festive and traffic-free pedestrian area of strolling-malls. Thousands of British shoppers come to this area, some just for the day, to browse among its extensive offerings.

So there you have the major features of Ostend: a busy port in the very heart of the city, a major beach and seaside promenade just to the side of the port, a large shopping area just below the beach; and now add the country's largest casino, a small but active nightlife district, dozens of fine restaurants—and a museum displaying the work of the city's most famous native son.

ENSOR, THE ARTIST OF OSTEND: In histories of modern art published all over the world, the Belgian artist Margritte is often omitted, and Delvaux may be missing, and the same with Permeke and De Smet—but Ensor (1860–1949), James Ensor, is always there. A seminal figure who grew up in the exciting era of the Impressionists in the latter half of the 19th century, he blazed a path through Impressionism into a different artistic style, one that sought to reveal the inner life of people, the fantasies, dreads, anxieties and terrors with which we all are afflicted. In one of his most distinctive post-Impressionist periods, when he led the Symbolist movement, he took the masks worn by revelers at Ostend's Carnival, and by placing them on the faces of large groups, evoked the kinds of emotion felt during nightmares. In other celebrated works, of grotesque human visages in pastel colors splashed upon largely white backgrounds, he made sardonic comments on the hypocrisy, vapidity and falseness of middle class society.

Though he loved Ostend, and scarcely ever left the city for a single day during the 87 years of his life there, he was the "bad boy" of the artistic scene, fiercely antibourgeois, flailing out against the establishment and institutions about him, quite obviously a Socialist, invariably blasphemous in religious themes. His most famous work, the 14-foot-long canvas of the procession he called "The Entry of Christ into Brussels" (1888), shows military bands, generals, churchmen and merchants, clowns and deathheads accompanying His arrival into the capital city. One marcher carries the sign, "Fanfares Doctrinaires Toujours Réussi" (Doctrinary Fanfares, Always Successful). Above the parade is flung a giant banner, inscribed "Vive la Sociale". The inscriptions, the crowd made to look like bizarre puppets, the pity so obviously felt for the central character, have all been subjects of intense controversy for decades, their meaning subject to numerous differing interpretations. A painting by Roger Raveel in the Brussels subway asks: "Qu'avait en vue Ensor par 'Vive la Sociale'?" (What did Ensor have in mind by "Vive la Sociale"?) When Ensor himself died, his hearse was pulled in a mammoth Ostend procession, resembling his painting, accompanied by ambassadors, generals and other dignitaries; the rebel had become a totem, honored by the very society he had scorned.

If you have not been aware of Ensor before, you will make his acquaintance in Belgium—through several major works in Antwerp's Museum of Fine Arts, and equal number in Brussels, two in Liège, one in Ghent—but especially in Ostend. On the **Wapenplein** (the town square) in the very center of the city, Ostend's **Museum of Fine Arts** ("Stedelijk Feest en Kultuurpaleis") devotes an entire section to Ensor—prints and drawings (with the impact of Goya) as well as paintings; it should not be missed. The museum itself is open daily except Tuesdays from 10 to noon and 2 to 5, is free on Wednesdays, and charges 30 francs (83¢) at all other times. But there is more here on Ensor. Running directly off the Wapenplein is the Vlaanderenstraat leading to the sea. At No. 27 Vlaanderenstraat, a block from the beach, is the restored, souvenirshop **home of James Ensor,** open daily except Tuesdays from June 1 to September 30, from 10 to noon and 2 to 5, in all other months on weekends only, from 2 to 5 p.m., always for a 30 francs (83¢) admission charge. In the studio-attic of that family house, wrote a noted art critic, "the future of modern painting was determined". Ensor, incidentally, was the son of a British (but Belgian-born) father, hence his English name.

THE OTHER KEY SIGHTS: Nearly everything of touristic interest (other than Ostend's important horse-racing track and the long extension of its broad beach) is found in a compact square no more than 400 yards on each side: the beach to the north, the open waters of the harbor to the east, the "Mercator" Yacht Harbor on the south, the broad Leopold II Laan to the west. The "Wapenplein" (town square) is almost in the center of the city, and also houses the **Folklore Museum** ("De Plate"). On the restaurant-lined, Fisherman's Quay ("Visserskaai") running along the waters of the port, is the interesting North Sea **Aquarium** open 10 to noon and 2 to 5, daily from April through September, weekends in other months, for a 40-franc ($1.11) admission fee; while in the Mercator yacht harbor is the three-masted former training ship of the Belgian Merchant Navy, the **"Mercator",** now a museum to be visited for a 60 franc ($1.67) fee; it's open daily from June to September, weekends only the remainder of the year. (Gerardus Mercator was the 16th-century Flemish map-maker and geographer, educated at the University of Louvain. Because he was threatened by charges of heresy in 1544, he moved to Germany. Amazingly for such a small country, Belgium also produced that other great map-maker and geographer, the Antwerp-born Abraham Ortelius, 1527–1598.)

Elsewhere in Ostend, the **Provincial Museum for Modern Art,** at 11 Romestraat, presents a complete survey of Belgian modern art from its origins to the present day, and is important for students of the subject. For indoor sea-water bathing, the mammoth, covered and heated **Municipal Swimming Pool** ("Stedelijk Zwembadcomplex"), at 1 Koninginnelaan, charges 50 to 100 francs ($1.39 to $2.78), depending on season, and also operates co-ed saunas, an unsettling experience for some. The **Wellington Racetrack** ("Wellington-renbaan") operates pari-mutual trotting races every Friday evening at 6:45 p.m. from May 13 to September 9, normal flat races on Mondays, Thursdays and weekends starting at 2:30 p.m. in July and August, for admission of 100 to 250 francs ($2.77 to $7). And there are so many other sports facilities, fishing trips, hikes and tours, other activities, offered in Ostend that a complete guidebook would be needed to detail them all. But where do you stay while enjoying the "city of a thousand possibilities"? Some suggestions follow:

HOTELS: The modern, balconied, 10-story **Hotel Andromeda,** 5 Kursaal Westhelling, phone 58-66-11, on the Albert I Promenade next to the Casino and directly on the beach, is in a class by itself. Through a slick, marble lobby, you step to modern rooms with hard, wide beds, Eames-armchairs for relaxing and reading, color TV and all else, for which the charge ranges (depending on season and seaside position) from 2000 francs ($56) to 4800 francs ($133) per double room, including breakfast for two, service and tax.

 Hotel Thermae Palace, at 7 Koningin Astridlaan (phone 80-66-44) on the sea; the **Bellevue-Britannia,** at 55 Albert I Promenade (phone 70-63-73) on the sea; and the **Hotel Imperial,** at 76 Van Iseghemlaan (phone 80-67-67) a block from the sea, form a closely-ranked grouping just below the standard of the Andromeda. The 60-room Bellevue-Britannia is fully as modern, a bit more strictly-functional and plain, but charges only 2500 francs ($70) for a twin room with bath and breakfast. The Thermae Palace is part of the 1930s-style, massive former baths establishment down the beach; it charges a uniform 4400 francs ($122) for twin rooms with bath and breakfast. The Imperial, across from the Casino, 50 yards from the beach, is a more traditional building with fairly large guest rooms, for which the charge ranges from 2200 to 2600 francs ($61 to $72) for a twin room with bath, including breakfast for two, service and tax.

 Another notch downwards, into a slightly lower category, and we find the **Hotel Bero,** 1A Hofstraat (phone 70-23-35), giving good value; as does the **Hotel Europe,** 52 Kapucijenstraat (phone 70-10-12), and the **Royal Astor,** at 15 Hertstraat (phone 50-49-70). The 60-room Bero, three blocks from the beach, is in its third generation of single family ownership, charges a reasonable 2000 francs ($56) for a twin with private bath and breakfast. The Royal Astor, a balconied building only 75 yards down a side street off the beach, charges only 1600 francs ($44) for its twin rooms with private bath, breakfast included. And the seven-story Europe, 60 yards from the promenade and the sea, charges from 1500 to 1750 francs ($42 to $49) for exactly the same.

For **budget-priced** rooms without private bath, but with hot and cold running water, try the cheaper **Hotel Pacific,** at 11 Hofstraat (phone 70-15-07) (1300 francs, $36, per double with breakfast).

The youth hostel of Ostend is **"De Ploate"**, 82 Langestraat (phone 80-52-97), charging 330 francs ($9.20) for bed-and-breakfast.

RESTAURANTS OF OSTEND: If you seek the classic *haute cuisine* of France/Belgium, you find it in two upper range establishments that dominate all the others: **"Au Vigneron"**, at 79 Koningstraat (phone 70-48-16; closed Sunday evenings and Mondays), and **Hostellerie Bretonne,** at 23 Vindictivelaan (phone 70-42-22; closed Wednesdays); best way to enjoy both is simply to order their periodically-changing "tasting menus" ("menus de degustation"): six courses for 2000 francs ($56) at "Au Vigneron", five courses for the same 2000 francs ($56) at the Bretonne. Learned food critics differ violently over which is the superior choice. Easily in third place is the upper floor restaurant (alongside the gaming tables) of the **Ostend Casino,** at the sea (the aptly-named **"Fortuna"**, open evenings only from 6:30 p.m. to 1 a.m.), of surprising quality for such a setting, yet at à la carte levels that permit you quite easily to eat for 1200 francs ($33), plus wine. Among the appetizers: a lobster bisque for 220 francs ($6.11), a salad of small shrimps ("crevettes") for 320 francs ($8.88), "Le Gratin de Fruits de Mer" (assorted sea foods, breaded and fried) for 400 francs ($11.11), and the seasonal asparagus, Flemish-style (with egg) ("Asperges à la Flamande"), 400 francs ($11.11). The always-exciting main courses: Half a Lobster with Belle-Vue Sauce, 700 francs ($20), a simple fried Sole of the North Sea "belle meunière" for only 600 francs ($17), a fish-and-seafoods stew ("Waterzooi van vis") for 700 francs ($20). With all the classic desserts priced at 170 to 180 francs ($4.72 or $5), including those cliché-like but luscious "crêpes 'Suzette'", you've had a memorable but fairly moderate meal that leaves you full, but light and unstuffed, as a great meal should.

Of **elegant, first class** quality, but priced to allow a dinner for 900 to 1000 francs ($25 to $28), is the **Old Shakespeare** at 18 St. Petrusen Paulusplein, opposite the station (phone 70-51-57;

leg of lamb is its specialty); the **Prince Albert**, at 44A Visserskaai (phone 70-60-63; and go there for its shrimp croquettes, its Normandy sole, its scallops "Coquilles St. Jacques"); the **Yacht Grill**, 61 St. Franciscusstraat (phone 70-29-79; closed Wednesdays).

In the **middle-class** area (600 to 800 francs $17 to $22, for a three-course meal), four restaurants—the **Chopin, Kwinte, Falstaff** and **Belgica**—are the consensus choice of a number of Ostenders with whom I recently argued the question. The **Chopin**, in the Hotel Ariel at 1A Adolf Buylstraat (phone 70-08-37, closed Thursdays) is proud of its roast crabs ("Geroosterde Zeekreeftjes"), its grilled and aromatically-seasoned lobster, its monkfish with leek ("Zeeduirel met prei"). The **Belgica**, at 42 Visserskaai (phone 80-48-00, closed Wednesdays), is priced even somewhat below the levels set forth above, yet again provides several usually higher-priced seafood specialities of Ostend, including its popular "Oostendse vissoep" (Ostend-style fish soup) and numerous shrimp-based dishes. **Kwinte**, at 28 Visserskaai (phone 70-13-43; closed Wednesdays), offers a great many regional specialties on its moderately-priced menu. And the **Falstaff**, with its unusually central location at 7 Wapenplein (phone 50-25-97), is a simple, narrow, beam-ceilinged and rather rustic room that attracts crowds with its hearty (for Europe) double entrecôte steak ("Dubbele Lendebiefstuk"), designed for avid beef addicts.

Your **cheapest** meals (under 400 francs ($11.11) are found in a number of popular but high quality "fritures" along the sea, on the Albert I Promenade high above the beach. Try the **Meridor**, the **Savarin**, the **Melrose** and **Splendid's**, at Nos. 48A, 62B, 63 and 67D Albert I Promenade, respectively.

Fishermen's Quay

The street along the dock where small trawlers deliver their catch of fish each day, is the **Visserskaai** ("Fishermen's Quay"), running on both sides of the **Vissersplein** ("Fishermen's Square"). In addition to several of the establishments listed above, no fewer than 31 other fish-specializing restaurants are found on it (amid fishing boats and fish stalls), of which the most expensive is the **Lusitania**, the cheapest the **Belgica**. It's an obvious point that in a city that lives from fish (fishing, shipping and tourism are Ostend's three main occupations), you ought to schedule at least one meal for the Visserskaai.

NIGHTLIFE AND NAUGHTINESS: Ostend's giant Casino on the sea ("Casino Kursaal Oostende"), largest in Belgium, has no closing days, is active as early as its opening hour of 4 p.m. (but heats up later in the night), operates several craps tables in addition to the more staid roulette, baccarat, "punto banco" and blackjack, and sells its chips for as little as 30 and 40 francs (83¢ and $1.11), although some few tables impose a 100-franc ($2.80) minimum. Admission to the building is 50 francs ($1.38). Gambling here is supplemented (and, to some, overshadowed) by the extraordinary weekend evening attractions in the Casino's 1,700-seat auditorium: the Royal Flemish Ballet, operettas, Philharmonic Orchestras of several Belgian cities, popular European performers; and seats, depending on the attraction, are priced for as little as 250 francs ($6.94), for rarely more than 450 francs ($12.50) or 600 ($17) . . . **Langestraat,** running parallel to, and two short blocks down from, the eastern end of the beach is the heart of the "Montmartre" quarter of Ostend, a "stay-up-late", neon-lit collection of bars, cabarets, discos, dance clubs, pubs and such, with enough variety to provide acceptable entertainment even to those who don't normally go in for this sort of thing . . . As elsewhere in Flanders, the movies are presented in their original languages, with sub-titles rather than dubbing; and since there are always U.S. or English films playing, they should provide excellent evening relaxation for the readers of this book. Several major cinemas are found on the Langestraat and intersecting Vlaanderenstraat, never more than three short blocks from the beach.

SOME OSTEND MISCELLANY: Ostend looks new by Belgian standards because it has been destroyed and rebuilt on several occasions. The once-strongly-Protestant city underwent a particularly harsh, three-year siege by the Spanish from 1601 to 1604, and later became known as "the new Troy" when its valiant citizens rebuilt. It was heavily bombed at the outset of World War II in May, 1940, was then selectively destroyed to build "the Atlantic wall" along its beaches by German strategists sure that Allied troops would invade there . . . Four trawlers based in Ostend go all the way to Iceland on their fishing expeditions, and the fish on your plate may very well come from there! . . . In few other cities is the harbor and port so centrally cut into the very heart of the city. One interesting activity is simply to walk along the pier at the entrance to the port, watching an endless succession of ships entering and leaving . . . Nearly 3,000,000 persons each year use Ostend for their crossings of the English Channel, either on the speedy "P. & O. Jetfoil" to Dover, or on the normal "P. & O." car-ferry to Dover or Folkestone . . . The peak of Ostend's fame occurred at the turn of this century—time of "la Belle Epoque" —when Ostend was the most fashionable resort of Europe, the summer home of King Leopold II of Belgium, a magnet attracting droves of wealthy Europeans to its race track and Casino, its Ther-

mal Baths and great seaside promenade where elegant ladies paraded with parasols. Nowadays that attraction can be felt almost as strongly. As you stroll along the fishing docks leading to the station, past a forest of masts and sails, then wander down the flower-bedecked shopping streets filled with crowds, and pause at an open-air café to hear a band perform from under a street-plaza cupola; as you buy a herring in an open air market, or lunch on mussels, french fries and beer in a promenade restaurant atop the embankment sloping to a beach filled with holiday-makers; and as you inhale the salty air and gaze out at the sparkle of light on a pearl-grey sea, all at the side of a large, bustling, friendly city, you'll agree that this is a remarkable resort, well deserving its fame.

Ostend is at the mid-point of the Belgian coast. As you proceed east, past Bredene, De Haan, Wenduine, Blankenberge and Zeebrugge, the economic level suddenly ascends as you enter the environs of glittering Knokke, once best known as the comfortable Knokke/Heist, now famous as the glamorous Knokke-le-Zoute.

KNOKKE

East Hampton and Palm Beach, Cannes and Cap d'Antibes, Portofino and Mar del Plata. What all these have in common is that they are glamorous vacation locales attracting the wealthy of the world and their hangers-on, scenes of elegant parties and frolicsome antics, subjects for boasting and name-dropping. Unless you are a Belgian, that is. To most Belgians, such talked-about towns are really quite *Ordinary. Overrun. Passé.* In Belgium, if you wish to impress, you say you are going for a holiday to **Knokke.** If you wish to appear more elegant still, you say you are going to Knokke-het-Zoute. If you wish to seem a veritable aristocrat, you talk airily about vacationing at "Le Zoute". Beyond "Le Zoute", there is nothing else to which man can aspire!

We are now at the extreme northeastern corner of the Belgian Coast, in the highest-category resort section of Belgium, one part of which—"Le Zoute"—is perhaps the richest vacationland in all of Northern Europe. In actual fact, the 12-kilometer coastline of Knokke is more properly known as "Knokke-Heist" and comprises five separate beach communities—from west to east, **Heist, Duinbergen, Albert Strand, Knokke, Het Zoute**—recently amalgamated into one. Not all are as affluent as the image of "Knokke" implies.

Heist is primarily a residential community of fishermen and construction workers sailing out of, or working in, nearby Zeebrugge. Its hotel capacity is small, and the tourists frequenting the area live mainly in flats and apartments rented by the month.

Duinbergen is also a family town of condominiums and apartment hotels, though it enjoys a dozen, charming, small transient-accepting establishments. The true tourist life—and the glamor—begins in Albert Strand ("Albert Plage") and moves on through Knokke, though even here, facilities are heavily of the upper middle class bracket, not higher, impressive but not yet overwhelming. Le Zoute is where the structures stun and are un-real, and residents are drawn from upper income Europeans, capitalists and celebrities of several countries.

THE KNOKKE CASINO: The centerpiece of the area is the grand and formal Casino of Knokke at 509 Zeedijk-Albertstrand, opposite the Albertstrand beach. Built in 1930, with numerous touches of "art deco", a giant central hall with one of the largest chandeliers in the world (made in Venice), and posh gaming rooms for roulette, baccarat and the like, it is a dressy place, but fun to frequent, after you've presented your passport and paid a 350-franc ($9.72) membership fee. Activities (apart from gambling) abound: motion pictures and cabaret shows, gala parties and changing exhibitions, all the high jinx of the wealthy set (including a discotheque for their children), and weekly "Gastronomic Dinners" in the important "Salle Magritte", which you should ask to see if you're not dining there. Here is Belgian Surrealism to intoxicate your every sense, eight giant murals by the famed René Magritte (see our chapter on Brussels): the man with a bird cage for torso and head, the plant that is at the same time a pigeon, the tiny chair upon a mammoth, canyon-sized stone chair, the nude that becomes a fish. You've seen them before in reproductions; imagine confronting them now in technicolor blow-ups 72 meters wide!

For several kilometers from the Casino in both directions, are tennis courts and small parks, golf and mini-golf, tasteful bowling alleys both indoors and out, 20 bicycle shops, a great sea-water thermal center (see below), congress and meeting halls, swimming pools and manicured grounds, hotels having the highest overall standards of any community in Belgium—and, of course, that 12-kilometer beach with all its shallow tides, sea sports and colorful kite festivals. Running diagonally off the beach at the center of Knokke: the mile-long Lippenslaan lined with the most numerous profusion of shops on all the Coast (about which more later).

HET ZOUTE: As you near the eastern edge of Knokke, suddenly all buildings—hotels and homes alike—turn white in color, sprout rust-red roofs, are 33-feet high and surrounded by grounds and gardens—even the Gulf Oil filling station, a gabled home, meets those specifications! You are in "Het Zoute" (the Dutch spelling), "Le Zoute" (in French). A private development of the city's leading family—the Messrs. (and Barons) Lippens—Le Zoute is an extraordinarily affluent community along the sea, through whose winding streets you can drive and observe, as you do in Beverly Hills, or in Juan-les-Pins. Captain Peter Townsend, ex-suitor of Princess Margaret of England, lives here, as do Belgian bank presidents, industrialists from the Ruhr, French and Bavarian film stars. Their presence, supplemented by the hundreds who come to stay in the exquisite hotels of Le Zoute, and the thousands drawn to adjoining Knokke (pronounced "kuh-nock-kuh"), have provoked the creation of restaurant and shopping facilities that are, in themselves, sightseeing attractions.

The main shopping street of Le Zoute is the **Kustlaan,** one block down from and parallel to the beach of Le Zoute. Worth Street and Madison Avenue, Rodeo Drive and Rue de Rivoli, pale (occasionally) besides the Kustlaan! Here, every renowned boutique and couturier, every gallery of note and jeweler-to-the-world, maintains a small shop behind a subdued and exquisitely-lettered sign. Some famous stores of Brussels deliberately close their premises on weekends in order to move their staffs and merchandise, and follow their clientele, to Le Zoute. In Le Zoute, everything is open on the weekends! Cartier and Cacharel, art dealers stocking an occasional Magritte or Delvaux, Giorgio Armani and Patek Philippe, are all crammed into a single, several-block street whose offerings are supplemented by the larger (but sometimes equally grand) stores of the long Lippenslaan.

HET ZWIN: To the immediate east of Le Zoute is the famous **Zwin,** that one-time estuary through which seagoing ships from remote lands across the waters sailed into medieval Bruges. Now it is a sandy marshland (see our Bruges chapter for the story and effect of its silting) and the ships you see from the beach are passing it by on their way to prosperous Antwerp. But on these marshes, covered in summer with sea lavender, is now maintained a 300-acre natural bird sanctuary much visited throughout the year by conservation-minded persons from both Belgium and abroad. Entering upon the nature-reserve for a 100-franc ($2.77) admission charge, 50 francs ($1.38) for children, you first visit aviaries maintained near the Restaurant "Chalet du Zwin", then proceed on your walk through the Zwin, seeing a most extraordinary assortment of bird-life, including white storks, plovers, gulls and geese—all viewed at close range as they breed in an area of unique vegetation. By climbing certain high sand dunes, you see all the way to the towers of Bruges and Damme, to the mouth of the Scheldt leading to Antwerp. You reach the Zwin by simply walking there from Zoute, along a clearly-identified road. And then you walk back. At 5 a.m. in the morning, as the gaming tables of the Knokke Casino are finally emptied of their addicts, ornithologists are already gathering on the Zwin!

HOTELS OF KNOKKE-HEIST: Because the Knokke area receives visitors all year around (especially on 52 busy weekends, when everything is open), its 120 hotels enjoy that asset denied to their counterparts in so many other resorts: capital to re-invest for upkeep, maintenance, improvements. The result: hotels of unusually high standard, bright and attractive. To single out a few is to neglect scores of equally pleasant, high quality properties. Nevertheless:

The top two establishments, generally conceded, are **La Reserve**, at 160 Elizabethlaan (phone 50/61-06-06) in Albertstrand, and the **Memlinc Palace,** on the Albert I Square ("Albertplein") (phone 50/60-11-34) in Zoute. The 120-room La Reserve, a city block long but only five stories high, is like a vast, elongated, country-lodge, its walls in white, its mansarded roof in rust-red, its massive lobby and restaurant subdued for tasteful, country living. Its location is two blocks from the sea, directly opposite the Knokke Casino, at the side of a tiny inland lake with boats, flanked by multiple tennis courts. Rooms are thoroughly modern, of Hilton-like standard, and comes with 12-channel color TV, mini-bar, small balconies, and high, high rates (by Belgian standards): 6500 francs ($181) double, 5800 francs ($161) single, breakfast and all else included, in high season (July, August, Easter and Christmas), 5300 francs ($147) double, 4300 francs ($119) single, at all other times. In one wing of the hotel is the important "Thalassa Center" (the watery health spa) of Knokke, described later in this chapter.

The Memlinc Palace, directly overlooking the sea in Zoute, affects the same Zoute-enforced design of red-and-white, mountain lodge-type shapes (and since Zoute makes such universal use of such colors, a great many structures in Knokke also follow suit), offers eighty-three rooms of somewhat prim, old-fashioned furnishings, but both rooms and their bathrooms are relatively spacious and comfortable, with heavy leather chairs, a small couch. Public areas downstairs are stunning, in a number of different styles ranging from "English gentlemen's club" to delicate French "Empire", but consistent within each area. Rates—for a hotel a tiny bit less desirable than La Reserve (though magnificently located)—are 4000 francs ($111) double, 2500 francs ($69) single, with breakfast, service and tax included.

The hotels in the category *just below* the two leaders are, on my list, eight in number, of which four are in Zoute and four in Albertstrand, all of them "little wonder" hotels of less than 40 rooms apiece. The Zoute contenders begin with the glamorous **Fairway Hotel** at 9 Tuineluiterspad (phone 050-61-14-67), with 14 rooms each designer-furnished in different styles and moods, and ranging in price from 3000 to 6000 francs ($90 to $180); a restaurant on the premises—the "St. Bernard"—is famous for its seafood specialties; followed by the elegant **Pauwels Hotel,** 353 Kustlaan (phone 50/61-16-17) (a block from the beach, amid the chic boutiques of Zoute's priciest shopping street; 3900 francs—$108—double, 2600 francs—$72—single, breakfast included); and go on to include the German-owned **Dorint-Hotel-Knokke,** 84 Kustlaan (phone 60/61-01-28) (totally rebuilt in 1983, and now consisting entirely of modern, suite-like units renting in the main for 3900 francs—$108—double in high season, 3700 francs—$103—double most other times, in a structure that includes enclosed swimming pool and sauna); the **Hotel Shakespeare,** at 795 Zeedijk-Zoute (phone 50/60-11-77) (doubles 4000 francs—$111—singles, 2750 francs—$76); and the **Hotel Lugano,** at 14 Villapad (phone 50/61-04-71), two blocks from the beach in the area closest to bustling Knokke. In Albertstrand, these upper-category properties include the trendy and chic **Hotel Lido,** at 18 Zwaluwenlaan (phone 50/60-19-25), two blocks from the sea, two blocks from the Casino (original modern art on the walls, highly modern and contoured furnishings throughout; 2400 francs—$67—twin, 1500 francs—$42—single); the tiny **Park-hotel,** 176 Elizabethlaan (phone 50/60-09-01), two blocks from the sea, with its highly-reputed, gastronomic restaurant downstairs (2600 francs, $72, double); the **Atlanta** at 162 J. Nellenslaan (phone 50/60-55-00), a block from the beach (2200 francs—$61, double; 1700 francs—$47, single); and the **Hotel Nelson** at 36 Meerminlaan (phone 50/60-68-10), less than two blocks from the beach (and a cheaper 2000 francs, $56, for a twin with bath, including—as do all these hotels—breakfast, service and tax).

More modestly priced, but of higher standard, with period furnishings throughout and enjoying a favored Zoute location, two blocks from the sea, is the 35-room **Britannia Hotel,** at 85 Elisabethlaan (phone 50/60-14-41) (2200 francs, $61, twin; 1120 francs, $31, single; and several rooms without bath for slightly less).

Cheaper still: **Hotel St. Christophe,** at 10A Ant. Bréartstraat in Zoute (phone 50/60-11-52) (1200 francs, $33, double without bath); the **Corner House,** at 1 Hazegrasstraat (phone 50/60-76-19), in Zoute, a pleasant, 22-room hostelry renting doubles without bath for only 1200 francs ($33), breakfast included, but a long walk from the extreme east corner of the beach, in the area just next to the Zwin nature reserve.

Finally, if you'll simply walk or drive down the broad Lippenslaan in Knokke, away from the beach, you'll pass numerous hotels—the **Westland,** at No. 253 (phone 50/60-20-01); the **Prins Boudewijn,** at No. 37 (phone 50/60-10-16), the **Prince de Liège,** at No. 34 (phone, 50/60-49-21), **Prince's,** at No. 171 (phone 50/60-11-11), still others—renting double or twin rooms without private bath for never more than 1200 francs ($33), breakfast included, in 1989.

CULINARY KNOKKE:
The area ranks just behind Brussels and Bruges in the number of outstanding restaurants found within it. And that's just as you'd expect in a near-permanent community of wealthy Belgians, experienced in the finest cuisine, demanding. Every Friday evening, they rush to book every table of the Casino's "Magritte Ballroom" for a "Gastronomic Evening" prepared each week by a different leading restaurant. The standards of that memorable, weekly feast are then freshly remembered, perpetuated, insisted upon, during the next six evenings of dining out!

What is less to be expected is that the chefs and proprietors at several of Knokke's leading restaurants—including its very best one—are women. You will quickly discard all your former beliefs about superior male chefs when you have tasted the dishes of Marguerite De Spae and her daughter, Rita, at Knokke's single-most-renowned, elegant and expensive **Restaurant Aquilon** (not to be confused with the Aquilon in St. Idesbald), at 70 Bayauxlaan (phone 50/60-12-74). That feminists can be tough indeed is proved by the price of their 2700 franc ($75), five-course, and very special menu (which you might as well order, given the level of à la carte rates): roast goose liver lightly spiced, lobster "Marguerite" with creamed spinach, "loup de mer" (grilled "sea wolf") with truffles, baby pigeon and accompaniments, light fruit tartes for dessert, with coffee, service included. Closed Tuesday evenings and Wednesdays.

In the category just below those heights, and at considerably lower cost, the male-operated **Restaurant Panier d'Or** and the male-operated **Restaurant Olivier** compete for honors. The Panier d'Or, at 656 Zeedijk (phone 50/60-31-89), is directly on the sea, near the tourist office, offers four-course "menus" for as little as 750 francs ($21), but charges 1000 francs ($28) for most, and is best known for its fish soup ("Vissoep") at 275 francs ($7.65), its lobster Flemish-style ("à la Flamande") priced according to weight, its well-garnished fish plates (sole, turbot and salmon) for 650 and 850 francs ($18 and $24), served with meticulously prepared sauces and from the freshest of ingredients. Twelve hundred francs ($33), plus wine, will be your average meal cost, astonishing in view of the restaurant's reputation and quality. Closed Tuesdays. Olivier, in the area of the Casino, a block from the beach of the Albertstrand ("Albert Plage") at 159 Nellenslaan (phone 60-55-70), rates third among the restaurant leaders, in my view, at rates that will average 1300 francs ($39) for the average meal.

Five other Knokke-area restaurants are among a larger number of very special establishments where dining becomes an occasion, yet at rates of only 1250 to 1500 francs ($35 to $42) for three courses of high quality. **"Le Chalet du Zwin"**, 8 Ooievaarslaan (phone 50/60-31-70), a former royal villa on the grounds of the bird sanctuary adjoining Het Zoute, is Swiss-operated, and serves a classic, three-course Swiss meal for 1000 francs ($30), service included: choice of Raclette Valaisanne, trout from Lake Leman or frogs' legs to begin, "Fondue Bourguignonne" (chunks of raw steak which diners dip into little bowls of boiling oil, and then douse with any of several Swiss sauces) as the main course, a lavish choice of desserts at the end. **Restaurant Ter Dycken,** a mile or so south of the Knokke beach at 137 Kalvekeetdijk (phone 50/60-80-23), is a large farm-style house behind green hedges, on whose lawn sits, quite improbably, a large, two-masted fishing boat of the Flemish style; inside, a three-course menu for 1750 francs ($49). Closed Sunday evenings and Mondays. **L'Echiquier,** upstairs at 8 De Wielingen (phone 50/60-88-82), just off the beach at Het Zoute, and now under the new management of Mr. Dejonghe, charges only 1000 francs ($28) for his three-course table d'hôte. **La Sapinière** at 7 Oosthoekplein (phone 050/60-22-71) (closed Tuesdays); and **Manderley,** at 53 Kustlaan (phone 050/61-14-69), are in a similar, 1000-franc ($28) price range.

Just plain Belgian waffles, for much less, are famous at **Siska's,** 177 Zoutelaan. And three-course Italian meals are only 425 francs ($11.80) at **"Ristorante-Pizzeria 'Il Pirata' "**, at 182 Lippenslaan.

MISCELLANY OF KNOKKE-HEIST: To arrive in the
Knokke area, and then not to tour the winding residential streets of Zoute, is to miss one of the world's richest and most extraordi-

nary communities. You tour it either by car or on foot or by bicycle, feeling awed or intensely indignant according to your political bent. It was possible to enforce the rigid aesthetic codes of Zoute because the entire vast expanse of land (entirely covered by dunes) belonged to one family, the Lippens. Maurice Lippens, grandfather of the current burgomaster of Knokke-Heist (Léopold Lippens), began the development in 1910 . . . The **"Thalassa Zeecentrum"** (Thalassa Sea Center), in Hotel La Reserve, 158 Elizabethlaan (phone 50/60-06-12) in Albertstrand, open daily from 9 to 6:30, sometimes later, is both a fitness club (seawater pool, sauna, gymnasium with elaborate equipment, low-calorie snack bar) as well as a thermal institute for the cure of varied illnesses through various applications of sea water (hot sea mud baths, jet streams, jacuzzis). "The sea cures all ills", wrote Euripides. Admission to the fitness club (saunas, pool, gymnasium) is free to hotel guests, 130 francs ($3.60) otherwise, and there are individual charges (490 francs to 900 francs) for the more elaborate treatments. The club sometimes closes between October and March; check . . . The bird sanctuary of the Zwin, measuring two kilometers by one kilometer, is open for visits as early as 4 a.m.— and some people arrive at that time! Cars are not allowed.

From the Belgian Coast, we turn south and then east, to a museum in the province of Limburg that hopes to change your life!

CHAPTER IX

LIMBURG: THE MUSEUM THAT WOULD CHANGE YOUR LIFE

□ □ □

The words were uttered with firmness and passion, almost as if he sensed they would be received with derision. "We must look to the ancients", he said. "They enjoyed a far greater sense of community than we do. They possessed knowledge and techniques scaled to the size of human beings. We must search their history for the wisdom they achieved, and apply those lessons to our own lives. We must extract from the past the most lasting values of that time, and learn how to reintegrate those values into our own daily existence. In this way we can improve the quality of our lives, and re-acquire a contentment that modern mankind lacks".

The speaker was referring to the late Middle Ages and other olden times of Western Europe. The knowledge, techniques, wisdom and values cited by him are primarily those of medieval people living 400 to 600 years ago. And the great Belgian museum of **Bokrijk** which he heads—the largest open-air museum in Europe—seeks nothing less than to change the consciousness of our own times by teaching its visitors to make use of that ancient knowledge today.

THE MESSAGE OF LIMBURG: The architect of this effort to

turn back the clock is a suave and sophisticated young Belgian with prematurely grey but curly hair, named Marc Laenen. He would not seem out of place on the most worldly boulevard of Brussels. But as curator-director of the **"Flemish Open-Air Museum of Bokrijk"** ("Provinciaal Openluchtmuseum Bokrijk"), located halfway between the cities of Hasselt and Genk, he lives and works in the most sparsely-populated and intensely-rural province in all of Belgium—that of "Limburg". An area of softly-rolling moors and heaths, pastureland and low forest, yet only 90 minutes to the east of Brussels on the Dutch border, Limburg is an ecologist's paradise, a preserve of nature and wildlife in which people picnic and hike in the sparkling open air. In it, the 1300-acre "Domain of Bokrijk"—a giant estate of land once belonging to an Abbey of Cistercian Sisters—is now among the most heavily visited recreational areas in Belgium, and justifiably so. For Mr. Laenen's Open Air Museum of Bokrijk (with its adjoining "arboretum" and children's park) is a joyous place for families spending the day on an outing—and a source of profound education as well. In that respect it differs from a number of its counterparts elsewhere in Europe:

THE CONCEPT OF THE OPEN-AIR MUSEUM: A great many international travellers have visited—and been vaguely disappointed by—open air museums in the countries of their origin: Norway and Sweden. Outside Oslo and Stockholm, at the turn of this century, preservation groups erected examples of the venerable, wooden rural architecture that would eventually have disintegrated if left untended in its original countryside locations. From remote areas, they uprooted barns, farmhouses, country churches; moved them all to the capital; and proceeded to scatter the structures about pleasant, forested, suburban settings, there to be visited one-by-one by persons interested in the rural past. For many, the visits proved sheer boredom. In other countries where I have seen them (such as Northern Ireland), these open-air museums of ancient farm dwellings seem almost purposefully bare and gloomy, as if to impress you with the economic poverty of the past. In still other countries, such as France, they are almost completely lacking in explanatory signs, commentaries, labels, inscriptions. "Res ipsa loquitur"—"the thing speaks for itself"—is the lawyer-like defense of these latter exhibits.

BOKRIJK—THE MUSEUM THAT TEACHES: Bokrijk follows an entirely different policy. First, it *clusters* its buildings into the same village or farmyard groupings from which they were taken. Each structure performs the contextual role or function for which it was originally designed. One sees a small village, or a complex farm, in its entirety, not scattered about in unrelated units. Three almost complete villages of the past—such as the dream-like hamlet of Kempen—result from the imaginative reconstruction of Bokrijk's historians. Second, Bokrijk displays medieval urban sights in addition to rural scenes. Now in construction (and partially completed) in a corner of the grounds are several squares of medieval Antwerp using transplanted buildings that, for one reason or other, could not be preserved *in situ* (on the spot) in that city. Third, Bokrijk exerts more than the usual effort to restore the interiors of its farm structures (but not its urban buildings) with the complete furnishings and decor, implements and tools, that would have been found there in the centuries of their use. Thus, Communal Brewery 12, from the 1600s, contains the actual, simple, beer-making equipment of that time; farmhouse 44, of the 1500s, contains the mid-wife's cloth mat on which a newborn baby would be clothed before the fire; mansion 76, from the 1500s, has tiny holes in its gable through which home-coming pigeons could enter into carefully-maintained roosts. And finally, Bokrijk goes to extraordinary lengths to explain and draw lessons from its structures and exhibits: by stationing elderly, retired commentators in each structure to explain its history and function (unfortunately, these ladies and gentlemen rarely speak English, although some do); through elaborate written signs and explanations accompanying special exhibitions (but in Dutch and French); through research projects; the housing of visiting scholars; the periodic issuance of monographs and other papers; the operation of classrooms to teach medieval construction skills and other topics; through the organization of special yearly exhibits ("the social value of medieval games", "keeping animals in the house", "beer-making at home", "fruit preserves"); and—most relevantly to the readers of this book—through the publication of a 75-franc ($2.08), 60-page, English-language guidebook to all the 120-plus structures and main exhibits; you can obtain that guide immediately upon entering the main gate. You can also, by phoning a day-or-so in advance to the museum at 011-22-27-11, reserve the services of a human, English-speaking guide to show you about, at a charge of 850 francs ($23.60), more on Sundays, for a complete tour presented to up to 20 persons. "The main purpose of a Museum is to inform", argues Mr. Laenen, "not simply to collect and preserve."

What sort of lessons does Bokrijk teach? They range from the simple to the complex and controversial. An example of the simple: the directional orientation of peasants' homes, in which sleeping rooms would wisely be placed to the east, cooling rooms and rooms for housing animals to the north, carrying their smells away from the house—for a similar reason, says the museum, a car garage should never be placed at the southern side of a house. A complex and controversial lesson: the belief by medieval people that some houses were conducive to sadness and sickness, while others were happy and healthy—the determining factor being the location of that house in a suitably beneficial setting. Before building a home, medieval people would look to see where their cattle and other farmyard animals habitually slept, and there they would place their homes. "Where my cat or donkey sleeps, there sleep I". An absurd superstition, right? Wrong. Eminent universities are now studying a contention, also advanced at Bokrijk, that radiation from the core of the earth may reach ground level at varying strengths; that persons sleeping in homes placed over low radiation emissions may enjoy healthier, happier lives than those situated over strong emissions. In fact, whole cities may suffer short-tempered, sickly attitudes and constitutions because of where they are located (New York? Paris?), a proposition derived from these same, simple beliefs as to where homes should be placed. While some of the propositions experimentally advanced at Bokrijk may cause you to sputter with protest, to feel your gorge rising, to roll your eyes, so did the argument of Galileo that the earth circled the sun. One thing about Bokrijk: it is never dull!

"Well-being" as the goal of life

Other passionate themes of the Bokrijk open-air museum are more familiar and congenial. In the years following World War II, says Mr. Laenen, the emphasis of Western European countries was on providing sufficient housing, income, forms of security—in short, welfare—to their citizens. Now the emphasis must shift from welfare to well-being, he contends. We must restore fresh air, unpolluted water, abundant greenery, to our lives; we must re-discover a sense of accomplishment and joy in our work and in the performance of daily household tasks. We must experience a sense of contentment in our family lives and communities; we must increase not the quantity of our possessions but the quality of our lives, not the high-tech industries in our midst, but the smaller, human-scaled activities of economic life. We can do that, in large part, by studying the architecture, environment, craftsmanship and social interaction of the pre-industrial past, by quickly re-discovering the valuable practices that succeeded for people in those times. And in performing these studies, Bokrijk can become an important educational instrument for wise policy.

As you wander through Bokrijk, you may suddenly (and for the first time) feel a sympathy and understanding for the "counter-culture" in your own country: for the people who pore through the Whole Earth Catalogue, the Mother Earth News, the Peoples' Yellow Pages, those skinny, bearded, pony-tailed types who bake their own (whole-grained) bread or weave their own coarse cloth. You will recall the insistence of Mohandas Gandhi on the development of small village crafts in place of foundries and steel mills. You may rush to re-read the passionate statement of the British economist, E. F. Schumacher, that "Small is Beautiful" (Harper & Row, 1973). In the Belgian museum of Bokrijk, you will be provoked to ponder the heedless urbanization of countries, the fearful exhaustion of natural resources, the de-humanization of work, the blighting of the landscape. And however you emerge on those questions, however violently opposed you may remain to Bokrijk's campaign against high-tech, you will agree that Belgium's museum-that-would-change-your-life is like few others you've visited before!

Games and refreshment

It is also sheer fun, for with typical Belgian concern for the sensual, no fewer than nine excellent restaurants and taverns are scattered over the grounds of the museum and near an adjoining chateau. One, the **St. Gummarus Inn** ("In Sint Gummarus"), is an actual, 18th-century tavern physically transplanted from the town of Lier near Antwerp; it is moderately priced for honest, home-like dishes; but even cheaper is **In Den Dolfijn** serving plates and specialties of West Flandria; while **"het Paenhuis"** is an old brewery serving hot plates in addition to beers of Brabant (kriek and gueuze). The most elaborate of Bokrijk's restaurants is **"'t Koetshuis"**, adjoining the 19th-century, neo-Renaissance castle of the Bokrijk estate ("Kasteel Bokrijk") just outside the grounds of the open-air museum. A place of high culinary quality, but with decor of rustic, rural style, it serves up a plate of Belgian asparagus cooked with egg ("Asperges Flamandes") that makes for a stunning feast. Eight hundred fifty francs ($23.60) are more than enough for a complete, three-course meal.

Around these major taverns and inns—especially near "Het Paenhuis", "St. Gummarus", "In Den Dolfijn"—are playing areas filled with medieval, wooden, games and toys at which gleeful children and adults engage in centuries-old contests and sports. Here again is a lesson of Bokrijk: the superb entertainment provided by these simple devices is achieved without electronics or coins, and calls simply upon energetic faculties of the flesh and spirit. Mankind needs less material affluence than we think, they seem to tell us; we can be self-sufficient by simply returning to basic joys. Visitors pursue that theme by picnicking on the grounds of Bokrijk, taking walks through its "aboretum" of scores of varieties of trees—but especially by playing the games!

The Open-Air Museum of Bokrijk is open daily from 10 a.m. to 6 p.m. from April 1 until the end of October, for an admission charge of 90 francs ($2.50) to adults, only 30 francs (83¢) for children or students.

GETTING TO BOKRIJK (AND STAYING OVERNIGHT):

From Antwerp, you drive on motorway E3 towards Hasselt (which then becomes E39), and look for the signs to the "Domein" about midway between Hasselt and Genk, an hour after leaving Antwerp. From Brussels, you drive towards Louvain and there pick up motorway A2 into the same E39. The latter trip requires about 1½ hours by car, and permits a day-long excursion, provided you set off for Bokrijk fairly early in the morning. For an overnight stay in the area, your best choice is the historic city of Hasselt, rather than Genk, staying at Hasselt's pleasant **Parkhotel,** at 350 Genkersteenweg (phone 21-16-52) for 1950 francs ($54) per double room, or—if you can afford the splurge—at:

Roger Souvereyn's "Scholteshof" (near Stevoort)

However one may assess the in-city hotels of Belgium, one stands in awe of its country inns: Belgium possesses scores of superb rural chateaus and farmhouses converted into restaurants and lodgings of the first order, comparable to any in the world. And high ranking among these luxurious inns is a Limburg establishment called **Scholteshof,** at 118 Kermtstraat (phone 011-25-02-02) in little Stevoort, eight kilometers to the southwest of Hasselt. A restored and gabled old farmhouse flanked by gloriously green pastures, with cobblestoned entrance and flagstone floors, its 18 guest rooms are as glamorous as any in Europe, with their leather covered desks, their futuristic but comfortable beds and easy chairs, their ultra-advanced TV sets and infra-red bathroom appliances. They range in price from 3300 ($92) to 5000 ($139) francs per room, breakfast for two included, and are rented by luxury loving types from nearby Hasselt (in Belgium), Maastricht (in Holland) and Aachen (in Germany), all equally drawn to a downstairs restaurant which is surely the most stunningly decorated in all of Belgium: like a layout from House Beautiful, with giant wicker chairs covered by pastel-colored cushions, at tables of fresh flowers upon lemon-yellow tablecloths. Through the massed ranks of stems and petal blossoms, across modern, frolicsome decor, one gazes through sparkling windows at cows grazing outside, and then enjoys a multi-course meal prepared by one of

Belgium's most celebrated chefs, the youthful Roger Souvereyn, who includes wine—successive servings of different, celebrated wines—in his all-inclusive menu prices of 2500 ($69) and 3500 ($97) francs per multi-course meal. Closed Wednesdays. Staying here (or in Hasselt or Genk) will supply you with the time to make a thorough tour of Bokrijk.

From north to south, from Dutch to French, we turn now to the unofficial capital of "Wallonia"—the vibrant city of Liège.

CHAPTER X

LIÈGE, LA JOIE DE VIVRE

□ □ □

Capital of Wallonia, Gateway to the Ardennes

"Could I have a cocktail or perhaps a strong drink?" I asked the tavern-keeper, knowing full well it was unlawful in Belgium for such a bar to serve anything other than beer. "Mais, bien sûr!" (But of course!), he shouted back. We were in Liège! And out came the familiar bottle of "peket" (pronounced peh-kay), fiery-hot, jolting liqueur of Liège, poured in full view of everyone there, just as it is each night for thousands of Liègeois. In lusty, free-spirited, independent "Wallonia" (the French-speaking, southern half of Belgium), there is occasional dissent, may we suggest, from the more strait-laced views of Flanders to the north.

"La Cité Ardente"—the "hot-blooded city"! Who coined the words we shall never know, but no one passing through Liège can ever doubt the sheer perfection of the phrase. Here are the modern-day versions of those unruly citizens of medieval Ghent! Politically intense, rebellious and sensitive to their rights, they are also fiercely democratic, quick to find excitement in lively debate, loving the sound of language, voluble, ever ready in the finest French/Belgian tradition to attend a party—or a protest demonstration! They adore the eccentric, admire the bohemian, encourage and support those civic "characters" who go wandering through town in outlandish costumes singing French ballads or selling lottery chances or flowers. If you're fortunate enough, you'll see two of the 80-year-old street-singers of Liège—Prosper and Joseph—who wear bowler hats and bright jackets, and are stood to drinks in every bar as they bellow out repeated choruses of "Non, je ne regrette rien".

Their night life, like Antwerp's, roars on till early morning, their brightly-lit restaurants until late at night. Their politics are primarily socialist, their policies at sharp variance with those of numerous other Belgians, making "Liège" a by-word for controversy. The city government owns the electric power company, the telephone system, the Opera and Philharmonic, numerous museums and hospitals. Twenty-five percent of the population are municipal employees. Heated to intensity by the latter's fiercely expressed views, a continual ferment in matters political is matched by lively commerce: 5000 shops draw crowds of daily shoppers—particularly to an area near the Cathedral from which traffic is barred—and a full 100,000 from three countries descend each Sunday morning on a riverside "flea market" daunting in its size. When it is properly explored, in depth and at length, Liège "grows" upon visitors, enticing them back again and again.

ORIENTATION AND GETTING AROUND: In geographical shape (not in appearance), the city resembles Paris, except for the fact that it is surrounded by foothills, first indication of the vast Ardennes. But it is traversed, like Paris, by a broad river—the important **Meuse**—in which a giant island—**"Outremeuse"**—resembles the position of Paris' "Ile de la Cité" and "Ile St. Louis" in the Seine. The "Outremeuse", birthplace and early home of writer Georges Simenon, contains one of the two major restaurant and nightlife districts of Liège in a picturesque quarter around the **Rue Roture;** it should be visited on at least one evening, crossing by foot or by car over the several auto and footbridges connecting "Outremeuse" to both the left and right banks of the mighty river. One of those bridges, the "Pont des Anges", bears striking resemblance to Paris' graceful "Pont Alexandre".

The "carré" and the shops

The other major nightlife district is in that web of narrow streets ("le carré", the square) west of the river that occupies an area looking like the tip of a thumb, held sidewise. Its borders are: the **Rue Pont d'Avroy,** the almost completely curving **Boulevard de la Sauvenière,** and the **Rue de la Regence.** Best way to approach it is from the brightly-lit, cinema-lined Rue Pont d'Avroy (pedestrians only), darting into the narrow streets and alleys to the left. The main shopping streets are in the same general area, closer to and beyond the Rue de la Regence, and along and below the department-store-lined Rue Joffre.

The "Old City"

Just above the entertainment district is the broad **Place St. Lambert,** site of the former Cathedral of St. Lambert (razed to the ground at the time of the religion-hating French Revolution) and of the monumental **Palace of the Prince-Bishops,** chief governmental center of Liège. In several years, when current excavations and construction are completed, this open square will have been restored to its former splendor; it now looks quite horrible.

The small **Old City** of Liège, site of nearly all the major museums and of St. Bartholomew's Church, starts at the Palace of the Prince-Bishops on that narrow strip of land between the River Meuse and the sharply ascending hill leading to the Citadel. The city tourist office is here ("Office du Tourisme", 92 En Féronstrée, phone 32-24-56, 32-20-95, or 23-92-00), and three short thoroughfares running roughly parallel to each other, enclose virtually every major sight in the "Old City": the continuous **Quai de la Goffe, Quai de La Batte,** and **Quai de Maestricht** along the River; the **Rue "En Féronstrée"** one block in; and the **Rue Hors Chateau** two blocks in.

WHY LIÈGE LOOKS AS IT DOES: Why is the "Old City" so small? And not so old? It is because in November of 1468, Liège experienced an event that robbed it of its medieval heritage.

Unruly and proud, stubborn and independent, 15th-century Liège had managed (through steps far too complex to relate here) to offend the equally hot-headed "Charles the Bold", last of the great Dukes of Burgundy. Feeling he had been ridiculed, Charles marched with his army in the last days of October, 1468, to the heights overlooking Liège, near the present site of the Citadel, intent on a revenge so severe that only a great Knight like Charles could have contemplated it. To head him off, 600 volunteers of Liège, under the command of Vincent de Bueren, crept up the side of the steep hill to Charles' camp and charged upon a particularly opulent tent hoping to assassinate him. They chose the wrong tent, and were slaughtered to the last man. Thereupon, calmly, methodically, almost without emotion, the great

Burgundian Duke set about the task—which required several weeks—of systematically leveling the entire city of Liège to the ground, killing its population at the same time. The flames could be seen from 50 kilometers away. Deeply devout, Charles left the Churches untouched, which is why we see them today, and also permitted eight houses to remain standing for the lodging of chaplains and priests employed in the churches.

Later, in 1477, when word arrived that Charles had met his own untimely end at the battle of Nancy, the miserable remnants of Liège crept out of the cellars and huts where they had been living like animals, and began rebuilding their city. Almost as a first act, they recovered their plinth-like **"Perron"**, symbol of their liberties, from the city of Bruges, to which it had been sent by Charles, and immediately re-erected it in the small market square of Liège where it continues to stand today. The resilience of the human spirit!

Because of the city's destruction by Charles the Bold near the end of the 15th century, and the long period before a new city emerged, nothing still stands in Liège from earlier than the late 16th century, except the churches. The so-called "Maison Havart" on the Quai de la Goffe, which presently houses the "Au Vieux Liège" restaurant, one of the city's best (see our restaurant discussion, below), is among the few examples in Liège of a structure surviving from even as far back as the late 16th century. And because Liège suffered occasional later bombardments (as from the French in 1691), and passed through a lusty phase of commercial expansion that favored replacing the old with the new, even the amount of that surviving ancient architecture is small indeed. As you walk through the "Old Town" of Liège today, along "En Féronstrée" and "Hors Chateau", you are primarily seeing structures from the "modern" (for Belgium) 17th and 18th centuries, except for the churches of course, and except for the Palace of the Prince-Bishops, whose major re-construction was begun in the early 1500s.

THE CITY OF THE PRINCE-BISHOPS: In their highly individual ways, the Liègeois uphold a tradition of independence more than 1000 years old; beginning that far back, Liège was the capital of a "country"—"le pays de Liège" or the "Principality" of Liège—which successfully maintained an aloof neutrality from European politics for longer stretches of time than any other such mini-state in Europe.

Like so many other communities in Europe, Liège arose on the site of a Gallo-Roman settlement, and developed there primarily because of the activities of churchmen who made it their headquarters for diocese activities. As happened in a handful of other European cities as well—Salzburg is one such instance—these church officials in Liège acquired secular as well as religious powers, became "princes" as well as "bishops", "prince-bishops" holding their "fiefs" in loose allegiance to the Holy Roman Emperor of Germany. In the year 972, the greatest of these Christian princes—a bishop named Notger—was appointed to rule Liège by Emperor Otto I, and enjoyed an illustrious reign in which the city developed to significant size. Already it was the capital of a much larger territory that extended over much of what is now eastern Belgium, and into Holland and Germany—"le pays de Liège" (the country of Liège). Astonishingly, these "Prince-Bishops" of Liège were able for centuries to resist takeovers by dukes of Brabant, kings of France, various counts and other temporal leaders, and to preserve an independent, neutral "Principality of Liège" until the time of the French Revolution.

They also developed into a rather democratic institution. Although occasionally resembling a dynasty—in which uncles would frequently be succeeded by their nephews—the "Prince-Bishops" were usually elected by the cathedral-chapter of Liège. Some were worldly men living far from Liège, "bishops" in name only, enjoying opulent lives; yet to their credit, they succeeded in keeping Liège removed from the fearful wars that swept over Belgium—and Europe—in the late 1500s and 1600s, preserving the economic base that was to make Liège an industrial pioneer in later times. Under their churchly administration, Liège developed Europe's earliest and most advanced coal mining industry, metallurgy plants, glassworks, and especially gunpowder factories, cannon and gun fabricators, armaments suppliers. Though Liège was neutral, it was happy to provide the rest of Europe with the arms for war!

Through much of this period, the people of the "country" (pays) of Liège spoke "Walloon"—a dialect of Latin—not French, and some are still able to speak Walloon today. Occasional television plays and theatre productions, menu items, and the like, preserve that ages-old dialect in the Liège of today, to a much greater extent than in most other Walloon cities. Liège considers itself the "capital" of Wallonia.

The detailed history of Liège and its "Prince-Bishops" is far too complex to be grasped by tourists on a short stay, but an appreciation of the city's proud tradition of independence is essential to understanding its current policies. And meantime, what about those coal mines, steel mills and armaments factories? You won't see them. The coal mines, some of them now museums, are all shut and depleted, and the smokestacks, mills and foundries are all in neighboring towns (such as Seraing) many kilometers away. The visitor to Liège sees an attractive commercial city of seemingly no industry at all, built with parks along a broad river, scarcely resembling its image as a major steel and armaments capital. If there is anything at all unattractive about modern Liège, it is that single, large, empty gap near the Palace of the Prince-Bishops, where zealots of the 1790s dismantled the Cathedral of St. Lambert, once the center of Liège.

HOTELS OF LIÈGE: Two hotels in a class of their own (the Ramada Liège and the Moat House), followed by a cluster of lower-category, railway-station-area hotels, are about the only choices available to you. A single, large motel—the Post House—on the motorway leading to town takes most of the overflow.

The **Ramada Liège**, 100 Boulevard Sauvenière (phone 32-59-19), is the leader, well located near all the centers of tourist interest, modern and efficient, with acceptably comfortable rooms of Ramada standard (105 of them spread over six floors of a 1960s building), and a surprisingly good restaurant (see below), among the best of Liège. Twin rooms with breakfast and all else are 3600 to 4000 francs ($100 to $111); singles 3000 to 3300 francs ($83 to $92), again with breakfast, service and tax.

The larger (224 rooms) **Moat House**, 2 Esplanade de l'Europe (phone 42-60-20), has bigger rooms, bigger beds and a swimming pool, but is located near the park-surrounded, city convention center on that needle-like extension of the broad "Outremeuse" island in the River Meuse. Though it's convenient to the center, its location doesn't match the Ramada's, from which you can walk almost anywhere. Still, the Moat House is attractive and fresh, charges about the same as the other (up to 3450 francs ($96) single, 4350 francs ($121) for twin, queen-sized beds, always with continental breakfast, service and tax included), and offers free parking in an enclosed garage.

Unless you're willing to stay in nearby Herstal, at the 100-room **Post House** (Rue Hurbise, phone 64-64-00) charging 3500 francs ($97), your remaining choices in Liège are pretty well limited to several older hotels over ground-floor restaurants in the streets around the Gare des Guillemins, Liège's railway station. The 80-room **Hotel de la Couronne**, 11 Place des Guillemins (phone 52-21-68), is the best of these, operator of a high quality restaurant downstairs and modern rooms in traditional and rather unimaginative furnishings upstairs, at rates of 2700 francs ($75) for a double with private bath, 1925 francs ($53) with private shower only, 1690 francs ($47) without private facilities; followed closely by the 27-room **Hotel Metropole,** 141 Rue des Guillemins (phone 52-42-93), charging 1400 to 1860 francs ($39 to $52) for a twin with bath and breakfast, 1400 francs ($39) for a single with bath and breakfast. Much cheaper is **Hotel du Midi,** 1 Place des Guillemins (phone 52-20-03), where doubles without private bath are 1040 francs ($29), breakfast for two included, and the larger **Hotel Univers,** 116 Rue des Guillemins (phone 52-28-04), doubles for 1380 francs ($38), sans bath but with breakfast. Students and other extremely cost-conscious travelers will like the rooms (10 of them) above the **Restaurant des Nations,** 139 Rue des Guillemins (phone 52-44-34), in which "demi-pension" arrangements—room and two meals—are 940 francs ($26) per person per day (or where you can simply order a two-course "menu" for 250 francs, ($7); or else the more centrally-located, and somewhat classier, **Pension Darchis,** 18 Rue Darchis (phone 23-42-18), charging 1000 francs ($28) for a twin with breakfast, but without private bath.

DINING IN LIÈGE:

The major restaurant, towering above all others, is a large villa known as **"Chêne Madame",** at 70 Avenue de la Chevauchée (phone 71-41-27). But the grand and expensive "Chêne Madame" is in the suburb of Neuville-en-Coudroz, high on a hill overlooking the valley of Liège, half in the woods, hard to find, and too much of a chore for most visitors. It specializes in game ("gibier").

Au Vieux Liège, 41 Quai de la Goffe (phone 23-77-48), rated second by everyone, is in the historic heart of Liège, a venerable, four-story townhouse of the late 16th century, decorated throughout with authentic 16th-century furnishings, enchanting to experience. The building is a national monument, the restaurant a living museum, the location on the corner of the Quai de la Batte, and the cost about 2000 francs ($56) per person (but with wine included), appropriate to a very special evening. Waiters in tails, serving candlelit tables, bring you a free "amuse-bouche" (literally, "amuse the mouth", a tid-bit) to begin (in my recent case, a fluffy shrimp paste in piping hot pastry squares). Appetizer can be a plate of paper-thin, smoked salmon as tender as butter, covered with tiny peppercorns, onions and greens, and accompanied by a small tumbler of red vodka encased in a bed of ice. I once went on to "côte à l'os bouquetière aux herbes", a flavored, rare steak surrounded by steamed vegetables, then a "Café Liègeois" and tea for dessert, and emerged from the ancient setting, at the side of the moonlit, broad river, feeling very pleased indeed, and impressed by the inclusive, 2000 franc ($56) charge, which you can even reduce to about 1650 francs ($46), including wine, through careful ordering. Closed Sundays, and from mid-July to mid-August.

More moderately-priced, but of top quality

Brasserie "As Ouhes", 21 Place du Marché (phone 23-32-25), the name a Walloon expression for heaven knows what, is the large and gracious restaurant on the narrow market square opposite the "Perron" (the obelisk-like symbol of Liège's independence), which comes as close to being the standard, staple, leading, normally-priced restaurant of Liège, as anyone knows. Its menu is the largest in town (and offers every "Liègeois" specialty), its near-30 appetizers average 250 to 300 francs ($7 to $9), main courses 350 to 500 francs ($9.72 to $13.88), and one eats an intriguing array of unusual dishes—Alsatian choucroute garnie, salads from the market place outside, garlic-laced fish soup (only 150 francs, $4.17), tender duckling in orange sauce, that chewy Belgian fish called "lotte"—for a total of 750 to 1000 francs ($21 to $28), including appetizer, dessert and wine. All this in the setting of a subdued dining room of impeccable taste. The prices of Liège are obviously a bit below those of Brussels. Closed Sundays, and Saturdays for lunch.

Rotisserie de la Sauvenière, restaurant of the Hotel Ramada Liège, 100 Boulevard de la Sauvenière, is a surprise standout, as elegant and removed from the Ramada image as if it occupied a townhouse on a suburban boulevard. How did it get there? Dishes are à la "nouvelle cuisine", adapted from all the classic French specialties; their appearance and service of the highest order; and yet relatively moderate for all that: a special three-course dinner sells for 950 francs ($26), a special "menu de chasse" (hunter's meal) for 1200 francs ($33)—terrine of wild boar or pheasant's soup to begin, various preparations of wild rabbit as the main course, then standard desserts—while à la carte choices permit three-course meals for 950 to 1150 francs ($26 to $32), plus wine.

Mamé Vi Cou (that means "nice old lady" in Walloon), 9 Rue de la Wache (phone 23-71-81), a hundred yards-or-so from the Royal Theatre, is Liège's most regional restaurant, the careful guardian of old-time recipes and plates, which are then described in big letters in Walloon, with smaller French sub-titles! You'll find various exotic stews, "black-and-white" blood sausages ("boudins"), chicken brewed in local beer, and my own favorite, quail flamed in burning gin, Liège-style. Prices are moderate: 160 to 180 francs ($4.44 to $5) for most appetizers, only 120 francs ($3.33) for large bowls of substantial soup, 320 to 460 francs ($8.88 to $12.77) for most main courses of fish or meat; the total averages 900 francs ($25) for a three-course meal with wine, in a colorful, brick-walled, multi-room atmosphere of friendly waitresses and exceptionally outgoing proprietor with handlebar moustache (his game specialties are costlier than the dishes I've quoted). This is all down an alleyway from the side of the Opera, next to the Bon Marché department store entrance at the Place de la Republique Française. Closed Wednesdays.

The standard meals for 500 to 750 francs

For the kind of meals you find by simply window-shopping, *most* tourists go to that brightly-lit, late-night street that forms one border of the nightlife section of Liège: the **Rue Pont d'Avroy.** At least a dozen restaurants await you here, of every size and description, but usually enabling a meal for just slightly more than 600 francs.

Tourists *in the know,* however, seek out the meals priced at 700 to 800 francs on the **Rue Roture,** in "Outre-Meuse", reached by foot-bridge over the river, or by giving in and taking a cab. This is the most "typical" area in all of Liège, a classic old street of barely-standing buildings housing as many as 25 restaurants (some with as few as 5 or 6 tables), a half-dozen discotheques or piano bars, a giant, student-style hangout and beer tavern called **Annexe 13,** 13 Rue Roture, all presented in quiet and rather subdued fashion, from behind glowing lights and shabby facades with understated signs, as if in a movie set of 19th-century life, and without the neon commercialism of the Rue Pont d'Avroy. While some rather expensive establishments have moved to Rue Roture in recent years (and therefore you must be careful), at least a dozen restaurants continue to price main courses for 350 francs ($9.72) and therefore permit dining quite easily for 600 to 700 francs ($16 to $19).

A tavern with all the Belgian specialties (400 to 500 francs, $11.11 to $14)

It looks like a dozen others you'll see, but the old-fashioned, wood-framed tavern called **Cafe Lequet,** at 17 Quai sur Meuse, directly on the river (phone 22-21-34), is a specially friendly place that makes more than the usual point of serving classic hot dishes on certain days of the week to accompany the Stella Artois beer in which it specializes: "potées" (mashed-potatoes-and-cabbage stews of the Ardennes area) on Wednesdays, "moules casseroles" (steamed mussels with french fries) on Fridays in season, and "boulets frites" (giant, hard balls of bread stuffing flavored with meat and soused in gravy, four inches in diameter; with french fries) every day of the week.

The meals for less

Le Palais des Mineurs, upstairs from that complex of shabby antique and second-hand stores at 23 Rue des Mineurs, directly in front of the Museum of Walloon Life, is a student restaurant open from 11 a.m. to dawn, charging 85 francs ($2.36) for an omelette with bread, 120 francs ($3.33) for spaghetti, 180 francs ($5) for lasagne, 45 to 60 francs ($1.25 to $1.67) for most sandwiches. . . . The fourth-floor cafeteria of the **Innovation** department store at 54 Féronstrée is a reliable stand-by for inexpensive, self-service meals. . . . And an extraordinary sandwich shop at 42 Rue Pont d'Avroy in the center of the nightlife district serves you a foot-long sandwich—literally, a 12-inch-long roll of fresh, crusty, Belgian bread—smeared with butter and heaped with meat, for exactly 50 francs ($1.39), a value of Liège.

DAYTIME SIGHTS OF LIÈGE: The major attractions are roughly a dozen in number, all but two located in and around the compact area of the parallel **Quai de Maestricht, Rue Féronstrée** and **Rue Hors-Château** in the "old city". At the tourist office of Liège, 92 Féronstrée, you'll be given a much-reproduced, illustrated map of the easy walking tour to be made from there to all 12 sights (and several more), on or off the three parallel and tightly-compressed streets named above. My own descriptions follow, not in the order in which they appear on the tourist office's walking tour, but in generally descending order of importance.

(1) **The Baptismal Font of Renier of Huy:** One of the "Seven Marvels of Belgium", this sculpted, brass tub of indescribable beauty is found in the **Church of St. Bartholomew** ("Saint Barthélemy"), at the extreme end of both the Rue En Féronstrée and Rue Hors Chateau, turning left or right from there (as the case may be) into the Place Paul Janson. Cast in the early 1100s by the most prominent metalsmith of an area that then, as now, is associated with metals, it was originally designed for the baptismal functions of an annex of St. Lambert's Cathedral, which revolutionaries of Liège dismantled in the 1790s. Appropriately, it was then moved to this historically-interesting, twin-towered, Ro-

manesque Church that also was begun, like the Baptismal Font, in the 1100s. Scholars have read opaque, symbolic meanings into the five sculpted scenes that surround the vast, cylindrical, brass bowl supported on the backs of 10 small oxen (the Apostles). The layperson needs to know, first, that the scenes depict (1) the baptism of Jesus by John the Baptist; (2) the baptism of the two neophytes by a later and emaciated John the Baptist, his ribs showing; (3) the baptism of a Roman centurion by St. Peter; (4) the baptism of the Greek philosopher Craton by John the Evangelist; and (5) the preaching by John the Baptist to four Romans (the two in the foreground seeming clearly impressed, the still-skeptical soldier holding up a finger for further information). That same lay observer should take in the obvious but harmonious mixture of both Greek and Byzantine influences on Renier's work, the expressions clearly apparent on the tiny, brass faces, his superb technical achievement in casting such a piece from a single mould of wax, but most particularly, the classic and almost perfect beauty wrought by this craftsman of genius at the summit of his career. Through this font, as babies, have passed most of the current population of Liège, brought there to be washed free of man's Original Sin. In gazing at it, one recalls the similar classic perfection of that Grecian urn (here given a third dimension) which provoked John Keats to exclaim that "Beauty is truth, truth beauty—that is all/Ye know on earth and all ye need to know". The Baptismal Font of Renier of Huy, in its brown-gold radiance, can be seen daily from 8 a.m. to 6:15 p.m., for no admission charge.

(2) **The Curtius Museum,** 13 Quai de Maestricht: On the banks of the Meuse in the "old city" district, this is the vastly impressive home of a 17th-century patrician/industrialist, Jean Curtius, now transformed into an archaeological museum of the "Mosan" (Meuse-related) area; it is among the truly important museums of Belgium. Its ground floor displays the most ancient treasures: Merovingian jewelry and swords, as colorful and decorative as modern art, yet of the *6th* century; Carolingian coins and rings, the surprising splendor and radiance—contrary to everything we've been taught—of the *early* middle ages; and then, from yet an earlier time, Gallo-Roman tomb objects from excavations in Liège: little metal bulls, lobsters, fish people, heads of the Roman gods, coins. Upstairs, the times move forward to the days of the extraordinarily capable Bishop Notger (late 900s), about whom the Liègeois say "we owe Notger to God, and everything else to Notger"; three recognized masterpieces here are associated with him or his times: the "Evangeliary" (prayer book) of Notger, with sculpted ivory cover, displayed in a glass, temperature-

controlled case; the "Dom Rupert Virgin"; and the "Mystery of Apollo". As the centuries unfold in lavishly-furnished exhibit rooms, we see portraits of those other remarkable Prince-Bishops of Liège, the actual, richly-embroidered clothing of 18th-century courtiers, the decorative arts of wealthy Liège in the days of its greatest influence. We leave with a sense of the historic role played by the unusual "Principality of Liège", from an impressive museum that is open to the public daily except Tuesdays from 10 to 12:30 and 2 to 5 p.m., and also open Wednesday evenings from 7 to 9 p.m., for an admission charge of 50 francs ($1.39), 20 francs (60¢) for children.

(3) **The Museum of Walloon Life,** at the Cours des Mineurs (which means Convent of the Minorites, a monastic order), is the most extensive folkloric museum of Belgium, a vast collection too varied for brief description, but conveniently grouped and vividly presented by multi-media effects in each exhibit room; even so grisly a subject as Walloon attitudes towards death and funeral ceremonies becomes utterly absorbing when viewed here. Ask at the cloakroom, at the conclusion of your visit, to be taken to the basement reproduction of a Walloon coal mine, accompanied by a guide delivering an indignant commentary (but in French only) on the hardships endured by 19th-century, Belgian coal miners of the Liège area. The "Musée de la Vie Walloone" is open daily except Mondays from 10 to 12 and 2 to 5 p.m. Admission is 50 francs ($1.39).

(4) **The Palace of the Prince-Bishops,** on the Place St. Lambert, admission free, flanks the gaping void left by destruction of the Cathedral of St. Lambert in the days of the French Revolution. It is a giant Gothic edifice of two adjoining rectangles (and therefore two adjoining courtyards) dating from the 1100s, but primarily appearing today in the form of its re-construction in the 1500s supervised by Cardinal Erard de la Marck, as later altered in part by a new and rather unsatisfactory facade placed on one portion in the 1800s; you can tell the latter by its coldness. Its outstanding features are the interiors of the two courtyards and not the facades. Because Cardinal de la Marck—a Prince-Bishop of Liège—was a devotee of Erasmus, the columns of the first courtyard are carved with 60 grotesque figures (and a self-portrait of the sculptor) illustrating the human "follies" of which Erasmus wrote. The second, and more perfectly-hushed, dreamlike courtyard is surrounded by the actual residence of the Prince-Bishops, and contained their gardens. This is among the largest, secular, Gothic buildings of Europe, and presently houses courtrooms of Liège, among other government offices, conducting trials open to

the public. Opposite the structure's eastern end is the ancient market place of Liège with its "Perron" column, symbol of the city's liberties, and the Town Hall, destroyed by the French in 1691 and then rebuilt, in its present style, in the early 18th century; it, too, should be visited.

(5) The **Sunday Market of "La Batte":** See our shopping discussion, below.

(6) The **Museum of Arms** ("Musée d'Armes de Liège), Quai de Maestricht: Another major European museum, repellant in its horror, yet dealing with a human activity uninterrupted since the dawn of time: the use of arms and the manufacture of them, in which Liège has led the world; even the mammoth American pistol company of Browning was recently acquired by Liège's "Fabrique Nationale" in Herstal. Here is perhaps the world's most impressive museum of arms, rivalled only by similar institutions in Dresden and Vienna, displaying every classic example of firepower and all forms of exotic weaponry, from a 14-barrel rifle to a breech-loading "arquebuse" (bow and arrow) of the 1500s; it inspires abhorrence or fascination, hopefully the former, and should heighten the visitor's desire for arms control internationally and strict gun controls domestically. The neo-classic, private mansion in which the museum is housed is itself a gem of stunning appearance, notable also for Ingres' painting of the young Napoleon as First Consul, done to commemorate his stay in Liège (with Josephine) in this very house, in August of 1803. The Museum of Arms is open daily except Mondays from 10 to 12:30 and 2 to 5 p.m., Sundays from 10 to 2 only, for an admission charge of 50 francs ($1.39) to adults, 20 francs (55¢) to children.

(7) The **Panorama of the Montagne de Bueren** (the de Beuren "staircase"): Off the Rue Hors Château, ascending higher than any outdoor steps or staircase one has ever seen, are these 373 steps built by a grateful city to honor the heroic but futile effort of 600 volunteers in the 15th century to thwart destruction of the city by Charles the Bold, last great Duke of Burgundy. Led by Vincent de Bueren, at a point near here, they climbed the steep hill on the night of October 29/30, 1468; the steps commemorate the deed. After they were constructed, burghers of Liège built homes along the steps, and there are present-day residents who climb more than 300 steps here each day to return home! You'll want to make the ascent for the spectacular vista of Liège from on top, stopping periodically to rest on park benches placed at merciful intervals. An almost equally steep, uphill street called **Rue Pierreuse** leads skyward in the same general area, but this time from behind the Place St. Lambert to the Citadel; along it are a

typical district and picturesque old homes of Liège. The life and activity of the low-income Pierreuse area are a "window" into the attitudes and politics of working-class Belgium.

(8) **Holy Relics in the "Treasury" of the Cathedral of St. Paul** (the main, central cathedral of Liège): For these, which may be seen only when church services are not in progress, you apply to the Sacristan of the Liège Cathedral at 2A Rue St. Paul, who will unlock the door to these extraordinary religious treasures, of which the best known is the sanctimonious gift proffered to the city by Charles the Bold after he had leveled it to the ground! It is an exquisite masterpiece of the goldsmith's art, done by Charles' own court jeweler, and depicts a penitent, beseeching Charles, kneeling, holding a phylactery-case containing skin from the hand of St. Lambert, while a hat-tipping St. George looks on, just as he does in the famous painting by Jan van Eyck. A photo of the "gift" of Charles the Bold to Liège appears in the color insert of this book. Was there ever such a donor? Alongside the tiny work, in this remarkable "treasury", is a life-sized effigy of St. Lambert; a bas-relief of the crucifixion in which the cross is allegedly made from a piece of the Real Cross; a 13th-century manuscript; and 13th-century paintings, all justifying the effort of requesting the Sacristan to show you around.

(9) **The Church of St. Jacques,** Place St. Jacques: In continuous construction or re-construction from the 1100s through the 1500s, and therefore part Romanesque, part "Gothic Flamboyant", part "Italian Renaissance" (the porch), the church should be visited for its interior, the most stunning in all of Belgium, with a valuted ceiling that can only be described as resembling braided epaulets of green, yellow and brown on stone. In its vastly intricate design and shimmering pattern, it can be challenged only by the intricate vaulted ribs and patterns of certain major English cathedrals, and it should be seen in the course of your visit. (See the photo insert in this book for a preview of what awaits you.) The church is open on weekday mornings from 8 to noon, weekends from 8 to 5, and all day on weekdays in July and August.

(10) **"Special Interest" Museums:** Several remaining museums will attract those interested in their specific subject matter, and these are the **Ansembourg Museum,** 114 Féronstrée (18th-century decorative arts, open daily except Tuesdays); the **Museum of Walloon Art,** 86 Féronstrée (local artists, open daily except Mondays); the **Museum of Architecture,** 14 Impasse des Ursulines (in a superbly restored building, but mainly documentation; closed Mondays); and the **Museum of Iron and Coal.** 17 Boulevard Poincaré (open on request only, afternoons).

To almost everything listed here, you walk; scarcely anything of tourist interest in Liège is so remote that a good, brisk walk can't reach it; and most is compressed, as noted before, into the "Old City" area near the tourist office.

NIGHTLIFE AND EVENING ENTERTAINMENT: We've earlier referred to the two major nightlife sections—the **carré** in central Liège (Rue du Pot d'Or, Rue St. Jean, Rue Tête-de-Boeuf), **Rue Roture** on the big island of Outremeuse in the center of the river. Both are replete with discobars and discotheques active late into the night, with cabarets and piano bars, taverns and cafes packed with lusty Liègeois. Though some are private clubs—like my own favorite, **La Canne à Rhum,** 2b Rue Tête-de-Boeuf—they nearly always admit well-mannered tourists appearing on the spot. Simply wander, look, and choose. If all you seek is a quiet tavern in which to relax and imbibe, you can scarcely do better than at the most picturesque **"Le Tchantches",** at 35 En Grande-Beche in Outremeuse, built around the theme of Liège's classic comic character dressed in blue smock, red kerchief, black hat, often portrayed as a marionette, always loud, brassy but warm-hearted: Tchantches. Ask about him, and you'll be drowned in anecdotes.

Movies in Liège are almost always dubbed from their original languages into French, and thus aren't usually suitable for tourists. But the rich musical theatre and concert world of Liège presents endless opportunities. As you'll soon learn, Liège was the home of Grétry, Cesar Franck, Eugene Ysaye, whose examples created strong traditions of excellence in music. Concerts of the renowned Liège Philharmonic are presented at that neo-classical building a block from the Church of St. Jacques; operas, operettas and ballets at the Théâtre Royal de Liège (Liège's major stage), classics at the "Théâtre de la Place", music hall variety at **Chez Sullon** (6 En Bergerue); and a dozen other theatres and halls accommodate the lesser productions. You will not be without distraction on any night in Liège!

SHOPS AND SHOPPING: When you have walked down the Pont d'Avroy towards the Cathedral, and then turned left just before the Cathedral square into the start of a sprawling shopping district, you'll have discovered that Liège is one city that needn't worry about the decay of its downtown district. Each day, thousands pour into the pedestrian streets of the center, from suburbs and surrounding towns, to enjoy one of Belgium's liveliest mercantile areas. Liège is the shopping capital hereabouts, and even French shoppers from Aix-la-Chapelle, the Dutch from Maastricht, Germans from Aachen, choose Liège for many of their shopping expeditions. A greater than normal number of Parisian establishments maintain branches in Liège, which adds to the cosmopolitan flavor of these pedestrians-only walking streets.

The same foreign shoppers flood into Liège on Sunday mornings to attend the world-famous, open-air market of **"La Batte"**, on the Quai de la Batte, and adjoining quais, along the left bank of the River Meuse. Extending for nearly a mile of the river's length, in a most picturesque setting of canvas stands and strolling shoppers of every age, "La Batte" mixes new goods with old, animals with plants, hot food stalls with antiquarian books. It accommodates every would-be seller of anything dredged from attic or cellar, and presents such a changing variety of goods each Sunday that residents of Liège, planning simply to "nip over" to "La Batte" for a specific purchase, are notoriously seduced into spending the entire morning there, to the detriment of Sunday newspapers and Sunday chores. Among the major sightseeing attractions (let alone the shopping opportunities) of Liège, one must list "La Batte"!

"LIEGEOISIANA"—SOME MISCELLANY: Jacques Brel wrote a song about Liège in which he achieved the rhyme of all time: "Il neige sur Liège" (it is snowing in Liege). . . . Experts have confirmed beyond doubt that the medieval city appearing in the background of Jan van Eyck's "La Vierge d'Autun" (Madonna with Chancellor Rolland), hanging in the Louvre, is Liège. . . . Liège, some of its Prince-Bishops, and the "wild boar of the Ardennes," figure prominently in Sir Walter Scott's historical novel, *Quentin Durward*. . . . Keep always in mind that most museums of Liège maintain evening hours on one night of the week, designated in our museum descriptions earlier in this chapter. . . . All museums of Liège are free on Sundays. . . . Georges Simenon was born and brought up in Liège, and uses the city in many of his novels. The tourist office will provide you with a written walking tour of Simenon's associations with Liège; in his crumpled raincoat, battered fedora and pipe, his image alone seems to capture the essence of this comfortable city.

EXCURSIONS FROM LIEGE: At numerous points near the River Meuse, a single word begins appearing on highway signs pointing to the south: "Ardennes". Liège is the gateway to Belgium's famed resort land. It is also a hub, a base for visiting sites in the Ardennes without moving from a hotel room in Liège. From Liège to the casinos of Spa and Chaudfontaine is a half hour by car or bus. From Liège to famous Bastogne is an hour, to historic Bouillon an hour and a half. To stay or not to stay in Liège (while visiting the Ardennes), to use it either as a base for the Ardennes or simply as the jumping off point for a further move south, is a closely-balanced decision, ultimately made on the basis of personal tastes. But it can also be influenced by an appraisal of the competing lures and facilities of the Ardennes itself.

Let us now be introduced . . . to the Belgian Ardennes.

CHAPTER XI

INTRODUCTION TO THE ARDENNES

□ □ □

BASTOGNE
LA GLEIZE

For seventy miles south of Liège, a thick blanket of calm lay over the great forest of the Ardennes. It was December 16 of 1944. Though war raged on the Western Front, here all was near-stillness. From the pastures of a hundred hillside villages, one could hear the clank of cowbells as cattle foraged through the snow. Here and there a farm vehicle left bluish wisps of smoke hovering in the crisp, mountainlike air.

And then bedlam erupted. From camouflaged positions in the forested hills, thirty panzer divisions of the German Wehrmacht roared forward into the allied lines, their goal Antwerp, their mission to change the course of the war. And suddenly the name "Ardennes" became burned into the memories of millions all over the world. Could it be? Could Adolph Hitler still win the war? For the next four weeks, during the saddest Christmas ever known, the world watched and studied and agonized over the Ardennes, the Ardennes, the Ardennes!

THE ARDENNES: This is the "mountain" land of Belgium, as different from level Flanders as a terrain could be; but its scenery is really one of high, rolling hills that only occasionally, and just barely, merit the title of "mountain". As you approach Liège, or Namur, or Charleroi—gateways to the Ardennes—and then proceed south of those cities, the land begins to rise and dip, sharply at times (as outside Spa and Durbuy), gently elsewhere (as in Bastogne or near Orval). Everywhere is forest—thick, natural forests covering the hills, spreading through valleys, surrounding the large, open spaces of the hillside towns, perfuming the air; and everywhere are cold, swiftly-flowing rivers cutting channels through the hills, or rushing streams gurgling among the trees and undergrowth. At multiple spots are famous grottoes or caves cut into the sides of hills, through which tourists enter into a dazzling, underground world; elsewhere are carefully-tended campsites along rivers, from which visitors hike on sign-posted walks maintained by an active and well-endowed forest service; and on the heights are "points de vue" from which one looks onto vistas comparable to any of the other finest sights of Europe. Nowhere are there billboards or other large commercial notices.

And throughout the vast expanse—covering the full southeastern third of Belgium—are no large cities at all, no urban sprawl, no pollution or giant factories. Rather, there are scores of small agricultural villages populated for generations by the same families, and a grand total of seven "towns"—Arlon, Bastogne, Dinant, Malmedy, Marche-en-Famenne, Rochefort, Spa—whose inhabitants barely manage to exceed 10,000 apiece. This is rural Belgium, "Alpine" Belgium, a "remote" Belgium in its disdain for urban attitudes, yet never more than an hour or two from Brussels, Namur or Liège.

FRESH AIR, SPORTS AND FOOD:
And this is also recreational Belgium, the Belgium of open-air sports and relaxation, where the chief industry is tourism and the cars are all headed to hundreds of small lodges and country inns, their average size no more than 10 to 15 rooms. Inside their timbered lobbies are warmly-blazing, wood-burning fireplaces in fall and winter; outside are verandahs overlooking the scene and equipped with reclining chairs for dozing, sunning or inhaling the forest-created ozone of an area called (for that reason) "the lung of Belgium". In varying months, the chief activities are fishing and hiking, canoeing (or kayak-ing), riding, rock-climbing, spelunking, and cross-country skiing, driving to look-out points ("points de vue") or shopping for farmhouse antiques, viewing exhibits of folklore or handicrafts, castles and abbeys—and finally, eating, eating, and

eating. Each lodge or hotel contains a restaurant, often more splendid and extensive than the hotel itself, and the food specialties of the Ardennes are themselves legion: smoked ham of the Ardennes, wild game (especially venison and boar), trout from the streams outside each lodge, choucroute (hot sauerkraut) and sausage doused in white wine, fresh farmyard breads and home-made jams, as well as "potées" (stews) of every sort, including the popular "potée ardennaise" of pigs' knuckles, potatoes and vegetables.

In our next two chapters, we'll survey the key resorts of the Ardennes, and then discuss its most historic sites. But before we do, let's first return to the great battle of World War II that provides so many additional reasons for a visit there today.

THE BATTLE OF THE ARDENNES: It appeared that the war was nearing its end. For six months since the D-day invasion, allied troops had remorselessly advanced on the German frontier, and now prepared for the last, great lunge across the Rhine. To concentrate their forces, they had, in a calculated step, left thinly defended the entire north-south line traversing the Ardennes: four under-manned and largely-untested American divisions were strung out along the entire mountain front. It was unlikely, reasoned U.S. generals, that the Germans would attack in such difficult terrain, and in the conditions of winter.

Two months earlier, Adolf Hitler had decided to do just that. From throughout the Third Reich he gathered and equipped every remaining division for this last supreme effort. The location of the attack? Like so many conquerors and military adventurers before him, he chose Belgium, poor Belgium, the eternal battlefield of Europe. Through the Forest of the Ardennes, the armies of field Marshal Gerd von Runstedt—General Sepp Dietrich to the north, General Hasso von Monteuffel to the south—would, if the plan succeeded, plunge through the American lines and then wheel northward to Antwerp, capturing the great supply port of all the Allied armies. In the process, they would cut the Allied forces in half, surround and starve the northern half, force Eisenhower to petition for surrender. It was a lunatic gamble, opposed by numerous German planners, but a barely feasible one—and it almost succeeded.

On December 16, after a savage barrage, the white-clad German armored ("panzer") divisions emerged from their forest concealment and overwhelmed the thin and outnumbered line of U.S. defenders. The surprise was total; the initial Allied defeat has been compared to Pearl Harbor. In the next several days, the

German juggernaut roared forward in a major advance that caused a giant "bulge" in the allied lines, reaching the outskirts of Dinant to the east, La Gleize to the north. The fighting was violent, furious, almost without quarter, often hand to hand, as desperately-outgunned American troops sought to stem the attack by a quarter of a million Germans. Every available unit was sent to the line. Cooks, typists, truck drivers, were handed rifles and sent forward to the Belgian front. As the German army advanced, they were followed by rear guard SS and Gestapo units who ruthlessly interrogated, and often executed, both Belgian resistance fighters and hostages rounded up from the young men of several towns. Whole Belgian villages of the Ardennes, the entire town of Houffalize, ceased to exist as they crashed to the ground from the shelling of opposing armies. Nearly two thousand Belgian civilians lost their lives in the crossfire, a larger number were wounded.

McAuliffe Says "Nuts!"

Of the many actions and counter-attacks that finally stemmed the advance, one in particular—at Bastogne—caused the world to hold its breath. Discovering that the town of Bastogne stood across the junction of several key roads and highways leading to the north and west, both German and American forces resolved to occupy the town first. In a desperate race from their base in France, the U.S. 101st Airborne ("Screaming Eagle") Division under Brigadier General Anthony McAuliffe, accompanied by elements of the 10th Armored Division, got there first—only to be immediately engulfed and surrounded by advancing German armies that outnumbered them four to one. Desperate fighting ensued. With fog and mist hampering their re-supply from the air, McAuliffe's men ran low on ammunition and food. On December 22, 1944, the German commander sent emissaries with a message giving them two hours to surrender, otherwise a German attack would annihilate them and the city of Bastogne. McAuliffe turned to his staff. "Aw, nuts", he said with scorn. "How am I to answer this?" One of them responded: "Why don't you use the same word you just spoke?" And McAuliffe scrawled a single word on a scrap of paper sent back to the German command: "Nuts!"

As some historians tell it, the German officer receiving the message was unfamiliar with the term. He asked the American lieutenant bringing it: "I do not understand. Is your commander's reply favorable? If it is, we are empowered to negotiate terms".

"My commander's reply is 'Nuts!'" answered the American

lieutenant. "It means 'Go to hell'. You understand that, don't you?"

U.S. forces at Bastogne never did surrender. Through Christmas day and almost until New Year's, still surrounded, they fought on, holding the road junction, causing serious dislocation to the entire German strategy of battle, destroying more than 200 German tanks and thousands of German troops, while suffering heavy losses themselves until rescued by the armies of Generals Patton and Hodges. Meanwhile, the words "Nuts!" and "Ardennes" appeared in the headlines of a thousand Allied newspapers to thrill the "home front"—I remember reading the front page exclamation as a child—and entered the history books to stand alongside the one-word retort of the French general, Cambronne, at the Battle of Waterloo. "Brave Frenchman, surrender!" had demanded a British commander on that day. "Merde!" responded Cambronne. Many believe that McAuliffe also used a stronger term than "Nuts!", but tourist officials of the city of Bastogne, who spoke with McAuliffe about it during his several postwar visits and prior to his death, confirm the version set forth above.

In the successful defense of Bastogne, causing extensive damage to the town and suffering, numerous Belgians lost their lives. One of them, a young nurse named Renée Lemaire, was killed by a shell as she tended to American wounded in an improvised hospital.

The "bulge" was eliminated, and the fighting subsided, by late January of 1945. A horrifying total of 76,890 Americans had been killed or wounded. The Germans had lost between 80,000 and 120,000 men. In German histories, the event became known as the "Battle of the Ardennes" or the "Von Runstedt Offensive". The Belgians call it "The Battle of the Salient"; the colloquial Americans call it "The Battle of the Bulge". And its aftermath, its cemeteries, its key battlefield sites, memorials, museums, can be viewed throughout the Ardennes—but especially in Bastogne.

BASTOGNE

For Americans certainly, but even for others, the visit is one suffused with emotion, a day when you are constantly aware of larger themes, when you experience a nervous undercurrent of history and great human endeavors, when you intensely appreciate the condition called Peace, and are determined to work for it.

It is the most "American" city in Europe. Its central square has actually been re-named "Place McAuliffe", and in it stands a damaged Sherman tank, a bust of McAuliffe, an American flag that flies every day of the year over Belgian soil. On the roads leading into town are markers of key battle sites consisting of the turrets of American tanks and armored cars set into concrete pedestals. Around the Place McAuliffe are cafes and restaurants whose plateglass windows are painted with the stars-and-stripes; and the continuing gratitude of the townsfolk towards their G.I. liberators is touching indeed.

THE AMERICAN MEMORIAL AND THE "NUTS" MUSEUM: The focus of your visit is the important "Mardasson Memorial" to the battle, and its adjoining "Nuts Museum" (more properly known as the "Bastogne Historical Center"). Both are on the historic Mardasson Hill a mile beyond the town, to which signs reading "Mardasson" point the way.

You will best appreciate the memorial by first visiting the museum, open daily from March 1 through mid-November, from 9 a.m. to 6 p.m., for an admission charge of 150 francs ($4.16) for adults, 80 francs ($2.22) for children. Here the battle is depicted and explained in every conceivable fashion: via a 20-minute audiovisual show presented throughout the day in a recessed amphitheatre at the center of the exhibits, via a constantly-projected film in a theatre portion of the museum, and most important, via a series of intricate, wax-model tableaux re-creating celebrated photos of the battle. Here is General Baron von Monteuffel meeting with his key aides; the uniform and coat are the actual vestments worn by him and later donated to the museum. Here is a jaunty General Anthony McAuliffe lifting the morale of his men by slouching insouciantly in his jeep, seemingly without a concern in the world, but studying a map. Here are Dwight Eisenhower, General Omar Bradley, General George S. Patton, conferring after the battle. Again the uniforms are authentic, donated by the participants, and the museum claims to possess the most comprehensive collection of World War II uniforms in the world, as well as the sort of light equipment that would accompany a parachute division. Dramatic dioramas, vitrines of exhibits well described, complete the extensive museum, which deserves a two-hour visit for a proper understanding of the battle.

A hundred yards uphill, on the crest of the "Mardasson" overlooking Bastogne and all its surroundings, is then the monumental, several-stories-high, hollow star that is the American Memorial, built by Belgian subscriptions in 1950. Underneath, carved out of rock, is a crypt containing three chapels—Protestant, Catholic, Jewish—decorated with the distinctive mosaic murals of Fernand Leger. Atop the star, reached via an interior spiral staircase, are viewing platforms set into each of the five points, looking out over key sites of the battle—and inscriptions at each point advise you of the highlights of each view, and of what transpired there. The names of 49 U.S. States, and of the army formations that took part in the battle, are carved into the stone sides of the star. Still to come, the most stirring portion of the memorial are ten, giant, stone slabs bearing a detailed account of the Battle of the Bulge by the distinguished U.S. military historian, S.L.M. Marshall. You will want to read every word of this statement of great dignity, phrased in a haunting pattern of rolling cadence that short excerpts can scarcely capture: "The battle began with fog and darkness. The thin defending line was overwhelmed and broken under weight of fire and metal. The Ardennes door lay open . . . The uniformed ranks of the United States fought for this soil as if it had been their homeland. The Belgian civilians, unarmed, refused to abandon it in the face of the oncoming enemy . . . 76,890 Americans were killed or wounded, or were marked missing . . . Seldom has more American blood been spilt in the course of a single battle. The number of Belgians who died or suffered wounds or great privation helping these friends from overseas cannot be known . . . This Memorial and the earth surrounding it are dedicated to the enduring friendship of the people of Belgium and the United States".

Unlike the Museum, the Memorial can be visited every day of the year.

TOURING THE BATTLEGROUND: Twelve explanatory
road signs, numbered 1 to 12, and containing illustrations, inscriptions, maps and sketches of the battle, as well as arrow-directions to the next numbered stop, identify the major battle points. In your car, on a 50-kilometer itinerary, you can drive along much of the perimeter of the lengthy siege.

Sign 1 is at Place McAuliffe, where you should pause to note the roads that fan out in all directions, reason for the struggle to hold the Bastogne Junction. No. 2 is the Mardasson Hill, 3 the German military cemetery at Recogne where 6,785 German soldiers lie buried. (Americans graves have long since been removed from the Bastogne area.) 4, at Noville, is where the battalion of then-Major Desobry (he's now a Lieutenant General, and makes frequent visits to Bastogne) held off the 2nd German Armoured Division for two days at the start of the battle, allowing a defense to form. 5, at Longwilly, marks the spot where a battalion of U.S. Lt. Colonel Cherry was virtually annihilated by the Panzer Lehr division. 6 at Margeret, 7 at Neffe, 8 at Mont, 9 at Marvie, are points where the German advance was stopped in brutal hand-to-hand combat. 10 is Hemroulle, where supplies dropped from the air saved the American garrison. 11 and 12 are Champs and

Mande-St. Etienne which German troops attempted to capture on Christmas eve as "a gift for our Führer"; they were stopped. From sign 12, one returns along the N4 to Bastogne.

THE LAST BATTLE ON BELGIAN SOIL? Is it possible, after all these centuries of interminable conflict, that the battle of Bastogne will have been the last to occur on Belgian soil? That the destruction of Belgian cities by foreign troops, the death and suffering of Belgian civilians in international conflicts, will have taken place for the last time at Bastogne? That this horror will finally have come to an end? We can only hope so. Bastogne's 10,000 residents are themselves working to that result by causing their city to be a founding member of the new "World Union of Martyred Peace Towns". Its other members: Verdun, Coventry, Volgograd (the former Stalingrad), Kalavrita (Greece), and several more cities largely destroyed in wars. Its purpose: to strive for "détente, disarmament, respect of human rights, of the rights of the child, and of the rights of nations to self-determination . . . [to end] hunger in the world". Somehow, by visiting Bastogne, by keeping alive the memory of its suffering, by paying tribute to its victory over militaristic bigots, the tourist seems to make a contribution to that same cause.

OVERNIGHT IN BASTOGNE: You can, of course, simply drive there from Liège (an hour away, now that motorway E9 has been completed), from Namur (one hour on Route N4) or even from Brussels (two hours on Route A40), or go there by train, returning at night to your starting point; but an increasing number of visitors now stay in and around Bastogne, savoring the friendship of a people whose international ties are strong. True, the hotels are small, and none are First Class, but the typical warmth of your Ardennes welcome, the home-style furnishings, and the scrupulous maintenance and cleanliness, result in a memorable interlude.

In the city itself are seven hotels and pensions having a total of 90 rooms, of which 27 are found in the city's leading establishment, the **Hotel Lebrun** at 8 Rue du Marché (phone 062/21-11-93), just off the Place McAuliffe. A plain-but-pleasant, low-lying, three-story building that extends for nearly a block, it charges 2195 francs ($61) for its 15 double rooms with bath or shower, as little as 1500 francs ($42) for the rooms without. Runner-up, directly on the central square, is the impressive, 16-room **Hotel "Le Borges"**, 11 Place McAuliffe (phone 062/21-11-00), whose doubles without bath are 1500 francs ($42), breakfast for two included. Budget champions hereabouts are: **Hotel du Sud**, 39 Rue du Marché (phone 062/21-11-14) (700 francs, $20 per twin), and **"L'Actuel"**, at 59 Avenue Mathieu (phone 062/21-45-05) (900 francs, $25, per twin).

If the hotels in Bastogne are full, then one proceeds to a larger cluster of good quality alternates (but tourist class only) in the picturesque little town (around 4,000 people) of La-Roche-en-Ardenne less than 25 kilometers away: **Hotel Belle Vue**, 10 Avenue de Hadja (phone 084/41-11-87); **Hotel des Ardennes**, 2 Rue de Beausaint (phone 084/41-11-12); **Hotel "La Claire Fontaine"**, at 64 Route de Hotton (phone 084/41-12-96); still others: most charging approximately 1700 to 2000 francs ($47 to $56) for a twin with bath. The particularly attractive **"La Claire Fontaine"**, with its 24 rooms, gastronomic restaurant, and situation at the side of the River Ourthe, is a bit more costly, at 2700 francs ($75) double. On the way to La Roche, you'll pass the rustic, 9-room **"La Ferme au Pont"**, in Ortho (1 Route de Bastogne, phone 084/43-31-61), which might also be considered, as should the **Hôtel Moderne** (26 Rue Châmont, phone 084/41-11-24) and **Hôtel de Liège** in La Roche.

Back in Bastogne (which people 40 years ago habitually referred to as "beleaguered Bastogne" or "once-beleaguered Bastogne"), the leading **Hotel Lebrun** (see above) also possesses the city's most "elegant" restaurant serving all the specialties from snails to trout, from locally-made patés to soufflés doused in Grand Marnier liqueur. Three-course meals average 1300 francs ($36), but can be had for as little as 800 ($22). No fewer than four much cheaper restaurants surround the Place McAuliffe—and these are the **"McAuliffe"**, the **"Leo"**, **"Le Midi"**, and **"Dany's"** —serving specialties of the Ardennes, and charging as little as 375 francs ($10.40) for three, simple courses. You walk from place to place comparing menus, then select. The 250-seat "Leo" is the one used for large groups of veterans visiting Bastogne; the 150-seat "bakery-ice cream parlor" called **"Le Melba"**, also on the Place McAuliffe, is where you go for snacks. A mile to the north of Bastogne, the pleasant **Restaurant "Au Coin Fleuri"** at 5 Chaussée d'Houffalize, is for relaxed meals in a rustic dining room at the side of a major road leading into town. My recent savory roast chicken there, with apple sauce, and a pitcher of white wine, came to 350 francs ($9.72), service included.

LA GLEIZE

The northernmost penetration of Belgium in the Battle of the Bulge, took place near a tiny mountain village called La Gleize. It is less than 40 kilometers from Liège, 15-or-so kilometers from

Spa. If you're in one of those two cities, but don't care to undertake the longer trip to Bastogne, you can secure a glimpse of the terrain of the battle, and one or two specific wartime sights, by making the short, pleasant drive to La Gleize through unusually scenic, hilly countryside of the Ardennes. Follow the road signs to **Stoumont** and just before arriving there, you'll encounter La Gleize; it is easily spotted despite the lack of signs. For on its "place communale" (city square), high up on the hill, stands a massive, German, Mark VI "Tiger" II tank of the armored regiment led by Obersturmbannführer Jochem Peiper. His was the spearhead force of Sepp Dietrich's 6th Panzer Army, assigned to cross the River Meuse within 24 hours after the launching of the attack, and equipped for that purpose with the most modern (early 1944) and massive of German tanks, the Tiger "II" manufactured by Porsche. Though the youthful officer wrought havoc with several American units, they dug in and stopped him at La Gleize. (The battle caused the incidental destruction of virtually every structure in La Gleize, and numerous civilian casualties.) The tank you see bears the hole of the shell that halted its advance on the night of December 22, 1944.

Peiper was preceded by English-speaking German troops under the command of the infamous Otto Skorzeny, all dressed in U.S. uniforms and driving captured U.S. jeeps. Their mission was to sow confusion behind the lines, to hold vital Meuse River bridges. To ferret out the imposters, American guards confronted suspicious groups with questions that only an American could answer. "Who won the World Series in 1940?" "What is the name of Betty Grable's husband?" (Band leader Harry James). One wonders how many Army intellectuals, unable to answer, were mistakenly taken for Germans!

Now look at the hills and ridges surrounding La Gleize. It was on these Ardennes-style heights that columns of the opposing armies moved and confronted one another. Was it realistic of German strategists to believe they could punch through such terrain? In even-numbered years (1990, 1992), the village of La Gleize maintains a small exhibition of the battle (models, uniforms, maps, weapons) that occurred here, in a small café at 51 Rue du Centre. Organized by the director of its tourist office, Gerard Gregoire, who also authored a book on those fateful events of December, 1944—"Les Panzer de Peiper Face à l'U.S. Army"— it is not to be compared with the elaborate museum at Bastogne, but is nonetheless a touching gesture on the part of the villagers. One of them described to me his emotions upon viewing the crumpled body of a young American soldier from California who had traveled thousands of miles to meet his death here on a hillside of La Gleize. "I do not always agree with your policies," he said, "but after seeing that, how could I ever be anti-American?"

SOME MISCELLANY OF THE ARDENNES: Roughly

speaking, the "Ardennes" are everything in Belgium found south of a line running, east-to-west, from Aachen on the German border, to Liège, to Namur, to Charleroi and Beaumont. It is French-speaking (except for a small border enclave of German-language Belgians)—and proudly Walloon . . . Though a few trains run through it (especially to such market towns as Bastogne and Saint Vith), it's obvious that your best means of transportation are cars and buses . . . Shakespeare placed his "As You Like It" in the Forest of Arden, which in this instance did not refer to the one in Warwickshire but to the "Forest of the Ardennes" . . . The name itself is thought to come from the Celtic *ardu-enna* ("highlands") . . . Belgium's compulsory replanting law requires that foresters replace every tree they cut down . . . Every Belgian you meet claims to have a second home in the Ardennes—yet it's a remarkably under-populated place! . . . Visiting a restaurant in the Ardennes, and in doubt over what to order, simply ask for an omelette with Ardennes ham; the latter ingredient turns this commonplace dish into the equivalent of anything you'd receive in a three-star restaurant! What is marinated for several days, salted for six weeks, then smoked for several months? Hams of the Ardennes ("jambon d'Ardenne")! You can't leave the area without tasting or purchasing one.

Why, in this introduction, have we so focused on war? Because all over the world, from the events of war, there are millions who know the Ardennes without ever having been there. But now we proceed to the peaceful attributes of this awesome vacation land.

CHAPTER XII

RESORTS OF THE ARDENNES: SPA AND DURBUY

□ □ □

One Where People Thin Out, The Other Where They Gorge

If you were to throw a dart at a map of the Ardennes, chances are you would hit a resort—a timbered hunting lodge, a luxurious castle hotel, a riding academy, a fishermen's camp. When Belgians go off for the weekend or on vacation, they head in the main for one of two destinations: the Belgian Coast—or the Ardennes. In the green/brown hills and valleys of the Ardennes, from a multitude of mountainside inns or rustic forest restaurants along rushing streams, from several scores of charming old villages clustered about 16th-century churches, from high-altitude "social hotels" maintained by labor unions, from holiday facilities too numerous to list, let alone describe, we've singled out two, key, recreational "resorts" favored by international visitors, that may whet the desire for more. Both are less than an hour south of Liège. They are the exquisite, little, toy village of **Durbuy;** and the city where half the royalty of Europe once "took the waters", soaked in mud of peat, tramped over mountainside trails, and then dispelled all the good effects of this at a late-night casino celebrated throughout Europe—just as thousands of less favored visitors continue to do today. We are talking not about any spa, or even about *a* spa, but about *the* **Spa,** where spas began—in the Belgian Ardennes.

SPA

It gave its name to a host of later imitators. Its precious riches are natural springs ("pouhons") dotted everywhere—in the town itself, in its grand and stately "Park of 7 Hours", in its forested hills, even atop high plateaus of peat. They gush forth waters that numerous physicians in Europe quite seriously believe are endowed with health-giving properties capable of ameliorating certain of the world's major diseases. Though most medical experts in other continents pay them no heed at all (just as they fail to study or practice Chinese acupuncture, or Indian meditation), Europeans in great numbers claim that "water cures" (the quaffing of great quantities of particular waters) or "thermal cures" (based on various baths and immersions, sprays, high-pressured hoses and other treatments associated with water) are beneficial to health. And Belgian physicians associated with Spa contend, in particular, that the waters of Spa are useful in treating *cardiovascular diseases* (hypertension, arteriosclerosis, venious thrombosis, obliterating endarteritis), *rheumatic diseases* (arthritis, arthrotis, neuralgia, sciatica, after-effects of accidents, cellulitis), and *diseases of the upper respiratory tract* (catarrh, rhinitis, pharyngitis, laryngitis, tonsilitis, tracheitis, voice fatigue and allergies), in addition to simply imparting a general feeling of good health. Add to all this a grand and elegant casino for evening distraction, superb restaurants, a huge building of baths, trails, every sport—and what more could you want?

THE DISCOVERY OF SPA: Water. Water everywhere. Water bubbling like champagne, gushing forth from among rocks in the midst of a forest ascending onto high hills. Water with exotic taste, lifting the spirit, causing a sense of well-being. A Roman soldier first noticed the phenomenon, and the Roman historian, Pliny the Elder, duly recorded the wonders of a place in northern Gaul called Spa, in his *Historia Naturalis* written nearly two thousand years ago. In the 1300s, medieval farmers and huntsmen rediscovered those curiously-refreshing, health-giving waters, and by the 1500s, Europeans were travelling in increasing numbers to Spa, in the Principality of Liège. At the peak of its fame, in the 18th and 19th centuries, it hosted every crowned head of Europe, as well as men of letters ranging from Montaigne (who called the waters "miraculous") to Bishop Berkeley. Its most celebrated visitor was Czar Peter the Great of Russia, suffering from severe forms of indigestion, and desperate for relief. He made the long trip to Spa in 1717, followed a meticulous program of mountainside walks interspersed with great, gasping, draughts of the waters of Spa ("the cure")—and soon pronounced himself restored! Then, after showering the city with medallions, awards, donations and letters of gratitude, he permitted his name to be placed on the central spring of Spa, the one you will visit in the very heart of the city in a quaint columnar building. It is the **"Pouhon Pierre-le-Grand"** (Spring of Peter the Great), open in "season" (from June 18 to September 11) from 10 to 2 and from 1 to 5:30 p.m.; from April to mid-June, and in later September, from 1 to 4 p.m., longer on weekends; most other times on weekends only, from 10 to noon and 2 to 4. Within those hours, an elderly lady sits at a desk at the entrance to the actual Spring down the interior steps, selling paper cups for 10 francs (27¢). As a marketing device, she permits unlimited multi-cup helpings of the pungent waters during the otherwise quiet time between 10 and 11 a.m., but so medicinal is the taste, so reeking with iron are these fluids from the single most ferruginous spring of Spa, that you won't want a second cup. They are most beneficial when taken on an empty stomach, and are "ferrugineuse, carbogazeuse, tonique, reconstituant, diurétique", in addition to being good enough for Peter the Great.

A later ruler, King Leopold II of Belgium, endowed the city with its great **Etablissement Thermal** (Thermal Establishment) in 1868. Again in the very heart of Spa on the Place Royale, and looking a bit like a small Paris Opera House, festooned with flags and fronted by great buckets of flowers, this is a renowned medical institution among that world of water-based treatment centers that later became known in every country as "spas", after Belgium's Spa. A block away, at the side of flowering gardens, are the gaming tables, restaurants and theatres of the equally splendid and grand **Casino of Spa,** on the Rue Royale, built in 1906. To follow the entire history of Spa, to see paintings and photographs of its famous visitors, historic posters advertising its claims, and correspondence of poets, authors and composers (Meyerbeer, Marguerite de Gauthier) enchanted with its atmosphere, you'll want to visit the **"Musée de la Ville d'Eaux"** (Museum of the City of Waters), at 77 Avenue Reine Astrid. Like everything else in this compact town, it is within easy walking distance from wherever you may be, and is open "in season" (June 12 to September 23) from 10:30 to noon, and from 2:30 to 6 p.m.; "out of season" on weekends only from 2:30 to 6 p.m. Note the especially florid posters by which Spa advertised itself in Britain at the turn of this century; they offer "a certain cure for Anemia, Chlorosis, Neurasthenia", a wonder-working series of "carbonic acid, gas baths efficacious in all heart troubles".

TAKING THE CURE: What exactly does one do in Spa to achieve such improved health? You "take the cure", and the people doing so are called "curistes". But cures come in different forms. There are simple "walking cures", usually combined with "drinking cures" (taking the waters); there are elaborate, classic "thermal cures" at the Thermal Establishment; and there are undoubtedly "eating cures" (for dieters), "sleeping cures", "exercise cures" (at multiple sporting facilities here), and any number of other cures springing from the fertile imaginations of the "spadois" (people of Spa) of Belgium.

"Walking cures"

At the **Tourist Office** ("Office du Tourisme") of Spa in the Pavillon des Petits Jeux on the Place Royale, maps are distributed for more than 100, sign-posted walks through the forests, hills and low mountains surrounding Spa, stopping along the way at successive, celebrated "pouhons" (Springs) for those life-enhancing waters. Where there's a "pouhon", there's usually a tavern or restaurant alongside, even in the deepest woods, to satisfy other needs. The classic walk, from two to 2½ hours in length, starts just behind the Casino and the Pouhon Pierre-le-Grand (where you take the first cup of water), proceeding along the **Route de la Sauvenière,** which you follow uphill until you see the **Route du Tonnelet** on your left. Turn left on the Route du Tonnelet until you reach your next "pouhon", the "Fontaine du Tonnelet" at an altitude of 325 meters. It is surrounded by a merry-go-round-type structure of white iron, flanked by a celebrated restaurant, "La Source du Tonnelet". Sip your second cup. Then continue walking uphill along the **Avenue Peltzer de Clermont** to the historic (reputed source of many miraculous cures, especially for childbearing) "Fontaine de la Sauvenière et Groesbeek" at 400 meters up. Sip your third cup. Or have lunch in the nearby, farmhouse-type "Relais de la Sauvenière". Then walk for half-an-hour down the **"Route des Fontaines"** to the "Fontaine de la Geronstère" (same altitude of 410 meters), whose slightly-sulphuric waters were the principal cure for Peter the Great; they also correct respiratory illnesses; and are found in the cobblestoned backyard of a stunning, white-stone cafe-restaurant, where you could have another snack, but should restrict yourself to a fourth cup of the waters. Now walk downhill back to town along the winding **Rue du Barisart** where you'll pass (and take a fifth, free, glass of water at) the Fontaine de Barisart, last of the major pouhons near the city, and possessing the very least amount of iron in its taste; it is also endowed with a tea-room/restaurant, this time ultra-modernistic in its setting of sloping lawns, giant trees, perfumed forest air. And from there you'll continue downhill again (and a bit waterlogged) into town.

There are, of course, numerous more extensive walks than these, though not all are along courses marked by "pouhons" (springs). There are half-day walks to the **Waterfall of Coo** ("Cascade de Coo") and adjoining pleasure park of carnival-like attractions; to the castles of **Franchimont** and **Anwaille,** to the celebrated caves and grottoes of **Remouchamps** (which operates the longest underground boat trip in the world), to the motor racing course of **Francorchamps** (site of the Belgian Grand Prix), and even (but for strong hikers only) to **Malmedy** and its World War II memorial, twenty kilometers away. While doctors may disagree about waters, they are unanimous in naming walking as the world's finest sport, exercising every muscle, engaging every faculty. When practiced in the heights of Spa, in the fir forests and peat plateaus that overlook this charming resort of the Ardennes, the activity entails a bonus: the inhalation of leaves and resins, the purest oxygen, a surcease from the pressures and noise of cities. No wonder visitors to Spa consider themselves cured!

"Drinking" cures

And, of course, you can simply drink the waters, with or without walking. Two different types are available to you: the iron-rich waters of the "pouhons" (springs) which you've encountered both in town (Pierre le Grand) and in the surrounding hills (Tonnelet, Barisart, Sauvenière, Geronstère), and a second category known as "Spa Reine" (the Queen's Spring) that is virtually without taste. Except for the nominal charge sometimes assessed for use of a glass, the first category is as free as the air to common use. You simply wander from spring to spring, gravely comparing their relative strengths of dissolved iron, the amount of their carbonic acid, their bubbly or non-bubbly quality, gaining strength as you pour successive cups into waiting gullet. You are "taking the waters."

The second type—"Spa Reine"—is a bit more special and of more limited supply. Pumped from a single spring named after Queen Marie-Henriette of Belgium, located in the peat uplands of the High Fagnes overlooking Spa, and protected from pollution by Draconian laws, Spa Reine is the purest water in the world—meaning that it possesses the lowest salt content of any water in the world, as well as the lowest quantity of any other type of mineral impurity, nitrates or calcium. And you can imagine what that means! In these days of low-salt diets combatting obesity and heart disease, the demand for Spa Reine is soaring each year.

A large part of the daily flow of Spa Reine is piped to Spa's **Thermal Establishment** (the baths) for use in various complex "thermal cures". Since most thermal treatments involve considerable sweating of both water and salt, the replacement of the lost water with Spa Reine effects a progressive reduction of salt in the body. And that pure, crystal clear, unpolluted Spa Reine washes out the body's kidneys in a spectacular fashion!

The remainder of nature's production of Spa Reine is piped to the bottling plant of Spa, operated under an exclusive concession from the city by the company called "Spa Monopole, S.A." (it holds the "monopoly" on Spa's waters). Naturally, an ample supply of bottled "Spa Reine" is on sale in the city's own restaurants, bars and groceries. Spa Monopole bottles not only the flat, quiet, non-bubbly "Spa Reine", with its almost complete absence of salt, but also a sparkling Spa water called "Spa Pétillant" (you'll find it sold throughout Belgium), "Spa Orange", "Spa Citron", "Spa Lemon" and "Spa Orania". While the latter are mixed with fruit juices and flavors, they contain no preservatives or colorings, but they do have some salt.

If you'd like a free taste, in fact a free bottle, of any of Spa's commercially-shipped waters, you can obtain one by simply taking the free, half-hour, guided and multilingual tour of Spa's bottling plant operated every weekday of the year from 9 to 11:30 a.m., and 1 to 4:30 p.m., and followed by unlimited servings of Spa. The bottling plant is an unusually modern one in which human hands rarely touch the bottles, and is found just behind the train station, a very short walk from the Casino and the Baths. If you've disliked the heavy taste of iron in the waters taken from the "Pouhons", you'll like the virtually tasteless nature of Spa Reine, or the bubbly fragrance of the other Spa brands, of which more than a million bottles are shipped each day.

"Thermal Cures"

Now for the serious plunge. In the exact center of Spa, in the spectacular, neo-classic building of the **Thermal Establishment** ("Etablissement Thermal"), otherwise known as "the Baths", white-jacketed doctors and attendants, nurses and researchers, pursue the science of hydrotherapy, in a labyrinthine structure of copper tubs and tiled showers, inhalation chambers and exercise rooms, intricate pipework sucking water from springs miles away. Every day of the year, upwards of 400 persons are seated here in mud baths made of the liquified, heated, decaying vegetable matter known as peat (from the stone-age-origin plateaus overlooking Spa), or immersed in gaseous, bubbling, mineral water tubs, or battered with jets of water, or asked to inhale mists of sulphurous steam, or given liquid treatments in which carbon dioxide is forced just below the surface of the skin, or simply seated in relaxing, wicker easy chairs sipping glasses of Spa Reine. No one is permitted to take a single treatment before first undergoing examination by a doctor of Spa attached to the Baths, who then carefully prescribes the entire course of treatment; and the activities of the doctors are themselves overseen by the prestigious Henrijean Institute of Spa, which exercises a form of "quality control" over the baths.

In an elegant, English-language booklet issued by the Baths, explanations are provided as to why these treatments are claimed to improve health or overcome disease. In some treatments, the waters are said to cause veins to contract, forcing blood into undernourished thoracic cavities. In others, certain chemical properties or mud-created heat cause a relaxation of hyper-tense muscles, a decrease of arterial pressures. Without further comment on these, or other far more complex assertions, it suffices to point out that thousands of European doctors prescribe such treatments for their patients, and numerous overseas visitors find their way to Spa, there to engage in the oldest therapy known to mankind. Didn't Eve take a bath in the Garden of Eden? And isn't Venus depicted as rising from the sea?

In most of the centuries prior to construction of the Thermal Establishment in the late 1860s, going to Spa meant drinking the waters, not bathing in them. Only in the late 1700s were first tentative attempts made to utilize bathing as a form of treatment; and these efforts of private entrepreneurs generally consisted of placing two or three primitive tubs into the precincts of their hotels.

Crude attempts to heat the waters generally deprived them of their mineral-laden qualities, and the resultant therapy—as ineffectual as it proved—was limited in any event to a class of people able to pay for the costly transfer and heating of waters from Springs to tubs.

In the 1860s, a strong Burgomaster of Spa, Joseph Servais, overcame ridicule and inertia to ram through the construction of this architecturally-tasteful and superbly-engineered building, serviced with sufficient quantities of water to process the needs of hundreds of "curistes" each day, at acceptable cost. He overcame doubts as to the efficacy of thermal cures, problems in the piping in of sufficient water. And what he built, under the patronage of Belgian King Leopold II, was a municipally-owned and operated structure that set new precedents for those times. It also democratized the practice of taking thermal treatments. Today, state-subsidized visits to the Thermal Establishment of Spa (and to two other institutions of "social thermalism" in Spa) are part of the National Health Care system of Belgium, available for little or no charge to low-income working people. One knows charwomen in Brussels who spend a month each year in the formerly-exclusive baths of Spa.

They also attract people of varying income from around the world. For the baths of Spa are amazingly cheap. The average complete "cure" at the Thermal Establishment requires about 18 days; yet such a course of treatment can cost as little as 7200 francs ($200), plus the cost of room and board at a nearby Spa hotel. And even as a day visitor, in a slow period, when there's unused capacity, you can sometimes drop in without appointment simply for a peat-mud bath ("bain de tourbe") followed by a carbo-fizzy bath and treatment ("bain carbogazeux"). That combination cost, in the summer of 1988, a total of 650 francs ($18). To apply for a thermal "cure", write or phone the Secretariat, **"L' Etablissement Thermal,"** Place Royale, 4880 Spa, Belgium (087/77-25-60), or write the **Spa Tourist Office,** 2 Rue Royale, 4800 Spa (087/77-17-00 or 77-29-13). Or simply apply at the reception windows, up the outside staircase and just inside the entrance of this splendid building—which is surely the jewel of this small city of Spa.

SPA'S EQUALLY GRAND CASINO: Gambling eliminates

additional bodily tension (or does it?). One of the eight casinos of Belgium is found in Spa, alongside the Baths, in a grand, turn-of-the-century building vastly superior to the other Liège-area casino at Chaudfontaine. It occupies the site of predecessor casinos dating back to 1769, and is thus the oldest casino in the world, predating Monaco's by a hundred years! There's European roulette (only one "0") here; Baccarat; Black Jack; a dressy, elegant atmosphere of silk, cloth-shaded lamps over gaming tables and tuxedoed croupiers; admission of 50 francs ($1.39); minimum bets of only 50 francs ($1.38); restaurants and exhibition rooms; a major theatre; and daily hours from 4 p.m. on. Go to 4 Rue Royale (phone 087/77-20-52).

HOTELS OF SPA AND NEARBY: We start with the sublime. The **Manoir de Lébioles** (phone 087/77-10-20) is an 18th-century castle next to the village of Creppe, three kilometers from Spa, on a plateau in the heights that dominate the "city of the waters". It is a turreted castle with entrance gate, a small complex of support structures (the former stable, the servants' quarters), immense surrounding lawns and formal gardens, a view over twenty miles of untouched countryside below, a giant reception hall of marble, stone, and exquisite period furnishings; and while it is not large enough for a king, it is the kind of castle his brother—the Prince—would have occupied. Upstairs is room enough for 30 guest rooms, yet there are only six—each the size of five normal rooms—supplied with country-estate furniture of the most modern comfort, an enthralling view, and open, wood-burning fireplaces that servants rush to ignite short minutes before you arrive. Each such immense room rents for 5000 francs ($139) to 5500 francs ($153) to 6500 francs ($181) to 7500 francs ($208), depending on size, including breakfast for two, service and tax, and while I've never seen the guests (who were all out, on a recent visit), they are undoubtedly couples anxious to capture moments of high romance and enchantment; the subdued dining-room restaurant downstairs (open also to non-guests; see our restaurant discussion, below), the sitting rooms where one takes tea before a fire, the grounds, are for tastes so demanding as to be positively decadent. Naturally you'll need a car for occasional forays into Spa —if you can ever break away from the paradise of your room!

Down from the clouds into the realm of normal hotels, but still on the heights overlooking Spa, the 95-room **Dorint Hotel Ardennes,** on the Route de Balmoral (phone 087/77-25-81), is less than a mile from the center of the city (looking almost straight down at it!), a modernistic, glass-fronted slab with big, red awnings, sticking out from the midst of a thick, pine forest; it is the top choice of the hotels actually associated with Spa, charging 1900 francs ($53) for a single room with bath and breakfast, 3400 francs ($94) for a double with private bath and breakfast. But you'll still want a car for reaching the Baths, although several walking trails into and around Spa start at the very entrance to the hotel. Rooms, all with balcony, are large and sunny, with modern, wide beds and sitting area; there are bars, restaurant, an indoor swimming pool and sun terraces outside, sauna, the links of the Royal Golf Club of Fagnes 500 yards away, every comfort and facility. If you can't get in, a more or less acceptable substitute is the smaller, modern **Hotel Olympic,** at Avenue Amédée Hesse (phone 088/77-25-48) nearby, again requiring a car. Motel modern in style and furnishings, it offers 12 rooms, 22 suites; charges only 1800 francs ($50) for two-people-and-breakfast; and is situated alongside the olympic-sized municipal swimming pool of Spa in another of those forest settings, high overlooking the city.

On the main street of Spa, in the very center of town, a two-minute walk from Baths and Casino, the always-reliable choice is the prim and old-fashioned **Hotel Cardinal,** at 21–27 Place Royale (087/77-10-64 or 77-19-64). Twenty-eight clean but dowdy rooms with private bath rent here for a maximum of 1860 francs ($52) single, 2720 francs ($76) double, always with continental breakfast included. The 27-room **L'Auberge-Spa,** at 3–4 Place du Monument (phone 087/77-36-66), nearby, is a close runner-up, with homey rooms and casement windows overlooking a small square, in a dramatic building of an almost-Tudor facade of brown beams criss-crossing through white stucco. A restaurant occupies the entire ground floor. Only 2100 francs ($58) for a double room with private bath and two breakfasts.

Other hotels in the actual town of Spa are almost astonishingly cheap, especially when you take the terms offered to guests pursuing a "cure"—room and meals. The old-fashioned **Park Hotel,** on the main street of Spa, 33 Avenue Reine Astrid (087/77-15-51), charges only 1450 francs ($40) for a double room with private bath and breakfast, only 950 francs ($26) double without private bath; the nondescript **Hotel de l'Avenue,** at 48 Avenue Reine Astrid (087/77-20-67), asks only 1100 francs ($31) per person for room and all three meals each day; **Chez Jean et Josien,** over a bar at 68 Reine Astrid (phone 087/77-12-21), asks 1050 francs ($29) per person for the same full-pension terms. For extremely cost-conscious visitors: the **Hotel du Chemin de Fer,** 25 Place de la Gare (087/77-14-15), charges only 800 francs ($22) for two persons, without private bath, but with continental breakfast included.

You'll like your hotels in and near Spa. Maintaining a proud, centuries-old tradition of hospitality, they're picturesque inside, full of charm. And if you have a car and the time to stay near villages 8 to 9 kilometers from Spa, you'll choose from a group of even more picturesque, farmhouse-style hotels, none charging as much as $40 a night for a double room with private bath and breakfast. Try, in particular, the specimens in and around "Sartlez-Spa", of which the **Auberge "Les Santons"** at 39a Cockaifagne, Route de Francorchamps (087/47-43-15), is outstanding, but priced at only 1900 francs ($57) per double room.

RESTAURANTS OF SPA AND VICINITY: The tingling, dazzling, classic, food experience of Spa is had at that castle-hotel-restaurant, **Le Manoir de Lébioles,** which led off our hotel discussion, and is located in Creppe, three kilometers from Spa (phone 087/77-10-20 or 77-02-76 or 77-02-79). In a dining room of satin covered walls and oil paintings looking out onto a sweeping valley view, it provides an unforgettable setting, the unaltered dishes, recipes and sauces of the traditional *haute cuisine,* memorable wines, but memorable prices as well. Except for soup at 120 francs ($3.33), you'll pay an average of 650 francs ($18) for most cold appetizers (oysters of Zeeland, paté de foie gras), an average of 980 francs ($27) for most main courses (cutlet of sweetbreads, side of lamb "Printanière"). Count on a total of $65 per person, plus wine, which is also the approximate cost of a five-course "Menu Gastronomique" at 2650 francs ($74), service included: it consists of oysters, then roast goose liver with points of asparagus, piping hot sweetbreads with red pears, a sorbet to prepare for the main course of lamb filet or pigeon, then cheese, and a choice of sweet desserts. For tiny eaters, there's a far more simple, four-course "Menu Traditional" for only 920 francs ($27.60): paté of duckling in port wine, a variety of small fish filets, braised quail with tiny potatoes as the supreme main course, desserts. Monsieur Jacques Cauwels-van Cauwenberg, proprietor of the Castle, is himself the chef for all this; he firmly believes he deserves a Michelin star, as yet unbestowed as of late 1988. Closed Sunday evenings, Monday, and the month of January.

In Spa itself, the classic restaurant is **Le Grand Maur,** at 41 Rue Xhrouet (phone 087/77-36-16, closed Mondays and throughout most of February, in the $50 per meal range; but a top value of the city is the restaurant of the **Hotel Cardinal,** at 25 Place Royale on the main street of Spa (087/77-19-64). Its decor hasn't changed in 80 years, nor its cuisine: standard, old-fashioned, bourgeois dishes, heavily-sauced, and bearing no resemblance at all to the kind of thinning plates and health foods you'd expect to find in a hotel catering to the "curistes" of Spa. One portly guest at the next table recently pondered the menu with great seriousness, sighed as he ordered a simple (but enormous) fried sole for his lunch, then proceeded to devour a plate of steamed potatoes alongside and washed everything down with a full bottle of white wine. I, more abstemious, recently had an enormous, old-fashioned bowl of creamed chicken soup to begin (accompanied by crusty bread), then limited myself to a healthy omelette "aux fines Herbes" (with green herbs), a simple fresh fruit salad for dessert, a bottle of Spa with the omelette. What restraint! Total cost: 425 francs ($11.80), and I have the check to prove it. Obviously, a normal fish or meat course in place of the omelette would have driven the total to around $16.

Does anyone diet in Spa? Are you serious? In *Belgium*? The *waters* are for that!

SOME MISCELLANY OF SPA: Say the word "Ardennes" and you immediately think of "forests"; but forests come in many forms and shapes. At the top of the forest overlooking Spa is an actual **"Museum of the Forest"** ("Musée du Forêt" or "Ferme-Musée de Berinsenne") offering instruction that justifies the brisk, uphill hike of an hour-or-so along the Vieille Route de Stavelot. Open from Easter through December from 1 to 7 p.m. on weekends and Wednesdays, daily except Monday in July and August, for no admission charge, it explores the intricate ecology of the great forest of the Ardennes, which accounts for more than 75% of all the forest land in Belgium: animals and plants, wild boars and trees, foxes and leaves. Surprisingly, as you'll learn from one exhibit, there's more forest now in Belgium than there was in the Middle Ages, because of the shift from wood-burning to other forms of energy. A museum sidelight, banal to some but riveting to me: the complete, standing reproduction of the dinosaur-like, skeletal structure of a simple chicken, a simple rabbit, a lizard. What a wondrous work is nature! . . . **Ceran,** an attractive family chateau in Spa, is one of the continent's most effective schools of the French language. For fourteen hours a day (quite literally from 8:30 a.m. to 10:30 p.m.), and for as little as one week to as many as four or five, in classes geared to your ability (but it's best to have at least a smattering of French before you arrive), Ceran plunges you, immerses, dunks and inundates you, in French, at classes and play, at hearty meals, at TV sets, movies and evening parties—for no matter what your nationality, previous linguistic training, age or ability, you communicate solely in French, living, eating and working in the Chateau, energized by the supportive air of the Ardennes. Room without private bath, all three meals each day (accompanied by wine at night!), all classroom instruction, tuition and language laboratories, amount to a total of only 15,000 francs ($416) a week, even less if there are two of you attending together and sharing the room. Write to **Ceran,** 144 Avenue du Château, Nivezé, B-4880 Spa (phone 087/77-39-16) . . . In winter, Spa has become a major center of cross-country skiing. In all other seasons, it offers every conceivable sport, from fishing and pedal-boating at its **Warfaaz Lake**, to kayak-ing down the **Amblève River** from its Telecoo Park, to golf on the course atop the **Balmoral** ridge, to a dozen such activities at **"La Fraineuse Omnisports Centre"** . . . In June of each year, the "International French Song Festival"—a fierce, several-day competition—takes place at the theatre of the Casino; in August, the National Belgian Stage Company appears there . . . To go to Spa from Liegè—a forty-minute trip by car—you take motorway E9 south to Remouchamps, and turn east from there to Spa; or you simply drive directly there on the (lesser) route N32 in a south-easterly direction from Liège. You can also reach Spa via train from either Liège or Brussels, by seeking out the rail schedules to Pepinster, where you then change to a little locomotive going to Spa. Amazingly, the one-way fare all the way from Brussels (via Pepinster) to Spa is less than $15.

EXCURSION TO THE MALMEDY MEMORIAL: If you have a car on your visit to Spa, you can drive it for twenty kilometers to a small patch of hillside outside the town of Malmédy, a name burned into the memories of people who lived during World War II. Who can forget the photograph of that snowy field in the Sunday newspapers of December, 1944, showing 85 bodies sprawled across its small expanse? They were soldiers of an American unit overrun in the first days of the Battle of the Bulge, captured by a German SS regiment, and then coldly machine-gunned to death in violation of every convention and rule of war. Today, on the small triangle of ground, Belgium maintains a low, roofed structure, a flagpole, and a memorial wall inscribed with the names of the men shot there: Jones, Davis, Murray, Rosenfeld, McGovern, Cohen, Brozowski, Lengyel, Bloom, McKinney, Piasecki . . . alongside a single quotation, in English: "We here highly resolve that these dead shall not have died in vain. A. Lincoln".

To make your own visit to the Malmédy Memorial, take Route 32 towards Malmédy and, on its outskirts, continue in the direction marked Waimes and St. Vith. At the intersection of Route 32 and Route 23 (the Belgians call it "la croix des Americaines") is the field where the infamous massacre took place.

A RE-ORIENTATION: Now glance at a map. The casino-baths-and-springs of famous Spa were 25 miles to the southeast of Liège. The fairytale town of **Durbuy** (pronounced "door-bwee"), to which we next turn, is 35 miles almost directly south of Liège, in an identical Ardennes setting of picturesque small mountains cov-

ered with forests and farms. Short minutes from Liège, you've moved from a major European city to the so-called "plus petite ville du monde" (smallest city in the world).

DURBUY

Some Belgians go there simply for the day, to shop, to browse, to dine, to seek a "quick high" from the penetrating air of the Ardennes. Some go there for an illicit weekend of candlelight dinners or earnest, romantic talks on the banks of the River Ourthe. Some go to propose, or to celebrate the anniversary of a wedding or liaison earlier made. It is a scene out of Disney, a pint-sized Rothenburg, an actual, olden city of closely-packed buildings around winding streets, yet so small that you could walk from one end to the other in twelve minutes. And every one of its architecturally-consistent, 17th- and 18th-century buildings is a hotel, restaurant, boutique, museum, archery range, art gallery, town hall, or travel agency—in short, it is a town devoted entirely to tourism. Where do the residents live? Mainly in homes or towns beyond the valley, unseen. Durbuy is too picturesque and idyllic to be sullied by baby carriages, or wash hanging to dry.

It all began, once upon a time, when an 11th century castle arose at this bend on the meandering River Ourthe. For protection, neighboring residents squeezed their homes up close to the walls of the Castle, built "dwellings near the fortress"—in Latin, "duro-bodions" (hence, "Durbuy"). The town grew to its present size, and in the year 1331 acquired a city charter and city rights from its medieval lord, the Count of Luxembourg (later succeeded by the Counts of Ursel). It never grew beyond its present size, and thus became "la plus petite ville du monde" (the smallest city in the world).

You approach the "city" through the equally small, neighboring hamlets of "Grand Han" and "Petit Han", themselves replete with hotels, restaurants, and the weekend or summer homes of true city folk from Liège. You then enter Durbuy along the **Rue Comte Theodule d'Ursel,** which immediately becomes a "flyover" spanning the so-called "Grand Place" and parking lots of the "new" portion of the town. On most weekends and in July and August, you'll be asked to descend immediately to those parking lots, and to drive no further into the winding streets of the "old city."

The River Ourthe runs alongside the north edge of town, providing the "city" with its official name, "Durbuy S/Ourthe" (Durbuy-on-the-Ourthe). The castle, dating from the 11th century, but now almost entirely composed of 19th century elements, is found along the river (it can be visited from 11 to 5 for 50 francs, but not on the fourth weekend of each month). On the south side of town, a low but almost vertical mountain rises from the area of the archery range ("tir à l'arc"), and the town itself is almost entirely surrounded by mountains and hills forming the Valley of the Ourthe. The compressed mass of structures and buildings along the winding streets of the old "city" are almost entirely 17th and 18th century in construction, but some go back earlier than that. Students of architecture marvel at the aesthetic consistency, and pleasant, peaceful flavor, of the small urban mass, and several modern city designers have sought to reproduce the same approach in contemporary forms. It is obvious that the absence of automobiles—that scourge of modern life—has much to do with the attractive and workable quality of this type of "city".

DAYS AND NIGHTS OF DURBUY: What do you do in Durbuy? First you wind down. You check into a charming hotel looking out onto a peaceful garden, and you read, relax, and doze. You browse through the quaint, narrow streets, window-shopping at the trendy boutiques, the numerous stores of antiques, the chi-chi (and usually expensive) establishments of all sorts. You visit the "jam factory". You shoot arrows on the archery range (6 for 60 francs—$1.67). You eat magnificent meals, and then stroll after lunch or dinner along the banks of the Ourthe. But mainly, you make hikes and walking excursions into the hills and forests of the Ardennes, communing with natural forces, devouring visual delights, clearing the lungs and the mind.

THE QUIET HOTELS OF DURBUY: When it's 5 p.m. and the tour buses have departed, and all remaining visitors are simply preparing for a memorable evening meal, silence descends over Durbuy, and people reflect on how favored they are to be staying overnight (the great majority of visitors simply come in for the day, or for a three-hour dinner). They sleep, as it were, in another century, in historic structures well furnished and maintained. The premier establishment is Maurice Cardinael's **Hotel Cardinal** in the old city (you won't need an address; phone 086/21-10-88) surrounded by small grounds. A member of the exclusive "Relais du Silence" association of particularly distinguished country lodges, it consists of eight magnificently-equipped, multi-room apartments looking out onto trees and birds singing, with every fine element of soap, linen, towels that the best of Brussels' shops could provide, and with its refrigerator already stocked with small tins of patés, cheeses, breads, beverages. When you go out for even a few minutes, an unobserved servant sneaks in and sets the table for a late snack! Remarkably luxurious, it nevertheless charges only 3200 francs ($89) to 4200 francs ($117) per apartment, per night, plus 200 francs ($5.55) per person for breakfast, a price value for quality so high. The 14-room **Residence le Vieux Durbuy** (086/21-10-88), under the same management, in a similar, isolated, old city setting, again birds singing outside your window, takes the overflow at rates of only 2200 francs ($61) for a twin-bedded room with private bath and breakfast, service included. The 9-room **Hotel du Prevôt** at the Rue des Récollectines (phone 086/21-28-68) in the old city, seems to me of equal desirability, a quiet and tastefully furnished hotel, but charges only 1800 francs ($50) for a double room with private bath and two breakfasts. For the most cost-conscious of visitors to the old city, the 7-room **Le Clos des Recollets,** on the Rue de la Prévôté (phone 086/12-12-71), offers rooms with and without private bath, charging 1400 francs ($39) for a double with bath, 1200 francs ($33) without, breakfast for two included. As you'd expect, Friday and Saturday nights are the most heavily booked at these old city hotels, as they are throughout Durbuy and vicinity.

The big, lodge-like building on the main street leading (in 50 yards) to the edge of the old city, is the **Hostellerie le Sanglier des Ardennes,** Rue Comte T. d'Ursel (phone 086/21-10-88), whose ground floor houses the renowned restaurant of the same name. Above its lounge of flower-designed chintz-cloth chairs and coffee tables piled high with well-thumbed magazines are 22 comfortable, old fashioned rooms, of which half look out on the swift-flowing waters of the River Ourthe, directly behind the hotel. Double rooms with private bath and continental breakfast are 2200 francs ($61) a night, while savings of about $10 per double are available to those who take the several doubles without private bath, using facilities "down the hall".

The other "big" hotel of Durbuy is the 29-room **Hotel des Roches,** on the Grand Place (086/21-11-68), above a large restaurant of the same name. Though an attractive establishment with reasonable charges—3000 francs ($83) for a double with bath and breakfast—and more modern (though in old stone) than its colleagues in the "old city", its setting on the car-filled square can't be compared with the dream-like situation of the others. The 20-room **Hotel Esplanade,** on the Grand Place (phone 086/21-16-81), again above a restaurant of the same name, is a still less expensive alternative, charging 1300 francs ($36) for a double with private bath and two breakfasts.

The "city's" cheapest hotel (with its cheapest restaurant; see below) is the 8-room **Auberge du Marcassin,** on the Rue Comte Theodule d'Ursel (phone 086/21-10-26), diagonally opposite

"Le Sanglier des Ardennes". It charges only 875 francs ($24) for a double room, breakfast, service and tax included!

THE GRAND CUISINE OF DURBUY: One establishment —Maurice Cardinael's **"Le Sanglier des Ardennes"** on the ground floor of the less important hotel bearing that name— dominates all others. Here is a serious, disciplined, culinary shrine ruled by a bearded, young chef who's given the acclaim of a movie star in Belgium. When Belgium recently sent representatives of its most important industries to Japan, Maurice Cardinael was included on the delegation. Primarily classic, but lightened just a bit by the "nouvelle cuisine", his appetizers include such imaginative combinations as "les filets de truites grillé"—three lightly-grilled, lemon-flavored strips of just-caught trout on a bed of hot, marinated lettuce, the taste subtle and superb (500 francs, $13.88). His main courses average only 600 francs ($17), such as "coquelet à l'estragon" (a deliciously tender, lightly-flavored guinea hen with tarragon and wild rice, the latter like none you've ever tasted). The wine is as little as 400 francs ($11.11) for a half bottle, from a wine cellar as extensive as any in the Ardennes (I visited it after my most recent visit, and ruined a 40-year-old, dust-encrusted bottle by incautiously turning it in its rack). And one can easily have three à la carte courses for $30, including wine; or a special five-course "menu gastronomique" for 1700 francs ($47) plus wine, or a once-in-a-lifetime, seven-course, 20th anniversary (of the restaurant) "menu gastronomique" *including* a different glass of wine with each course, for 2750 francs ($76) per person: salmon "gelée", warm goose liver, baby lobster with drawn butter, sweetbreads with herbs, roast pigeon in sage, chèvre cheese of Durbuy, fruit platter and strawberry tart. You must phone first for reservations (086/21-10-88), and should note that the restaurant (but not the hotel) on the Rue Comte Theodule d'Ursel is closed on Thursdays, and rarely available (unless you've booked well in advance) on Saturdays in season.

Diagonally opposite the mini-golf course on the south edge of the old city, the restaurant **Le Moulin** is a picturesque, two-story, stone farm structure of the 14th century—oldest building in Durbuy—where guests dine on the second floor, amid rustic, mill-style decor. It attracts a chic crowd, who are immediately served a free glass of raspberry-flavored champagne and "amuse-gueules" (tid-bits) as they sit down. A choice of seven different appetizers—assorted sea foods, fish paté, scallops, goose liver in port wine jelly, among them—are priced at 500 to 550 francs ($13.88 to $15.27), six main courses—grilled duckling with fresh spinach salad doused in strawberry vinegar, rare filet mignon with fricassee of field mushrooms in cream of shallots sauce, saddle of hare in heavy cream, with Swiss-fried potatoes, among them —are uniformly 500 francs ($13.88), and cheese and a choice of dessert are offered at no extra charge! With a $10 bottle of wine for two persons, your total meal will come to $40 per person, and I'd choose Le Moulin as a lower priced alternative to Le Sanglier des Ardennes, or if you can't obtain a table at the latter.

Your less costly meals should be sought at the ground floor restaurants of the hotels on the more modern Grand Place at the side of the old city. There, the **Hotel des Roches** offers a three-course "menu", service included, for 950 francs ($26), while the big **L'Hacienda,** also on the square, offers considerably cheaper à la carte selections priced at only 60 francs ($1.66) for soup, 300 francs ($8.33) for grilled steak and potatoes, 275 francs ($7.63) for half-a-roast-chicken and french fries. And consider the "boulets"—two giant, heavy, flour dumplings doused in a brown sauce/gravy, for only 180 francs ($5). With a glass of red wine, they make a filling refreshing meal at L'Hacienda.

Cheapest, three-course meals in town are served at the **Auberge du Marcassin,** diagonally opposite Le Sanglier des Ardennes on the Rue Comte Theodule d'Ursel: 325 francs ($9) for one that includes side of pork as the main course, a more elaborate variety for 600 francs ($17). Ordered à la carte, most appetizers here are only 140, 170 or 190 francs ($3.88, $4.72 or $5.27), most main meat courses garnished with vegetables 275, 300, or 440 francs ($7.63, $8.33 or $12.22). As you will have noted, hotel rooms in Durbuy are quite remarkably low-priced, but only L'Hacienda and Auberge du Marcassin are correspondingly cheap for meals; to eat for less, you'll have to leave the chic, and often artsy-craftsy, confines of Durbuy for the more ordinary life of the neighboring villages.

DEEPER INTO THE ARDENNES: Spa and Durbuy, so close to Liège, are only hors d'oeuvres in the feast of sights and experiences offered by the Ardennes. The tourist with a car will now push further south to the Valley of the Semois near the border of France, and to the historic castle-town of Bouillon and the great abbey-monastery of Orval. In Belgium, where all distances are short, they lie only 150 and 160 kilometers from Liège, only 160 and 170 kilometers from Brussels.

CHAPTER XIII

HISTORIC GEMS OF THE ARDENNES: BOUILLON AND ORVAL

□ □ □

Center of the First Crusade, Cockpit of Religious Conflict

The setting may be a vast primeval forest, of small villages alongside rushing mountain streams, but the most remarkable political upheavals, philosophic disputes, social struggles, have been played out in the Ardennes! If you will travel with us now to Belgium's southernmost border with France, two hours by car from either Brussels or Liège, we will promise you a spine-tingling glimpse of important history, yet all of it viewed in an area of Tyrolean-like scenery, perfumed air, charming country inns, richly satisfying beer, and once-in-a-lifetime meals!

BOUILLON

In the lushly-green valley of the **River Semois,** of all things, the scene suddenly shifts to a time hundreds of years before the age of the Gothic Cathedrals or the painting of the Holy Lamb. We are, instead, in a city founded in the days of Charlemagne, viewing a Feudal castle of the 10th and 11th centuries, a museum of the early Middle Ages. The mists of time roll back. Before us now are visions of lords and serfs, of knights in armor on horses armored too, of fortresses besieged by stone-throwing catapults on wooden towers rolled to their crenellated walls. Bouillon brings us those images with astonishing force—not simply through its mammoth, military castle on heights of stone that rise straight up from the center of the city, but from a little known, somewhat neglected, but absolutely chilling museum near the entrance to that castle, which tells of life in the year 1000, and 1100, and relates the story of a key Walloon figure of those times who led the First Crusade. His story is essential to the enjoyment of Bouillon:

GODFREY OF BOUILLON (BORN 1060, DIED 1100):

He was the next to the oldest son of a French count and "Ida of Ardennes"—a young man of uncertain prospects raised to be a Knight. At the age of seven (if his tale followed the traditional course of knighthood), he becomes a page boy in the home of another seigneur, lives off scraps from the family's table, grooms the horses, learns to wield a sword and shield, graduates to jousts atop a charging steed, is put to sleep by tales of chivalrous deeds, prays and fasts throughout the night on the eve of his manhood, and is dubbed a holy Knight—at the age of sixteen. Almost simultaneously, his childless uncle, Godfrey the Barbu (the bearded one), Duke of Lower Lotharingia (consisting mainly of the Province of Lorraine in France and the Duchy of Bouillon in what later became Belgium) bequeaths to him the Duchy of Bouillon, its magnificent castle, and numerous neighboring estates and villages. He is now "Godfrey of Bouillon". Within months, other powerful lords aided by Pope Gregory VII descend on Bouillon to wrest it away from its youthful chief. Besieged for several weeks in his great castle on the rocky heights, Godfrey proves a superb strategist, defeats them all. He immediately offers his troops and services to his own liege lord, the Pope-opposing Emperor of Germany, Henry IV. The latter is the man who, at Canossa, had done penance to the Pope while standing barefoot and barely dressed in the snow. Now, accompanied (among others) by the young Duke of Bouillon and his troops of Bouillon, Henry marches on Rome and deposes Pope Gregory. Godfrey, heaped with honors, an acknowledged military leader, returns to Bouillon and awaits the next call. It is not long in coming.

The call for crusade

From the Holyland, now held by the Seljuk Turks, a Christian monk named Peter the Hermit returns to tell of the sufferings of the Christian population in Jerusalem. A charismatic new French Pope, Urban II, preaches to thousands at Clermont that Western Europe must recover the Sacred City. He sets the date—August 15, 1096—when the Knights of Christ must march. "Deus lo Volt!" (God wills it!) roars back the frenzied crowd. And in Bouillon, Godfrey hurls himself into action. From the Prince-Bishop of nearby Liège, he obtains a three-year mortgage on his Duchy, castle and lands, acquiring the funds (1300 pounds of silver, three pounds of gold) with which to finance an army for the great march. (He counts on repaying the loan with riches of the Middle East.) He obtains another 100,000 "écus" by selling freedom to the residents of the city of Metz (which he owns). An imposingly tall figure made more impressive by obvious piety and towering military reputation, he also possesses that special talent common to many Belgians of today: he is multi-lingual (in French, German and Dutch)! Whether it was this Belgian attribute that dictated his selection to head an international army, we will never know. But Godfrey of Bouillon—Bouillon!—is chosen to lead the First Crusade.

A courtly knight. In gleaming armor covered by a tunic of pristine white linen bearing a Red Cross. From Bouillon, from Blois, from Toulouse and from Palermo, other such knights and their armies (among them, Baudoin of Brussels, Jean of Namur, barons from Tournai, Liège and Brabant) converge first at Constantinople, and then, suffering indescribable hardship and losses over three ensuing years of struggle, they take Antioch, gateway to Jerusalem. Godfrey distinguishes himself by cutting a Muslim in half, at the waist, with a mighty swipe of his razor-sharp sword. Of the original army of 600,000, less than 50,000 survive to assault the walls of Jerusalem with their battering rams, catapults, buckets of fire. After three days of battle, Godfrey, followed by his brother Baudoin, leaps the wall crying "Deus lo Volt!" On the 25th of July, 1099, Jerusalem is taken, its Moslem and Jewish population put to the sword, and Godfrey—having refused the title, "King of Jerusalem"—is named "Protector of the Holy Sepulcher", in which he now kneels, tearfully, for a prayer of thanksgiving. A year later, consolidating the victory in Syria, he dies of a draught of poisoned cider, allegedly proffered him by the Emir of Caesarea. He is buried in the "Church of the Holy Sepulcher", under an almost-rhyming quatrain flatly naming him as the architect of victory: "Ici repose Godefroy—Le célèbre duc de Bouillon—Qui conquit cet terre au culte chretien—Que son ame regne avec le Christ—Amen" (Here lies Godfrey, celebrated Duke of Bouillon, who conquered this land for Christianity. May his soul rest with Christ, Amen).

In the sorrow of the moment, no one seems to notice that the mortgage is in default. In Liège, the priestly holder of the pledge calls the loan! And Bouillon quietly passes into the hands of the Prince-Bishops of Liège, there to remain for the next 500 years.

The Museum "Godfrey of Bouillon"

Now we walk into history. At the start of the esplanade leading to the great castle of Godfrey of Bouillon, high over-looking Bouillon, are multiple buildings housing two museums, of which the first celebrates the era and deeds of Godfrey, Duke of Bouillon. It is a thousandth the size of the Tower of London, yet it conveys much of the emotional impact of far larger structures in the latter. And though nominally devoted to Godfrey, clearly it is a much broader, and virtually unique, Museum of the Crusades. "En 1096" (In 1096), says a large and chilling inscription at the entrance, "au cri de 'Deus Lo Volt" (to the cry of "God Wills It!"), "les peuples de l'Occident" (the people of the West) "se mirent en marche vers Jerusalem" (set off for Jerusalem!). There follows, on two floors, remarkable artifacts of that millenium year—coats of mail, axes, swords, maces and armor, copper bas reliefs of 11th-century scenes, life-sized effigies of early medieval figures, illuminated manuscripts devoted to the Crusades; copies of later parchment Papal "bulls" granting indulgences to those who did the Church's work; and equally important, large blow-ups, maps and models explaining and instructing in the events of that important stage of European history. There are mock-ups of the catapults, battering rams and other assault machines used against the walls of a dozen cities of Islam; models and paintings of armor-clad knights juxtaposed against the cloth-clad Turks; examples of Eastern Art and practices at the time of the Crusades which, when brought to Western Europe, softened the harsh, Frank-ish life of the times; giant maps showing invasion routes, stages of the advance against both Byzantine and Moslem cities; a detailed model of the Castle of Godfrey of Bouillon (which you soon will be seeing) showing phases of its construction; and there are, in particular, against the staircase linking the two floors of display rooms, lighted transparencies of 13th-century illustrations that thrilled the populace of medieval Europe with epics of the grand movement, each bearing a tabloid-style, yet utterly authentic, Latin "headline": Pope Urban II Preaches the Crusade—Pierre the Hermit, the March of the Poor—Godfrey Crosses the Ocean—Battle of Constantinople!—Baudoin Takes Leave of His Brother, Godfrey—The Taking of Thrace!—The Battle of Antioch—Bohemond Takes Antioch by Assault—Discovery of the Holy Lance!—Miracle at the Mount of Olives—Godfrey Goes Beyond the Jordan—Baudoin Comes to Jerusalem—The Coronation of Baudoin".

Most of what we've cited is on the upper floor of the museum. Downstairs are two relatively unimportant rooms on more modern times, and two other final rooms that hold highly significant treasures: a recently-unearthed Paleo-Christian shrine of the 7th century; a 13th-century statue from the nearby Abbey of Orval; an interesting Papal Bull of Pope John XXII granting a remission from sin to those volunteers of Bouillon who would build its Church of St. Peter. But most fascinating is the upstairs area that tells of the European march to the Middle East, and of the Christian communities and states they founded or strengthened there. You may wonder whether it was from here, from tiny, medieval Bouillon, that the seeds were planted of the present Christian-Moslem conflict in Lebanon. The Museum of Godfrey of Bouillon is open daily from April 1 to November 1, from 9 a.m. to 6:30 p.m., for an admission charge of 60 francs ($1.66) to adults, 30 francs for children. In July and August, to accommodate the demand, hours are extended until 7:30 p.m.

The Castle of Godfrey of Bouillon

Though there's yet a second worthy museum ("Le Musée Ducal") only steps away from Godfrey's, it's appropriate at this point that we immediately turn to the great **Castle of Godfrey of Bouillon** ("Le Chateau Fort", or military castle) at the end of the high plateau on which the museums sit. It is the key sight, heavily visited, of Bouillon, and claimed by the city's tourist board to be "le plus ancien vestige de la Féodalité en Belgique" (the oldest vestige of feudalism in Belgium). While that assertion is strongly arguable, the castle is truly thought to date from the 8th century, and is definitely mentioned in literature of the 10th. Note how it commands a clear view of the nearby French border, as if it was built to watch movements from the important French city of Sedan, just 15 kilometers away. The first sight of it is tingling. It soars from the long, thin spine of an almost vertical hill flanked on both sides by the rushing River Semois, and by the charming town of Bouillon, below. Surely as Godfrey lay dying in Syria, his last thoughts must have been of this deep, green, Eden-like valley of the Semois, of the River snaking a sharp "U" around his towering castle, of the thickly-matted forests on the surrounding hills.

Note, as you approach the castle, how you walk over two successive wooden bridges flung over gaping precipices. Once these were movable drawbridges, with counterweights, designed to be raised at the first sign of attack. Below, the rock has been worked in such a way as to prevent ladders from being placed there by invading troops. You first enter the immense, vaulted "Salle de Turenne" (Room of Turenne) with its imposing chimney/fireplace in white stone. You follow a 50-meter-long, curved corridor to the 11th century "Salle Primitive" commanding the defense of the second drawbridge. You enter the "Salle Godefroid de Bouillon" with its chilling sight of a mounted and armored Godfrey seated on a horse also covered with armor, the knight grasping a 12-foot lance, the wall behind him adorned with heraldic shields of the Duchy of Bouillon. Inlaid into the stone floor is a giant wooden cross worn by time. (Professors have ransacked whole libraries, in vain, to determine its origin.) You pass through the "Cour d'Honneur", then into the torture room with its "oubliette" for disposing of prisoners, a cellar for food and ammunition, a prison closed by three consecutive doors, with but a tiny opening for discerning whether it is day or night, then proceed along a corridor going to the one-hundred-square-meter cistern containing the castle's water supply (which was in contact, many believe, with an underground source of water). Except for an occasional weapon, or racks or screws in the room of torture, most of these dank chambers are today empty; your imagination must furnish them. Wherever you see stairs of stone, climb them; your objective is the highest point of the Castle, the "Tour d'Autriche" (Tower of Austria), with its eagles' nest affording a clear view of the bulk of the Castle behind, the town of Bouillon below. The flag of Belgium flies here. Nearby, cut into rock, is the "Fauteuil Godefroid" (Armchair of Godfrey). Who sits in it will marry within the year.

The Castle of Godfrey of Bouillon ("Le Chateau Fort") is open from 9 a.m. to 6 p.m., daily from April through November, daily except Mondays and Tuesdays in December, January and February. Admission is 60 francs ($1.67) for adults, 50 francs ($1.39) for children.

THE POST-GODFREY ERA—IN THE "DUCAL MUSEUM": Time marches on. Upon the very same castle heights, at the start of the esplanade leading to the great Chateau, and adjoin-

ing the Museum of Godfrey, is now the **"Musée Ducal"** (Museum of the Duchy of Bouillon) dealing with a later era fully as troubled and turbulent as Godfrey's. You will savor its exhibits best by first reviewing that later history of Bouillon. Start by recalling that upon Godfrey's death in 1100, the Prince-Bishops of Liège "called" the awesome mortgage and assumed ownership of the entire Duchy of Bouillon. They ruled it until the late 1500s, acting through governors who sometimes did, and sometimes didn't, obey orders. Again and again throughout that time, other powerful seigneurs, pretenders, usurpers, challenged the absentee owners from Liège, besieged the castle, fought bloody battles on the esplanade leading to it, repeatedly demolished the city of Bouillon.

Great dramas of medieval politics were played out here. One colorful siege, among many, lasted for forty days, caused starvation within the Castle. To show their disdain, to feign that they had supplies aplenty, the defenders hurled a live pig over the walls. From Liège, the Prince-Bishop sends a reliquary of the bones of St. Lambert to give heart to his army; they prevail. Another episode, in 1380: two ecclesiastical parties contend over the post of Prince-Bishop in Liège. They fight in Bouillon. One wins and reduces the town of Bouillon to ashes. Two years later, he loses and *his* home city is reduced to ashes. 1480: a young nobleman named William de la Marck is expelled from court for a deed of violence, becomes deranged, forms a Robin-Hood-style army of bandits in the great forest of the Ardennes, causes such havoc that he becomes known as "Le Sanglier des Ardennes" (The Wild Boar of the Ardennes, title of Durbuy's famous restaurant of the same name), advances on Liège with his bandit army bearing images of a boar on their right shoulders, himself murders the then-Prince-Bishop of Liège (Louis of Bourbon) with an axe, requires that his brother be given the Duchy of Bouillon. Though the despotic "Wild Boar" is later executed, his brother Robert, supported by the King of France, holds on tenaciously to Bouillon. But his own son, Robert II, turns lunatic. In 1521, in the name of the 5,000-man army of the Duchy of Bouillon—Bouillon!—he declares war on the Hapsburg Emperor Charles V. The riposte of Charles is quite terrible. He hurls the troops of Bouillon over the walls of the Castle to their deaths in the rushing waters of the Semois below, dismantles large portions of the Castle, and returns Bouillon to the Prince-Bishops of Liège. If those stones could talk!

In the late 1500's, Bouillon passes from the ecclesiastics of Liège to a noble French family, de la Tour de l'Auvergne. Gradually, it comes under the effective control of Louis XIV, who in 1680 sends his great military architect, Vauban, to rebuild the castle to its former eminence. A plaque on the archway beyond the second drawbridge—be sure to see it—expresses the "reconaissance éternelle" (eternal gratitude) of Henri de la Tour d'Auvergne to the great Sun King.

Throughout most of the 1700's, the Duchy of Bouillon sleeps peacefully under the benevolent rule of the largely absent de la Tour d'Auvergnes. But beneath the surface there is intellectual ferment that makes a true bubbling bouillon out of Bouillon. A minor French author named Pierre Rousseau (1716–85) moves to Bouillon in 1760, where he becomes a much greater printer and publisher of the works of the French "philosophes" and "encyclopédistes". Because their books attack the established order, they cannot be published in France, and it is little Bouillon, in the depths of the Ardennes, that becomes the publishing capital for the emerging Revolution. In the Ducal Museum, you will see the epochal books and broadsides issued by Pierre Rousseau, all bearing elaborate frontispieces identifying them as coming from "L'Imprimerie (Printing Shop) de Bouillon". You will also see copies of "La Revue Encyclopédique", one of the world's first newspapers, published in Bouillon by Pierre Rousseau. Naturally, these revolutionary ideas also have an impact on Bouillon. When the French Revolution occurs, the people of Bouillon instantly chafe over the fact that they are governed by a particularly dissolute Duke, a certain Godfrey Charles Henry de la Tour d'Auvergne pursuing the life of a Parisian boulevardier; he is scarcely ever seen in Bouillon. Though he writes sympathetically to the civic assembly of Bouillon, they respond that they are fed up with the spectacle of "des hommes commandant aux hommes pour satisfaire leurs caprices" (men lording it over other men to satisfy their whims). By early 1794, they have decided to break with the Duke and create an independent republic, La Nation Bouillonaise! And the tiny new country then proceeds to issue laws and proclamations—you will see them in the Ducal Museum —that rival in lofty phrase and deed those of its revolutionary neighbor, France. Feudalism is abolished; all "nobles, procureurs et prêtres" (noblemen, lawyers and priests) expelled from their positions; all Augustins and other foreign religious orders suppressed, their convents and monasteries sacked; the power of the aristocracy is replaced by that of the people; "la Liberté et l'Egalité" are proclaimed to be the new basis of society. "Le Peuple Bouillonais", says their declaration, "ont juré de vivre libre ou de mourir" (The people of Bouillon have resolved to live free or to die!).

An independent nation. But it was not to last. In 1795, the revolutionary government in Paris annexes little Bouillon to

France. And in 1815, following the defeat of Napoleon, the Congress of Vienna awards Bouillon to the Netherlands, from which it then becomes a part of Belgium in 1830. The proud, little Duchy, with its nearly-independent Duke, its pretention to being a Country, fades into history.

Knowing all this may aid your enjoyment of the Ducal Museum, may bring it alive and vibrant, as you pass exhibits of Bouillon from the 16th through the early 19th centuries. Though a part of the museum is "folkloric" and deals with everyday life (the building itself is a typically bourgeois house of the 18th century), the more important sections are historic, and the most fascinating of these are the editions of Voltaire and de la Fontaine printed by the "underground" press of Bouillon. What a role it played on the European stage! What a tormented history of invasion, occupation, pillage and sack—like Belgium itself! Yet what glorious achievements of intellect and culture! The Ducal Museum maintains the same hours as the Museum of Godfrey of Bouillon, and the 60-franc admission at one, admits you also to the other.

ENJOYING THE VALLEY OF THE SEMOIS: The other principal distractions of Bouillon are "promenades"—guided walks through its remarkable scenery—or drives through it, stopping at look-out points ("points de vue") for panoramas of awesome hills and river valleys. It can never be sufficiently stressed that this is one of the most scenic concentrated areas in all of Europe. The landscapes are like masterful paintings of hills and plateaus covered with lush greenery, the tiny villages found throughout are architecturally historic, free from commercial ugliness. You pass a partly-stone barn and realize it dates from the 17th century; you pause at an old cemetery set next to a mountain stream, and see headstones bearing dates and inscriptions of the 1600s. In the management and preservation of its natural environment, mainly due to an inspired forester, Jean-Etienne Hallet, Bouillon has set a standard for the rest of the world. And so proud is the city of its forest walks that it will provide you with a *free* guide to accompany groups of at least six persons who phone for that service a day in advance. Dial (061) 31-27-26 and ask for Monsieur Allard, or dial (061) 46-76-41 and ask for Madame Crasset. Both are members of the **Union St. Hubert Service Guide-Nature,** an example of that Belgian propensity to provide visitors with hospitality "on the house." What other country would do the same?

Making the same "promenades" or auto tours without a guide is done by simply picking up a walking map, "La Carte des Promenades du Grand Bouillon", for 60 francs ($1.67) at the tourist office in town ("Syndicat d'Initiative") or at the entrance to the Castle of Godfrey of Bouillon. Red lines bearing numbers are the routes to follow, and the numbers correspond with easily-spotted numbered signs along each road or path—not a single tourist has yet been lost. The broad red lines are for motorists; the narrow ones are the more interesting paths for hikers (some of the routes dating back for centuries, and recently discovered and re-opened by Mr. Hallet). If you do drive, you stop wherever you see the initials "P.V." ("point de vue"—look out points) and by walking in off the road at those points, you follow paths to magnificent vistas. Ninety-nine different routes are listed, each further designated as "F" (facile) for easy, "M" (moyen) for medium, "A" (accidenté) for hilly and uneven, "D" (difficile) for difficult, "A.D." (a déconseiller) for not recommended to easily frightened persons. Although the area's most spectacular view is at the hilly outcropping known as the "Tombeau du Geant" (Giant's Tomb) reached from the village of Ucimont north of Bouillon, I'd go there only by car, limiting the walking tours to "easy" itineraries 4, 5, 7 and 8 starting from the Pont de Liège (Liège Bridge) or Pont de France (French Bridge) in Bouillon itself. Other walks (including shorter ones) start from the Hideous Windmill ("Moulin Hideux"; see below) in nearby Noirefontaine, from Dohan, Les Hayons, Bellevaux, and other villages in the region of the "Moyenne Semois" immediately to the north and east of Bouillon. Each of the latter villages is itself a sightseeing attraction.

THE ENGINEER OF THE FORESTS: Walks like these didn't

simply happen. They are the work, in large part, of the proud, Belgian forest ranger earlier named, M. Jean-Etienne Hallet, whose family has lived here for centuries in a huge, stone chalet that makes a rather affluent country squire out of the 40-ish Monsieur Hallet. Yet every morning he puts on the heavy boots, green knickers, green flannel shirt and silver officer's bars of an official forester, and strides forth to protect the delicate, fragile "ecosystem" of the forest he loves. Large crews of workmen under his supervision clear underbrush, prune trees, create paths that channel tourists into limited areas protecting the forests from indiscriminate wanderings and damage; create clear fields of vision for the forest's many "P.V.'s" (points de vue), plant new trees, instruct visitors in the proper treatment of the forest, post signs and admonitions: "le bruit pollue" (noise pollutes), my own favorite. From early in this century, the city has tenaciously protected its forest from private developers, and the results are many thousands of acres of ethereal beauty preserved for all the people of Belgium, and not simply for a few wealthy owners of "second homes". Indeed, almost the entire Forest of Bouillon now belongs to the municipality of Bouillon, and income from the logging of dead trees is an important source of city revenues.

As you tour it, and especially as you thrill to the views from M. Hallet's favorite "P.V.'s" near Dohan, created or improved by him—"la Saurpire", "la Grande Dampirée", "le Rocher Lecomte"—think of the Engineer of the Forest, and of hundreds of other unsung figures throughout the world who fight to preserve our natural heritage. Here, their work has created a compelling reason for travel to the southernmost portion of the Belgian Ardennes.

LODGINGS AND MEALS: Food first. Though some are
maintained as separate establishments, the outstanding restaurants of Bouillon are those in hotels—and vice versa. And the leader by far is a country lodge spoken about in hushed awe, whose name is actually placed on maps of the region: **"Le Moulin Hideux"** (The Hideous Windmill), at 1 Route du Dohan (phone 061-46-70-15) on the outskirts of Noirefontaine, three kilometers from the center of Bouillon. This appears at first to be simply an elongated, brick, three-story farmhouse building, though an elegant one, set near a tiny lake in the very center of the forest, isolated, silent, surrounded by trees. But inside, in its 13 guest rooms, you discover the meaning of the term "in good taste". The soap in the bathrooms is by Jean Patou; little tubes of toothpaste are inconspicuously available; knitted caps of wool cover rolls of toilet paper; tiny candies are placed near your pillow; rooms (large and airy) look out onto gardens. Coming downstairs for dinner, you first sip aperitifs as you sink into the softness of leather armchairs scattered through a rustic lounge; you scan the leather-covered menu while doing so, place your order for dinner, and are only later gently invited to carry your drink into the dining room when the appetizer is ready. There you enjoy a classic French-Belgian meal, best begun with a plate of three fluffy "mousses de paté"—ham, beef, lamb—whipped into feathery clouds of meat having the texture and weight of cotton candy, then followed by other supreme concoctions of subtly-flavored soups, aromatic dishes of fish, celestial-tasting wild game from the forest. The prices are also stratospheric—figure on spending at least 2250 francs ($63) per person and often more, including your aperitif but not including wine. The rate for rooms is far more moderate: 4800 francs ($133) including breakfast for two, for a twin-bedded room with private bath. And breakfast includes marmalades and jellies of the Ardennes, spread on oven-warm rolls, that lift those prosaic food items to special heights. In this land of luxury country inns—and it is these, rather than in-city hotels, that are the par-

ticular glory of Belgium's lodging industry—the "Auberge du Moulin Hideux" occupies a commanding place. If the Hideous Windmill is full, and you're desirous of a similar breathtaking situation in the open grounds of the Ardennes Forest near Bouillon, try the **Hostellerie "Le Prieuré de Conques"** at 176 Route de Florenville (phone 061/41-14-17) in Herbeumont, 20 kilometers from Bouillon, along the banks of the Semois. Thirty-two hundred francs ($89) per double room with breakfast, but its restaurant obviously can't compare with that of the renowned Hideous Windmill. The **Hotel "Un Balcon en Foret"** (A Balcony on the Forest), at 120 Route d'Alle (phone 061/46-65-30)—quite literally arranged like a viewing balcony along the side of a hill—is a third such comfortable country lodging, this time in Rochehaut, less than 12 kilometers to the northeast of Bouillon. Its particularly tempting highlight is a heated indoor swimming pool. Twin rooms with bath and breakfast: from 2000 to 2800 francs ($56 to $78).

Back in the actual town of Bouillon, the hotel/restaurants are all in quaint, but unpretentious, 19th-century buildings just across the Semois from the hill of the Castle. The top-rated choice for both rooms and meals is the pleasant **"Aux Armes de Bouillon"**, at 9 Rue de la Station (phone 061/46-60-79), with flowered wallpaper throughout, copper pans hanging from brick fireplaces, velvet covered chairs, heavy flowered carpets—you perhaps get the picture! Remarkably, there's also a heated indoor swimming pool (to 27 degrees centigrade), a sauna and solarium, in this 65-room "hostellerie", yet rates (with breakfast and various supplements included) are only 2600 francs ($72) per twin room with bath. A high-standard restaurant, where three-course "menus" range from as little as 750 francs ($21) to as much as 1750 ($49), serves classic dishes prepared by the hotel's much-decorated, heavily-awarded chef, Guy van Hal, a "maitre rotisseur", a "chevalier du Tastevin"! Cheaper, almost as pleasant, are the 45-room **Hotel de la Semois**, at 44 Rue du College (phone 061/46-60-27) (1680 francs ($47), per twin room with bath); the attractive, 20-room **Hotel Central "Au Duc de Bouillon"**, at 2 Rue des Hautes-Voies (phone 061/46-61-38) (1700 francs, $47, per twin with bath); and the 73-room **Hotel de la Poste**, at 1 Place Saint Arnould (phone 061/46-65-06) (2050 francs ($57), per twin with bath). At the last named, table d'hote meals of simple, home-style dishes, are priced as low as 500 francs ($14). Bouillon is so small, its hotels so clustered, that you'll scarcely need the addresses given above. A particular value for our most cost-conscious readers: the 40 rooms without private bath at the big **Hotel Panorama**, high up on the hill overlooking the Tyrolean-setting of Bouillon, at 25 Rue "Au-

Dessus de la Ville" (phone 061/46-61-38); those rooms rent for as little as 1500 francs ($41.67) double, with two continental breakfasts included. And moderately-priced "menus" are had down the street in the restaurants of the **Hotel Tyrol** at 23 Rue "Au-Dessus de la Ville" (for about 500 francs, $14) and **Hotel "Le Gai Repos—Chez Patate"**, at 4 Rue "Au-Dessus de la Ville" (for as little as 600 francs, $17, although they can run considerably higher). The youth hostel, accepting people of all ages, is the **Centrale Wallonne**, at 16 Chemin du Christ (phone 061/46-62-26).

A BOUILLON OF MISCELLANY: Trains don't service Bouillon (although buses do), and a car is the preferred mode of travel; with one, you can drive to the hilltop chateau ruins of **Herbeumont**, 20 kilometers from Bouillon. This is a 12th-century castle destroyed by soldiers of Louis XIV, where it's strangely affecting to clamber over the remaining walls and floors of a once-great structure dominating the countryside for miles around. As you peer into the ancient cistern, scrape dirt away from the floor of a former dining room, discern a fragmented, Romanesque arch, you feel like an archaeologist—and indeed, imagine what further excavations could reveal here! . . . The River Semois, as it loops around Bouillon, is like a sharply compressed and upside-down "U" whose shape could have been chosen by providence to frame the magnificent "chateau fort". The buildings of the town are squeezed on both sides of the eastern leg of the "U". . . . The chief crop of the valley of the Semois? Tobacco. The chief recreational activity (apart from hiking and eating)? Fishing in the Semois itself. Stop in first at the Tourist Office ("Syndicat d'Initiative") for a 300-franc ($8.33) permit. . . . Though the story of Godfrey is a stirring one, it is darkened, for many, by the ugly excesses of his troops. As they moved, successively, through European, Byzantine and Islamic cities, the crusaders murdered, pillaged, raped and stole, herded whole communities of Jews into synagogues and burned them alive, later waded knee-deep through blood of the "Saracens" (read: muslims) they slaughtered in Jerusalem. Some zealots joined the crusaders because local preachers had promised them "plenary indulgences": direct admission to heaven without first passing through purgatory. The analogy to current-day religious fanaticism in Iran and the Middle East is startling. Through it all rode a pious Godfrey, the "perfect, gentle knight". . . . Other easy car excursions from Bouillon: to forts of the Maginot Line of World War II fame, in La Ferte, France (40 kilometers); to the "Chateau Fort" of Sedan, France (25 kilometers); to the Grottoes of Han (50 kilometers to the north); to Bastogne and its war museum and memorial (60 kilometers to the east); but especially to Orval, final stop on our tour of the mighty Ardennes.

ON TO ORVAL: From Bouillon, an excellent road leads in 20 kilometers to a country village (and ski center) called Florenville, and 8 kilometers from there is the celebrated **Abbey,** or **Monastery of Orval.** In this giant complex, set against low, forested mountains, of church building, sweeping gardens, pilgrims' retreat, housing quarter, medieval ruins, museum and shop, brewery, and more, only 40 monks live. Yet for 900 years, tiny bands of men such as these, other-worldly mystics, have exercised an influence great beyond their numbers over the life and development of the Roman Catholic church.

THE GREAT MONASTERY OF ORVAL

Every day of the week, every week of the year, throughout their entire lives, they observe the liturgical hours: Matins, Lauds, Prime, Terce, Sext, Nones, Vespers, Compline.

Matins. At 3:30 a.m., in total darkness, they arise in their cells and hurry to the Church to intone the Psalms, the Scripture, the "Te Deum" with which they await the coming of a new day.

Lauds. At 6 a.m., having prayed for an hour and strolled for an hour in the still-dark gardens of the cloister, in silent meditation, they return to their choir stalls to resume the chanting of psalms, the singing of hymns, the recital of the Gospel.

Prime. Their prayers continue till that moment, between 7 and 7:30 a.m., when light filters through the colored windows of the lofty church, and each day, as they tell it, they experience radiant joy, an almost ineffable calm and security, at the approach of another dawn.

Terce. Sext. Nones. Throughout the day, they labor in the fields, or in the "scriptorium" (writing room) or library of the Abbey buildings, or in its famed brewery, stopping briefly for the three daytime "offices"—the recital of short prayers—designated above.

Vespers. At 5:30 p.m., they take their dinner at two long marble tables—a simple meal of vegetables and bread—as one of their number reads aloud from the Holy Gospel.

Compline. At 7 p.m., they step again to the Church for one last fervent session of prayer ending in the *Salve Regina* to the Virgin Mary. By 8 p.m., they have returned to their simple cells and are asleep.

As Trappist monks, they do not speak to one another unless the demands of work require it, but they will quite readily converse with visitors or outsiders in those one or two areas on the monastery grounds (see below) where contact can be had. And although they brew one of the world's most acclaimed beers, "Orval", they drink water with their meals, and rarely taste their own creation.

In the colorful, Catholic land of Belgium, there are six major Trappist orders, and numerous monasteries and convents that maintain the 1300-year monastic tradition of Western Europe. But it is primarily in Orval that a visitor can gain at least a partial look, however guarded and limited, at this strange way of life, so very remote from our own personal experience.

THE BEGINNINGS OF ORVAL—AND ITS NEAR-DESTRUCTION: Early in the life of the Church, monastic orders arose of men and women anxious to escape what they considered its worldly deficiencies, to reform its abuses, to consecrate their own lives with an almost inhuman passion and intensity. By the mid-500s, a large number of them had organized their communities according to the stern "Rule" of St. Benedict, a detailed prescription of practices stressing self-imposed poverty, strict obedience to the Abbot of each order, a constant application to manual labor. In later years, some monasteries proceeded to make a mockery of the Rule, became rich, luxury-loving and indolent. Others angrily condemned violations of the Rule, and led great reforming efforts—of which the Cluniac movement of the 900s, from the Monastery of Cluny in the Burgundy region of France, is a prime example. But regardless of the ebbs and flows, these periodic alternations between idealism and baser urges, the monastic orders of Western Europe were continual seedbeds of important theologic developments. In their chapter houses occurred the most vital religious debates of the early Middle Ages. From their monks' cells emerged the missionaries that were to convert entire continents. In their "scriptoriums", classic manuscripts were laboriously copied by monks performing their obligation of manual labor—and thereby the knowledge of the Roman and Greek civilizations, the light of learning, was preserved.

In the 1100s, the particularly important "Cistercian reform" emerged from the Abbey of Citeaux (hence, "Cistercian") near Dijon in France—and it is from there that we pick up the story of Orval. Reacting to increasing corruption and worldliness in the other Benedictine orders, the Cistercians placed their monasteries in the midst of great forests far from the taints of civilization. They stressed austerity in church decoration, church clothing, liturgy and practices, placed a renewed emphasis on hard manual labor for all monks. And they were a proselytizing, organizing, expansive breed who founded more than 300 abbeys (monasteries and convents) in the first half of the twelfth century. One of them was Orval. It occupied the site of a Chapter House founded in 1070 by Benedictine monks coming from far-off Calabria. When they later abandoned the site in 1110 for unexplained reasons, the Cistercians moved in and created an institution of such size and scope as to forcefully impress the medieval world. Over the next 700 years, Orval's religious influence over hundreds of surrounding towns and churches was immense, and the exhibits in its underground museum—which you soon will be visiting—confirm its importance in the theological world. Among other things, Orval was a particular leader in the Trappist reforms of the Cistercian order in the late 1600s (originally emanating from the Abbey of La Trappe), which stressed the importance of perpetual silence and strenuous fasts. It reached the height of its spiritual fame and material prosperity in the late 1700s.

And then: disaster, in the form of the French Revolution. In 1791, King Louis XVI escapes from Paris, headed—it is said—across the border to refuge in none other than the Abbey of Orval. He is stopped short in Varennes, arrested, returned to Paris, and Orval is indelibly tainted as anti-Revolution. For two successive years, war rages in the area as Austro-Prussian troops move back and forth over the border in their effort to overthrow the new French state. Aristocratic French emigrés seek shelter in Orval; French ire rises against the monastery. In 1793, a victorious French army under the youthful General Loison trains cannon and dynamite upon the vast Monastery of Orval and reduces it to jagged ruins. From their sanctuary in nearby Conques, the 37 surviving monks of the order are deported and dispersed. For 130 years, Orval exists only in ruins, yet it is visited by such illustrious figures as Victor Hugo, who stares entranced at its shattered walls.

In 1926: rebirth. Father Marie-Albert van der Cruyssen, a Belgian army officer grievously wounded after four terrifying years of near-continuous battles in World War I, becomes a Trappist monk. He conceives the idea of re-building and refounding Orval, and shoulders the 22-year task of financing and engineering the monastery complex. In 1948, Orval reopens, as grand and vital as ever.

YOUR VISIT TO ORVAL: Daily from 9 a.m. to noon and from 1 to 6 p.m., from April through October, and on Sunday mornings only during the remainder of the year, visitors are admitted to much of Orval for an admission charge of 60 francs ($1.67). Obviously you cannot go into the cloister where the monks live, or into the fields, workshops or brewery where they labor. But what you do see is well worth the trip.

You first enter upon the ruins of the medieval monastery destroyed by the French in 1793. If, by this time in Belgium, you have gained a liking for medieval church architecture, you will be enthralled by the original Romanesque basilica of the Abbey of Orval—even in ruins. Enough remains to reveal its total design and conception. You see the magnificent Rose Window (now bereft of its glass) of the former transept; you see long series of Romanesque capitals in the nave and transept, the finest of their kind in Belgium. You pass the delicate vaulted entrances of the 12th-century chapter house; the prominent tomb of Wenceslas, first duke of Luxembourg; the great, vaulted hall of the former cloister, still largely intact; the multitude of intricately-carved, Romanesque pillars and supports for an early medieval church that surely was one of the most impressive of its time.

From the ruins of the old abbey, you descend into a cellar underneath the giant, new basilica, where a permanent museum displays treasures of Orval's past, maps and models of the former Orval, explanations and histories of monastic life and institutions. If your tour is taking place at the time of Orval's twice-daily public masses—at 11 a.m. or 5:30 p.m. weekdays and Saturdays, 9:30 a.m. on Sundays—you can, upon request, ascend a staircase at this point to the church gallery, where you will witness a service of the monks. It is now that you will thrill to the modern reproduction of the starkly unadorned, strong, neo-Romanesque style in which the new basilica was designed by its renowned Belgian architect, Henry Vaes. Earlier on your tour, from vantage points near the old ruins, you were able to see the striking entrance of the new basilica, with its giant elongated statue of the Holy Mary with Child, which extends for almost the entire height of the front facade.

While the former, ruined basilica and buildings may seem small in relation to the new Church and adjoining modern cloister buildings—a vast complex—keep in mind that the new cloisters have been built upon the precise site of other cloisters destroyed by the cannonading French. Thus, Orval, even as of the 1700s, was nearly the size it is today—an awesome fact to contemplate.

Either before or after your visit to the old basilica, you will be able to witness an audio-visual presentation of monastic life in the ancient guesthouse building near the area of the ruins. A sensitive film on the puzzling topic of the monk's vocation, it asks the question: "Mais, pourquoi?" (But why?). Why should men subject themselves to such a life? On my own recent visit to Orval, having been specially permitted to enter the cloister portion of the Abbey, I asked a monk whether he was happy. "I am very happy," he replied. "I cannot imagine any other life for me". Orval's complement of 40 monks presently includes two former lawyers, a chemist, a prominent businessman. One studied for the priesthood in his late 40s, after a life in commerce; he was quickly made a senior administrator of the Abbey. Other monks, regardless of background, perform such lowly tasks as mending clothes, cleaning the kitchen. One elderly monk I observed, wiping dishes, took pains to insure that the glassware sparkled, as if he were a kitchen employee at the Ritz. A sparkle for a water glass, at a frugal monk's meal!

On visiting the tasteful souvenir shop at the entrance to the Abbey, you will see at least one and perhaps two of the monks, in their impressive, Cistercian garb: a white woolen robe, over which hangs a dark brown "scapular" (a long, narrow cloth hanging in front and in back of the robe, and girdled round by a broad, black leather belt). A cowl, or hood, hangs on the back. One monk assists the other secular sales personnel, rotating this task with other less public ones. An elderly, retired monk usually sits among the crowds, benignly smiling over all, and enjoying the busy atmosphere of the shop. On sale, apart from books, posters, other literature and subdued souvenirs, are the famous beer, cheeses and breads made at Orval. They sell for the remarkable price of only 330 francs ($9.17) for a case of 12 bottles of the celebrated Orval beer, 290 francs ($8) for half a platter of the cheddar or roquefort cheeses.

BEER AND CHEESE OF ORVAL: Benedictine monasteries have traditionally engaged in such production not simply to earn revenue for their needs, but to provide work for the surrounding populace; the largely-automated brewery of Orval employs only two monks, but over a score of "civilians" from neighboring towns. Its production is limited to only 100 decaliters per day, far less than could be produced or sold, an amount carefully calculated to cover the financial needs of the Abbey, and nothing more. The process of production, following an age-old recipe, is a painstaking one of fermentation at high temperatures (completely contrary to the low temperature fermentation of normal beers), after which the beer is actually stored in open vats, in a cool cellar, for two months before it is bottled. Because it then contains a sediment of yeast at the bottom of each bottle, it must gently and carefully be poured, leaving the yeast within; and because of this, very little Orval is transported or sold outside of Belgium. Needless to say, Orval is a superb beer with a unique grainy taste, as are the four other "Trappist" beers made and sold in Belgium, from the monasteries of Westmalle, St. Sixtus, Chimay and Rochefort.

LODGINGS FOR OVERNIGHT: The nearest town is Villers-devant-Orval, where the stately **Hostellerie d'Orval** (phone 061/31-34-44) offers seven rooms with bath and breakfast for about 1300 francs ($36) per room, and multi-course meals in its restaurant for a costlier (relatively) 850 to 1100 francs ($23 to $31). The larger town of Florenville, ten minutes away, possesses the old-fashioned **Hotel de France,** at 28 Rue Généraux-Cuvelier (phone 061/31-10-32), where 8 of 32 rooms are with bath, the rest without; the former rent for as little as 1120 francs ($31) twin, the latter for 1885 francs ($52) twin. And there are excellent, two and three-course meals for from 600 francs ($17) to 850 francs ($24). You are, of course, so close to Bouillon that you can also stay at the latter's hostelries, and still easily visit Orval.

Bouillon and Orval: they bring to you what you bring to them. As so often in Belgium, a prior glance at history eases the way to enjoyment, understanding and growth.

CHAPTER XIV

THE VALLEY OF THE MEUSE

■ ■ ■

NAMUR

DINANT

CASTLES AND CAVERNS

Here, now, is the glittering "Chateau Country" of Belgium, the area of castles in profuse array, on sharply-jutting bluffs of hills or alongside crucially-situated waterways. You are in the French-speaking, French-flavored Province of Namur, whose center is a western segment of the River Meuse, anchored at top and bottom by the ancient cities of Namur and Dinant. And everywhere are castles: castles at Vêves and Lavaux-Sainte-Anne, castles at Corroy-le-Chateau and Spontin, castles at a dozen different locations, awesome structures with turrets topped by pointed cones, sights that suddenly loom up before your car to jog your memory about the crazy quilt of fiefdoms that made up medieval Europe.

By simply driving, or taking the train, for about ninety kilometers south of Brussels, you enter a once-upon-a-time land of now-departed courtiers, jousts and banquets, of chivalry and knighthood, in a scenically-awesome land of forested heights and steep cliffs overlooking rushing rivers. Atop the cliffs: former citadels of military importance, now reached by cable cars and winding mountain roads, now occupied by mountain lodges and restaurants looking out onto gaily-beflagged sightseeing boats that cruise the waters beneath.

What do you do in Namur? You visit those magical castles, as well as monasteries (especially Maredsous and Floreffe), and ancient churches; see special-interest museums of considerable appeal (like one on the sport of hunting, another on the artist, Felicien Rops); descend into subterranean caves of world renown; test your luck at roulette or blackjack at the popular Casino of Namur; attend folkloric festivals throughout the year in virtually every main town; go kayaking along the rivers and their tributaries; or simply book a sightseeing boat. In this southwestern segment of Belgium, adjoining farm areas of France, there is little heavy-industry and no mammoth cities, which leaves the region perfect for tourism and especially for tourists with cars. Simply look at the map, mark off the key sites, and then begin your tour from a single "base" (for the distances are short), which will probably be either Namur or Dinant.

NAMUR

On the triangle of land formed by the confluence of the Meuse and Sambre Rivers, there rises a sharp, stone hill, thousands of feet high, that obviously commands the entire area. For two thousand years, military architects have used it as a fortified castle, and it was around this massive "citadel" that the ancient city of Namur developed in the 11th century. In the lay-out of its streets, undisturbed since then, it is—with Bruges—the best-preserved city of Belgium.

The Citadel of Namur can be visited throughout the year by "téléphérique" (cable-car), on foot (via a 408-step stairway), or by car. You ascend it to enjoy a breathtaking vista of "the Valley of the Meuse"; to visit the largely-underground fortifications that withstood some twenty-odd sieges over the centuries; to visit its high-altitude amusement parks in summer; to dine in its several restaurants. The famed Casino of Namur (which opens at 2 p.m., for a 100-franc entrance charge) is down below, on a street that roughly parallels the river.

HOTELS OF NAMUR: The Citadel is also the site of your leading accommodations choice: **Le Chateau de Namur** at 1 Avenue de l'Ermitage (phone 081-22-26-30). A stately, lofty, Renaissance structure surrounded by quiet gardens, and with views "to die from", it also serves as the hotel school for the province. Result: you are served by an eager staff of neophytes who haven't lost their enthusiasm for the trade. Guest rooms are large, with plain, traditional furnishings; public areas are large and calm, with comfortable easy chairs; a ground-floor restaurant is similarly-spacious and features the regional cuisine of the Ardennes (for Namur vies with Liège as "Gateway to the Ardennes"). Figure 1000 francs ($28) for the average meal; figure 1950 francs ($54) per single room; 2700 francs ($75) double, including breakfast.

Back down the hill, at river level, a number of desirable and relatively-modern hotels are found along the street of the railway station: the 14-room **La Porte de Fer,** 4 Avenue de la Gare, phone 081-23-13-45 (1500 francs, $42, single; 1900 francs, $53, double, with breakfast); and the 21-room **Queen Victoria,** at 11 Avenue de la Gare, phone 081-22-29-71 (1400 francs, $39, single; 1700 francs, $47, double, with breakfast).

The area's best-endowed hotel (in facilities; it has a swimming pool, partially indoors, among other amenities) is the modern **Novotel,** about six kilometers from town at 1149 Chaussee de Dinant in Wepion, phone 081-46-08-11. Singles here rent for 2525 francs ($70), doubles for 3225 francs ($90), breakfast included.

MEALS: The leading restaurant of the area (about $50 for the average meal, not including wine) is **Les Rumiers,** 32 Rue Basse, in Crupet, ten miles from the center of Namur. Within Namur, I like the medium-priced establishments (slightly under $20 per meal) clustered in great profusion along the Rue des Brasseurs (the city's oldest street, a national treasure), a block from the River Sambre. These include **Le Temps de Cerises, Le Campagnard, La Gousse d'Ail,** still others, charging 160 francs ($4.80) for superb fish soup, 385 francs for a well-garnished steak au poivre. Thus, your average, two-course meal will total to well-under 700 francs, with wine. (If your waiter seems unusually easy to understand in French, that's because the people of Namur are reputed to speak very slowly; their civic symbol is the snail (l'escargot). On my next trip to Namur, I'm going to try the similarly-priced **Le Petit Bedon** at 3 Rue Armée Grouchy, highly touted to me by several "Namurois", and I'm also going to stop at the roadside fruit stands of nearby Wepion, reputed for their strawberries and fresh strawberry jam ("fraises de Wepion").

THE CHIEF ATTRACTIONS: Apart from the Citadel, and a boat ride along the Meuse (you'll see multiple sightseeing docks), the "must-see" attraction is the **Museum of Felicien Rops,** at 12 Rue Fumal, open 10 to noon and from 2 to 5, daily except Sundays. A Namur-born (1833) impressionist, who initially studied and painted in France, but returned to Namur to complete the body of his mature work, Rops is a stunning talent too often overlooked, but here given a proper showing for his sensual, earthy paintings of 19th-century life. Among a dozen other museums, important are: the **Namur Museum of Ancient Art,** 24 Rue de Fer, closed Tuesdays, Saturday mornings and Sunday afternoons (Meuse goldsmiths' and silversmiths' works of the 11th and 12th centuries, pre-Van Eyck paintings from the end of the 14th century, its highlights); and more compelling still, a collection of artifacts officially designated as one of the "Seven Wonders of Belgium" ("the Magnificent Seven"): the **Treasure of Hugo d'Oignies,** in the Institut des Soeurs de Notre-Dame, 17 Rue Julie Billiart. Hugo of Oignies was a 13th-century metalsmith of Namur, who used his craft to create engraved, religious articles of surpassing beauty: a golden chalice, an outer bookbinding—the famed "Evangelarium"—for the holy scriptures, a jewel-encrusted cross, plates for the Host, reliquaries, and other articles of wrought metal fashioned with such artistic talent and religious fervor that they were already regarded as masterpieces in his own time. As an example of the perfect, unquestioning faith of those days, they are unequalled, and should be seen.

DINANT

Though it's but an eighth the size of Namur, the town of Dinant presents much the same breathtaking appearance, along the River Meuse, dominated by a sharply-rising, stone mountain topped by an expansive, 11th-century citadel (fort), which looks down directly onto an imposing, 13th-century "collegial" church with bulbous main tower. The citadel is open all year, and, like Dinant's, can be visited by téléphérique (cable-car), on foot (400 steps), or by car.

Down below, the sightseeing boats leave on daily, hour-long tours of the river, from April through October, and on longer excursions—even to the French border—in summer. Generally, you'll want to consider using Dinant as a base (or stopping point) for your excursions to the castles further south, or for your trip to the caves at Han-sur-Lesse, which we've discussed further on. If you do stay over, you'll need to know about the lodgings set forth immediately below:

HOTELS OF DINANT: As the town is small, the hotels are tiny —but select. Probably the most suitable for a passing tourist are the 20-room **La Citadelle,** 5 Place Reine Astrid, phone 082-22-35-43 (1110 francs, $31, single; 1800 francs, $50, double); and **La Couronne,** 1 Rue Adolphe Sax, phone 082-22-24-41 (1200 francs, $33, single; 1900 francs, $53, double). Location of the latter should alert you that Adolphe Sax, inventor of the saxophone, was a resident of Dinant, the city's pride and joy.

RESTAURANTS OF DINANT: Vivier d'Oies, at 7 Rue de l'Etat in Dorinne, about seven miles away, is the region's outstanding restaurant, at rates of about $50 for the average meal, not including wine. Still high in quality, closer, and far less costly is **La Cremaillère** in suburban Anseremme, at 2 Rue du Velodrome, where you can eat well for about $20, not including wine. In town, your standard meals might be taken at **Bouboule "Au Roi de la Moule"**, 34 Rue Sax, which specializes in mussels served 26 different ways.

CASTLES AND CAVERNS

Outside its two main cities, the province requires a car for thorough touring. With one, you can—in a day—take in the major "chateaux" (castles), and then devote another day to exploring the region's world-famous caves.

Chateaux

Though everyone will have their own favorite, mine is the thoroughly-medieval, fairytale castle of **Vêves,** seven miles from Dinant; you'll spot it quite easily from its elevated height in a hilly forest, and with its six, cone-shaped towers. Open from Easter through October, for a charge of 100 francs, its interior—surprisingly to some—is of 17th-century furnishings left there by the more recent successors of the medieval family whose heirs continue to own the Chateau de Vêves down to the present day. This is at Celles-sur-Lesse, 12 kilometers from Dinant, six kilometers from the E40 highway, exiting at 20, Achêne.

Different in tone, with new portions added in post-medieval times, is the rather remarkable **Lavaux-Sainte-Anne,** in the "lowlands" of Namur, surrounded by herds of grazing deer encouraged to stay there (you'll always see a few). The original, moat-surrounded structure was built in 1450. Here, you'll visit medieval towers surmounted with restored, rounded domes; pass through a succession of magnificently-furnished family rooms (including one whose fixtures are adorned throughout with deers' antlers); and then visit the Museum of the Hunt ("Musée de la Chasse et de la Nature") in one of the more recent buildings, designed not simply to display trophies of the hunt, but to argue the necessity for hunting (various, claimed, ecological reasons). The visit is intriguing, provocative. Take E411 or N94 to get there.

Then, on your map, you'll want to search out the 13th-century **Corroy-le-Chateau,** with 18th-century apartments and appointments; it's owned by direct descendants of the counts who built it seven hundred years ago; the 14th-century chateau of **Spontin;** and the more recent castles of **Franc-Waret** (18th century) and **Annevoie** (mainly 18th century), the latter surrounded by the most famous gardens of Belgium, an important attraction.

At all the castles, expect to pay a quite reasonable entrance charge ranging from 90 francs ($2.50) to 120 francs ($3.33).

Can you stay overnight in a castle? At **Chateau d'Hassonville,** built in 1687 as a turreted, four-story, 50-room "hunting lodge" for Louis XIV of France, you'll sleep like a king, in grounds surrounded by a giant forest preserve. A downstairs castle restaurant is elegant, the views unforgettable, and double rooms range from 4000 to 6000 francs ($111 to $167) a night, the latter rate for those with special vistas onto the verdant scene. All this is but an hour from Brussels by car, or 1½ hours on the direct train from Brussels to Luxembourg, getting off at Marloie; the hotel will pick you up at the station.

Spelunking

The caves of the province are another compelling attraction, drawing visitors from all over Europe. Largest (and indeed, the largest of Europe) are those at **Han-sur-Lesse,** south of Dinant, where you'll enter by "panoramic train" and exit by boat on a subterranean river. Two hundred thirty francs ($6.40) for the combined tour, March through December. Almost equally impressive are the **Caves of Rochefort,** six kilometers from Han; the **Caves of Neptune** ("les Grottes de Neptune") to the south-west of Dinant near Petigny-Couvin (visited by boat on an underground river; take the Route de Frasnes to get there); and especially the **Caves of Goyet** ("Cavernes Prehistoriques de Goyet") near Namur (on the Nameche-Mozet-Gesves road). One of the most important prehistoric sites of Europe, sheltering people from both the Neanderthal and Cro-Magnon Ages, the last-named is wonderfully-preserved, kept free from pollution, and well-described by multi-lingual guides. Open April through September, daily from 9 to 6, for an admission charge of 150 francs.

Throughout your stay in the Province of Namur, you'll also see signs and brochures for the sport of river-kayaking, in two-person "vessels" that somehow, miraculously, stay upright and afloat on the gentle rapids that periodically appear on various streams of Namur. Simply stop at the nearest municipal tourist office—even tiny villages hereabouts have one—to ascertain specific locations for the activity in which only the eskimos of Alaska surpass the Belgians of Wallonia.

CHAPTER XV

ART CITIES OF WALLONIA

□ □ □

TOURNAI
MONS

The eye must be taught to see. As we near the end of our journey through Belgium, we are at least ready for Tournai, the oldest city (with Tongeren) in Belgium. If we had not first gone to Bruges or Ghent or Liège, we could not have appreciated the subtleties of difference that one or two hundred years of earlier development brought about in architecture and crafts, in cathedrals and homes. Indeed, if we had not already been medievalists, we could not have appreciated Tournai at all without first training our eyes in those other "modern" medieval cities that reached the peak of their development in the thirteenth, fourteenth and fifteenth centuries.

TOURNAI

The twelfth century. The 1100s. Those are the years reflected in the key surviving structures of medieval Tournai. A cathedral of the 1100s, perhaps the greatest in Belgium, representing the flowering of the style of the Romanesque. A belfry of the 1100s. Churches of the 1100s. A city wall of the 1100s. And best yet, homes of the 1100s—the oldest examples of burghers' homes still remaining in Western Europe!

THE PROVINCE OF HAINAUT: We are in the heart of French Belgium ("Wallonia"), in the Province of Hainaut adjoining France and periodically annexed by France (or owing loyalty to its King) over the ages. The scenery is lush and varied, both hilly and flat, dotted here and there with 18th-century castles or stately homes that make it another "chateau country" of Belgium—we'll be visiting two such castles later in this chapter. Though Hainaut is the most heavily industrial section of Belgium, the average visitor is scarcely ever aware of that activity, so verdant and rural is most of the scenery through which he or she passes. And though segments of Hainaut were once known as "the black country"— because of the coal mining that fueled its industrial might, especially in the "Borinage" district outside Mons, where a young Vincent van Gogh shared the grinding poverty of 19th-century coal miners in his days as an evangelist—all coal mining has come to an end in Belgium, and no longer bespoils the city of Mons, or Hainaut.

Three major cities dominate Hainaut. Largest is **Charleroi,** commercial/industrial capital of Hainaut, flanked on its outskirts by concentrated stretches of foundries and mills, modern in both contemporary appearance and history—it was not founded until the 1600s, which is "yesterday" by Belgian standards! Though a progressive and gleaming metropolis of 250,000 residents (in an area of 250,000 more), it is bypassed by tourists short on time—and writers short of space.

Second is **Mons,** of 100,000 residents, administrative capital of Hainaut, with ancient structures and fascinating museums, to which we'll soon be turning.

And then there is **Tournai,** Art Capital of Hainaut, the medieval home of craftsmen and sculptors, the makers of tapestries and porcelain chinaware, goldsmiths and stonecutters—who spread the artistic fame of Tournai throughout the ancient world, and left awesome vestiges of their work in the Tournai of today.

THE FIRST CAPITAL OF EUROPE: A Roman settlement— "Tornacum"—as early as the century before Christ, Tournai was sufficiently mentioned in histories and ancient maps to convince the medieval world of its undoubted eminence. But it took a chance discovery in 1653 to reveal how truly important it was. Like the excavators of Troy or the tomb of King Tut—but without their intent—a severely-handicapped workman of the 17th century, digging the foundations of a wall in the garden of Tournai's Church of St. Brice, found that he had broken into a tomb of dazzling sights, its contents an explosion of colors that leaped and sparkled even in the dim light. On the decaying remains of a royal cloak were hundreds of "bees" made from pure gold—the symbol of majesty. Underneath them: a skeleton. Around it: hundreds of gold and silver coins bearing a single, kingly image; several weapons; the ornately-decorated, exquisitely beautiful handle of a sword; rings and bracelets; and most important, a date and an inscription that stunned the experts who came to see it. "482". "Childerici Regis". They had found, in 1653, the fifth-century tomb of Childeric, King of the Franks, father of the great Clovis, founder of the Merovingian Dynasty! And this—Tournai—had been their capital, the first capital of the newly-restored Europe!

The story fell into place. At the beginning of the modern era, Julius Caesar had cruelly conquered Gaul. There followed three and a half centuries of relative peace, after which invasions from the east—including those by Franks living on the banks of the Rhine—had finally broken the rule of Rome. In the year 432, Salic Franks chose Tournai as their capital of the area emerging as "Francia". Their later chieftain, Childeric, consolidated the royal power, handed a kingdom to his son Clovis in 482. And Clovis, from the royal seat of Tournai where he lived until 10-or-so years before his death in 511, created the Empire of the "Merovingians" which was to last and loosely govern for three centuries. Though its capital moved (with Clovis) from Tournai to Paris, Tournai remained an ecclesiastical capital of immense authority, the head of a diocese that ruled all of Flanders, vast sections of France. Quarreling Merovingian rulers ceded civic powers to the Bishop of Tournai, and it was as a virtually independent city ruled by its Bishop (a later vassal of the King of France) that Tournai developed from the year of Childeric's death in 482, through the time of the Merovingian Empire, through Charlemagne, and indeed until the early 1500s, when the Hapsburgs—Charles V—reduced the temporal powers of the Bishop and removed Tournai from its allegiance to the French King.

Throughout the city are relics of the Merovingians—6th century, 7th century, 8th century. They are found in the great Treasury of Tournai's Cathedral of Notre Dame (described below). They exist in the form of jewelry left in tombs, funeral urns, buried coins and pottery, other artifacts, displayed in Tournai's important **Museum of History and Archaeology.** So fresh and vital was the Merovingian story to the builders of Tournai's great 12th-century Cathedral that they related various epics from it (for example, Chilperic—another Merovingian—receiving a sceptre from his demented wife, Frédégonde) in bas-relief sculptures on the "capitals"—the uppermost parts—of Romanesque columns scattered through the Church. Other Merovingian stories are told in extraordinary 16th-century stained glass windows of the transept. And meanwhile, where are the treasures of Childeric's tomb now? They were sent by one of those tiresome foreign rulers of Belgium to Vienna, and from there to Paris. And in Paris, all but a few were stolen and presumably melted down, to the enrichment of a French thief, with no benefit to Belgium.

The later story

Tournai reached the peak of its power and influence in the 11th and 12th centuries, long before either Bruges or Ghent. In this, the most important ecclesiastical city of the area, the arts flourished, and craftsmen brought economic wealth to their fellow citizens. The blue stone of Tournai was sent to construction projects all over the known world. Goldsmiths thrived, as did carvers of ivory, sculptors of stone, jewelers, architects of the famous "Tournaisienne" style. In 1187 the city became a part of France and stayed that way for more than 300 years; it was briefly retrieved in 1667 by Louis XIV, whose elegant structures and riverside quays still adorn the city today.

But alongside the triumphs of its craftsmen class, were ceaseless wars ending in destruction; few cities have been as repeatedly besieged and pillaged as Tournai. Religious wars contributed to general decline. In 1566, Protestant iconoclasts sacked the churches; in 1568, Philip II responded with the wholesale burning of heretics, banishments, confiscations of goods. When the time later came to replace works of art destroyed by the Calvinists, there were no artists left in Tournai to perform the work! They had all fled, some to Antwerp, others to Holland, Germany, Switzerland, America. The population of Tournai fell, its economy declined even further.

And then the cruelest blow. In 1940, German bombers levelled 60% of the city. Yet miraculously, the key sites—belfry and Cathedral, most churches, historical museums, towers and the city's unique military bridge—escaped unscathed or easily repairable. Soon the Grand' Place was restored to its earlier magnificence, and tourists today see a city that, though hardly what it was, is still a scene of grandeur and beauty.

THE MAJESTIC CATHEDRAL OF NOTRE DAME: The
12th-century cathedral is the supreme sight, surmounted by the

startling combination of five, pyramidal, bell towers ("les cinq clochers") seen from any spot in the town. To many—not only those from Tournai—it is the most remarkable cathedral in all of Belgium; to all observers, bar none, it is the most remarkable *Romanesque* cathedral in all of Europe.

When it was completed in the late 1100s, it was entirely Romanesque, of heavy walls, small windows and circular designs, relatively low in height, its nave lined on both sides with four successive stories of rounded arches atop each other—an enthralling sight. Fifty years later, a new, "modernist" Bishop of Tournai became swept up in the excitement of the new Gothic style, concluded that the Cathedral was behind the times and should be replaced with an entirely Gothic structure. He proceeded as far as the choir of the Cathedral, demolishing it and substituting a new and soaring Gothic choir twice the height of the nave and almost as long, a wing of soaring, pointed arches, thin walls, stained glass windows, a magnificently symmetrical series of flying buttresses to support the new, light walls. For unexplained reasons (which were probably financial), the re-construction then stopped. And thus it is that the Cathedral of Tournai has come down to us today as a "dual" building of totally contrasting but strangely harmonious styles: a soaring, graceful, pointed choir, twice as high as the nave and almost as long; a low Romanesque nave; the two buildings intersected by a vastly spacious Romanesque transept with circular chapels at each end, and with those five, famous bell towers atop the transept, somehow joining the two disparate wings into a "marriage" that works.

The mammoth, 435-foot-long Cathedral owes its fame not simply to the majesty of its grand design, but to the ancient stone work and glass that adorns its facade and decorates its pillars and interior walls. The main entrance (on the little Place de l'Evêché), above which is a "rose window" (rose in shape, not in color), is preceded by a porch entirely covered with statuary, of which the Old Testament examples in the bottom rows are by Tournai sculptors of the 14th century. Many of the statues still show damage or decapitation by Calvinist rioters in 1566. The "capitals" at the top of columns show other secular and biblical scenes; pillars at the side doors (north and south) are twisted like licorice candy, and decorated above with stone bas-reliefs (of Virtues battling Vices) that date from the original construction of the edifice in the 1100s. Those of the north door (facing the River Scheldt) are widely proclaimed to be the finest surviving examples of Romanesque sculpture in all of Belgium. Chapels in the choir still contain their original 16th-century illustrated windows, while two chapels in the transept display unique wall murals of the 12th century, still clearly discernible. The huge transept, itself the size of a cathedral, should be viewed on its own; at one side of it, separating the nave from the choir, is a graceful marble rood-screen (or "ambo") done in Renaissance times.

Though much of the artwork of the Cathedral was either destroyed by the aforementioned Protestant iconoclasts, sold at auction by commissionaries of the French Revolution, or burned to cinders by German incendiary bombs in 1940 (the fire was heroically extinguished by prisoners from the Tournai jail), numerous pieces have been re-installed, of which the greatest are surely the **Crucifixion** by Jacob Jordaens (1593–1677) (in the Chapel of St. Louis, to the right of the nave as you walk towards the transept), the triptych **Scenes from the Life of the Virgin** by Martin de Vos (1531–1602) (in the chapel at the extreme rear of the ambulatory at the back of the choir), and a badly-restored **Deliverance of Souls from Purgatory** by none other than Peter Paul Rubens, in a room at the right of the choir as you enter it. The second woman with the outstretched arms is Rubens' wife.

Taken as a whole, the Cathedral captures the exotic, fervent religiosity of the Middle Ages as do few other structures.

The "Treasury" of the Cathedral

And there is still far more, of importance and magnificence, this time in the famed "Treasury" of the Cathedral containing one of the "Seven Wonders of Belgium"—the reliquary casque by metalsmith Nicholas of Verdun. In the Latin inscription at the bottom of it, we are advised not only of the year of its completion (1205), but that it required 109 "marks" (27 kilos) of silver, and six "marks" (1½ kilos) of gold to adorn.

A "reliquary" is a wooden chest or box lavishly covered with sculpted metal, and containing holy relics: bones of a saint, patches of skin, the instruments by which martyrs were tortured, thorns or fragments of wood from the crown and cross of Jesus. In the sculptures covering the small, gold-plated casque (sometimes known as "The Shrine of Our Lady"), Nicholas of Verdun reached near perfection, creating tableaux of New Testament scenes so vital and alive that the little gold statues seem to be walking out of the box whose sides they line. The scenes are not in chronological order, but you will easily place them: in one, the Archangel Gabriel, holding a long, rectangular tablet (a phylactery) on which is written the words of the Ave Maria, delivers the Annunciation to Mary; elsewhere, Mary and Elizabeth, two slim ladies standing in conversation, tell one another that each is ex-

pecting a child. One scene is of the Adoration of the Magi (at one
end of the casque), as a seated and crowned Mary holds the infant
on her lap. There is the Flight into Egypt; the presentation of the
Baby to the veiled hands of the High Priest, Simeon; the Baptism
of Christ; the Whipping of Christ; Christ rises, shows his spear
wound to a doubting Thomas. At the end, Christ sits with angels,
holding a globe topped by a cross. The grace and proportion of the
figures, the style, elegance and drama of the whole, are all remarkable, and deeply beautiful.

This golden shrine by Nicholas of Verdun has been named
one of the seven greatest masterpieces of Belgium. And each year,
on the Sunday nearest to the 8th of September, leaving the Cathedral at 3 p.m., it is carried (along with other works of art) in the
great **Procession of Tournai** (originally instituted to protect Tournai from the plague) that has been conducted annually since the
year 1092 through the streets of the town. It is accompanied, at
that time, by three other great reliquaries of the Cathedral Treasury: the **reliquary of St. Eleutherius** (1247) (first Bishop of Tournai, in the sixth century, whose sculpted image symbolically
holding the five towers of the Cathedral—the ones you see today
—appears at the side of the 13th-century box; the bulging rectangle of metal statues and decoration rivals the great achievement of
Nicholas of Verdun; its filigreed metalwork, all done by an anonymous master, undoubtedly required painstaking labor over several years); the later **reliquary of the Damoiseaux** (1571); and,
oldest of all, a marvelously abstract, 7th-century **ivory reliquary**
of the Merovingian times, looking as if it had been decorated by
Henri Matisse. There is, as well, in this great Treasury—this treasured storehouse belonging to the entire world—the 8th century,
ivory "diptych" (two sculpted ivory panels) created by St. Nicaise
in the last days of the 700s; an oft-pictured, sixth-century Byzantine cross studded with chunky rubies, emeralds and pearls, with
an alleged fragment of the true cross embedded in the center; the
red-silk chasuble worn by St. Thomas à Becket, Archbishop of
Canterbury, on his visit to Tournai in 1170, short weeks before his
assassination in his own English cathedral; the red velvet cloak
worn by Charles V at a meeting in 1531 of the Order of the Gold-
en Fleece in the choir of the Tournai Cathedral; the 14th-century
sheet music of the famed **Mass of Tournai,** first polyphonic chant
to be composed for three harmonizing voices; a renowned, 72-
foot-long 14th-century tapestry of Arras, depicting the lives of
Tournai saints Piat and Eleutherus; and there are manuscripts,
paintings and other extraordinary pieces. In all the history of theological arts and crafts, in all the cathedrals, temples and mosques
of the world, it is only occasionally that one finds a single room to

rival the Treasury of Tournai's Notre Dame Cathedral in historic importance or artistic achievement.

The Cathedral is open from 8:30 to noon, and from 1 to 6 p.m.; the Treasury from 10 to noon and 2 to 6 p.m. Admission to the Treasury is 30 francs (83¢).

TOURNAI'S MUSEUM OF HISTORY AND ARCHAE-OLOGY:

The Cathedral is two short blocks to the east of the triangularly-shaped Grand' Place. Three and a half blocks in the other direction (from the Grand' Place, walk up the Rue des Maux to the Place de Lille, and turn right onto the Rue des Carmes) is the collection that supplements that of the Treasury: the **"Musée d'Histoire et d'Archaeologie"** in a former 17th-century pawnhouse on the Rue des Carmes—it completes the story. On its ground floor is a vast exhibit of Roman-Gallo relics and artifacts of the 1st through the 4th centuries, all excavated from the soil of Tournai as recently as the 1950s. See, in particular, those pieces from a luxurious Roman villa found in the city's district of La Loucherie. In successive rooms: stone sculptures of the following centuries, through the 14th. And then, on both ground and upper floors, one is finally face to face with those two exquisite crafts that brought fame to Tournai in more recent times: the priceless 15th-century **tapestries** of Tournai, and the equally precious, 18th-century Tournai **porcelain** and **china**—both producing the sharpest sense of awe and delight in visitors who normally don't have the slightest interest in tapestries or china.

The tapestries, all telling dramatic stories, are bold, colorful and immensely graphic; their stories flow and develop from one side of the great hanging cloths to the other, without division or grouping into separate scenes; one could stare at their detail for hours. Some are quite malignantly propagandistic: the "Siege of Jerusalem", subtitled "The Revenge of the Savior", takes obvious glee from the sufferings and famine of the Jewish population surrounded by the Romans; we see, among other things, a famished mother cooking her newborn infant over a spit. Another depicts the courage of Charlemagne's officer, Roland, at the battle of Roncevaux; another the adventures of the Greek "Argonauts" led by Hercules, the feats of Hercules and Jason in the Trojan War. We are already witnessing the evolution of art towards secular, non-Biblical themes, though not yet divorced from ancient religious hatreds. Every tapestry here was made in ateliers of Tournai in the mid-to-late 1400s.

Upstairs are the artistic, 18th-century master-works of Tournai that rely simply on the delicacy of color and form, the abstract beauty of swirling designs, the most basic flowers, birds and pastoral scenes (in cameo blue, in pale rose, in lavendar) on the famed "faience"—the priceless porcelain china—of Tournai. In showcase after showcase of plates and cups that differ from anything we see today in even the finest store windows—quite literally soaring above the finest contemporary product of Messrs. Wedgwood or Rosenthal—we learn that any art is great when greatly pursued. For a short 120 years, from 1752 towards the end of the 1800s, the porcelain makers of Tournai pursued the art of producing and decorating porcelain with a zeal and skill no longer found in the world we know, and that even then, in other cities, was normally directed to great paintings or statues. In this field, as in metal, Tournai had few equals.

Like all the museums of Tournai, the Museum of History and Archaeology charges no admission, and is open daily except Tuesdays from 10 to noon and 2 to 5:30 from April 1 to October 31, in all other months on weekends only during the same hours. The Museum of Paleontology and Pre-History occupies another wing of the same building, charges no admission, and maintains the same hours.

THE MUSEUM OF FINE ARTS: The third great gem of Tournai, little known outside of Belgium, is its "Musée des Beaux-Arts", small but *select*. It is distinguished almost as much by the building in which it is housed, a new-Greek masterpiece designed in 1928 by the great Belgian architect of "l'art nouveau", Victor Horta (see our Brussels chapter). Built of giant, white, stone blocks in the Courtyard to the immediate left of the Tournai Town Hall (a 500-yard walk to the south of the Grand' Place, on the Rue Saint-Martin), it softly curves and undulates, in the style of this under-appreciated master, and is illustrated inside almost entirely by natural light flooding through ingenious glass apertures and panes. Horta was selected for the building by the skilled Belgian art collector, Henri van Cutsem, of Brussels, whose collection forms the heart of this museum limited to 700 pieces.

Forty works, filling one of the five basic exhibition rooms, are by Tournai-born (1810–1887) Louis Gallait, whose large and painstakingly realistic tableaux—almost in the style of a Flemish primitive!—are a veritable and extremely dramatic history course in the origins of the revolt of the Netherlands against Philip II of Spain: the panoramic "Abdication of Charles V", "Reading of the Death Sentence to the Counts of Egmont and Horne", "Last Moments of the Count of Egmont", the particularly masterful "Last Honors Rendered to the Counts of Egmont and Horne". And then, among many portraits, is a work of deep affection and genius inscribed to his best friend, a pensive, human Colonel Hallart portrayed with double chins and unruly hair.

One noted ancient painting is the ravishing **Virgin and Child** by another Tournai-born (1400–1464) artist who went on to found a celebrated school for the Flemish primitives further north, the great Roger de la Pasture, as he is called here, but better known in the Dutch as Rogier van der Weyden. In this enthralling masterpiece, Mary is shown offering her breast to the Infant as a mother would, protruding the nipple with her forefinger and middle finger as all of us have seen new mothers do. And then there are two often-reproduced works of the French impressionist, Edouard Manet (1832–1883): **Chez la Père Lathuille** (though painted in 1879, we have all seen that mildly-reproving French waiter in the background, undoubtedly in his current reincarnation, during our own, late–20th-century trips to France) and **Argenteuil.** Add, in alphabetical order, Bruegel the Younger's **Hunters in the Snow;** five works by the immensely accomplished Henri de Braekeleer (1840–1888); Charles Degroux' (1825–1870) **Pilgrimage to Dieghem;** Sir Anthony Van Dyck (1599–1641, two pieces); James Ensor (1860–1949, two pieces); Jean Gossart's (1472–1531) **Saint-Donatien,** another much-acclaimed masterwork of a "Primitive"; Jacob Jordaens (1593–1678); Robert Campin (born 1378 in France, died 1444 in Tournai), the probable "Master of Flemalle", and perhaps the greatest of the Tournai painters; Bernard van Orley (1488–1541); a tiny but masterful Rubens sketch and larger painting; Georges Seurat's (1859–1891) pointillist **Shore at Honfleur,** Joseph Stevens (1832–1892); Theodore Verstraete's (1851–1907) **Funeral at Campines** and several other fine works; and many other mainly-Belgian painters of the 15th through 19th centuries. As you will note, the museum displays no 20th-century paintings (as yet), and that limitation, avoiding the clashing departures and styles of our own day, makes the museum's collection even more pleasant to peruse and comprehend. You will have an enjoyable, two-hour interlude at this surprising institution which retains the tone and flavor of a private collection. The museum is free, and open from 10 to noon and 2 to 5:30 p.m. from April 1 through October 31, on weekends only (same hours) in all other months.

THE ROMANESQUE HOUSES OF THE LATE 1100'S:
And at some point in your stay, you will want to seek out the **Rue Barre Saint-Brice** in front of the Church of St. Brice (this is on the other side of the River Scheldt from the Grand' Place) for a view of the two noted houses of the late 1100s—oldest bourgeois houses

in Europe. Later examples are found further along the street, while Gothic-style homes of the 13th century are on the Rue des Jésuites, short steps away.

OTHER MAJOR SIGHTS OF TOURNAI: The **Town Hall** ("Hôtel de Ville") of Tournai, which is not on the Grand' Place, occupies the classic 18th-century palace of the Abbot of an important Benedictine Monastery outlawed by the French Revolution, converted into a "Temple of Reason", and taken over by the city shortly after that. It should be visited only for a view of its spectacular, 12th-century Romanesque crypt (cellar), sole remains of a far more ancient building once occupying the site. . . . The impressive **Belfry** ("Beffroi") of Tournai does stand on the Grand' Place, from which you hear the 44 bells of its carillon on Saturday mornings at 11:30 a.m. in June, July and August. Oldest Belfry in Belgium, oldest even in all of northern Europe, its bottom half dates from the late 1100s. You can climb its 265 spiral steps (20 francs, 56¢) for a view of Hainaut. . . . **"Le Pont aux Trous"** (Bridge of Holes; you'll see why) is the 13th-century military bridge that spans the north segment of the River Scheldt ("L'Escaut"), just below the peripheral Boulevard Delwart. It was connected to the old city walls, and could block access on the river, as it did in the course of several notable, bloody battles. . . . For five strange years, from 1513 to 1518, Tournai belonged to England following its capture by Henry VIII. Claiming also the throne of France, Henry VIII was at least the king of Tournai, and his Cardinal Wolsey became Bishop of the Tournai Cathedral (and is still carried as such on the Cathedral's records). What a team! Henry built, and left behind him, the 80-foot-high **Tower of Henry VIII** off the Place Verte, now serving as the **Military Museum** ("Musée d'Armes") of Tournai. It houses a particularly interesting exhibit relating to the underground Belgian Resistance in World War II. . . . The central portion of the city is studded by eight other major churches, of which four—**St. Piat's, St. Brice's, St. James'** (here, St. Jacques'), and **St. Quentin's**—date from the 12th century. Most impressive is St. James' (whose later alterations have made it almost entirely Gothic); most architecturally interesting is St. Brice's, with three separate naves and a "triple roof"—an example of the endless innovations in design of even that ancient time. . . . The **Museum of Folklore** ("Maison Tournaisienne"), showing articles and settings of daily life that were obviously collected and displayed with great love by its post-war staff, is no more than a short block from the Belfry Tower of the Grand' Place, down the Rue Saint-Martin. Its display rooms occasionally use wax models of the Tournaisiens who used the implements they display; its table-top model of Tournai in the 1700s is enchanting; its most affecting sight is of the apparatus that Marie-Thérèse of Austria had designed for placing abandoned children in convents of the town (a box with hinged doors at both sides, set into the convent walls). With the child went the torn half of a piece of paper; if the poor family or mother were later able to retrieve the child, they presented the other half of the paper as identification. This apparently was Marie-Thérèse's solution to the problems of Tournai's 18th-century poverty! The museum (an important visit to be ranked high on your list) is open daily except Tuesdays from April through October, on weekends at all other times, always 10 to noon and 2 to 5:30 p.m., and charges no admission.

TOURNAI'S HOTELS AND RESTAURANTS: The hotel situation is not outstanding in this city devoted to Art, and most visitors bed down for the night in the several larger hotels near Mons (45 kilometers away; see below), in Kortrijk ("Courtrai", only 30 kilometers distant), or—best yet—in an exquisite country lodge, "Le Prieuré", less than 10 kilometers from Tournai itself. Top hotel in the center of town is the 20-room, tourist class **"Aux Armes de Tournai"**, at 24 Place de Lille (phone 69/22-67-23 or 22-57-89), charging 1100 francs ($31) for a single with bath and breakfast, 1500 francs ($42) for a double so endowed; and if they're booked up, you might then turn to the even smaller **Hotel de l'Europe** at 36 Grand' Place (phone 069/22-4067), charging 1200 francs ($33) single, 1800 francs ($50) double with bath. Better than the latter, but about 5 kilometers from the heart of Tournai in the heights of little Mont St. Aubert, and enjoying a view of Tournai, is the modern, 29-room **Centre Le Panoramique**, at 2 Place de la Trinité (phone 69/23-31-11) with rates similar to the de l'Europe. Try, alternately, La Tour Saint Georges at 2 Place de Nédonchel (phone 069/225-300), charging 1050 francs single, 1500 francs double.

The larger Mons-area hotels are described in our Mons section, below. The major hotel of nearby Kortrijk, directly to the north of Tournai, is the 50-room **Hotel Broel**, at 8 Broelkaai (phone 56/21-83-51), charging 3800 francs ($106) for a double room; but cheaper rates are available in a near-equivalent establishment called the **Damier**, at 41 Grote Markt (phone 56/22-15-47) (only 1550 francs, $43, per double).

The restaurant situation improves considerably, and there's no need to leave the center of town unless you're anxious to climb to the very summit of the culinary scene. That latter condition is found, for prices ranging from 1550 francs ($43) to 1800 francs ($50) for the average dinner, plus wine, at the **Le Prieuré,** in

Blandain-lez-Tournai (7 Rue du Prieuré, phone 69/35-25-06), 10 kilometers from Tournai, where the specialties are duck with fresh figs, and slivers of veal with baby vegetables steamed in lime (closed Sunday evenings and Mondays); at the quite elegant, red-carpeted **Le Cristal,** 20 kilometers from Tournai at 1 Rue du Roi Baudoin in Monscron (phone 56/33-28-40, order the baby lamb of Pauillac, the lobster "en papillotte"; closed Monday evenings and Tuesdays); and at the funny, whitewashed, two-story structure called **"L'Ousteau au Vert Galant",** in a little park of its own at 106 Chaussée de Lannoy at Froyennes-lez-Tournai (phone 69/22-44-84), closed Monday evenings, Tuesdays and the entire month of July; the latter's giant shoulder steak served with three sauces—"La côte à l'os grillé aux épices aux trois sauces"—is particularly popular.

Back in the very center of Tournai, five high-quality restaurants whose à la carte prices total 900 to 1200 francs, $25 to $33, for three courses, sometimes with, sometimes without, wine (depending on your skill in ordering), are located directly on the Grand' Place. Typical, but elegant, and heavily booked for week-day lunch, is the **Charles Quint** (Charles V), at 3 Grand' Place (phone 69/22-14-41), where a 240-franc ($6.67) appetizer (say, "escargots", snails, a half dozen of them), followed by a 500-franc ($14) main course ("rognons de veau Dijonnaise", veal kidneys with mustard sauce; or "filet poivre vert crème", pepper steak with cream sauce; or "Sole Charles Quint", and a 200 franc ($5.50) dessert ("Parfait au Grand Marnier" or "Poire Belle Helene" or "Dame Blanche"), leaves plenty of space for a half bottle of Beaujolais in your 1200 franc ($33) per person budget (remember that service charge is already included in these prices in Belgium). And since main course of chicken—"poulet au curry" or simple "poulet roti"—are priced well below 400 francs ($11.11), it's quite easy—even at these rather impressive restaurants on the Grand' Place of Tournai—to keep your total meal check to 950 francs ($26) per person.

Elsewhere in Tournai, it's easy to eat for less—as, for example, on the Place Crombez in front of the station (400 to 500 francs, $11.11 to $14, per meal, at several establishments located there).

MISCELLANY OF TOURNAI: The vicissitudes of Tournai! It was sacked, pillaged, besieged or occupied by (among others) the Vandals in 406, the Franks in 440, Siegebert (King of "Austrasie") in 564, the Norsemen in 881, Henry III in 1053, the Emperor Henry IV in 1103, Baudoin of Constantinople in 1197,

Fernand of Portugal (Count of Flanders) in 1212, the Flemish city armies in 1302, Edward III, King of England, in 1340, Charles V in 1521, The Prince of Parma in 1581, Louis XIV in 1667, Prince Eugene in 1709, Louis XV in 1745, the new French Republic in the 1790s, the Germans in 1914 and 1940. Here, in microcosm, is Belgium. . . . A brand-new, one-hour **"Bateaux-Mouche"** ride on the River Scheldt is offered from May through September, departing from the Quai Taille-Pierre daily except Monday at 2 p.m., 3:45 p.m. and 5:30 p.m., with a supplementary departure at 10:30 a.m. on weekends, for an 85-franc ($2.36) fee. . . . The destruction of Tournai in World War II can be compared in scope to that of Conventry. Yet which of us has ever heard of the bombing attack on Tournai?. . . . The **Cathedral of Tournai** is considerably longer in size than the cathedrals of Brussels, Bruges, Antwerp and Mechelen; and even longer than the cathedrals of Paris and Chartres! (But that of Amiens is exactly the same size). . . . If you are driving to Tournai from Flanders, you'll be guided by highway signs identifying the city as "Doornik", the Dutch for Tournai. Conversely, on maps of the city issued in Tournai, the familiar River Scheldt appears as the French-styled "L'Escaut"!

MONS

The capital of Hainaut, Mons is yet another of those ancient Belgian cities—this one 1300 years in existence—that is carpeted with cobblestoned streets, dotted with massive churches (12 of them), endowed with (in this case) especially interesting museums (10 of them), and possessed of many scores of distinguished period buildings (almost all from the 17th and 18th centuries) in its central quarter, where it is always interesting to stroll. Although the outlying neighborhoods are modern and planned, with apartment blocks and factory plants, and although the larger district of Mons (the "Borinage") was once the unpleasant coal mining center of Belgium (mining ceased in 1976), you can spend a pleasurable day or half-day in the museums and historic sites of central Mons, and you may also decide to use its modern hotels in the suburbs as your base for exploring other highlights of Hainaut.

It is a hilly city. The Romans used it as a fortified camp commanding the countryside below nearly 2000 years ago; the N.A.T.O. nations use it today as the site of their military arm, the "Supreme Headquarters of Allied Powers in Europe" *("SHAPE"),* which currently employs nearly 15% of the population. Mons, in Latin, means "hill" or "mount", as does "Bergen" in Dutch; and the city variously referred to in Belgium as "Mons/Bergen" occupies an area of softly rolling hills topped by a tall Belfry Tower at its highest point. Driving into town, you'll want to park as close as possible to the central Grand' Place, because most everything of interest is within easy walking distance of there.

ON AND OFF THE GRAND' PLACE: An impressive, 15th-century **Town Hall** ("Hotel de Ville") occupies the central position on this central square; and as a minor note, a gesturing, 15th-century iron monkey on the building's facade bears a shiny head because of the tradition that those stroking its head will marry within the year. Everyone does.

Directly behind the Town Hall, reached by simply walking through its arched entranceway, is a courtyard known as the "Jardin du Mayeur" that leads to no fewer than six important museums, of which four—**"Le Musée de Guerre 1914–1918 et 1940–45"** (Museum of World Wars I and II), the **Ceramics Museum, Museum of Pre-History,** and **Museum of Medals and Coins**—occupy a single crowded and rather shabby, but quite fascinating, old structure known as the "Centenary Museums". The museum of the wars displays a particularly comprehensive collection (World War I on the musty ground floor, World War II on the third floor) of photos, posters, leaflets and proclamations of both sides, uniforms and guns, reflecting especially the key role played by Mons in both conflicts. In the midst of these horrifying struggles, Belgium never ceased to be a colorful, resilient, somewhat mystifying place—and perhaps one of sardonic, ironic story-tellers. Thus it is claimed that in August of 1914, German troops coming from their conquest of Brussels and marching on Paris were successfully checked, for a time, outside Mons, by retreating British troops heartened by the alleged appearance in the sky of Angels in the form of British Archers—so goes the famous legend of the "Angels of Mons", which is also depicted by artist Marcel Gilis in a painting that hangs in the nearby Town Hall. Whether this story originated with the British or the Belgians is a much-disputed point. The museum is open daily except Mondays from 10 to noon and 2 to 6, for an admission charge of 20 francs (56¢), and its unusually complete World War I collection, thought provoking and evocative, deserves to be seen.

Other visits are easily made only a few yards away. To the side of the "Mayor's Garden", but this time on the Rue Neuve off the Grand' Place, is Mons' **Museum of Fine Arts** (Musée des Beaux-Arts"), whose 19th- and 20th-century paintings and sculpture are considerably stronger than those of earlier centuries; though lacking the depth and the several masterpieces of its counterpart in Tournai, it provides a pleasant display of several lesser and local Hainaut figures, among whom you may find occasional standouts. The museum is open 10 to noon and 2 to 6, daily except Mondays, and charges no admission. Almost next door, the **Museum of Mons Life,** in a 17th-century home on the Rue Neuve, exhibiting local folklore and crafts, is also without admission charge and maintains similar hours and Monday closings.

THE "CHATEAU HILL" AND THE COLLEGIATE CHURCH:

Just to the north of the Grand' Place, on a sharp rise of land, you find the hilltop park on which the Castle of the Counts of Hainaut stood until the 1860s (when "improvement minded" city fathers tore it down!). Still standing is the 17th-century Belfry Tower with its decorations likened by Victor Hugo to several "teapots"; you may climb the Belfry (20 francs) for an even more spectacular view of Mons (including the battlefields of 1914) than the excellent one afforded by the hill. Fifty yards away, still on the hill, the **St. Calixte Chapel,** dating from the year 1051, is the oldest structure in Mons, and open for a view of its three recumbent tomb figures (some dating to the 9th century) daily except Mondays from 10 to noon and 2 to 6, for no admission charge. The "Hill of the Chateau" or "Place du Chateau" dominating Mons is still referred to as such, though the Chateau no longer exists.

To the west of the hill, but below it, is Mons' great, Gothic, **Collegiate Church of Ste. Waudru** (15th/16th century), named after the daughter of the Count of Hainaut who established a convent near here in the 7th century and thus founded the city of Mons. Its interior is a soaring, vaulted room that stretches into the distance; its most famous decorations are the epic sculptures and Renaissance-style wall-carvings of a 16th-century native son, Jacques du Broeck, whose greatest work here is the alabaster bas-relief "Résurrection du Christ" in the north side of the transept (among numerous other works by du Broeck found in this collegiate church); but its most notable features, to me, are its 16th-century stained-glass windows encircling the entire oval of the choir, that tell the more-or-less sequential story (from left to right as you face the rear of the choir) of the Annunciation, Visitation, Nativity, Adoration (by the Magi), Purification, Flight to Egypt, Meeting with the "Doctors", Crucifixion, Apparition, Ascension, Pentecost, Assumption, Trinity, Saint Francis of Assissi Stigmatized, Elders of the Apocalypse—in that precise order, left to right. Each window is the gift of a wealthy, and usually princely, figure of the 1500s, such as Philip the Handsome or Maximillian the 1st.

And then there is the giant, gilded coach called the **"Car d'Or"** (Golden Chariot), covered with cherubs, rococo beyond belief, standing just inside the church's entrance. It leads the "Procession of the Golden Chariot" on a day each Spring when Mons explodes into a revelry that takes several different forms.

CARNIVAL!

Most countries enjoy one great carnival—a single, long weekend in Rio, a single period of Mardi Gras in New Orleans. Belgium celebrates at least two dozen! They take place in Binche (near Mons), in Nivelles and Ath, in a score of other cities that each explode into color and festivity on at least one or more days of the year—and in Mons on "Trinity Sunday" (in the late Spring of each year).

On that morning, the Golden Chariot is drawn through the streets of Mons by several white horses, followed by an exotic ecclesiastical procession that includes young girls in Belgian brocades and laces, solemn clerics, and a group carrying the skull of Ste. Waudru encased in a silver reliquary. The procession no sooner returns to the church than a boisterous, rollicking, simulated battle breaks out in the Grand' Place, witnessed by thousands of jubilant spectators who sing the ancient "Song of the Doudou" (accompanied by the Carillons of the Belfry) as they wait for the fight to start. In a ritual unchanged since the year 1490, there now occurs the ancient combat of St. George against the Dragon (the "Lumecon"), a rocket-shaped beast wielded around the square by white-clad attendants as it faces the valiant knight of the Crusades mounted upon a charger: the legendary Gilles of Berlaymount, who became "St. George". All this is surrounded by such surprising grotesqueries and anomalies as to best await the viewing of it, rather than to rely on any description. The feasting, celebration and carousing continue through the day, and culminate at night in an historical "Pageant of Mons" presented by 2000 actors, musicians and singers in the square before the Cathedral. If you possibly can, try to be in Mons on Trinity Sunday to attend the festival known technically as the *"Ducasse"* but colloquially as the *"Battle of the Lumecon"*, preceded by the procession of the Golden Chariot.

THE CARNIVAL OF BINCHE:

Greatest of all the Belgian carnivals, attracting tens of thousands of outside visitors each year, is the one held in the town of **Binche** (it rhymes with "ranch") only 20 kilometers from Mons. It lasts for three days, from Sunday ("dimanche gras") through Tuesday ("mardi gras"—Shrove Tuesday), culminating on that last day in the famed **March of the "Gilles"**. The latter are those carefully costumed figures appearing on posters and paintings all over Belgium (see the photo inserts in this book), wearing hats of ostrich plumes three feet high, light khaki pantaloons colorfully embroidered with the profiles of lions reared upon their hind legs, matching tunics stuffed with straw to create a barrel-chested look, large lace collars, and masks of an astonishingly modern mien (despite the fact that the "Gilles" date back to the 14th century!): stark, white faces bearing orange moustaches and eyebrows, and small green-glass spectacles. At dawn on the appointed Tuesday, almost as if they were preparing for a bullfight or a religious ritual, the "Gilles" are solemnly dressed by their wives or families at home, then proudly emerge in ones and twos onto the street, and converge to the sound of eery drumbeats into the Grand Place of Binche around 10 a.m., from which they then continue to parade throughout the day and well into the evening, tossing oranges to the crowds from small and periodically replenished wicker baskets held in one hand. It is as if they are flinging stars into the sky. All around them is the insistent drum beat of scattered bands, playing rhythms as unique to Binche as the samba is to Rio. Earlier, on Sunday, and to a certain extent on Tuesday as well, other citizens of Binche (those not belonging to the carefully-selected, exclusive corps of "Gilles"), cavort about town in garish and grotesque costumes and masks, a large number of them men dressed as women. The festivities start as early as 9 a.m. on Sundays and reach a climax of crowds, music and parades towards 3 p.m. On Tuesday, the Gilles reach the Town Square towards 10 a.m., but matters continue to peak as late as 3 p.m., and resume at 7 p.m.

Carnival festivities and the wearing of fanciful costumes and masks, is a tradition found all over the world, in differing religious and secular societies, apparently fulfilling a deep human urge. Binche possesses an intriguing **International Museum of Carnival and Masks** (two blocks from the Grand Place, around the corner from the Rue St. Paul), displaying, explaining and discussing carnival costumes and objects from around the world. Its exhibits are so well presented, so provocative of thought, so handsomely mounted on wax models in fascinating tableaux, that it ought definitely to be on your list of attractions if you should ever find yourself in Binche. And if you are in Belgium on or near Shrove Tuesday, you have the opportunity to witness one of the world's great spectacles, strangely affecting, in the "March of the Gilles" of Binche.

The colorful country of Belgium, its people in love with life! What better note on which to end our visit to Wallonia, than with the Gilles, flinging oranges—like stars—into the sky!

ABOUT THE AUTHOR: Arthur Frommer is a graduate of the Yale University Law School, where he was an editor of the Yale Law Journal, and he is a member of the New York Bar. After service with U. S. Army Intelligence at the time of the Korean War, he practiced law in New York City with the firm of the late Adlai Stevenson until the growing demands of travel writing and tour operating required that he give them his full attention. He is the author of *The New World of Travel 1989,* of *Europe on $5 a Day* (now in its 32nd yearly edition as *Europe on $30 a Day,* and largest selling travel guide in the United States), of guide books to New York and Amsterdam, and of two books dealing with legal and political subjects. He is also the founder of Arthur Frommer Holidays, Inc., one of the nation's largest international tour operators, and lectures widely on travel subjects.

NOW, SAVE MONEY ON ALL YOUR TRAVELS!
Join Frommer's™ Dollarwise® Travel Club

Saving money while traveling is never a simple matter, which is why, over 27 years ago, the **Dollarwise Travel Club** was formed. Actually, the idea came from readers of the Frommer publications who felt that such an organization could bring financial benefits, continuing travel information, and a sense of community to economy-minded travelers all over the world.

In keeping with the money-saving concept, the annual membership fee is low—$18 (U.S. residents) or $20 U.S. (Canadian, Mexican, and foreign residents)—and is immediately exceeded by the value of your benefits which include:

1. The latest edition of any TWO of the books listed on the following pages.
2. A copy of any Frommer City Guide.
3. An annual subscription to an 8-page quarterly newspaper *The Dollarwise Traveler* which keeps you up-to-date on fastbreaking developments in good-value travel in all parts of the world—bringing you the kind of information you'd have to pay over $35 a year to obtain elsewhere. This consumer-conscious publication also includes the following columns:

> **Hospitality Exchange**—members all over the world who are willing to provide hospitality to other members as they pass through their home cities.
>
> **Share-a-Trip**—requests from members for travel companions who can share costs and help avoid the burdensome single supplement.
>
> **Readers Ask . . . Readers Reply**—travel questions from members to which other members reply with authentic firsthand information.

4. Your personal membership card which entitles you to purchase through the club all Frommer publications for a third to a half off their regular retail prices during the term of your membership.

So why not join this hardy band of international Dollarwise travelers now and participate in its exchange of information and hospitality? Simply send $18 (U.S. residents) or $20 U.S. (Canadian, Mexican, and other foreign residents) along with your name and address to: Frommer's Dollarwise Travel Club, Inc., Gulf + Western Building, One Gulf + Western Plaza, New York, NY 10023. Remember to specify which *two* of the books in section (1) and which *one* in section (2) above you wish to receive in your initial package of member's benefits. Or tear out the next page, check off your choices, and send the page to us with your membership fee.

FROMMER BOOKS
PRENTICE HALL PRESS
ONE GULF + WESTERN PLAZA
NEW YORK, NY 10023

Date_____

Friends:
Please send me the books checked below:

FROMMER'S™ $-A-DAY® GUIDES

(In-depth guides to sightseeing and low-cost tourist accommodations and facilities.)

☐ Europe on $30 a Day $14.95	☐ New Zealand on $40 a Day $12.95
☐ Australia on $30 a Day $12.95	☐ New York on $50 a Day. $12.95
☐ Eastern Europe on $25 a Day $13.95	☐ Scandinavia on $60 a Day $13.95
☐ England on $40 a Day. $12.95	☐ Scotland and Wales on $40 a Day $12.95
☐ Greece on $30 a Day $12.95	☐ South America on $30 a Day $13.95
☐ Hawaii on $50 a Day $13.95	☐ Spain and Morocco (plus the Canary Is.)
☐ India on $25 a Day. $12.95	on $40 a Day. $13.95
☐ Ireland on $35 a Day $13.95	☐ Turkey on $25 a Day. $12.95
☐ Israel on $30 & $35 a Day $12.95	☐ Washington, D.C., & Historic Va. on
☐ Mexico (plus Belize & Guatemala)	$40 a Day. $12.95
on $25 a Day. $13.95	

FROMMER'S™ DOLLARWISE® GUIDES

(Guides to sightseeing and tourist accommodations and facilities from budget to deluxe, with emphasis on the medium-priced.)

☐ Alaska $13.95	☐ Cruises (incl. Alask, Carib, Mex, Hawaii,
☐ Australia $14.95	Panama, Canada, & US) $14.95
☐ Austria & Hungary. $14.95	☐ California & Las Vegas $14.95
☐ Belgium, Holland, Luxembourg $13.95	☐ Florida $13.95
☐ Brazil. $14.95	☐ Mid-Atlantic States $13.95
☐ Egypt. $13.95	☐ New England $13.95
☐ France $14.95	☐ New York State $13.95
☐ England & Scotland $14.95	☐ Northwest $14.95
☐ Germany $13.95	☐ Skiing in Europe. $14.95
☐ Italy. $14.95	☐ Skiing USA—East. $13.95
☐ Japan & Hong Kong $13.95	☐ Skiing USA—West. $13.95
☐ Portugal, Madeira, & the Azores . . . $13.95	☐ Southeast & New Orleans $13.95
☐ South Pacific. $13.95	☐ Southeast Asia $14.95
☐ Switzerland & Liechtenstein $13.95	☐ Southwest $14.95
☐ Bermuda & The Bahamas $13.95	☐ Texas $13.95
☐ Canada $13.95	☐ USA. $15.95
☐ Caribbean $13.95	

FROMMER'S™ TOURING GUIDES

(Color illustrated guides that include walking tours, cultural & historic sites, and other vital travel information.)

☐ Australia $9.95	☐ Paris $8.95
☐ Egypt. $8.95	☐ Scotland $9.95
☐ Florence. $8.95	☐ Thailand. $9.95
☐ London. $8.95	☐ Venice. $8.95

TURN PAGE FOR ADDITIONAL BOOKS AND ORDER FORM.

FROMMER'S™ CITY GUIDES
(Pocket-size guides to sightseeing and tourist accommodations and facilities in all price ranges.)

☐ Amsterdam/Holland	$5.95	☐ Minneapolis/St. Paul	$5.95
☐ Athens	$5.95	☐ Montreal/Quebec City	$5.95
☐ Atlantic City/Cape May	$5.95	☐ New Orleans	$5.95
☐ Belgium	$5.95	☐ New York	$5.95
☐ Boston	$5.95	☐ Orlando/Disney World/EPCOT	$5.95
☐ Cancún/Cozumel/Yucatán	$5.95	☐ Paris	$5.95
☐ Chicago	$5.95	☐ Philadelphia	$5.95
☐ Dublin/Ireland	$5.95	☐ Rio	$5.95
☐ Hawaii	$5.95	☐ Rome	$5.95
☐ Las Vegas	$5.95	☐ San Francisco	$5.95
☐ Lisbon/Madrid/Costa del Sol	$5.95	☐ Santa Fe/Taos (avail. May 1989)	$5.95
☐ London	$5.95	☐ Sydney	$5.95
☐ Los Angeles	$5.95	☐ Washington, D.C.	$5.95
☐ Mexico City/Acapulco	$5.95		

SPECIAL EDITIONS

☐ A Shopper's Guide to the Caribbean	$12.95	☐ Motorist's Phrase Book (Fr/Ger/Sp)	$4.95
☐ Beat the High Cost of Travel	$6.95	☐ Paris Rendez-Vous	$10.95
☐ Bed & Breakfast—N. America	$11.95	☐ Swap and Go (Home Exchanging)	$10.95
☐ California with Kids	$14.95	☐ The Candy Apple (NY for Kids)	$11.95
☐ Guide to Honeymoon Destinations		☐ Travel Diary and Record Book	$5.95
(US, Canada, Mexico, & Carib.)	$12.95	☐ Where to Stay USA (Lodging from $3	
☐ Manhattan's Outdoor Sculpture	$15.95	to $30 a night)	$10.95

☐ Marilyn Wood's Wonderful Weekends (NY, Conn, Mass, RI, Vt, NH, NJ, Del, Pa) . . . $11.95
☐ The New World of Travel (Annual sourcebook by Arthur Frommer previewing: new travel trends, new modes of travel, and the latest cost-cutting strategies for savvy travelers) . . . $12.95

SERIOUS SHOPPER'S GUIDES
(Illustrated guides listing hundreds of stores, conveniently organized alphabetically by category)

☐ Italy	$15.95	☐ Los Angeles	$14.95
☐ London	$15.95	☐ Paris	$15.95

GAULT MILLAU
(The only guides that distinguish the truly superlative from the merely overrated.)

☐ The Best of Chicago (avail. April 1989)	$15.95	☐ The Best of New England (avail. June 1989)	$15.95
☐ The Best of France (avail. July 1989)	$15.95		
☐ The Best of Italy (avail. July 1989)	$15.95	☐ The Best of New York	$15.95
☐ The Best of Los Angeles	$15.95	☐ The Best of San Francisco	$15.95
		☐ The Best of Washington, D.C.	$15.95

ORDER NOW!

In U.S. include $1.50 shipping UPS for 1st book; 50¢ ea. add'l book. Outside U.S. $2 and 50¢, respectively. Allow four to six weeks for delivery in U.S., longer outside U.S.

Enclosed is my check or money order for $_____

NAME _____

ADDRESS _____

CITY _____ STATE _____ ZIP _____